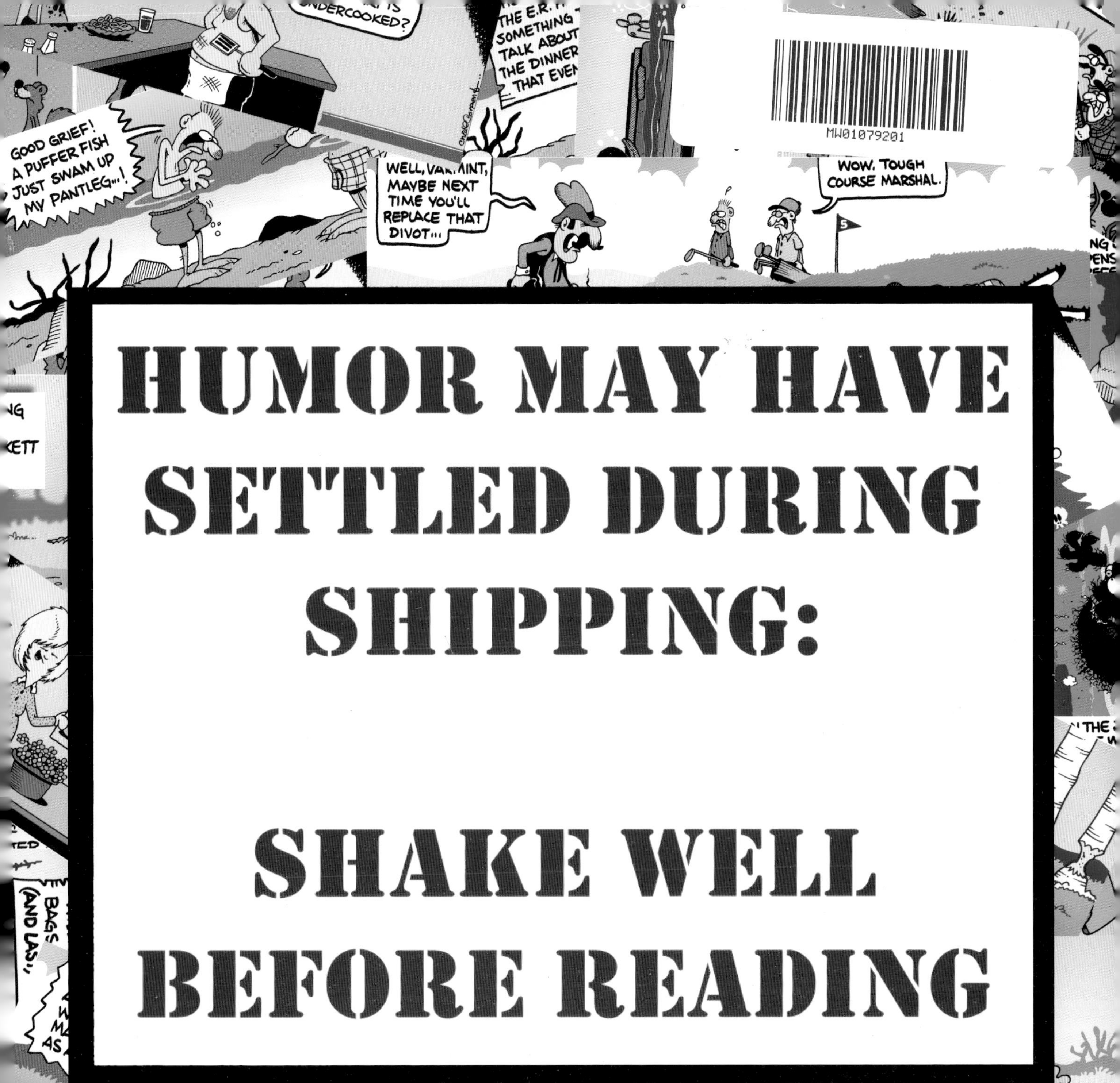
GOOD GRIEF! A PUFFER FISH JUST SWAM UP MY PANTLEG...!
WELL, VARMINT, MAYBE NEXT TIME YOU'LL REPLACE THAT DIVOT...
WOW. TOUGH COURSE MARSHAL.

HUMOR MAY HAVE SETTLED DURING SHIPPING:

SHAKE WELL BEFORE READING

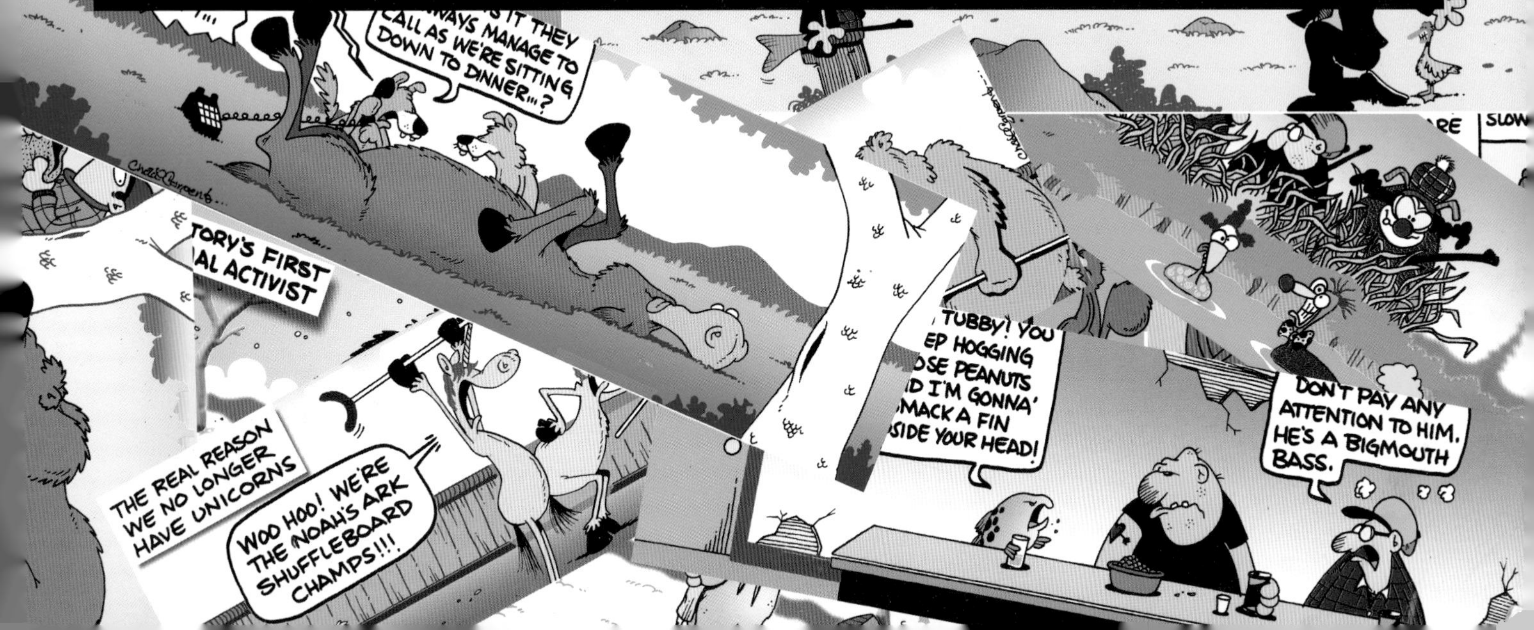
THE REAL REASON WE NO LONGER HAVE UNICORNS
WOO HOO! WE'RE THE NOAH'S ARK SHUFFLEBOARD CHAMPS!!!
DON'T PAY ANY ATTENTION TO HIM. HE'S A BIGMOUTH BASS.

Chad Carpenter presents...

TUNDRA

IN FULL COLOR!

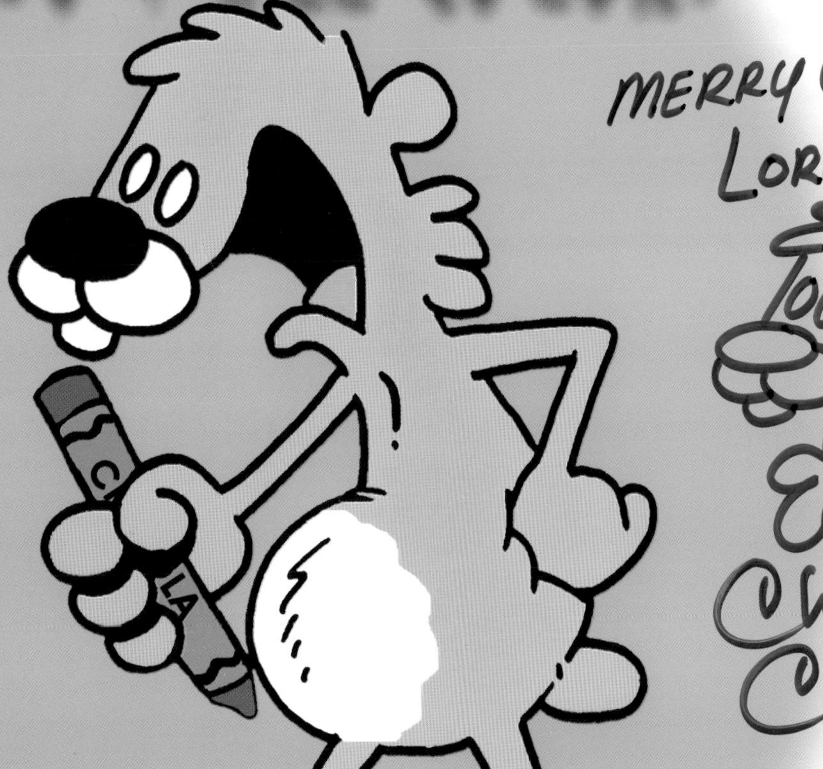

MERRY CHRISTMAS
LORRAINE!

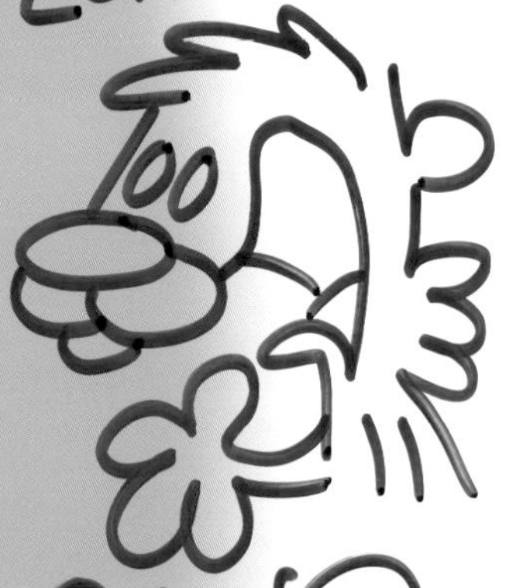

Chad Carpenter...
'2002

FROM THE NORTH'S MOST POPULAR COMIC STRIP!

PUBLISHED BY TUNDRA & ASSOCIATES

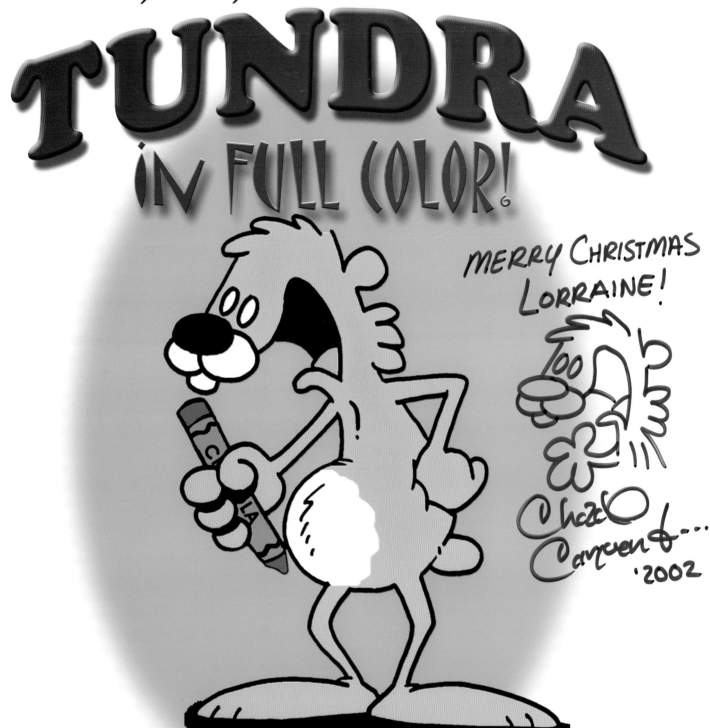

Published by Tundra & Associates
PO BOX 770732
Eagle River, Alaska 99577

FOR ADDITIONAL COPIES OF THIS OR OTHER TUNDRA BOOKS, AS WELL AS CALENDARS, MOUSE PADS, SCREEN SAVERS, ETC. PLEASE VISIT THE OFFICIAL TUNDRA WEBSITE AT:

www.tundracomics.com

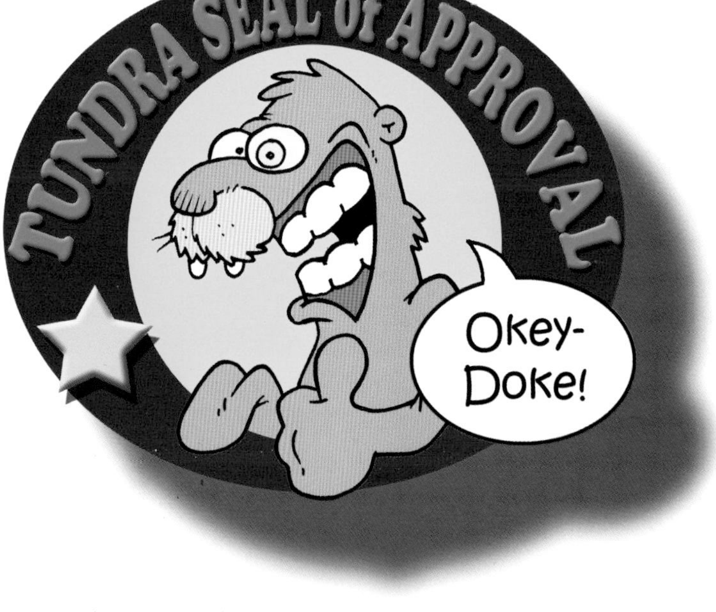
TUNDRA SEAL of APPROVAL
Okey-Doke!

Library of Congress Catalog Card Number: 2002107457
First Printing: August 2002
ISBN: 1-57833-193-5
Printed by Samhwa Printing Co., Ltd., Seoul, Korea

Dedicated to:

DOUG & MORRIS

If it wasn't for the opportunities you gave me, I probably would've ended up as a successful attorney or politician...

THANK YOU!

Foreword
By Sherman Squirrel

When Chad first asked me to write the foreword for his new book, I was honored. Then I realized that the reason he asked me in the first place was because he was too lazy to do it. If you look back through the past Tundra books, you'll notice that he has almost always managed to sucker someone else into doing this tedious chore for him. Granted, in the book previous to this one (THE REALLY BIG TUNDRA TREASURY) he did .echnically write his own foreword, but it consisted mostly of his mother's ecipe for potato soup.

In spite of Chad's flagrant disregard for a work ethic, I have decided to step up to the plate and write a worthy foreword.

A tome of this magnitude can only occur with incalculable hours of blood, sweat and tears. Since Chad gets squeamish at the sight of blood; has never broken a sweat (except to open a bag of cheese puffs); and hasn't shed a tear since Laverne & Shirley went off the air, very few of those hours were devoted by Chad. So I would like to take this opportunity to thank some of the folks that made this book possible:

Thanks to Jennie "Bean" Carpenter for her countless hours of suffering due to Chad's incessant whining about not being able to meet the deadline to get this book finished. She eventually got fed up, shoved Chad into a closet, and completed the entire task in just under 20 minutes.

Thanks to "Mr. Dale" Chavie for taking the time out of his busy schedule to color a very large portion of the strips in this book. He managed to accomplish this feat during the time it took Chad to sharpen his crayons.

And of course, thanks to Big Brother Darin for using his incredible wit & talent to help keep Tundra going strong all these years. And a very special thanks to him for coloring & writing the wonderfully witty storyline for the "MAJOR NUT" comic book enclosed within these pages.

I'm sure Chad would also like to thank his incredibly talented support staff: Mark Dickerson & family, Dudley Bear, Andy Lemming, Whiff Skunk & of course ME, Sherman Squirrel... In fact, especially ME, for writing this stupid foreword and not interrupting Chad's precious naptime...

Sherman Squirrel

Gangrene Gulch, July 15, 2002

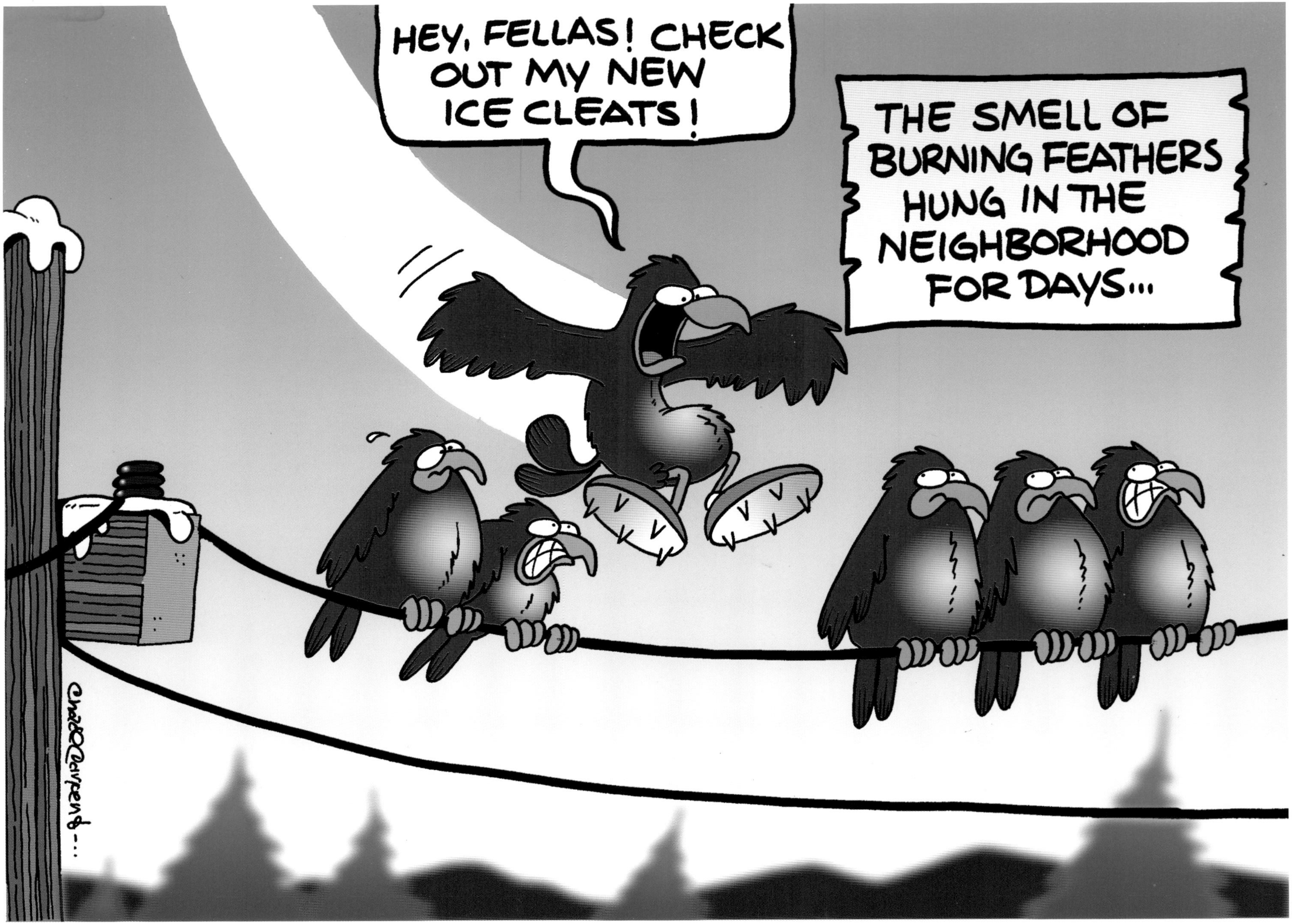
HEY, FELLAS! CHECK OUT MY NEW ICE CLEATS!
THE SMELL OF BURNING FEATHERS HUNG IN THE NEIGHBORHOOD FOR DAYS...

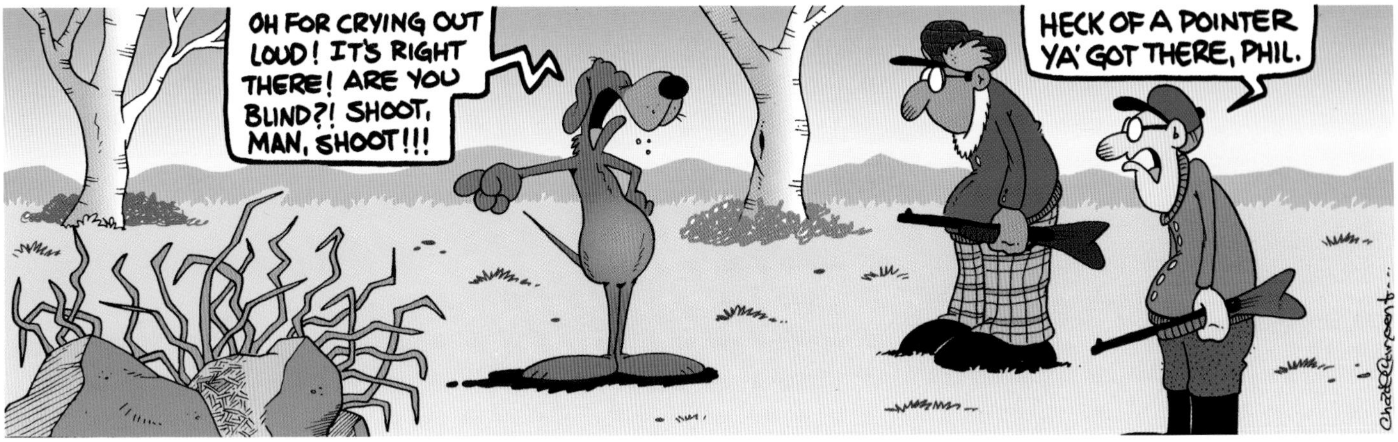
OH FOR CRYING OUT LOUD! IT'S RIGHT THERE! ARE YOU BLIND?! SHOOT, MAN, SHOOT!!!
HECK OF A POINTER YA' GOT THERE, PHIL.

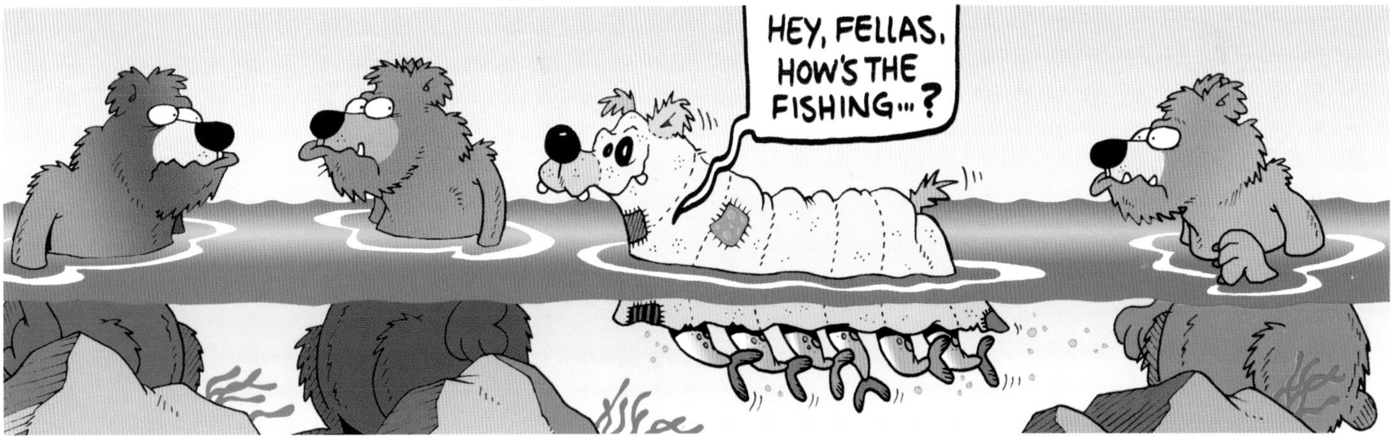
HEY, FELLAS, HOW'S THE FISHING...?

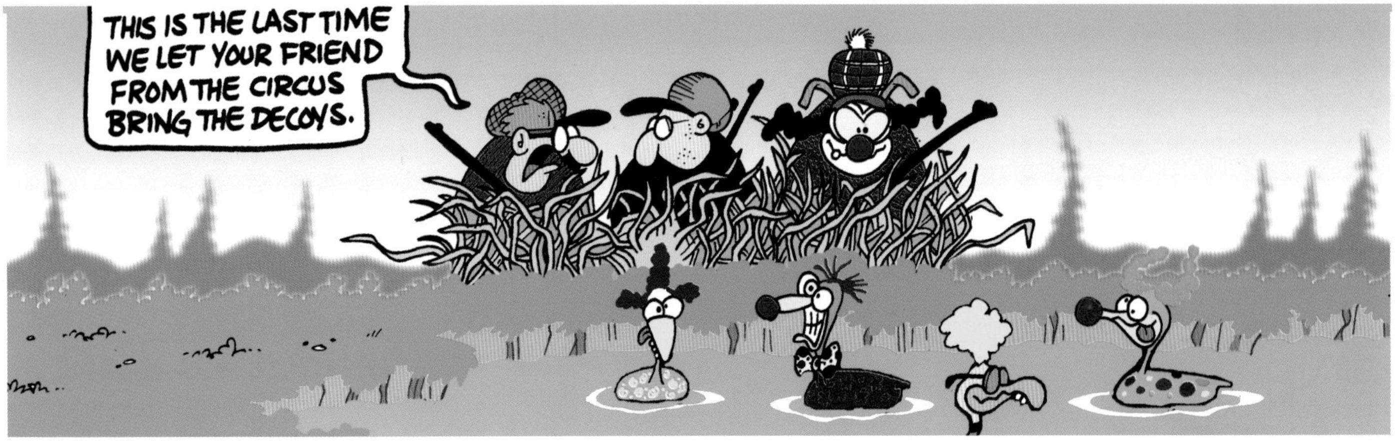
THIS IS THE LAST TIME WE LET YOUR FRIEND FROM THE CIRCUS BRING THE DECOYS.

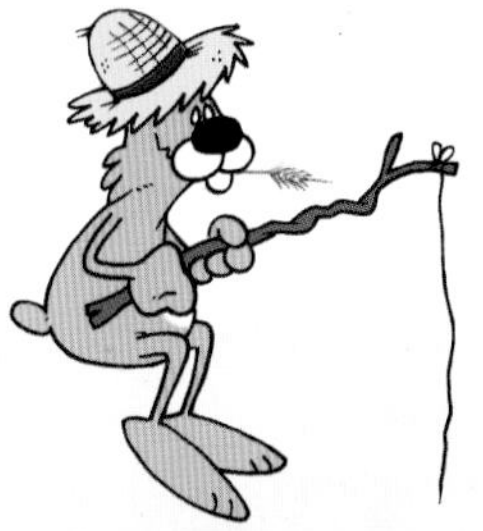

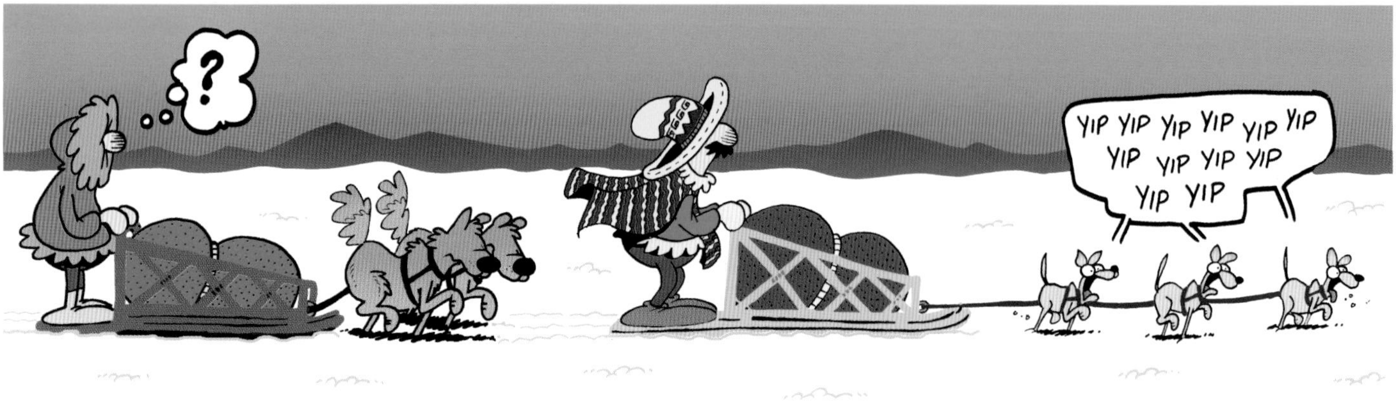
?
YIP YIP YIP YIP YIP YIP
YIP YIP YIP YIP
YIP YIP

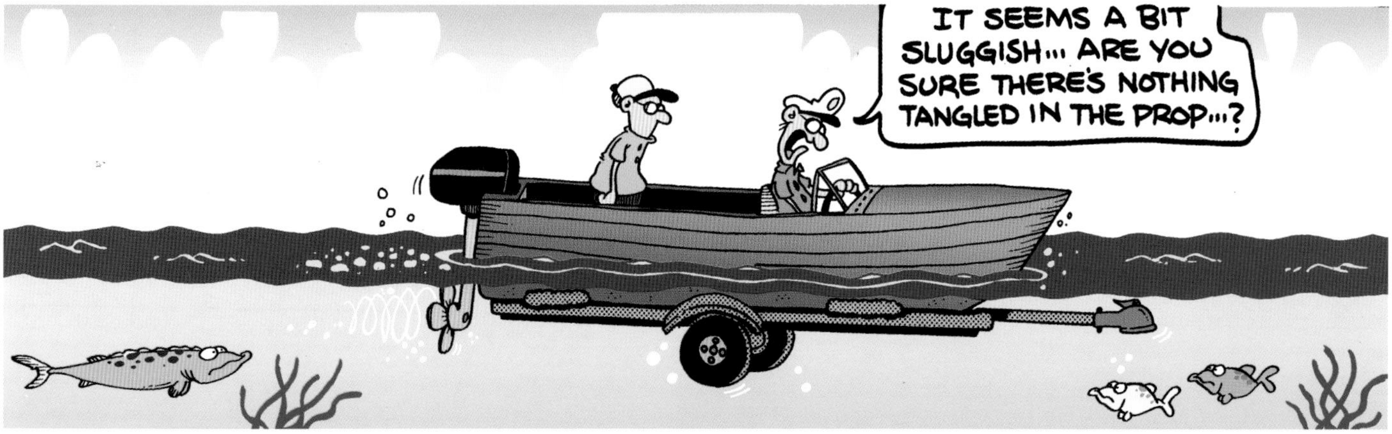
IT SEEMS A BIT SLUGGISH... ARE YOU SURE THERE'S NOTHING TANGLED IN THE PROP...?

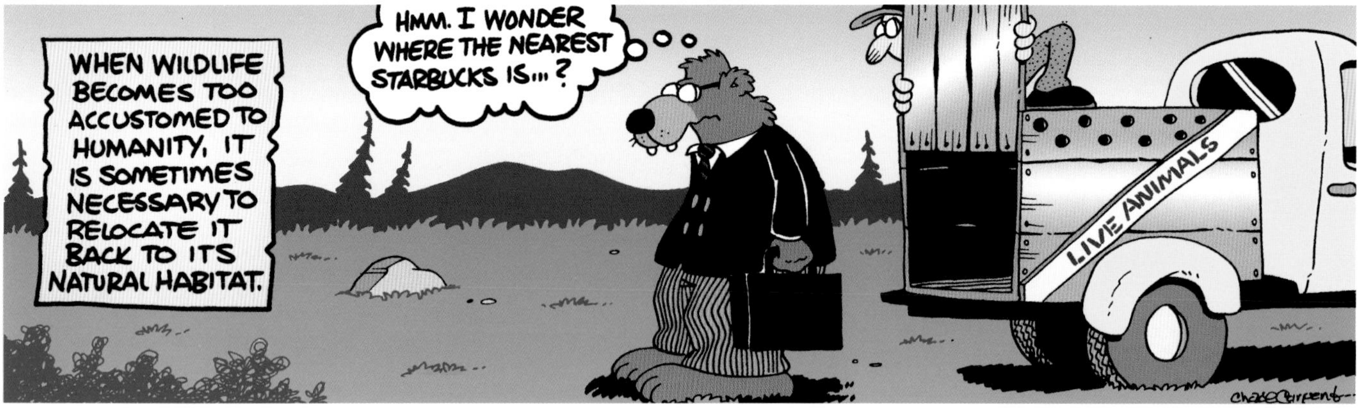
WHEN WILDLIFE BECOMES TOO ACCUSTOMED TO HUMANITY, IT IS SOMETIMES NECESSARY TO RELOCATE IT BACK TO ITS NATURAL HABITAT.
HMM. I WONDER WHERE THE NEAREST STARBUCKS IS...?
LIVE ANIMALS

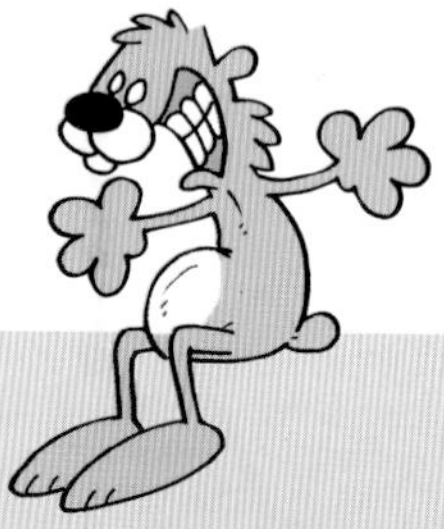

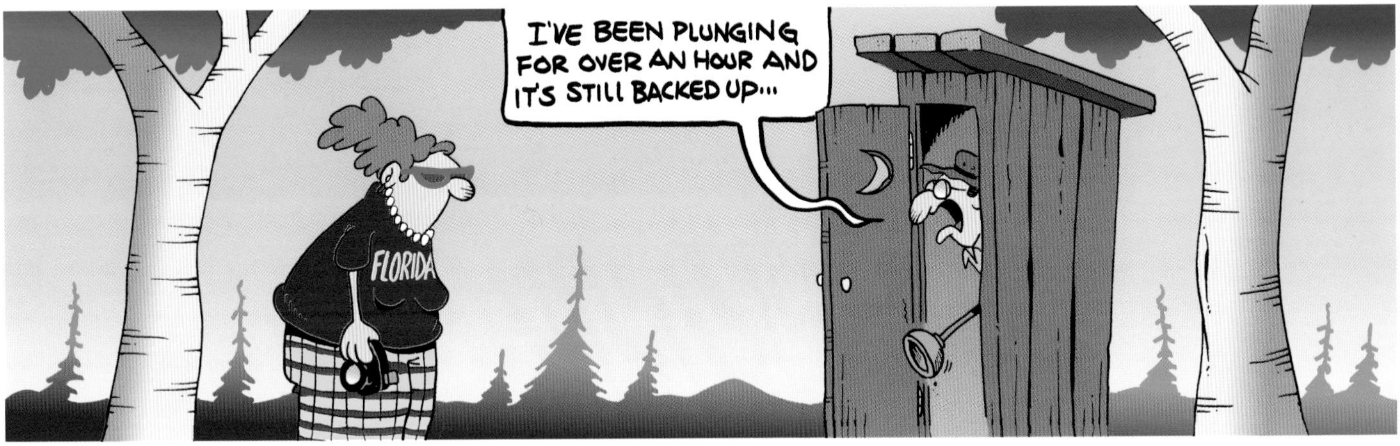
I'VE BEEN PLUNGING FOR OVER AN HOUR AND IT'S STILL BACKED UP...
FLORIDA

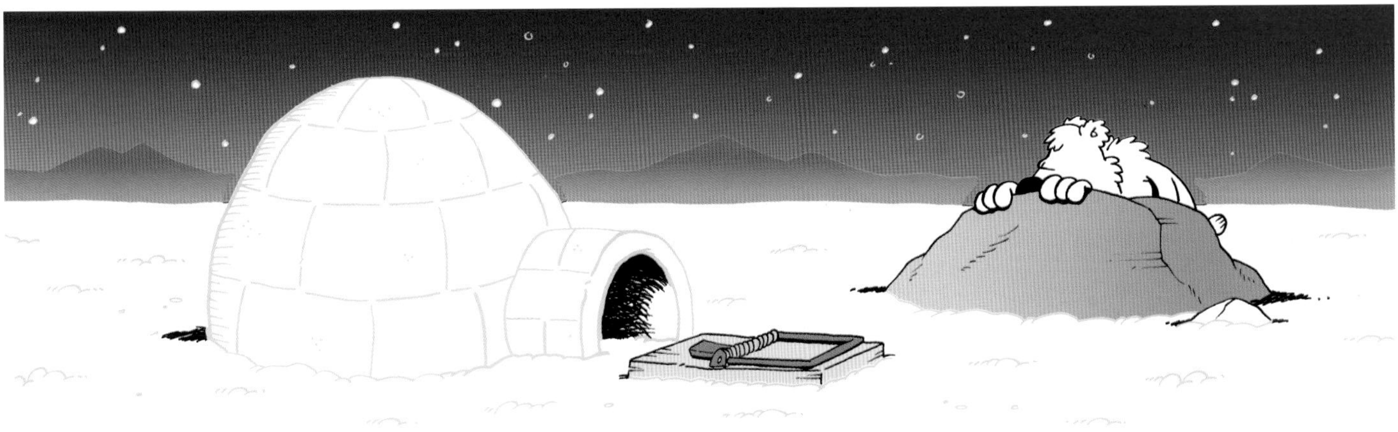

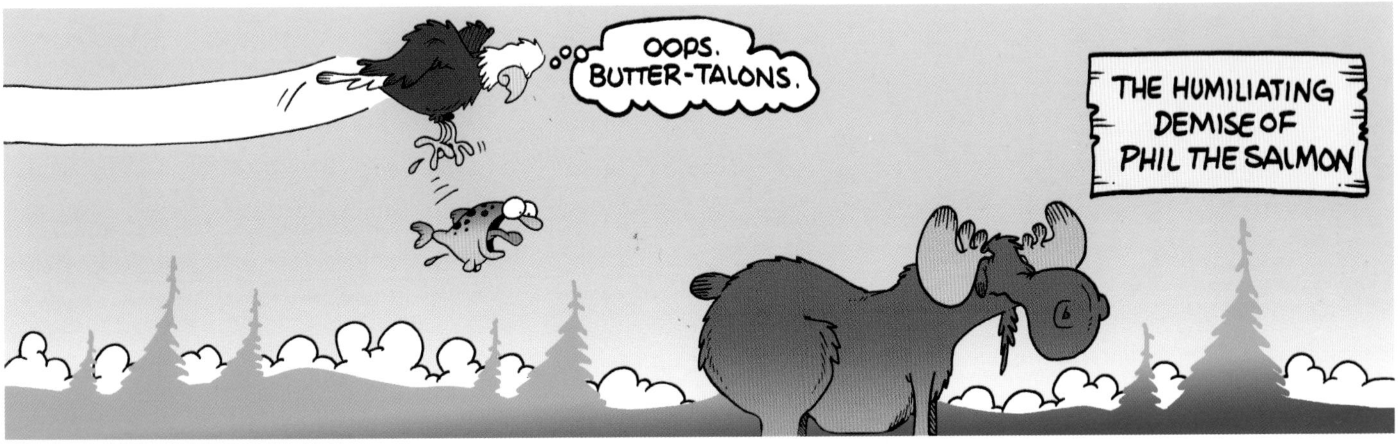
OOPS. BUTTER-TALONS.
THE HUMILIATING DEMISE OF PHIL THE SALMON

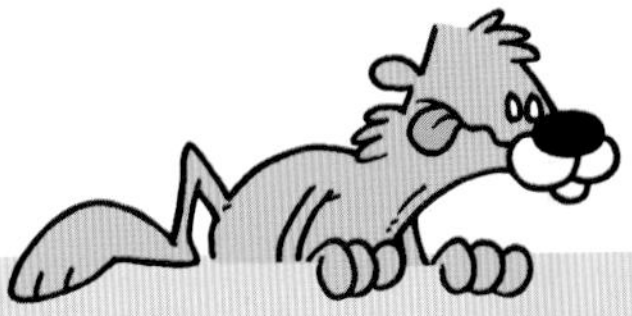

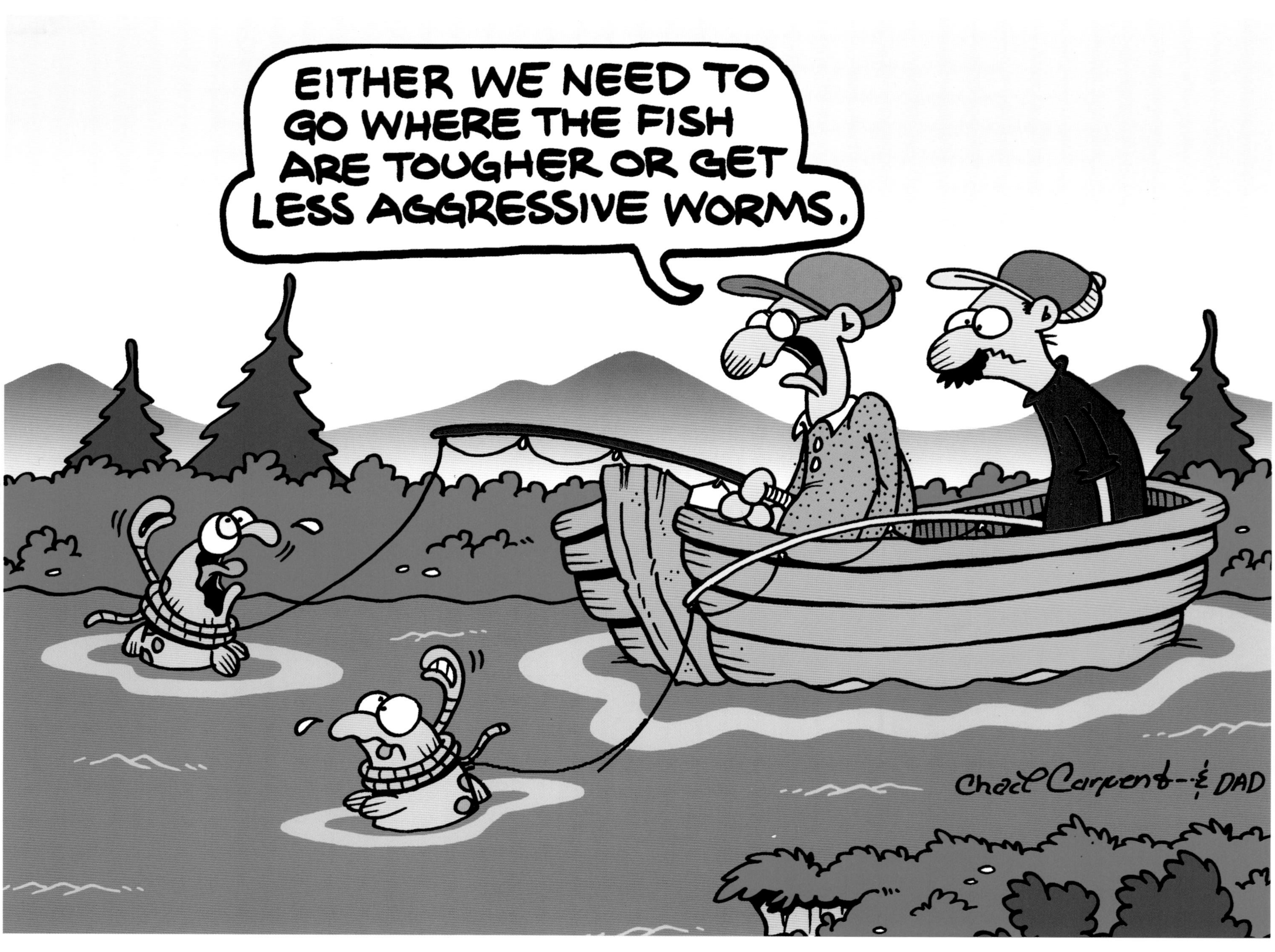
EITHER WE NEED TO GO WHERE THE FISH ARE TOUGHER OR GET LESS AGGRESSIVE WORMS.
Chad Carpenter -- & DAD

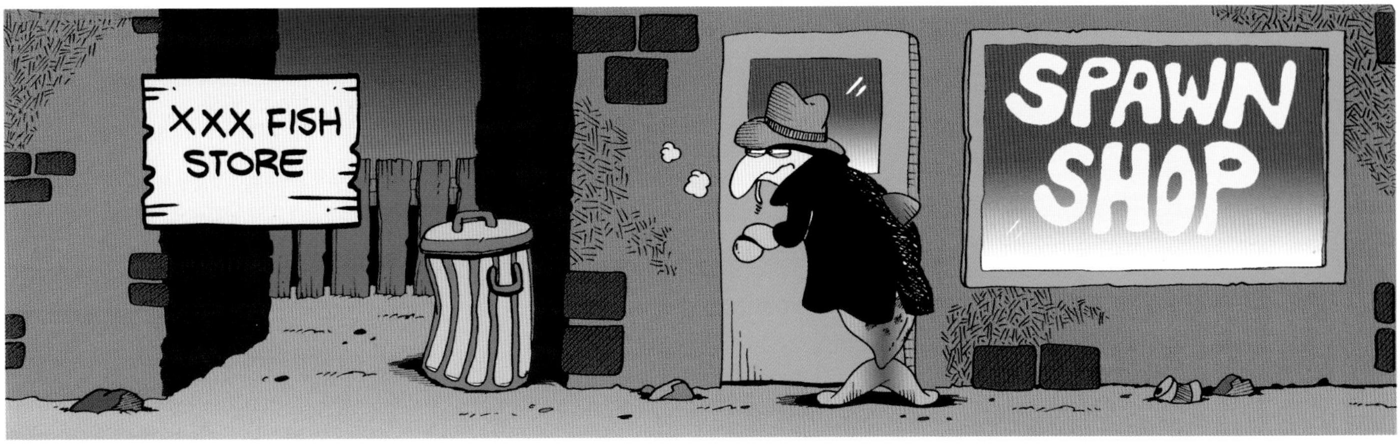
XXX FISH STORE
SPAWN SHOP

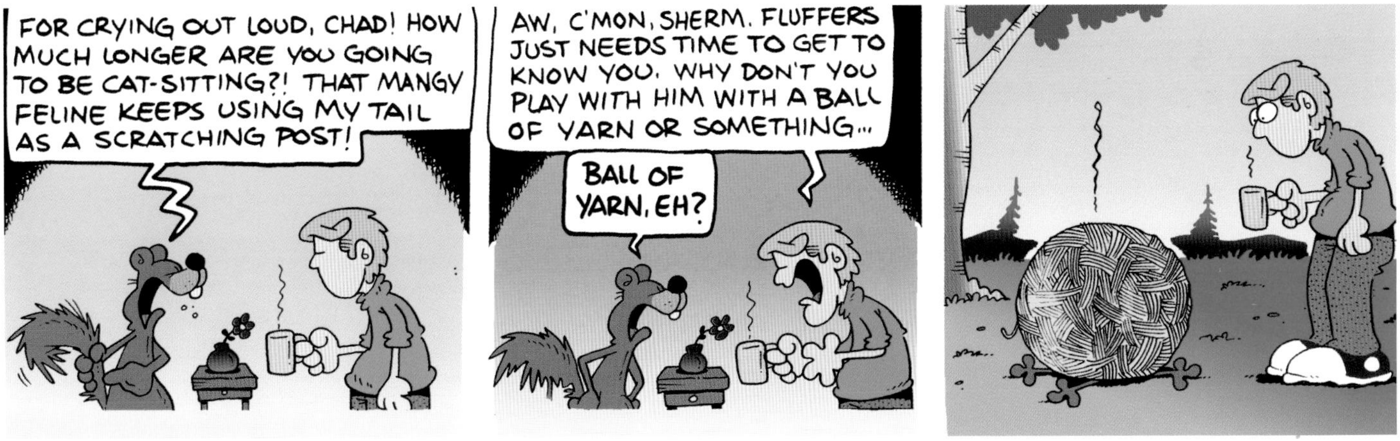
FOR CRYING OUT LOUD, CHAD! HOW MUCH LONGER ARE YOU GOING TO BE CAT-SITTING?! THAT MANGY FELINE KEEPS USING MY TAIL AS A SCRATCHING POST!
AW, C'MON, SHERM. FLUFFERS JUST NEEDS TIME TO GET TO KNOW YOU. WHY DON'T YOU PLAY WITH HIM WITH A BALL OF YARN OR SOMETHING...
BALL OF YARN, EH?

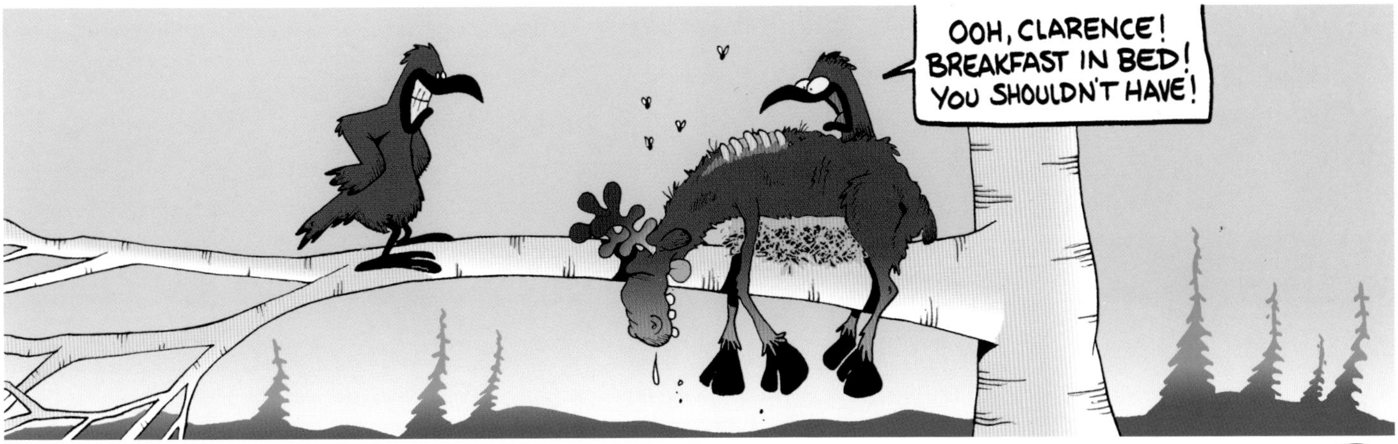
OOH, CLARENCE! BREAKFAST IN BED! YOU SHOULDN'T HAVE!

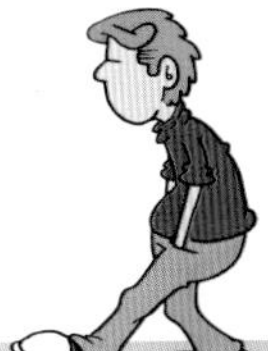

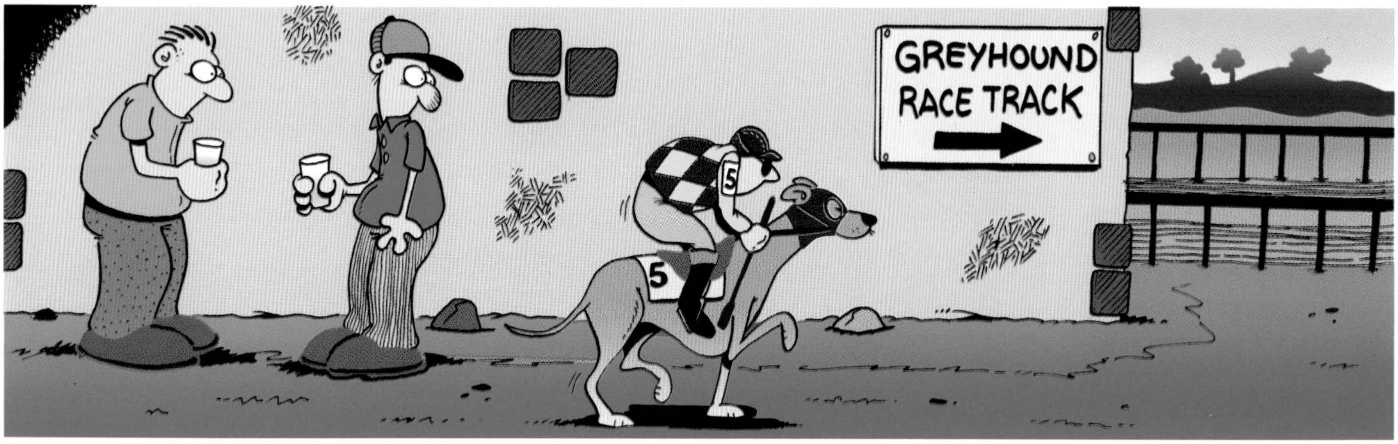
GREYHOUND RACE TRACK
5
5

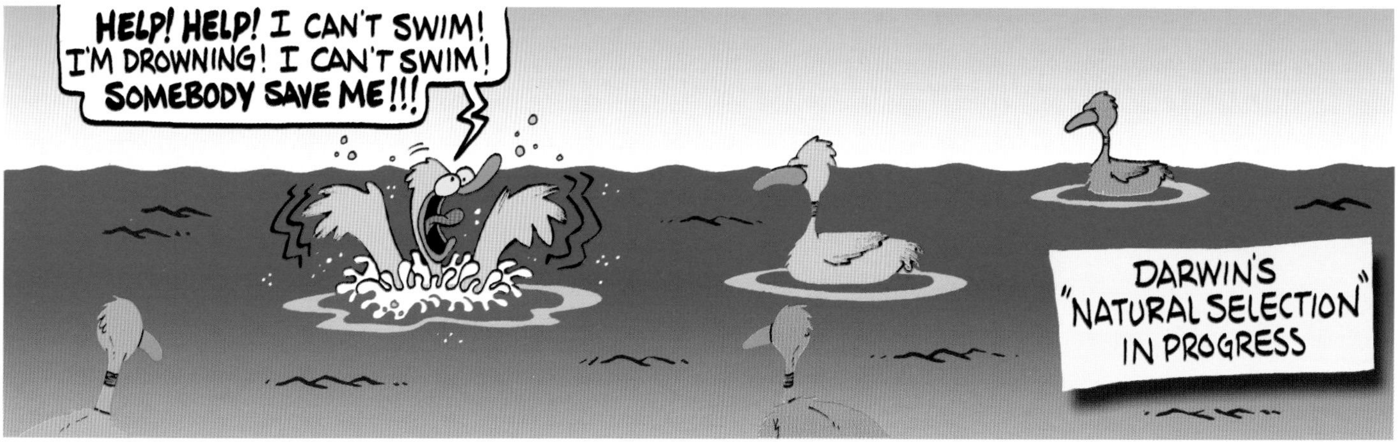
HELP! HELP! I CAN'T SWIM! I'M DROWNING! I CAN'T SWIM! SOMEBODY SAVE ME!!!
DARWIN'S "NATURAL SELECTION" IN PROGRESS

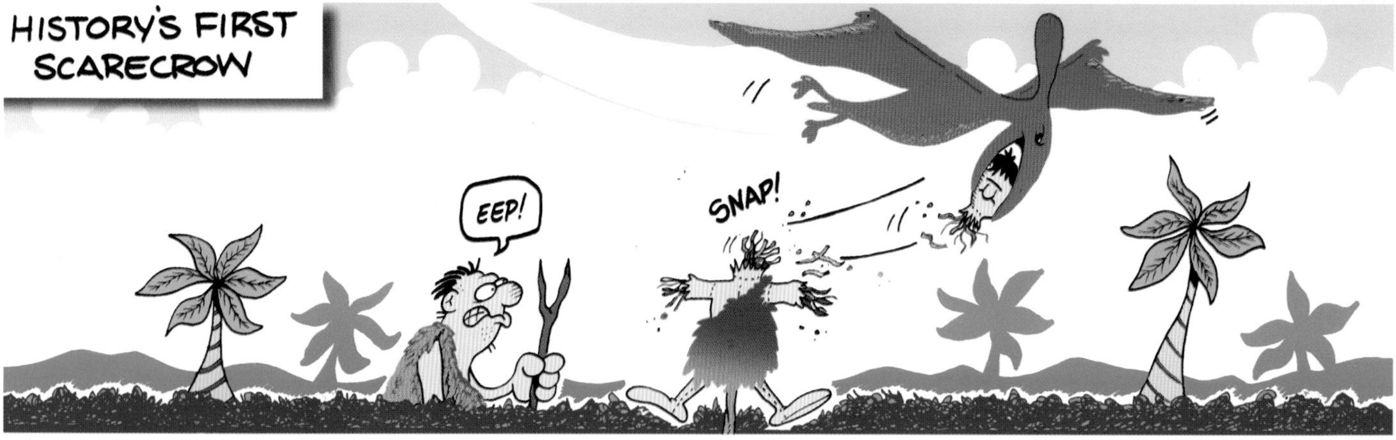
HISTORY'S FIRST SCARECROW
EEP!
SNAP!

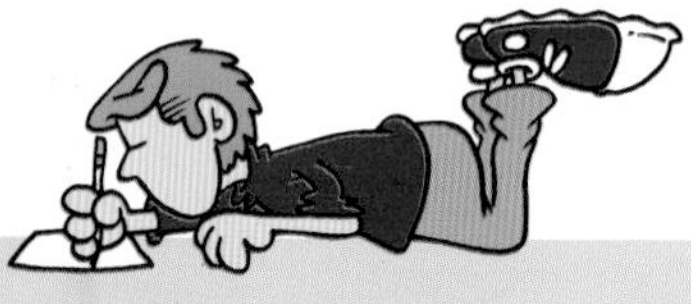

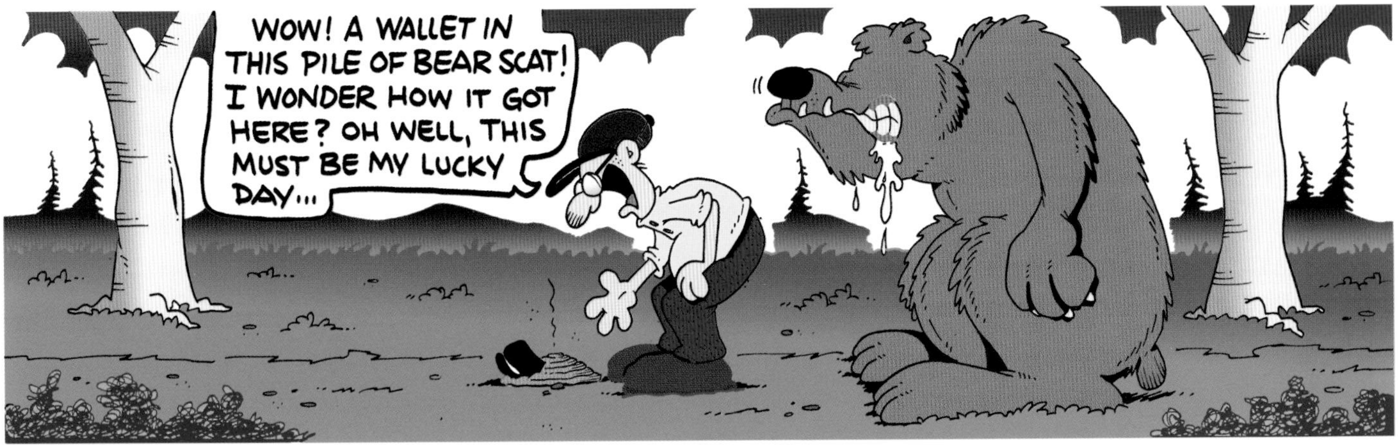
WOW! A WALLET IN THIS PILE OF BEAR SCAT! I WONDER HOW IT GOT HERE? OH WELL, THIS MUST BE MY LUCKY DAY...

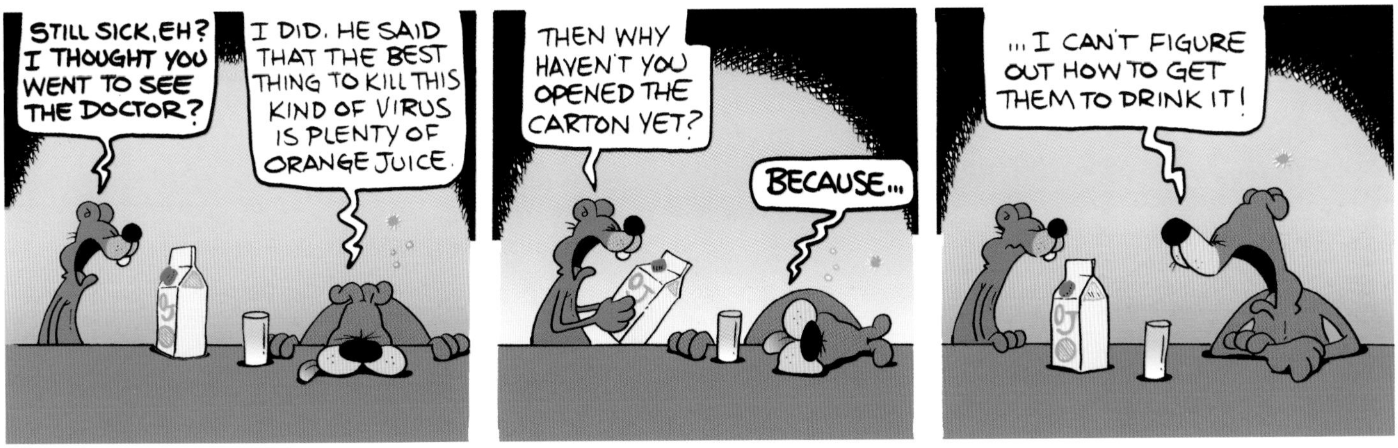
STILL SICK, EH? I THOUGHT YOU WENT TO SEE THE DOCTOR?
I DID. HE SAID THAT THE BEST THING TO KILL THIS KIND OF VIRUS IS PLENTY OF ORANGE JUICE.
THEN WHY HAVEN'T YOU OPENED THE CARTON YET?
BECAUSE...
...I CAN'T FIGURE OUT HOW TO GET THEM TO DRINK IT!

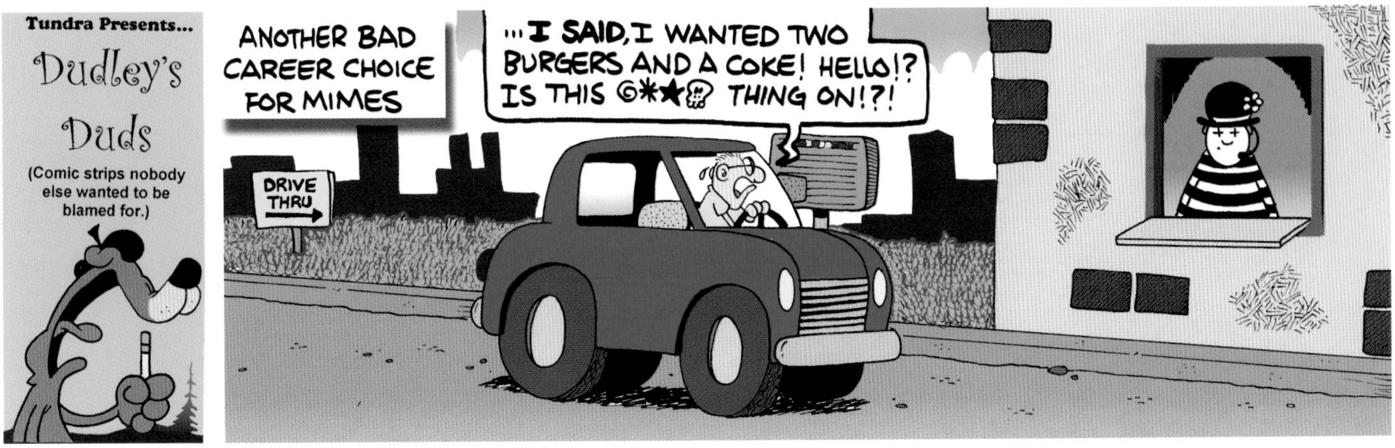
Tundra Presents...
Dudley's Duds
(Comic strips nobody else wanted to be blamed for.)
ANOTHER BAD CAREER CHOICE FOR MIMES
...I SAID, I WANTED TWO BURGERS AND A COKE! HELLO!? IS THIS ©✱★!? THING ON!?!
DRIVE THRU

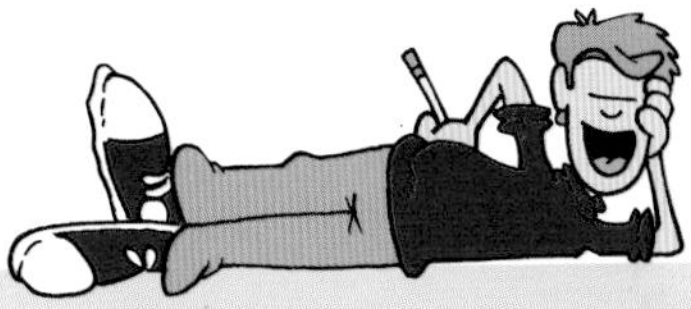

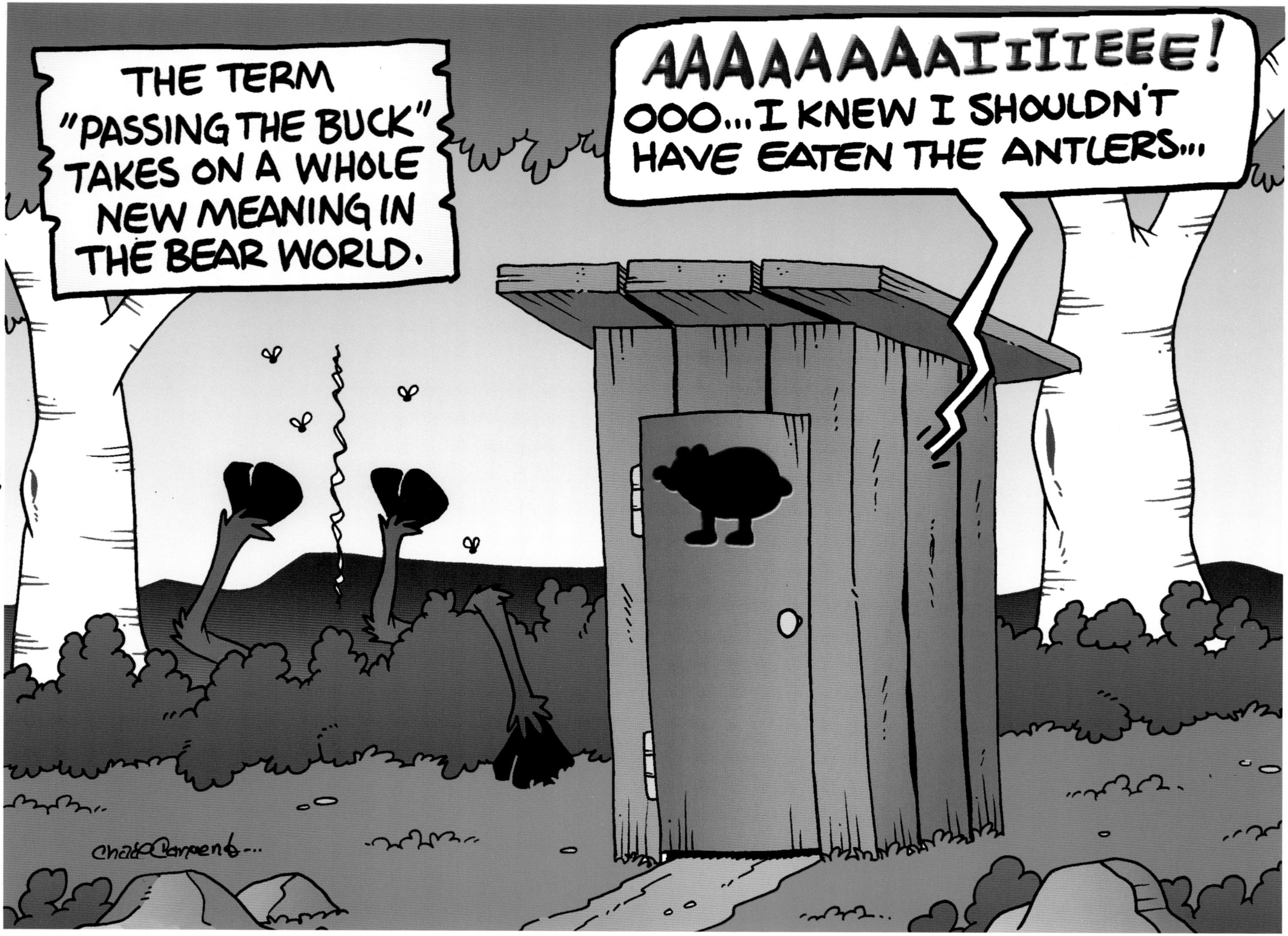
THE TERM "PASSING THE BUCK" TAKES ON A WHOLE NEW MEANING IN THE BEAR WORLD.
AAAAAAAAIIIIEEEE! OOO... I KNEW I SHOULDN'T HAVE EATEN THE ANTLERS...
Chad Carpenter...

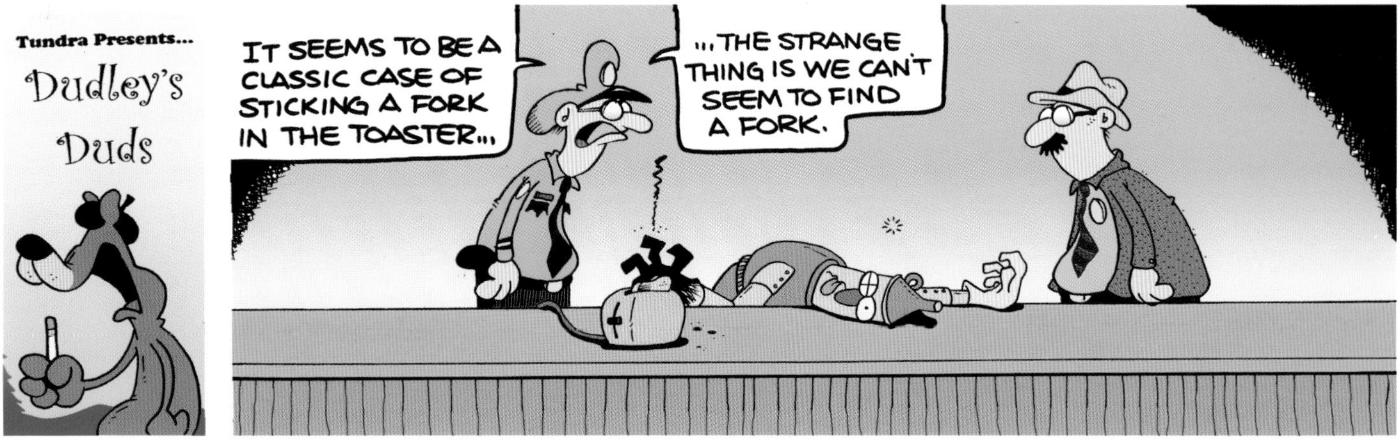
Tundra Presents...
Dudley's Duds
IT SEEMS TO BE A CLASSIC CASE OF STICKING A FORK IN THE TOASTER...
...THE STRANGE THING IS WE CAN'T SEEM TO FIND A FORK.

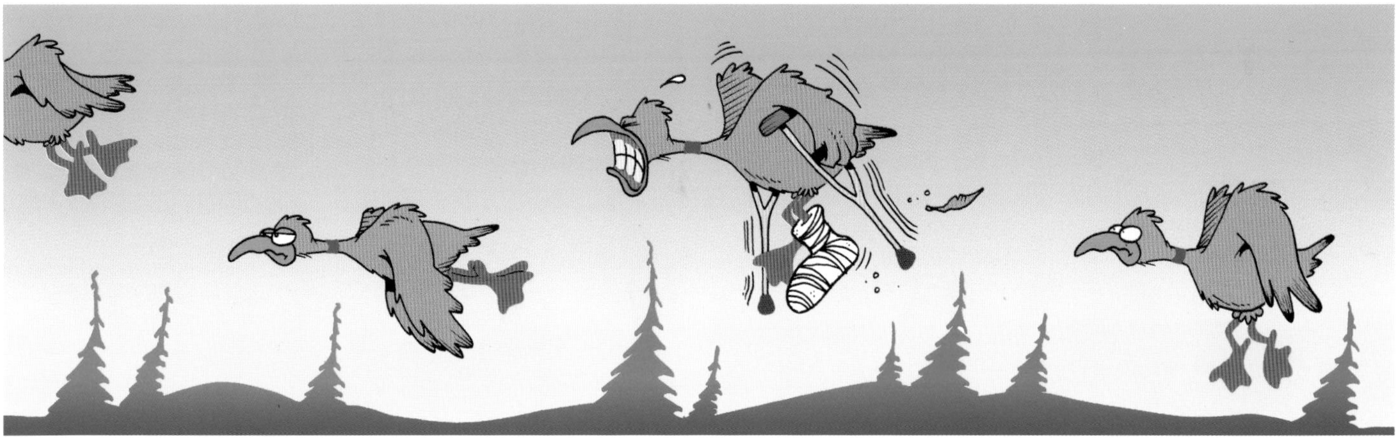

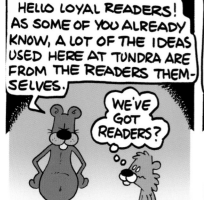

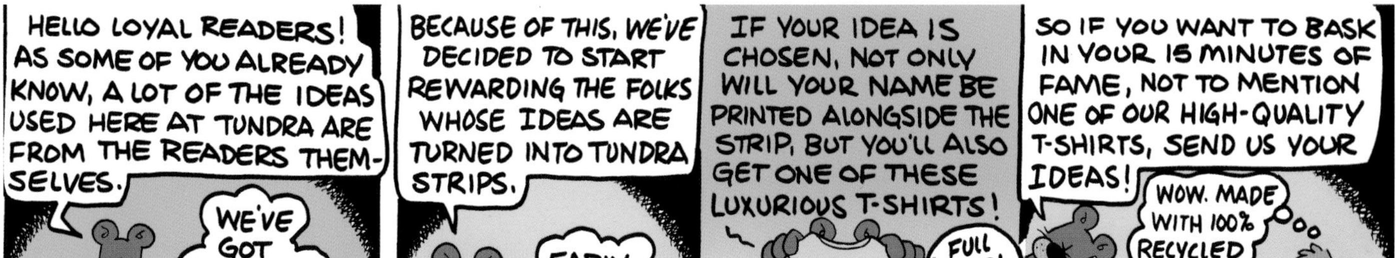
HELLO LOYAL READERS! AS SOME OF YOU ALREADY KNOW, A LOT OF THE IDEAS USED HERE AT TUNDRA ARE FROM THE READERS THEM-SELVES.
WE'VE GOT READERS?
BECAUSE OF THIS, WE'VE DECIDED TO START REWARDING THE FOLKS WHOSE IDEAS ARE TURNED INTO TUNDRA STRIPS.
EARLY PAROLE?
IF YOUR IDEA IS CHOSEN, NOT ONLY WILL YOUR NAME BE PRINTED ALONGSIDE THE STRIP, BUT YOU'LL ALSO GET ONE OF THESE LUXURIOUS T-SHIRTS!
My idea was used as a TUNDRA comic strip...
...and all I got was this lousy T-shirt.
FULL COLOR!
SO IF YOU WANT TO BASK IN YOUR 15 MINUTES OF FAME, NOT TO MENTION ONE OF OUR HIGH-QUALITY T-SHIRTS, SEND US YOUR IDEAS!
WOW. MADE WITH 100% RECYCLED GOAT HAIR...
www.tundracomics.com
- or - TUNDRA PO BOX 770732
Eagle River, AK 99577

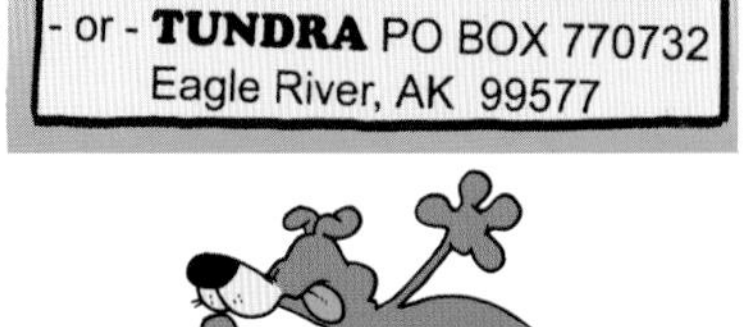

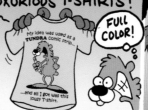

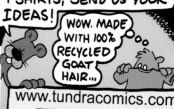

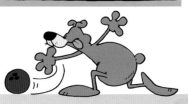

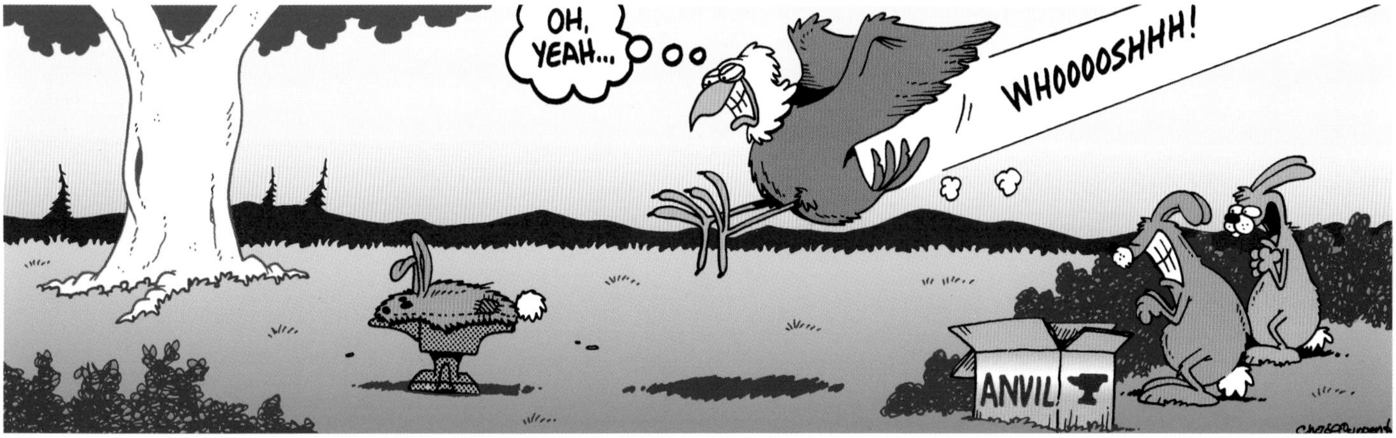
OH, YEAH...
WHOOOOSHHH!
ANVIL

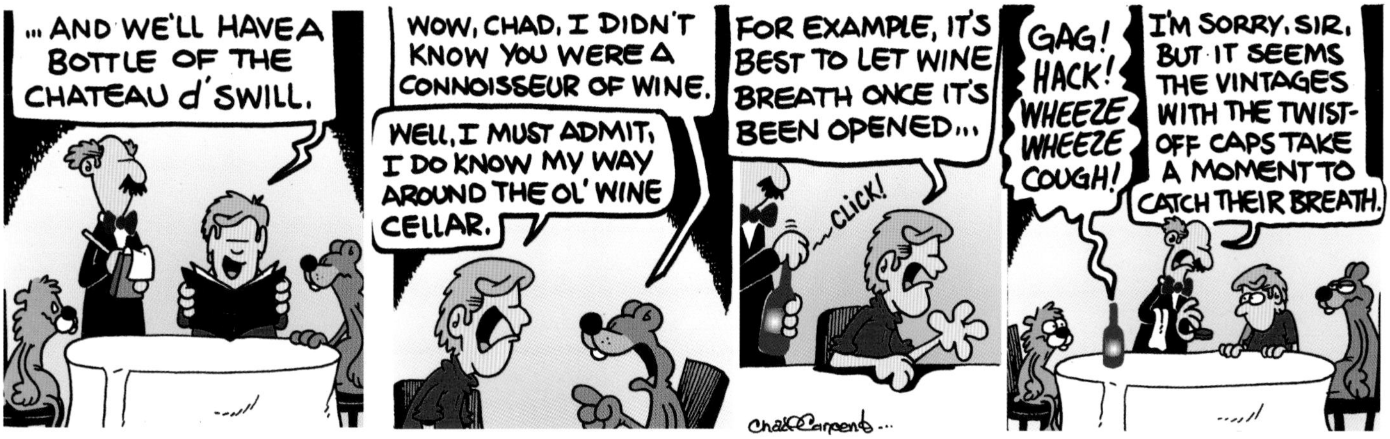
... AND WE'LL HAVE A BOTTLE OF THE CHATEAU d' SWILL.
WOW, CHAD, I DIDN'T KNOW YOU WERE A CONNOISSEUR OF WINE.
WELL, I MUST ADMIT, I DO KNOW MY WAY AROUND THE OL' WINE CELLAR.
FOR EXAMPLE, IT'S BEST TO LET WINE BREATH ONCE IT'S BEEN OPENED...
CLICK!
GAG! HACK! WHEEZE WHEEZE COUGH!
I'M SORRY, SIR, BUT IT SEEMS THE VINTAGES WITH THE TWIST-OFF CAPS TAKE A MOMENT TO CATCH THEIR BREATH.

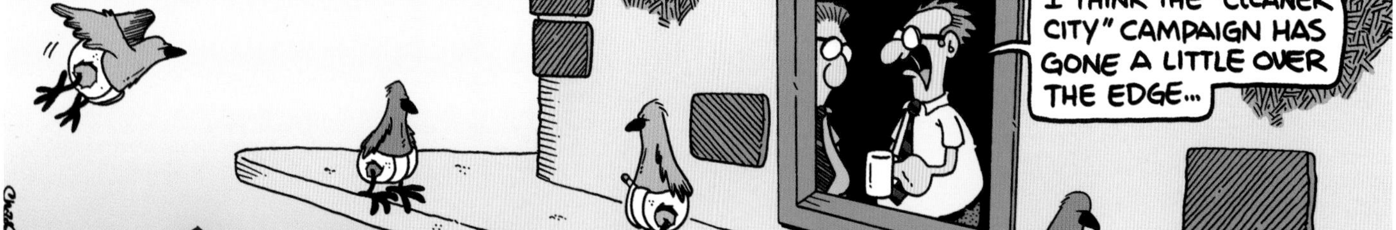
I THINK THE "CLEANER CITY" CAMPAIGN HAS GONE A LITTLE OVER THE EDGE...

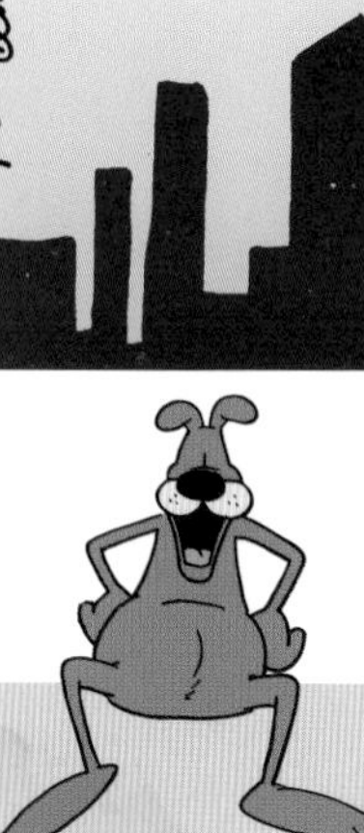

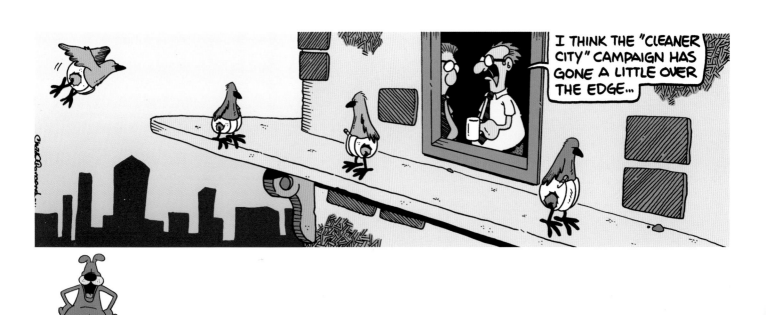

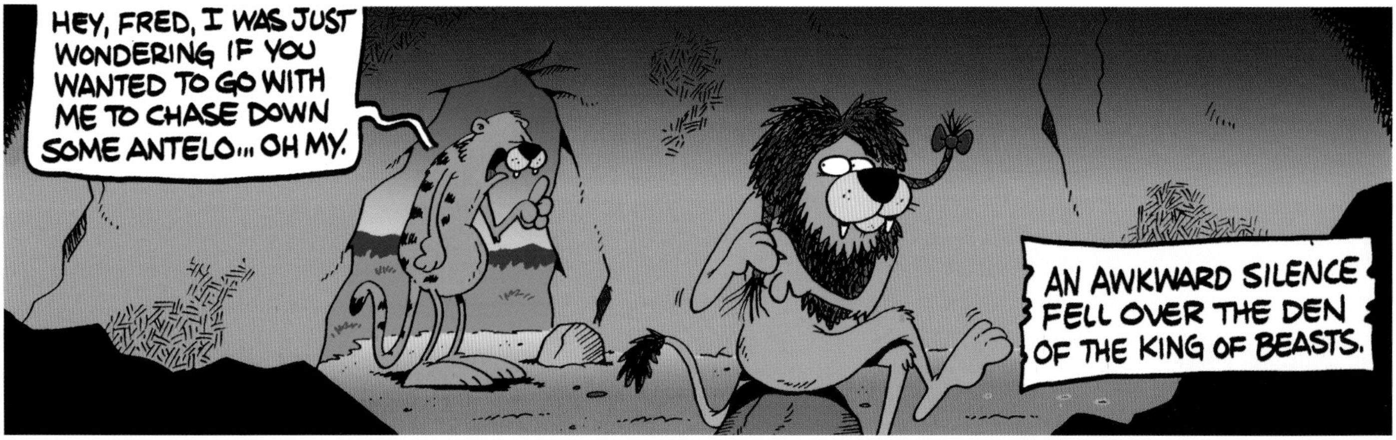
HEY, FRED, I WAS JUST WONDERING IF YOU WANTED TO GO WITH ME TO CHASE DOWN SOME ANTELO... OH MY.
AN AWKWARD SILENCE FELL OVER THE DEN OF THE KING OF BEASTS.

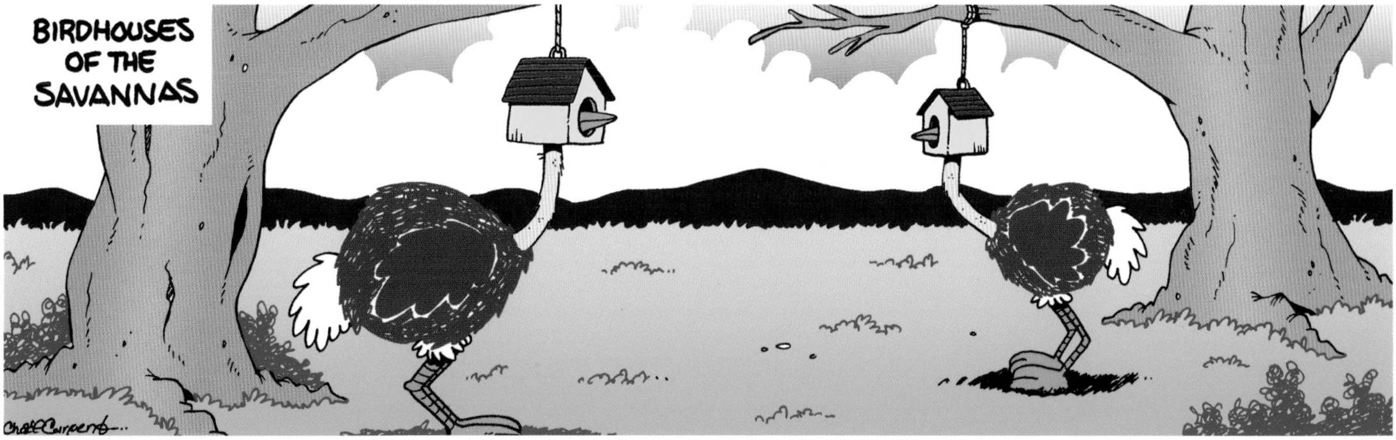
BIRDHOUSES OF THE SAVANNAS

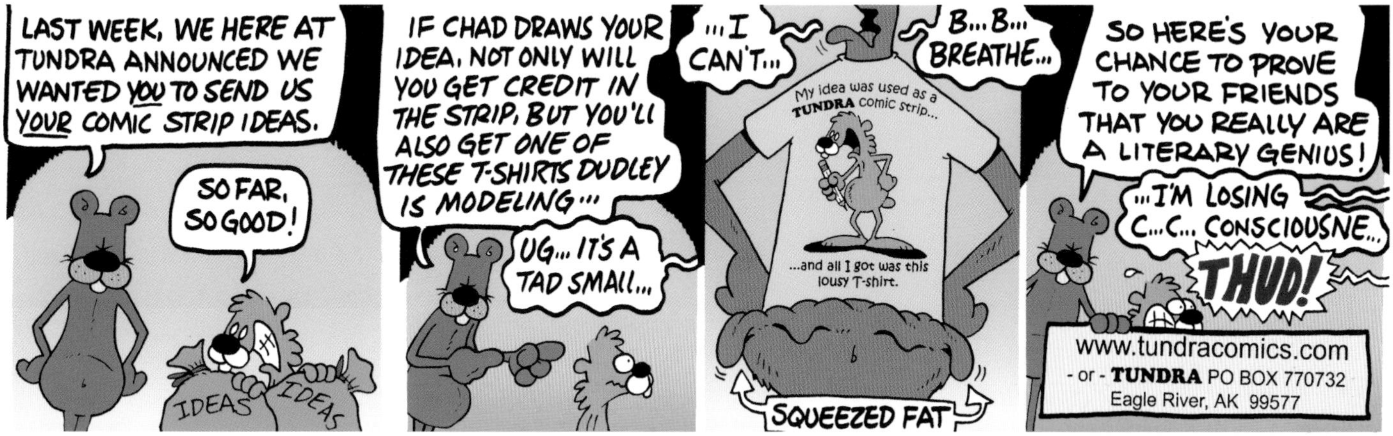
LAST WEEK, WE HERE AT TUNDRA ANNOUNCED WE WANTED YOU TO SEND US YOUR COMIC STRIP IDEAS.
SO FAR, SO GOOD!
IDEAS
IDEAS
IF CHAD DRAWS YOUR IDEA, NOT ONLY WILL YOU GET CREDIT IN THE STRIP, BUT YOU'LL ALSO GET ONE OF THESE T-SHIRTS DUDLEY IS MODELING...
UG... IT'S A TAD SMALL...
...I CAN'T...
B... B... BREATHE...
My idea was used as a TUNDRA comic strip...
...and all I got was this lousy T-shirt.
SQUEEZED FAT
SO HERE'S YOUR CHANCE TO PROVE TO YOUR FRIENDS THAT YOU REALLY ARE A LITERARY GENIUS!
...I'M LOSING C...C... CONSCIOUSNE...
THUD!
www.tundracomics.com
- or - TUNDRA PO BOX 770732
Eagle River, AK 99577

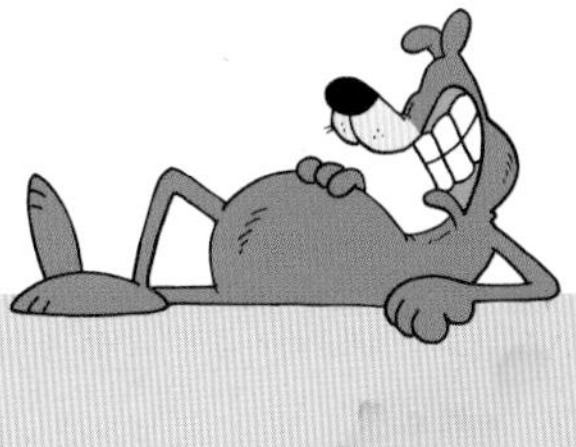

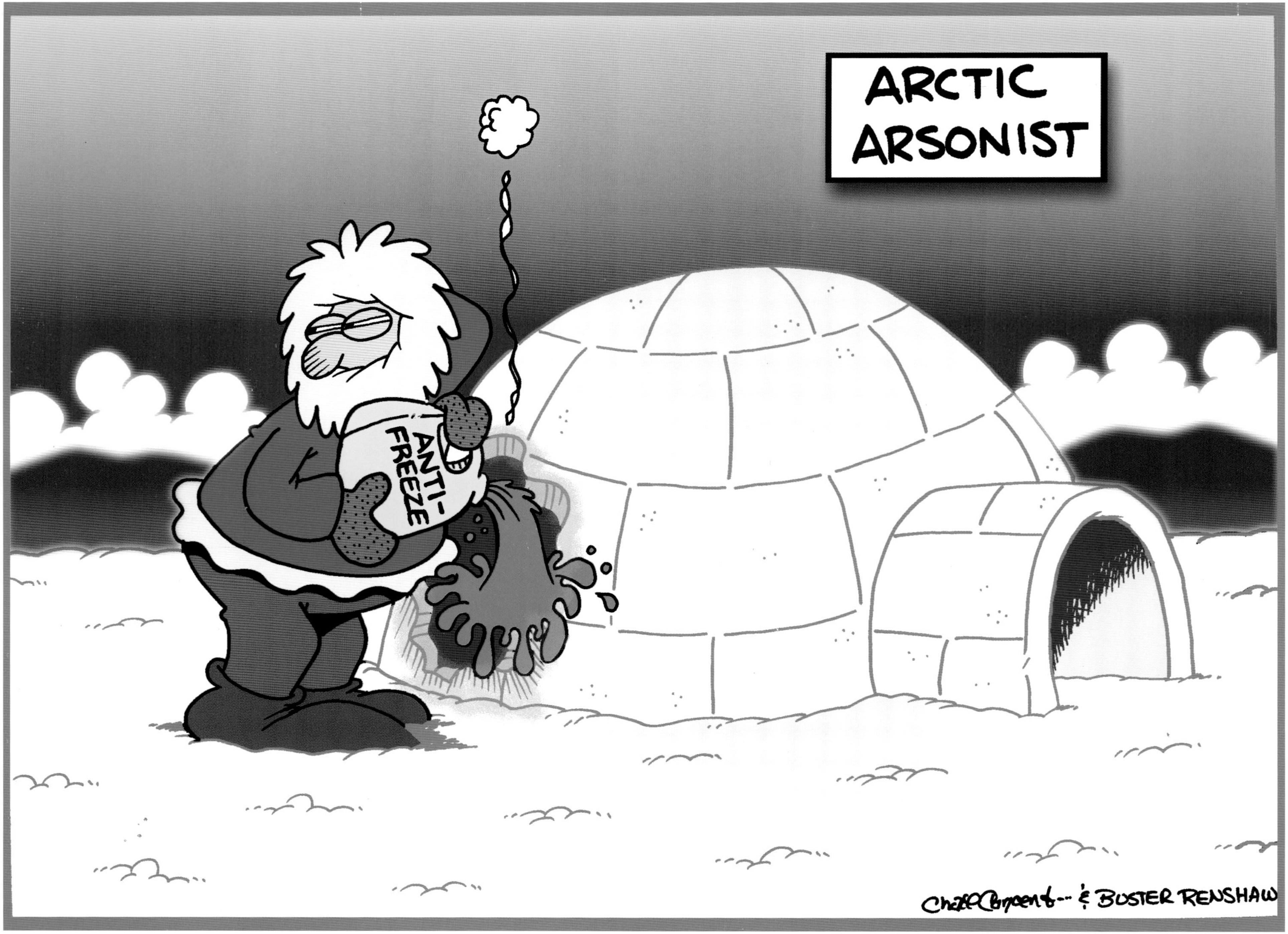
ARCTIC ARSONIST
ANTI-FREEZE
BUSTER RENSHAW

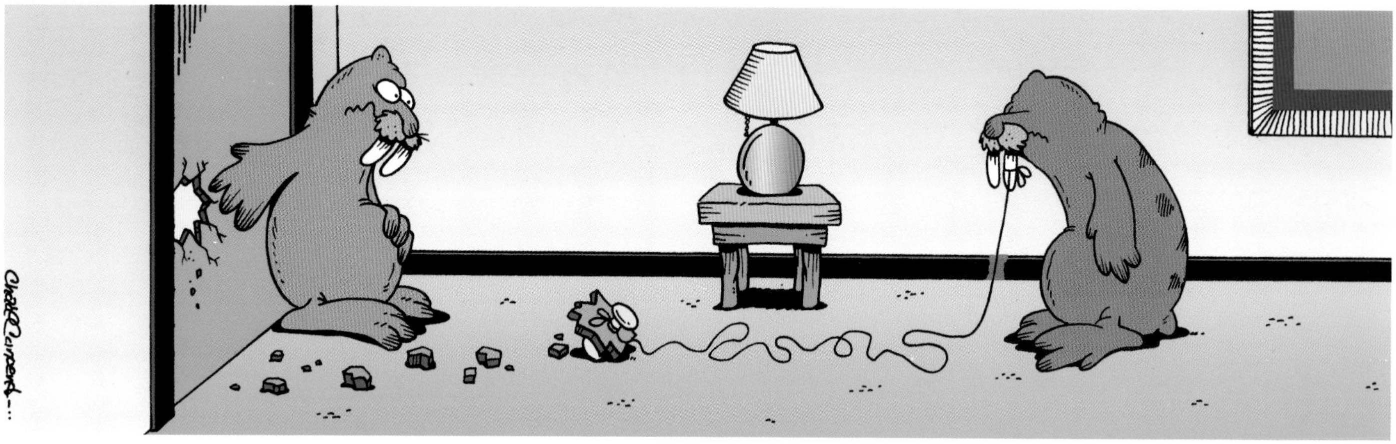

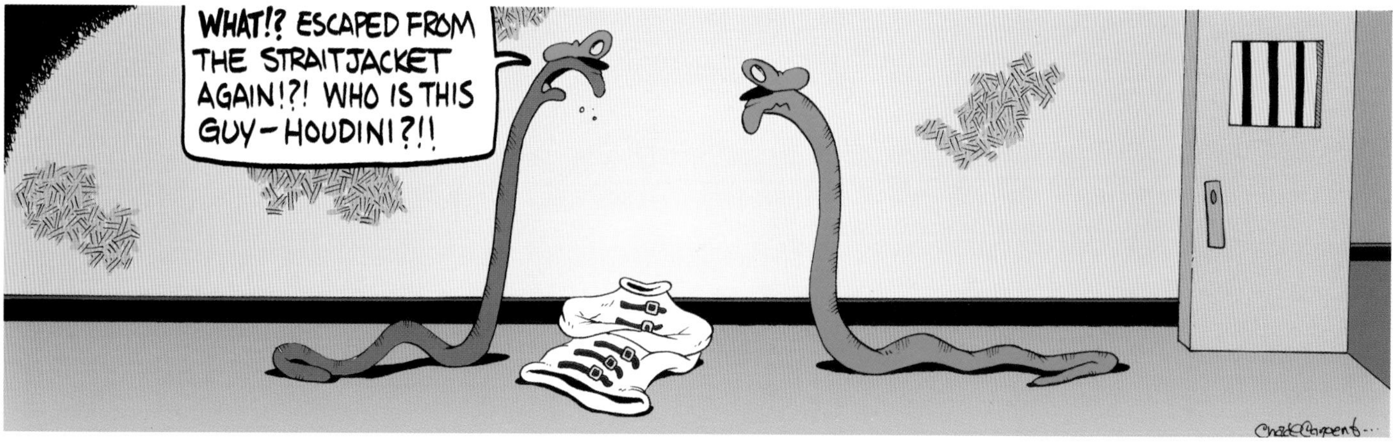
WHAT!? ESCAPED FROM THE STRAITJACKET AGAIN!?! WHO IS THIS GUY – HOUDINI?!!

This comic strip is based on the idea of Curvin Metzler Anchorage, AK

Do you have an idea that would make a great comic strip? Send it to:

www.tundracomics.com

or

TUNDRA IDEAS
PO BOX 770732
Eagle River, AK
99577

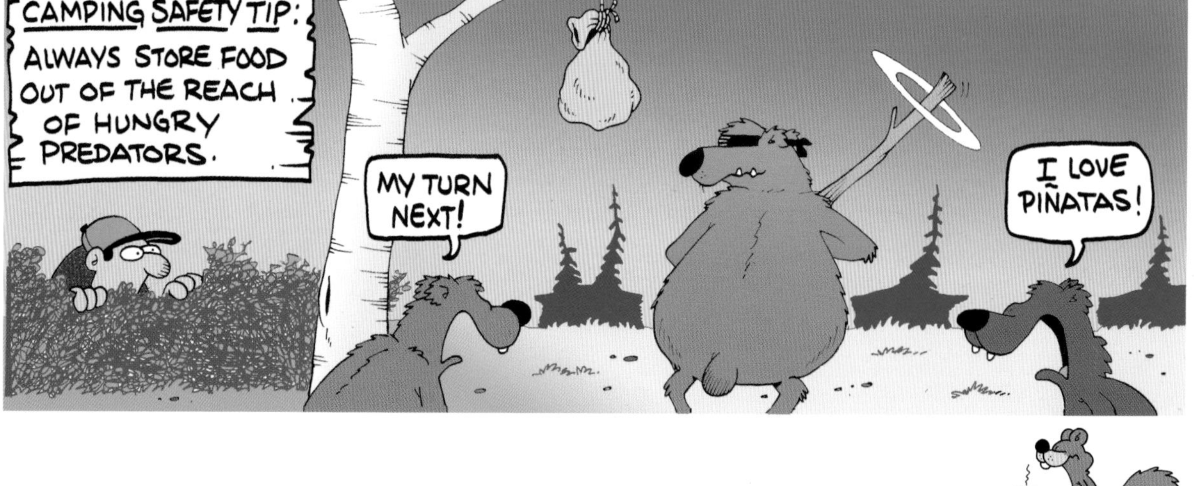
CAMPING SAFETY TIP: ALWAYS STORE FOOD OUT OF THE REACH OF HUNGRY PREDATORS.
MY TURN NEXT!
I LOVE PIÑATAS!

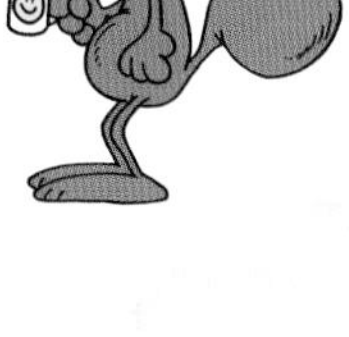

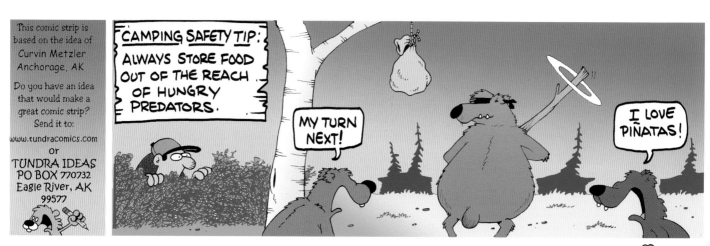

This comic strip is based on the idea of

Mark Wilkerson
Anchorage, AK

Do you have an idea that would make a great comic strip? Send it to:

www.tundracomics.com
or
TUNDRA IDEAS
PO BOX 770732
Eagle River, AK
99577

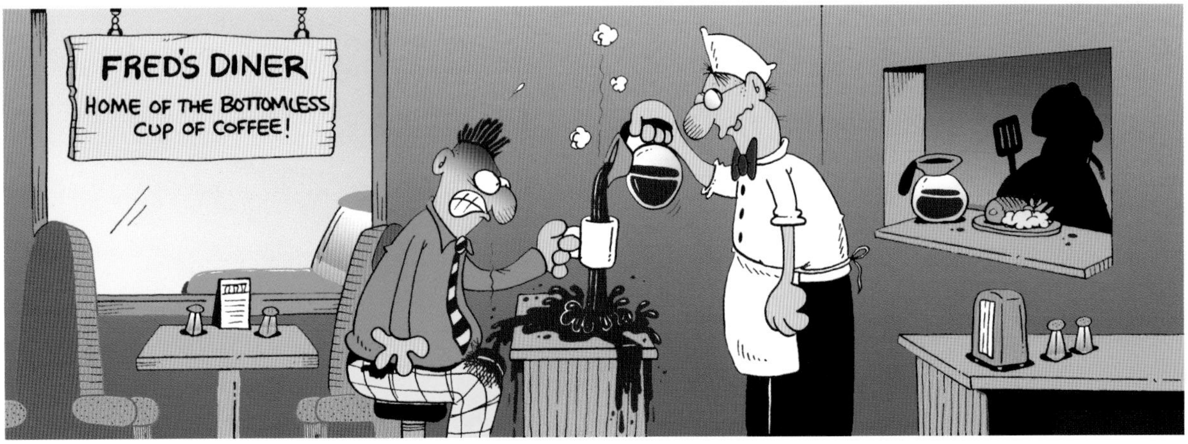
FRED'S DINER
HOME OF THE BOTTOMLESS CUP OF COFFEE!

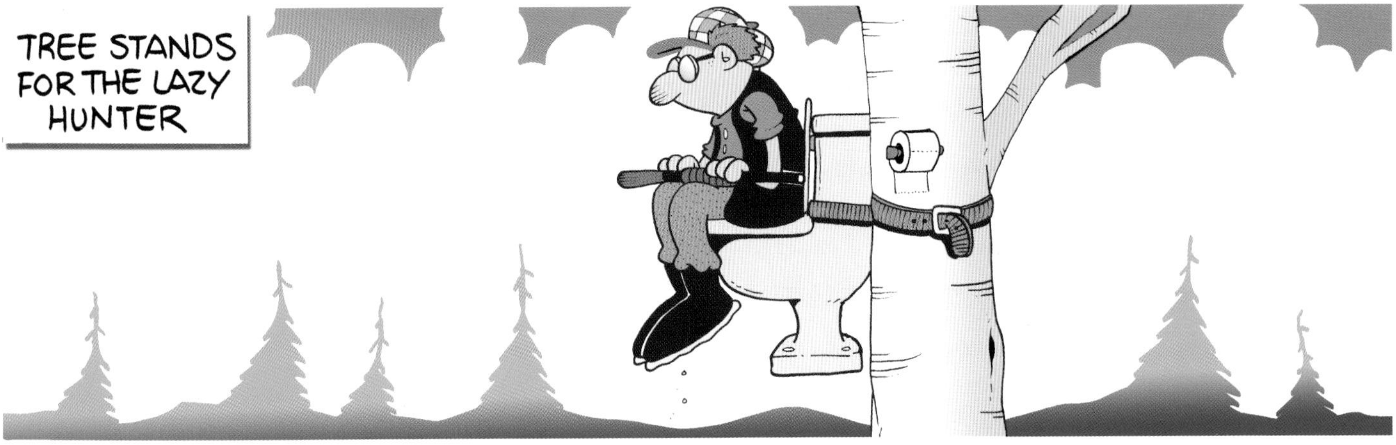
TREE STANDS FOR THE LAZY HUNTER

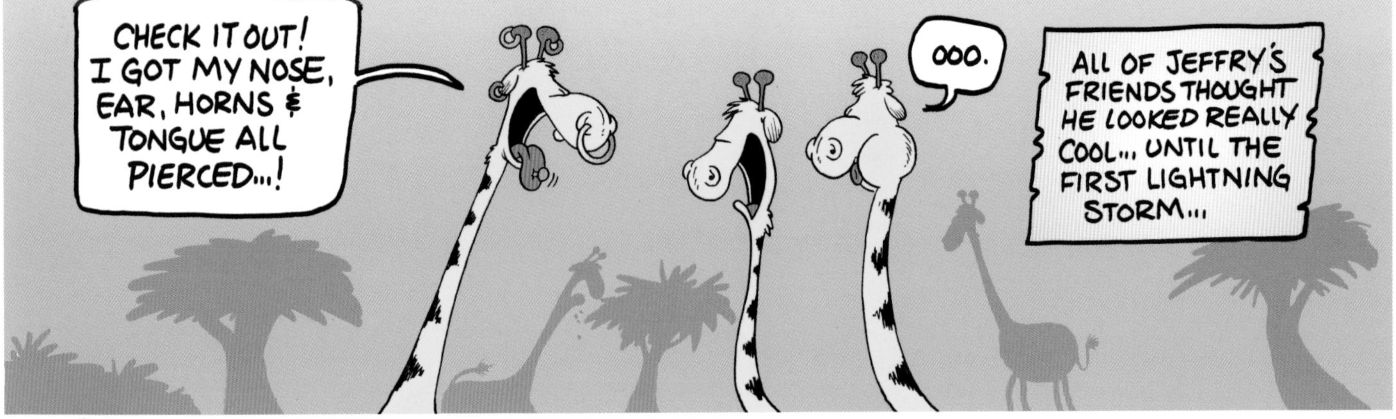
CHECK IT OUT! I GOT MY NOSE, EAR, HORNS & TONGUE ALL PIERCED...!
OOO.
ALL OF JEFFRY'S FRIENDS THOUGHT HE LOOKED REALLY COOL... UNTIL THE FIRST LIGHTNING STORM...

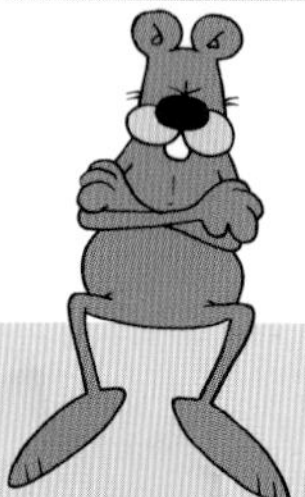

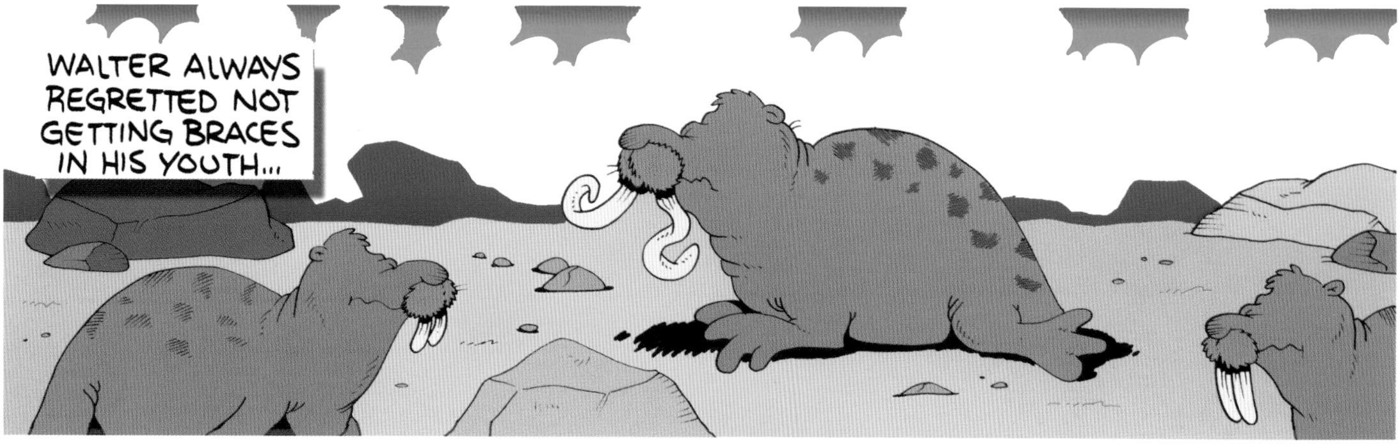
WALTER ALWAYS REGRETTED NOT GETTING BRACES IN HIS YOUTH...

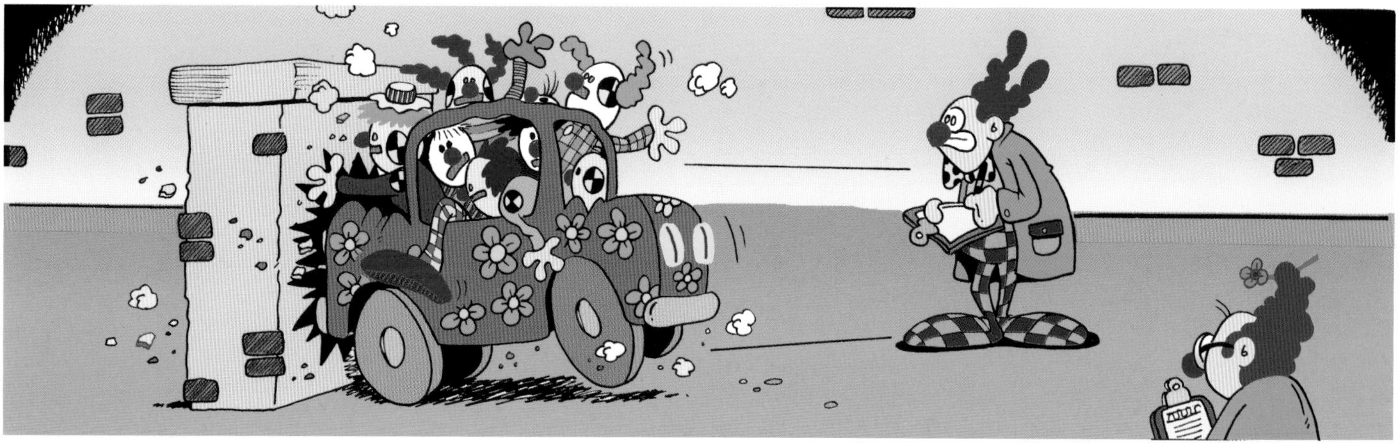

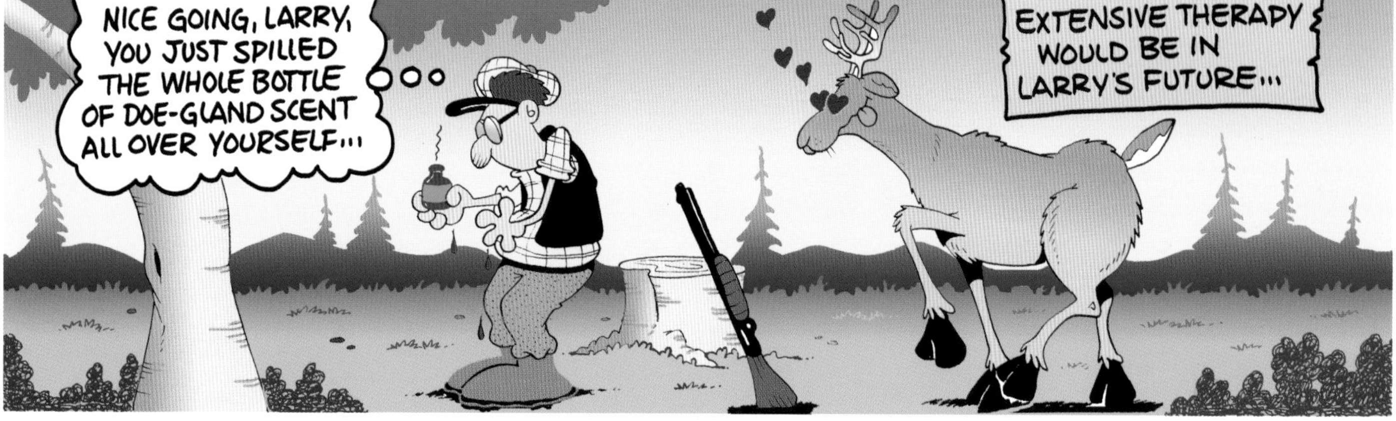
NICE GOING, LARRY, YOU JUST SPILLED THE WHOLE BOTTLE OF DOE-GLAND SCENT ALL OVER YOURSELF...
EXTENSIVE THERAPY WOULD BE IN LARRY'S FUTURE...

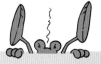

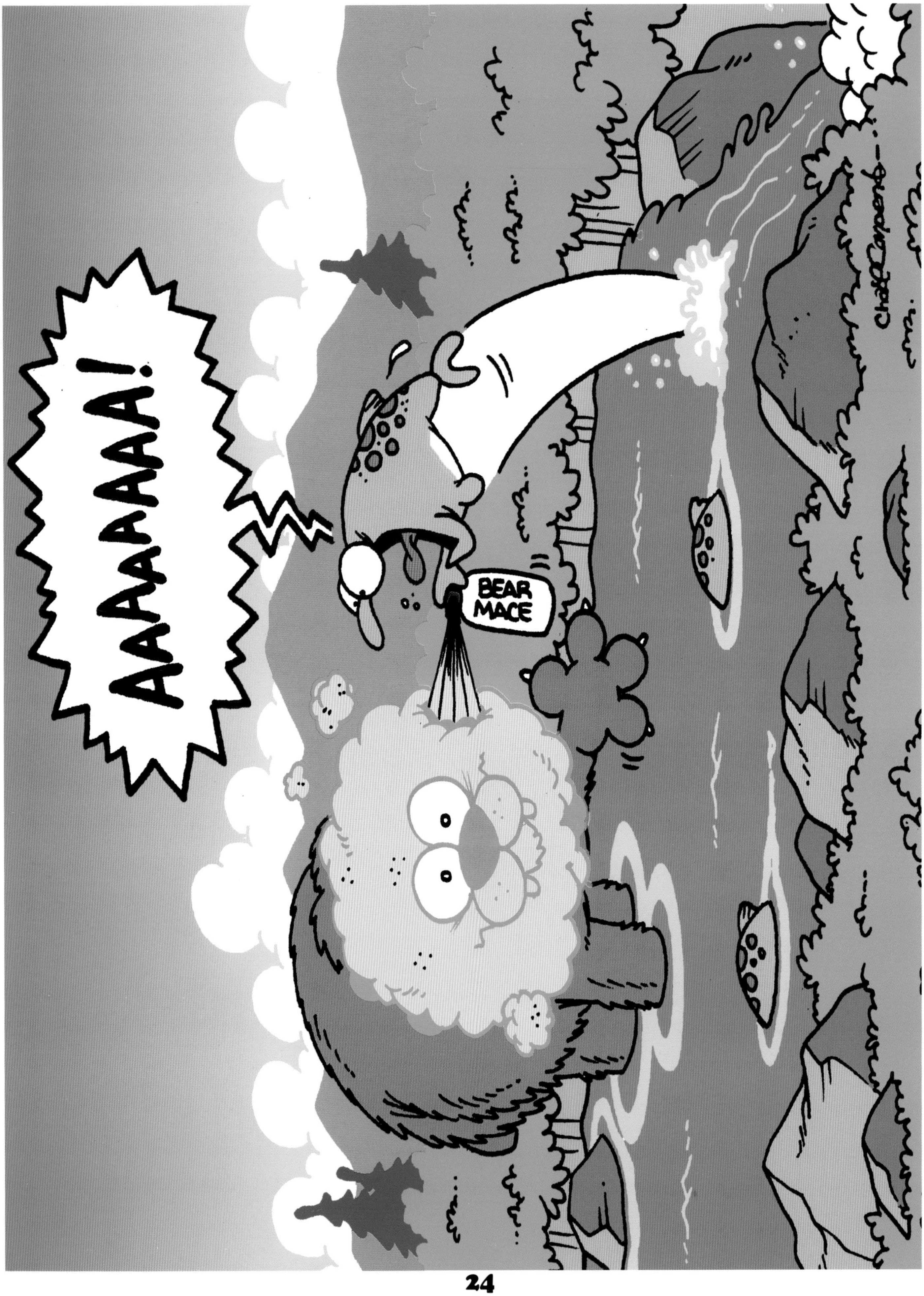
AAAAAAA!
BEAR MACE

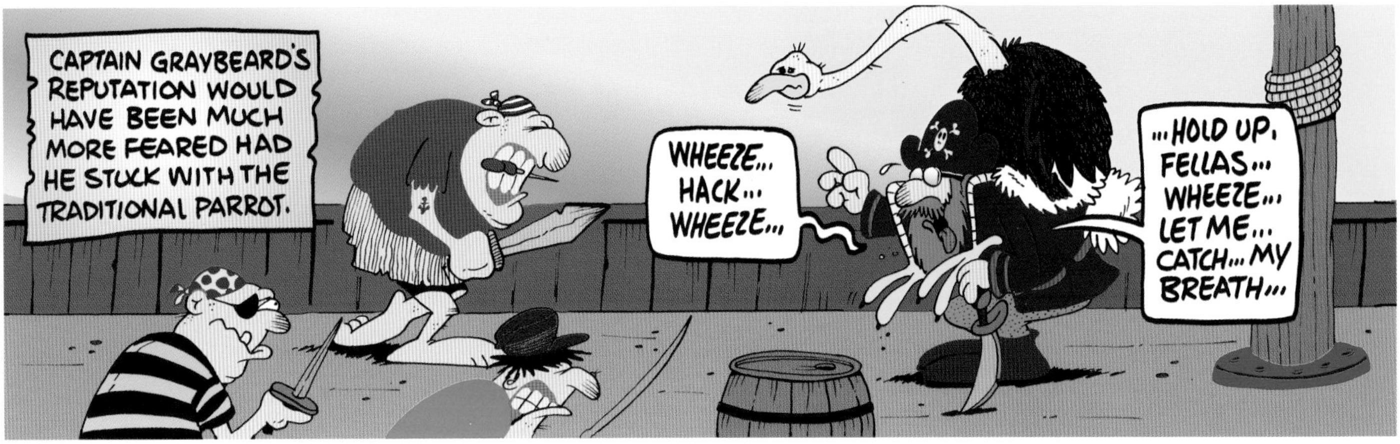
CAPTAIN GRAYBEARD'S REPUTATION WOULD HAVE BEEN MUCH MORE FEARED HAD HE STUCK WITH THE TRADITIONAL PARROT.
WHEEZE... HACK... WHEEZE...
...HOLD UP, FELLAS... WHEEZE... LET ME... CATCH... MY BREATH...

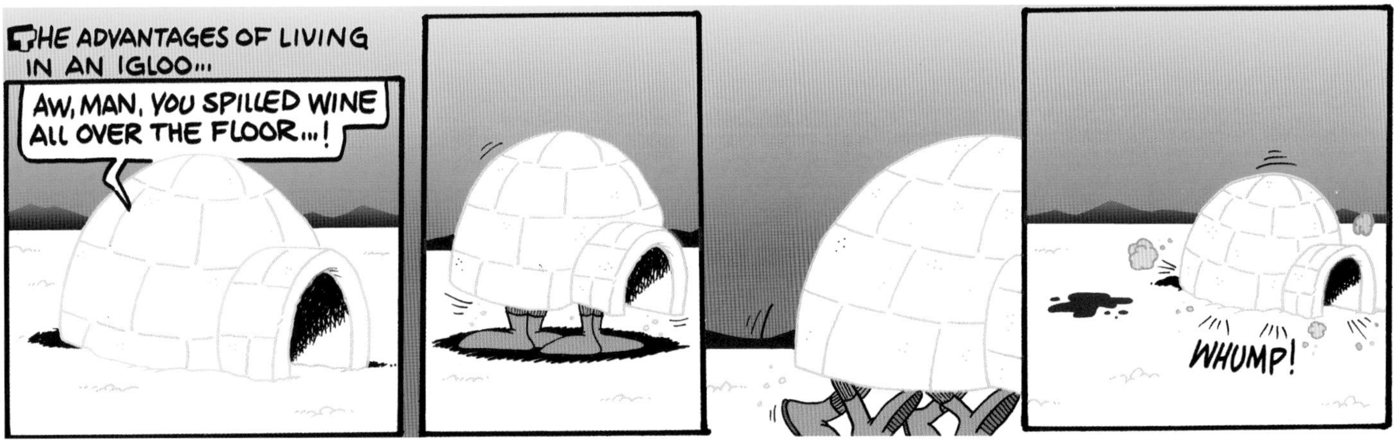
THE ADVANTAGES OF LIVING IN AN IGLOO...
AW, MAN, YOU SPILLED WINE ALL OVER THE FLOOR...!
WHUMP!

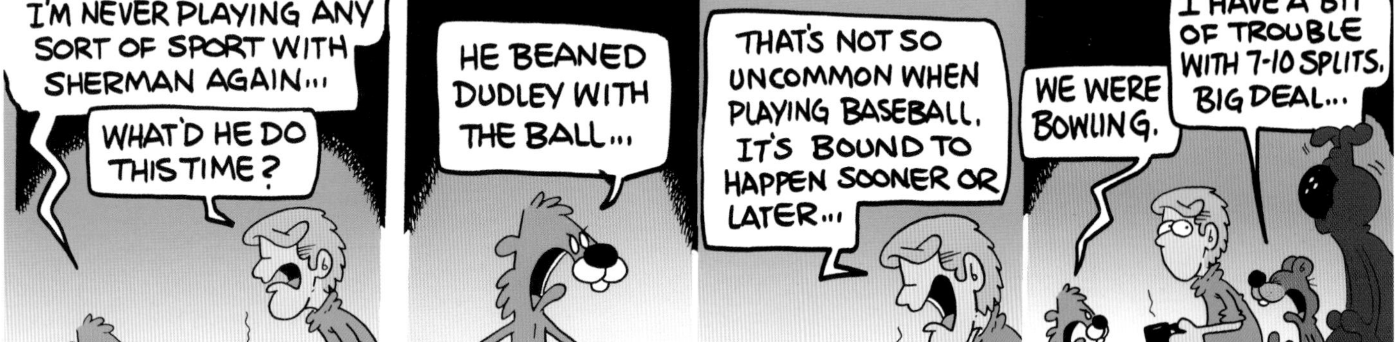
I'M NEVER PLAYING ANY SORT OF SPORT WITH SHERMAN AGAIN...
WHAT'D HE DO THIS TIME?
HE BEANED DUDLEY WITH THE BALL...
THAT'S NOT SO UNCOMMON WHEN PLAYING BASEBALL. IT'S BOUND TO HAPPEN SOONER OR LATER...
WE WERE BOWLING.
I HAVE A BIT OF TROUBLE WITH 7-10 SPLITS. BIG DEAL...

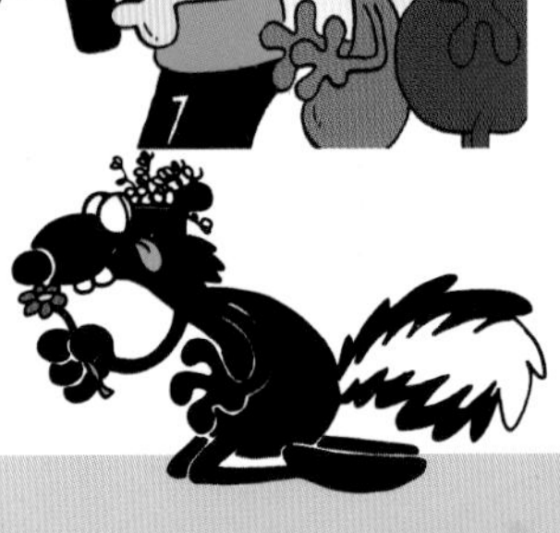

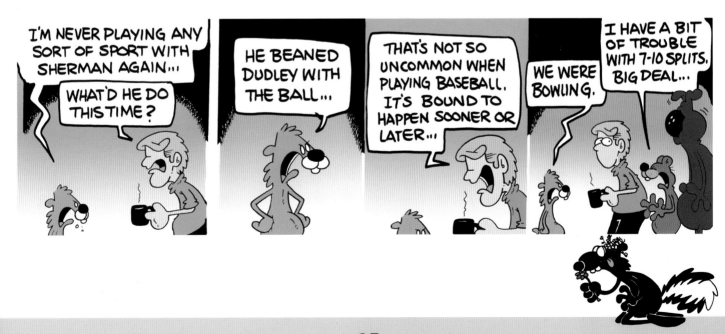

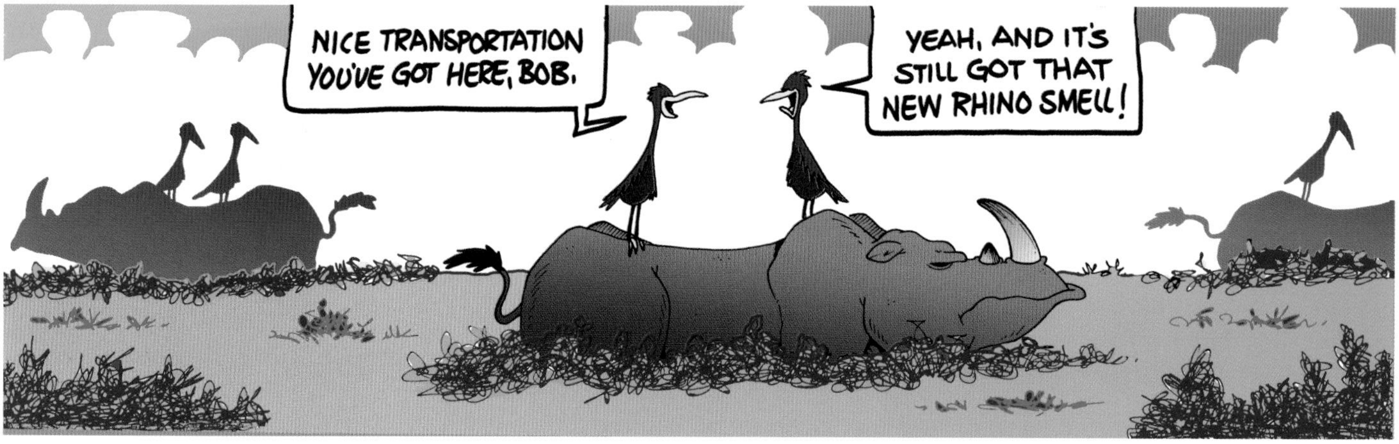
NICE TRANSPORTATION YOU'VE GOT HERE, BOB.
YEAH, AND IT'S STILL GOT THAT NEW RHINO SMELL!

This comic strip is based on the idea of
CAMERON McCLURE
Anchorage, AK

Do you have an idea that would make a great comic strip? Send it to:
www.tundracomics.com
or
TUNDRA IDEAS
PO BOX 770732
Eagle River, AK
99577

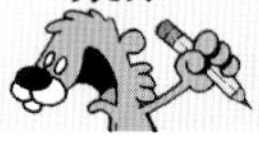

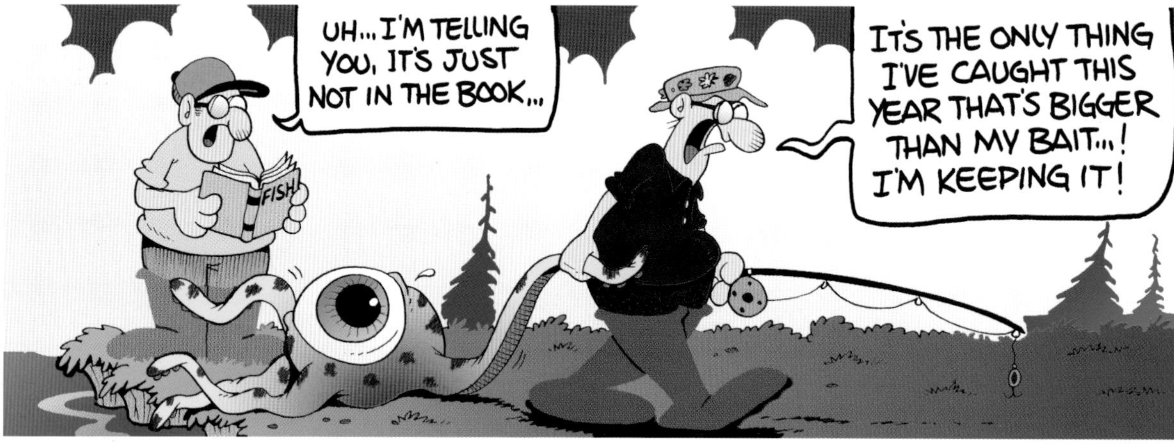
FISH
UH... I'M TELLING YOU, IT'S JUST NOT IN THE BOOK...
IT'S THE ONLY THING I'VE CAUGHT THIS YEAR THAT'S BIGGER THAN MY BAIT...! I'M KEEPING IT!

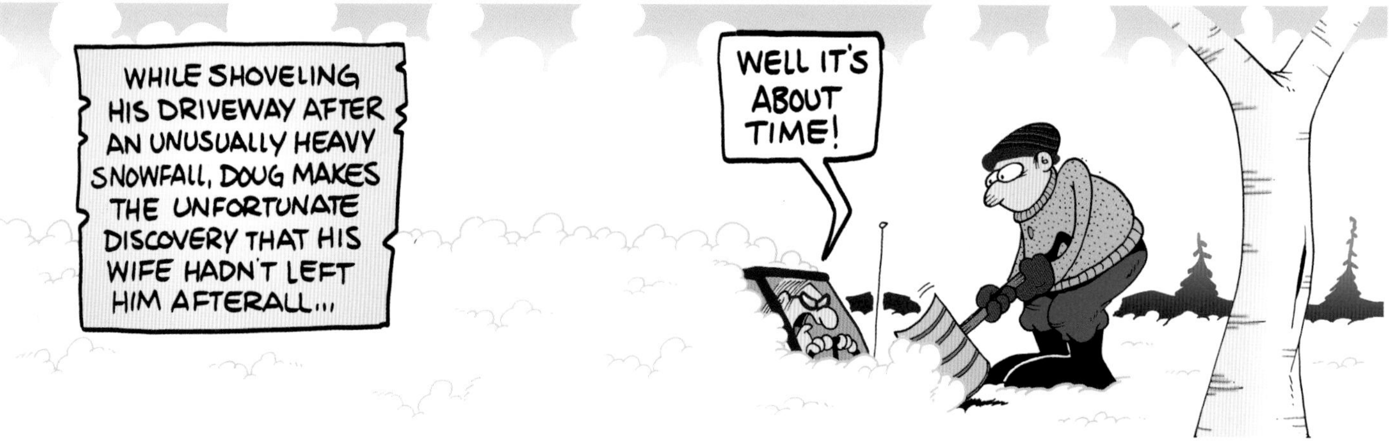
WHILE SHOVELING HIS DRIVEWAY AFTER AN UNUSUALLY HEAVY SNOWFALL, DOUG MAKES THE UNFORTUNATE DISCOVERY THAT HIS WIFE HADN'T LEFT HIM AFTERALL...
WELL IT'S ABOUT TIME!

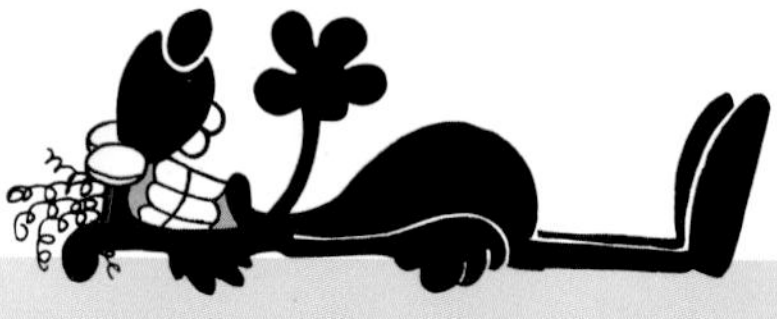

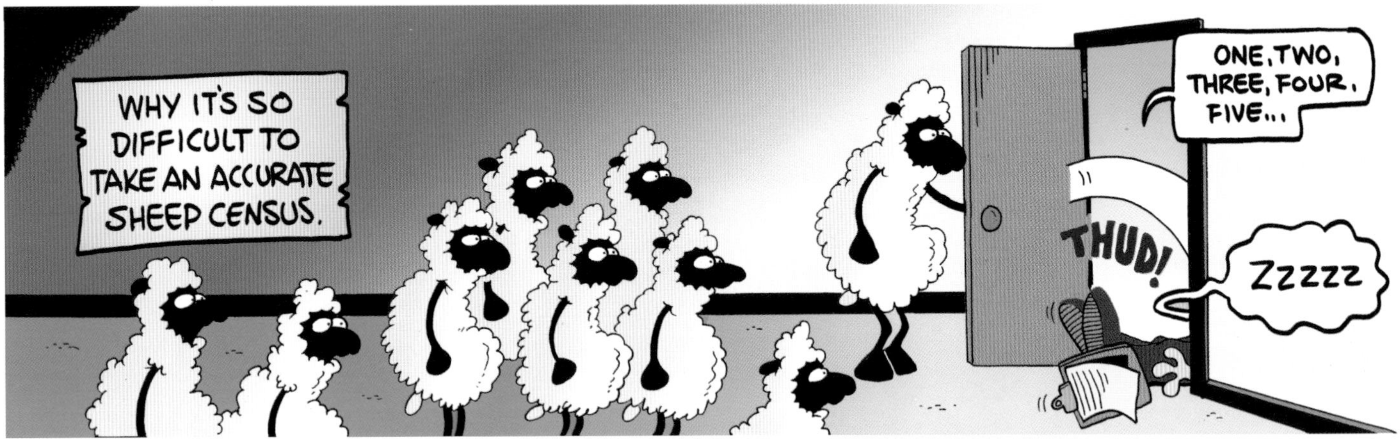
WHY IT'S SO DIFFICULT TO TAKE AN ACCURATE SHEEP CENSUS.
ONE, TWO, THREE, FOUR, FIVE...
THUD!
Zzzzz

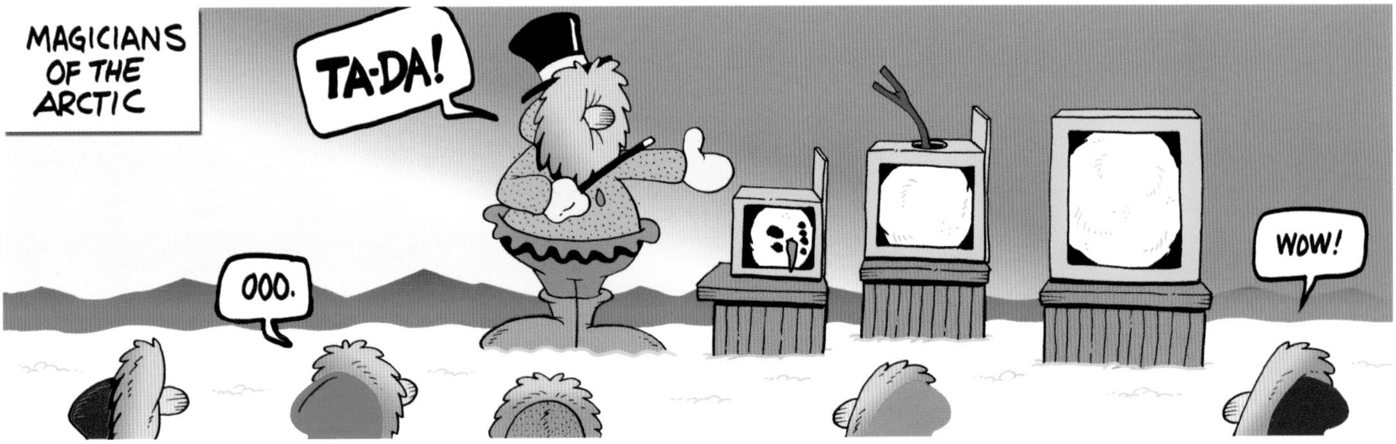
MAGICIANS OF THE ARCTIC
TA-DA!
OOO.
WOW!

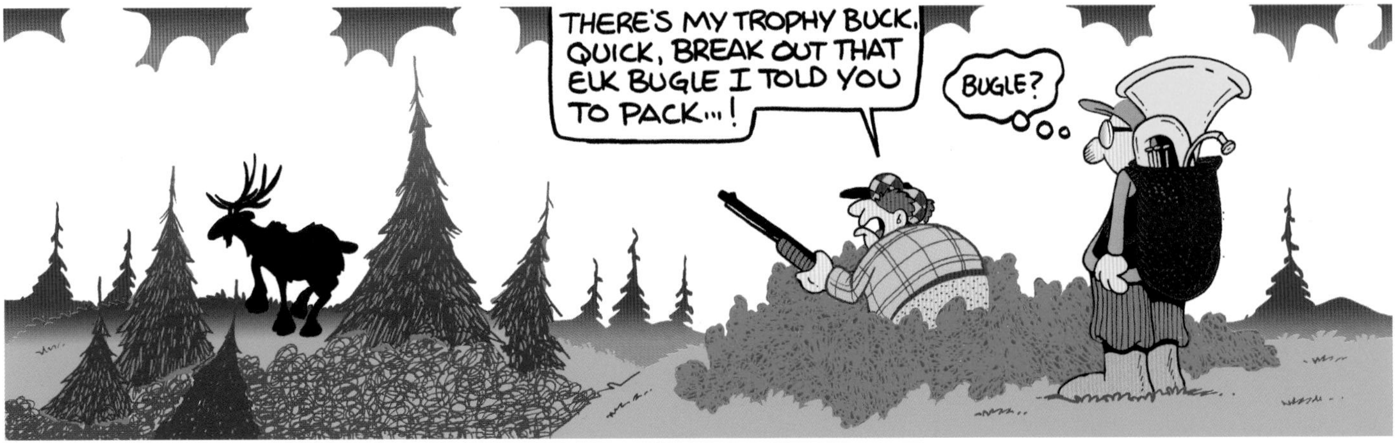
THERE'S MY TROPHY BUCK. QUICK, BREAK OUT THAT ELK BUGLE I TOLD YOU TO PACK...!
BUGLE?

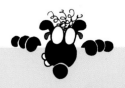

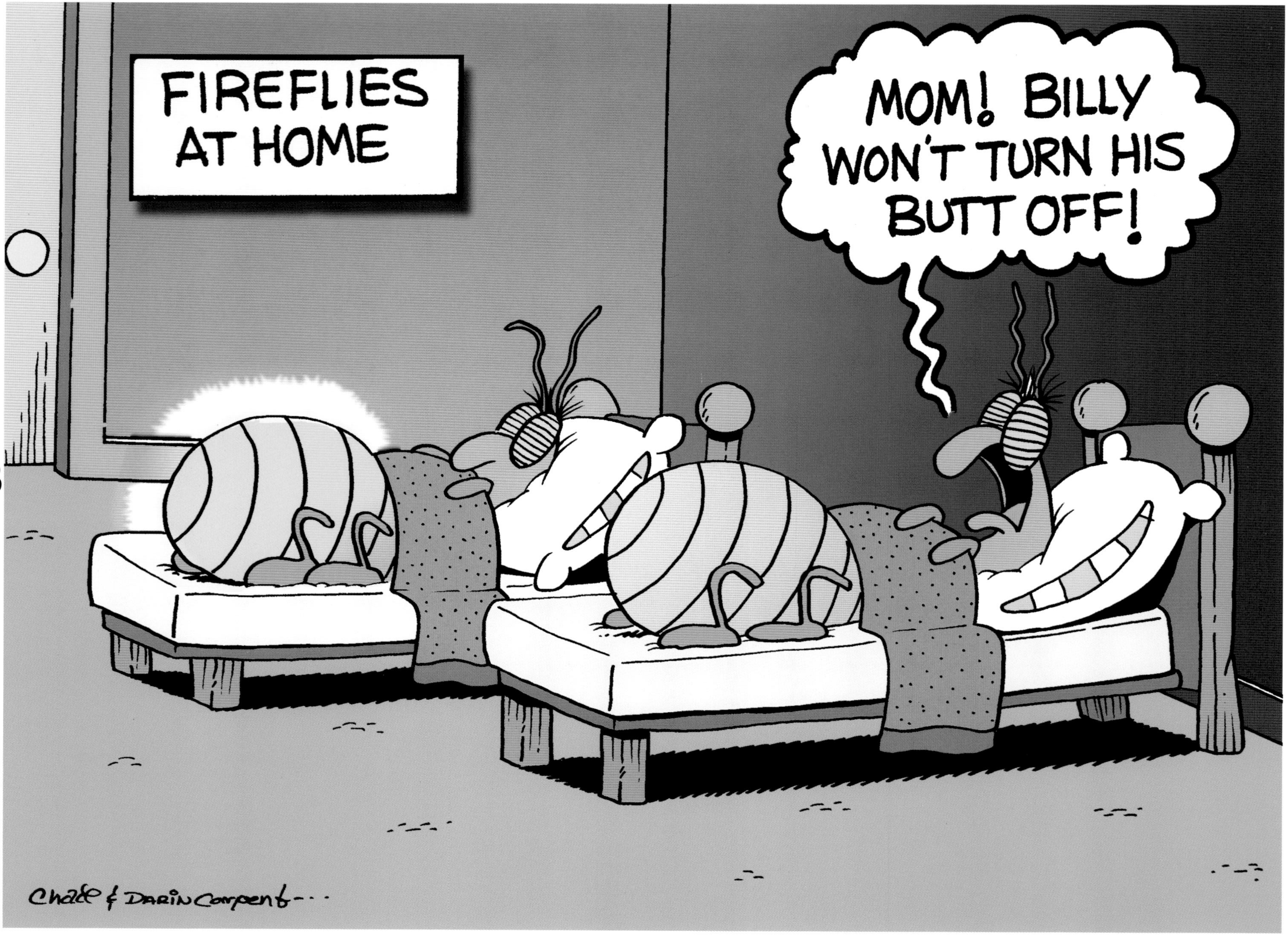
FIREFLIES AT HOME
MOM! BILLY WON'T TURN HIS BUTT OFF!
Chad & Darin Carpenter...

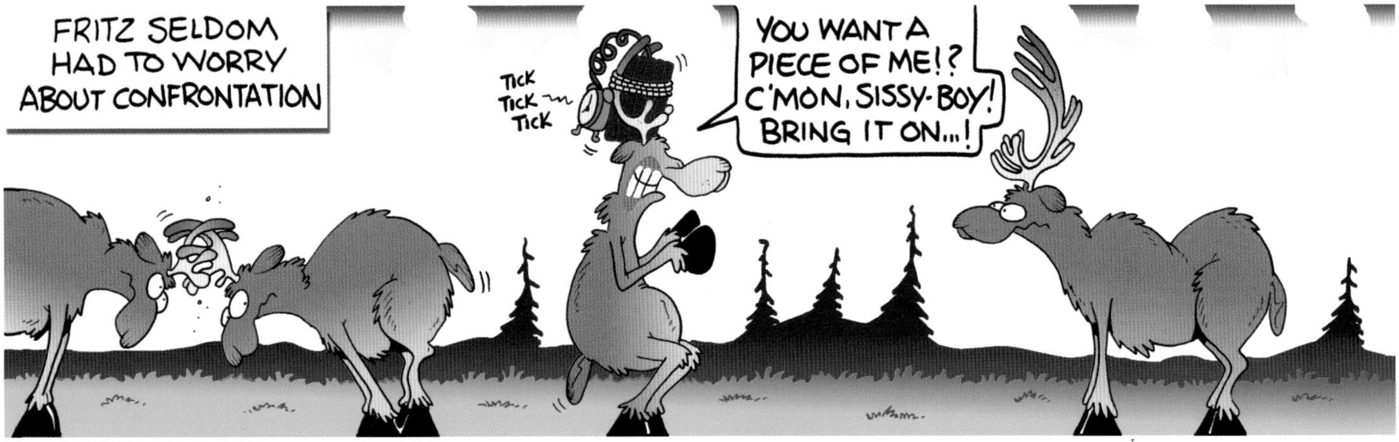
FRITZ SELDOM HAD TO WORRY ABOUT CONFRONTATION
TICK TICK TICK
YOU WANT A PIECE OF ME!? C'MON, SISSY-BOY! BRING IT ON...!

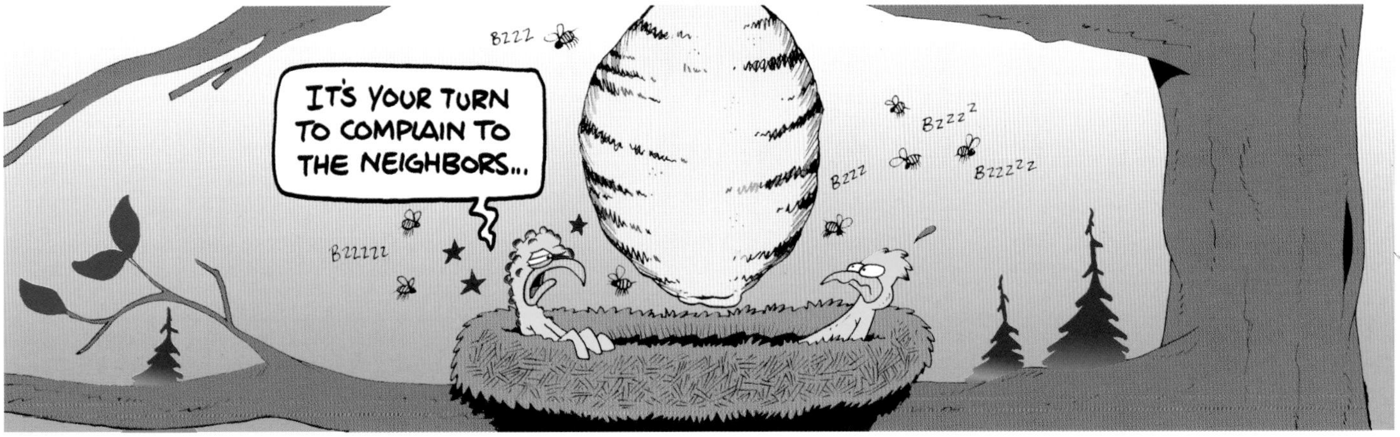
BZZZ
IT'S YOUR TURN TO COMPLAIN TO THE NEIGHBORS...
BZZZ^Z
BZZZ
BZZZZZ
BZZZZZ

This comic strip is based on the idea of
John Laux
Anchorage, AK

Do you have an idea that would make a great comic strip? Send it to:
www.tundracomics.com
or
TUNDRA IDEAS
PO BOX 770732
Eagle River, AK
99577

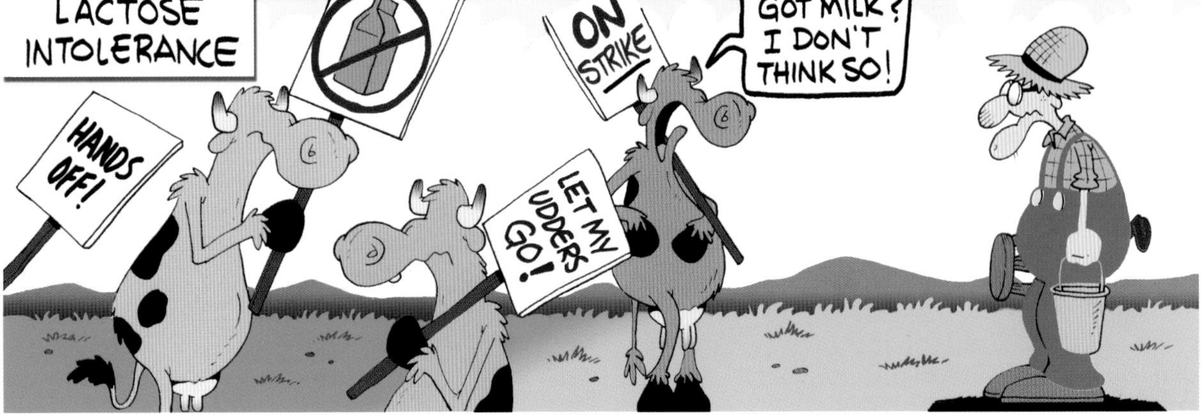
LACTOSE INTOLERANCE
HANDS OFF!
ON STRIKE
LET MY UDDERS GO!
GOT MILK? I DON'T THINK SO!

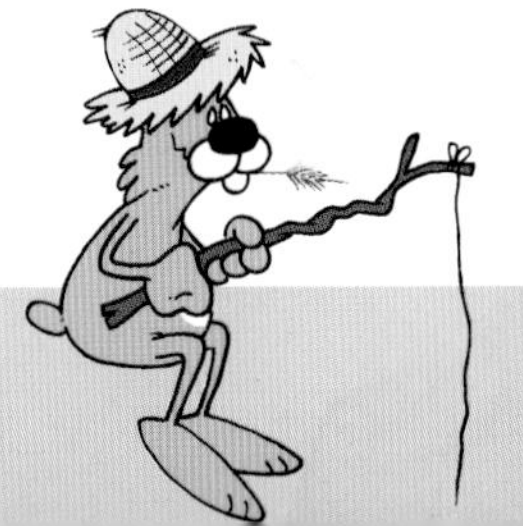

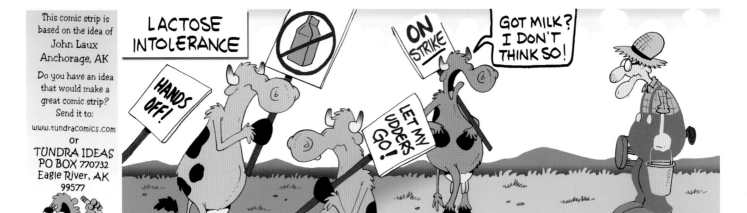

This comic strip is based on the idea of

Alicia Greene
Wasilla, AK

Do you have an idea that would make a great comic strip? Send it to:

www.tundracomics.com
or
TUNDRA IDEAS
PO BOX 770732
Eagle River, AK
99577

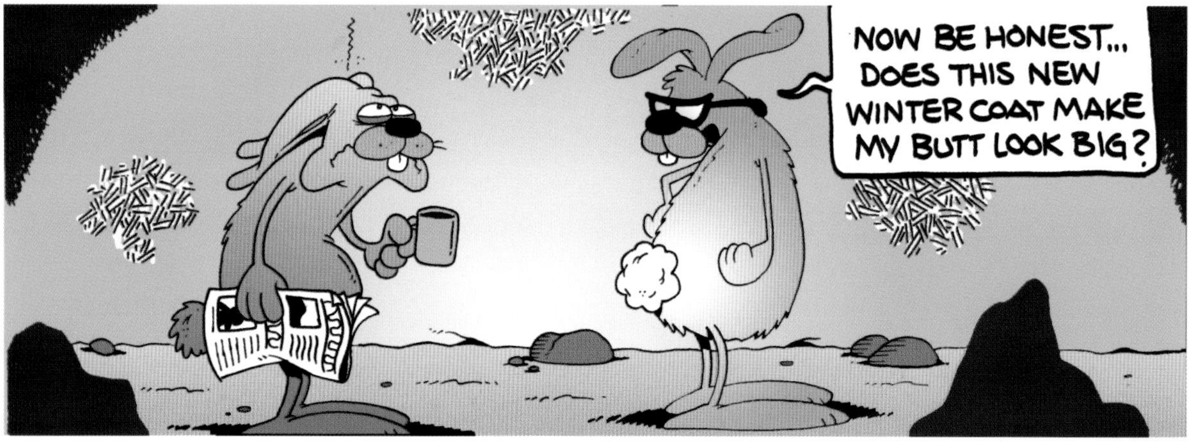
NOW BE HONEST... DOES THIS NEW WINTER COAT MAKE MY BUTT LOOK BIG?

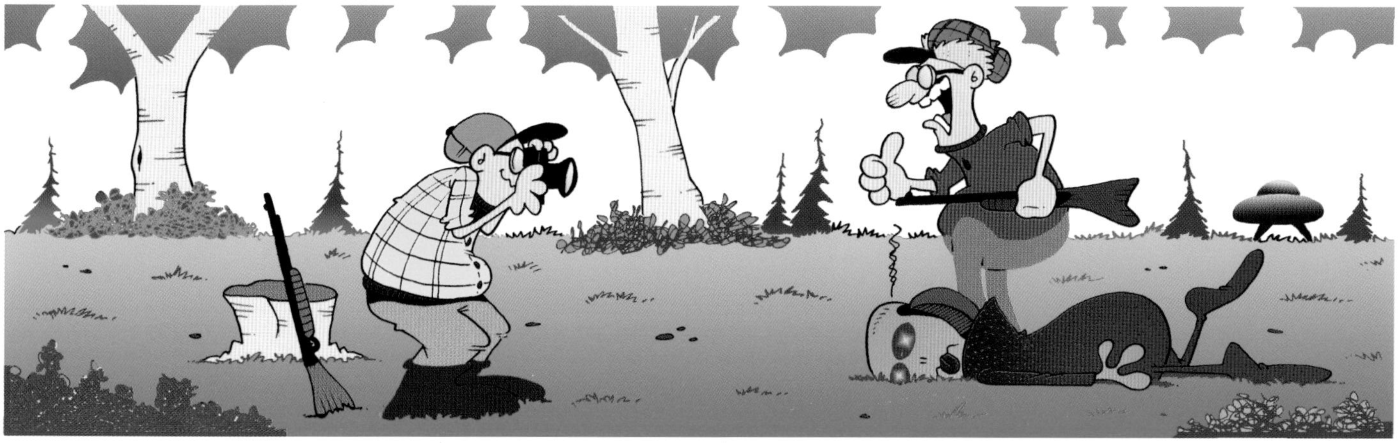

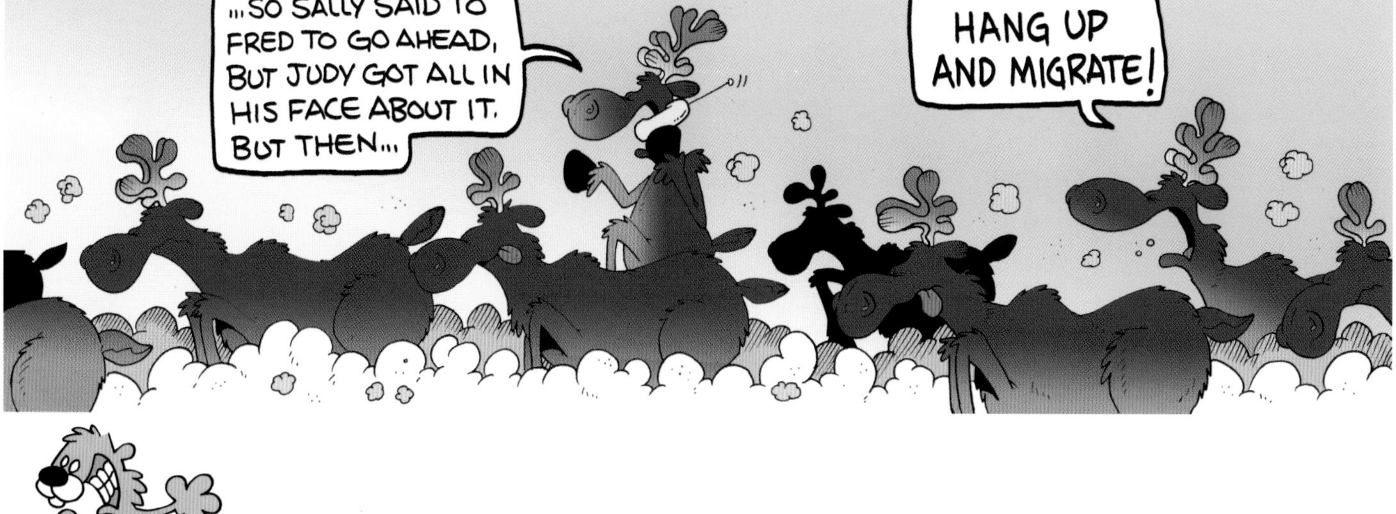
...SO SALLY SAID TO FRED TO GO AHEAD, BUT JUDY GOT ALL IN HIS FACE ABOUT IT. BUT THEN...
HANG UP AND MIGRATE!

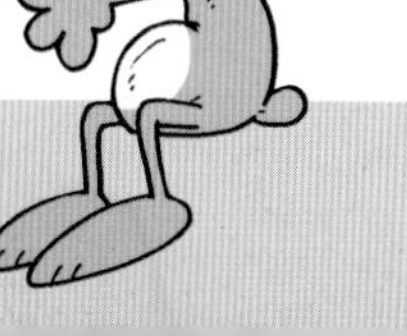

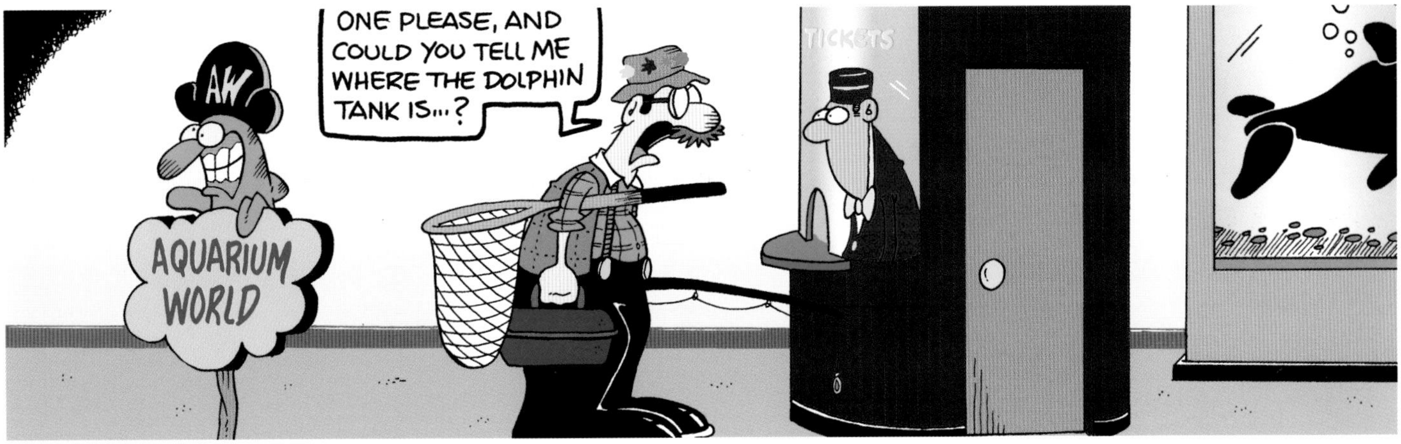
AW
AQUARIUM WORLD
ONE PLEASE, AND COULD YOU TELL ME WHERE THE DOLPHIN TANK IS...?
TICKETS

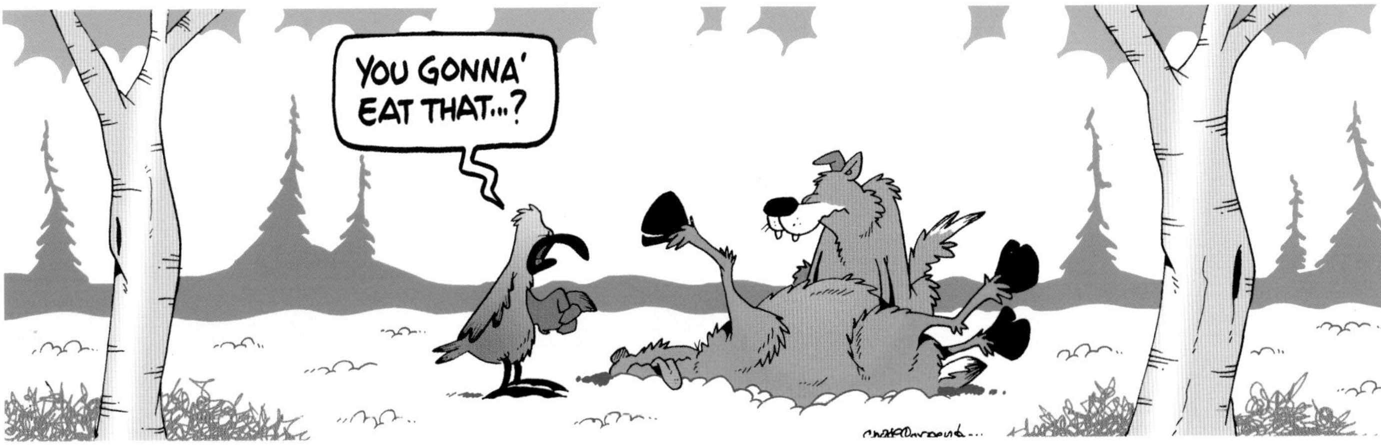
YOU GONNA' EAT THAT...?

This comic strip is based on the idea of
David Hendry
Delta Junction, AK

Do you have an idea that would make a great comic strip? Send it to:
www.tundracomics.com
or
TUNDRA IDEAS
PO BOX 770732
Eagle River, AK
99577

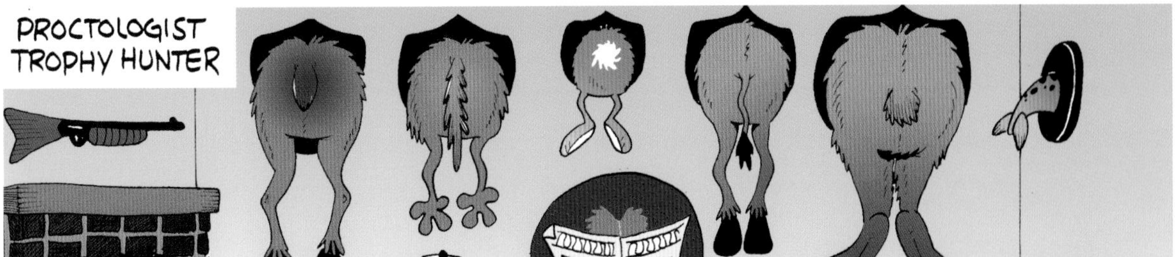
PROCTOLOGIST TROPHY HUNTER

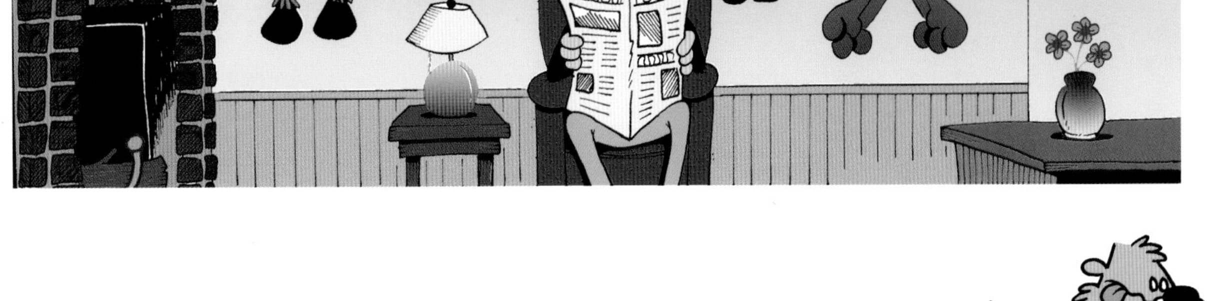

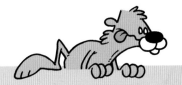

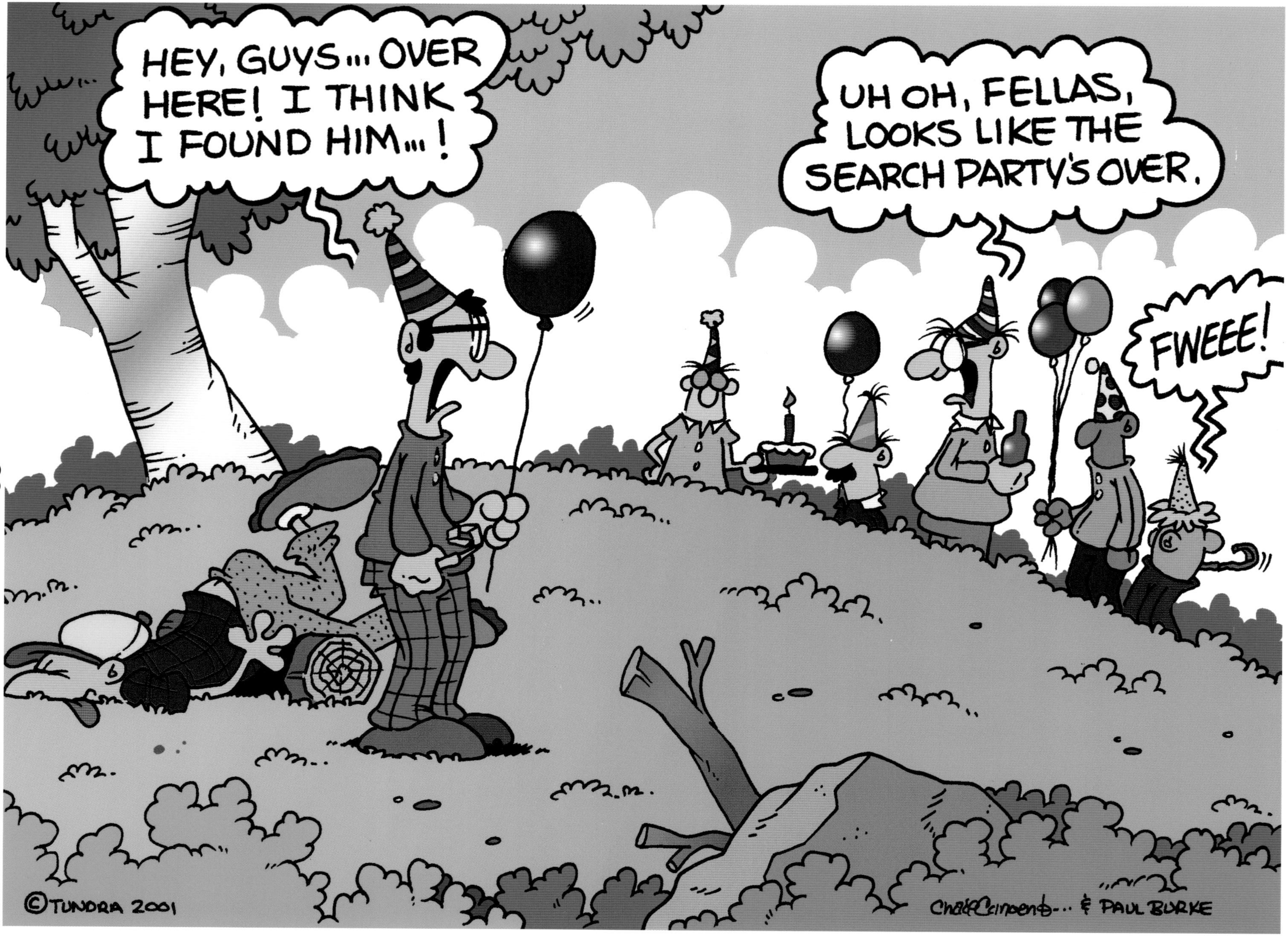
HEY, GUYS... OVER HERE! I THINK I FOUND HIM...!
UH OH, FELLAS, LOOKS LIKE THE SEARCH PARTY'S OVER.
FWEEE!
©TUNDRA 2001
& PAUL BURKE

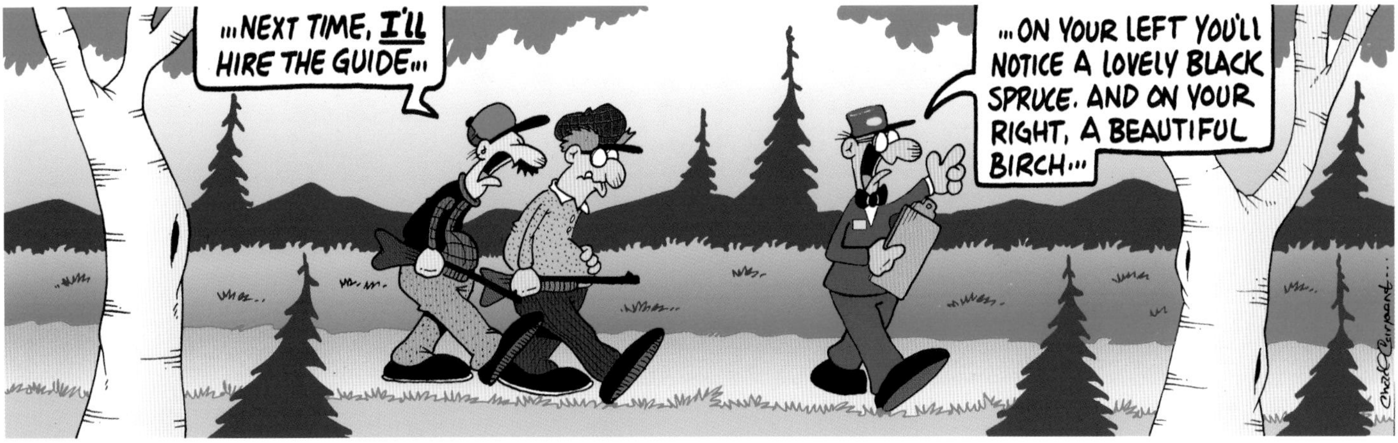
...NEXT TIME, I'LL HIRE THE GUIDE...
...ON YOUR LEFT YOU'LL NOTICE A LOVELY BLACK SPRUCE. AND ON YOUR RIGHT, A BEAUTIFUL BIRCH...

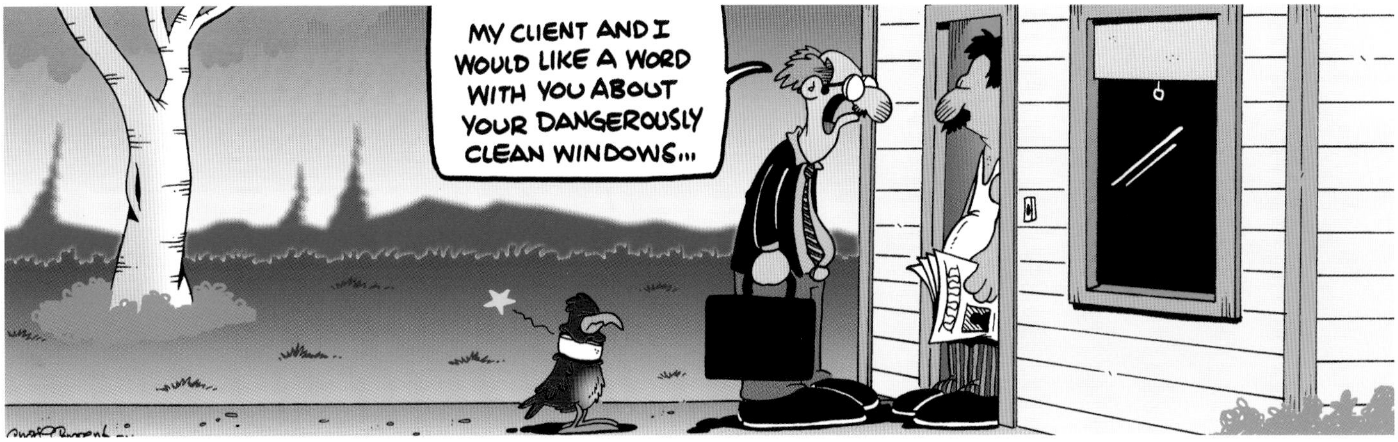
MY CLIENT AND I WOULD LIKE A WORD WITH YOU ABOUT YOUR DANGEROUSLY CLEAN WINDOWS...

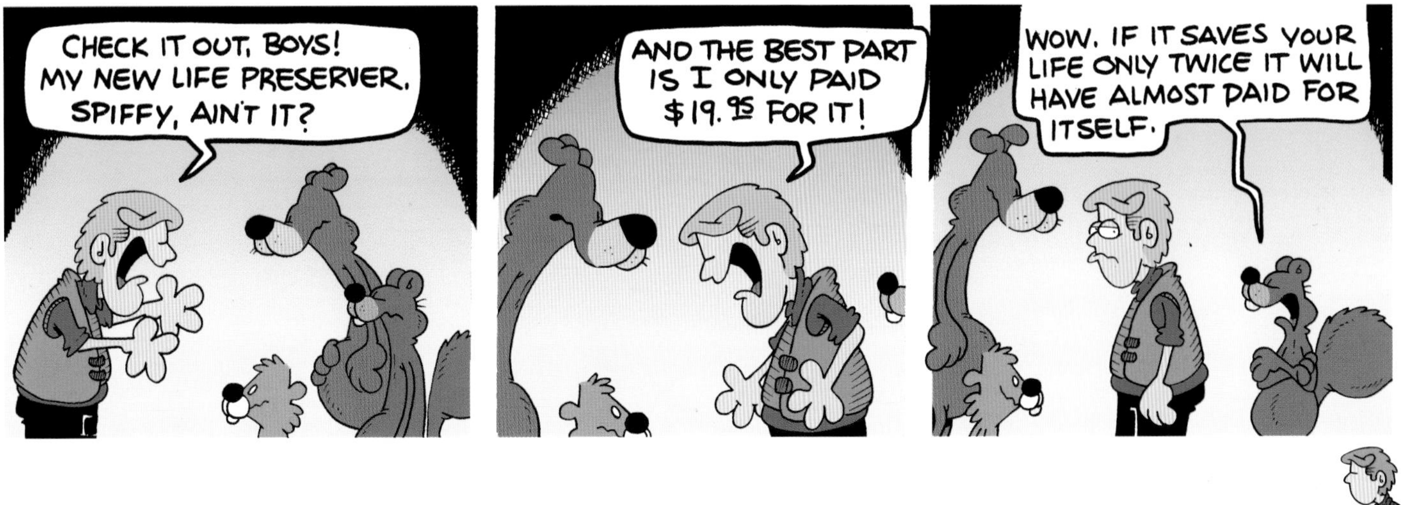
CHECK IT OUT, BOYS! MY NEW LIFE PRESERVER. SPIFFY, AIN'T IT?
AND THE BEST PART IS I ONLY PAID $19.95 FOR IT!
WOW. IF IT SAVES YOUR LIFE ONLY TWICE IT WILL HAVE ALMOST PAID FOR ITSELF.

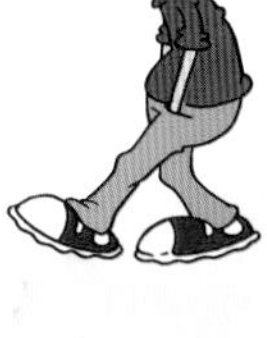

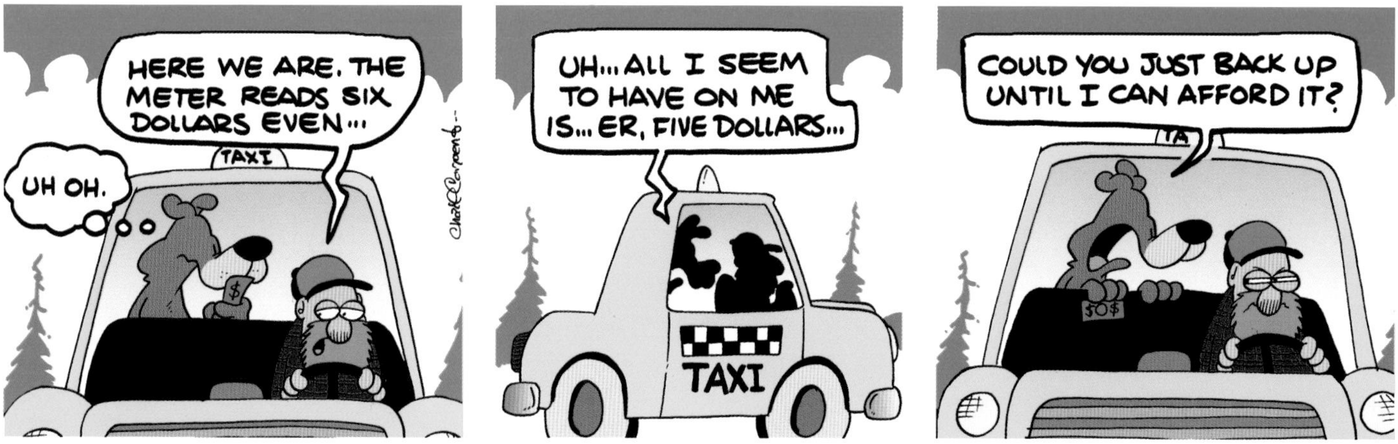
HERE WE ARE. THE METER READS SIX DOLLARS EVEN...
UH OH.
TAXI
UH...ALL I SEEM TO HAVE ON ME IS... ER, FIVE DOLLARS...
TAXI
COULD YOU JUST BACK UP UNTIL I CAN AFFORD IT?

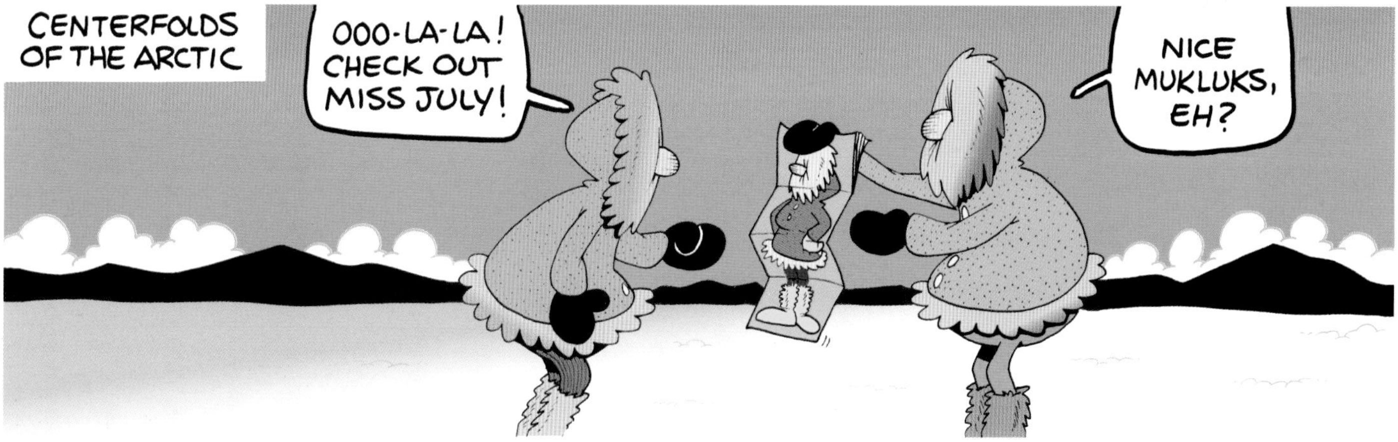
CENTERFOLDS OF THE ARCTIC
OOO-LA-LA! CHECK OUT MISS JULY!
NICE MUKLUKS, EH?

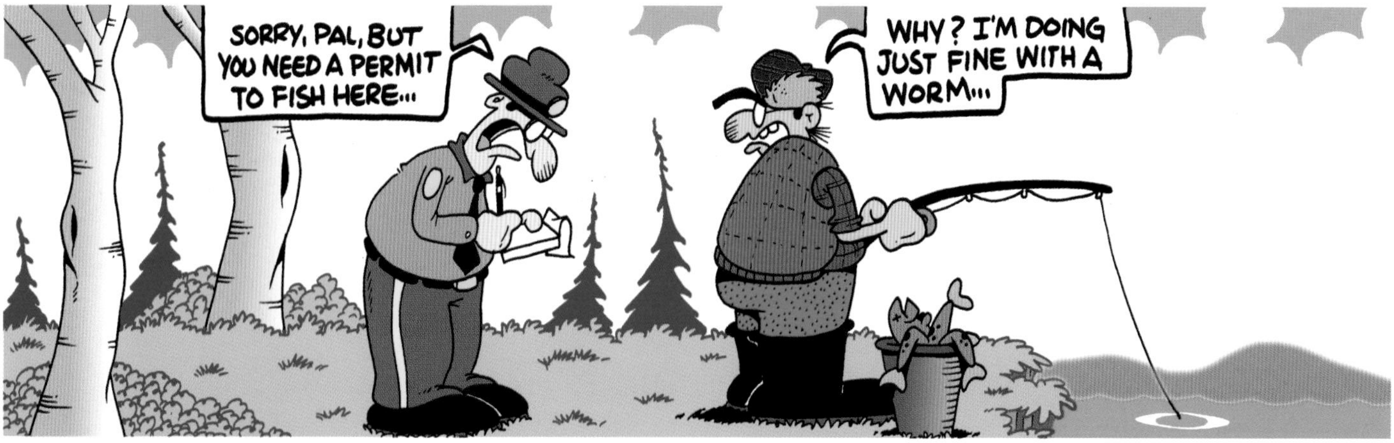
SORRY, PAL, BUT YOU NEED A PERMIT TO FISH HERE...
WHY? I'M DOING JUST FINE WITH A WORM...

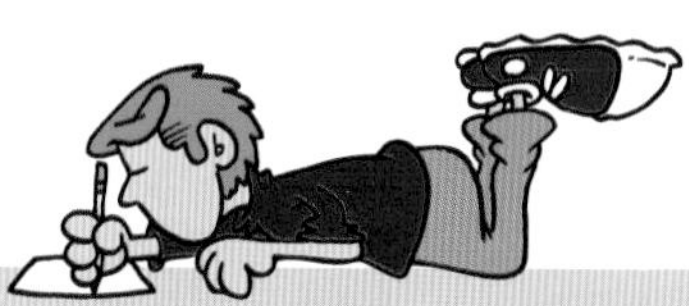

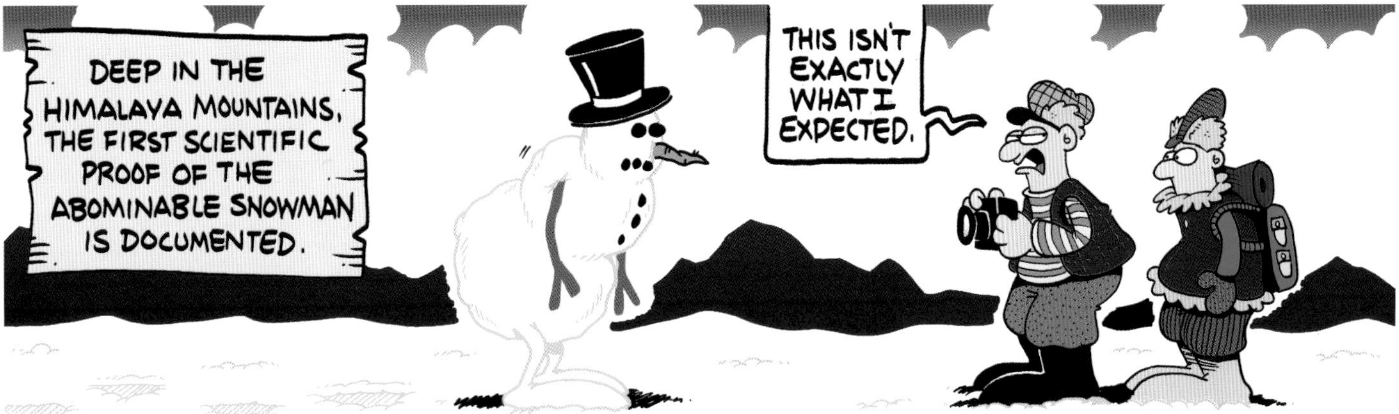
DEEP IN THE HIMALAYA MOUNTAINS, THE FIRST SCIENTIFIC PROOF OF THE ABOMINABLE SNOWMAN IS DOCUMENTED.
THIS ISN'T EXACTLY WHAT I EXPECTED.

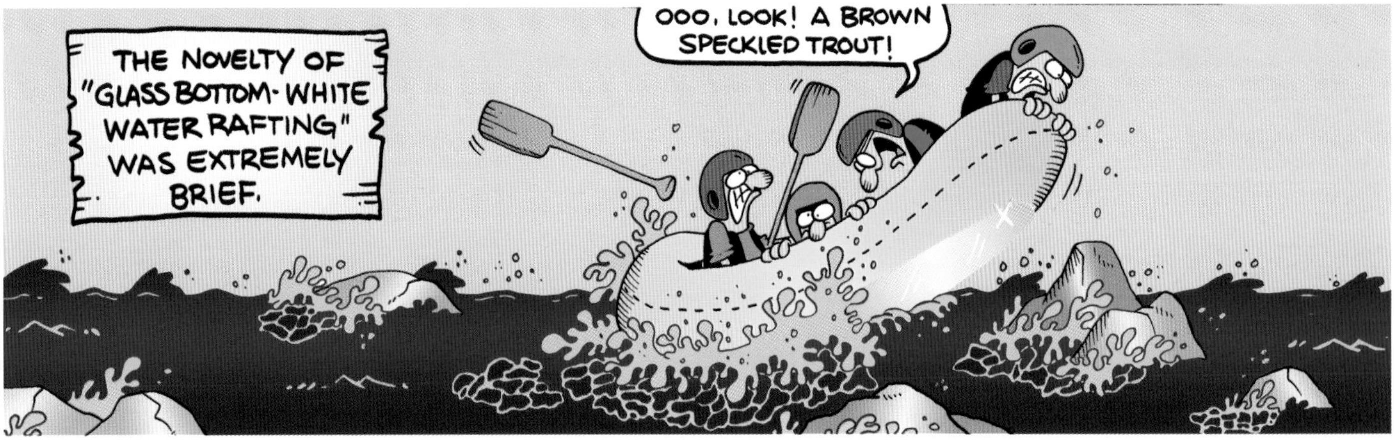
THE NOVELTY OF "GLASS BOTTOM-WHITE WATER RAFTING" WAS EXTREMELY BRIEF.
OOO, LOOK! A BROWN SPECKLED TROUT!

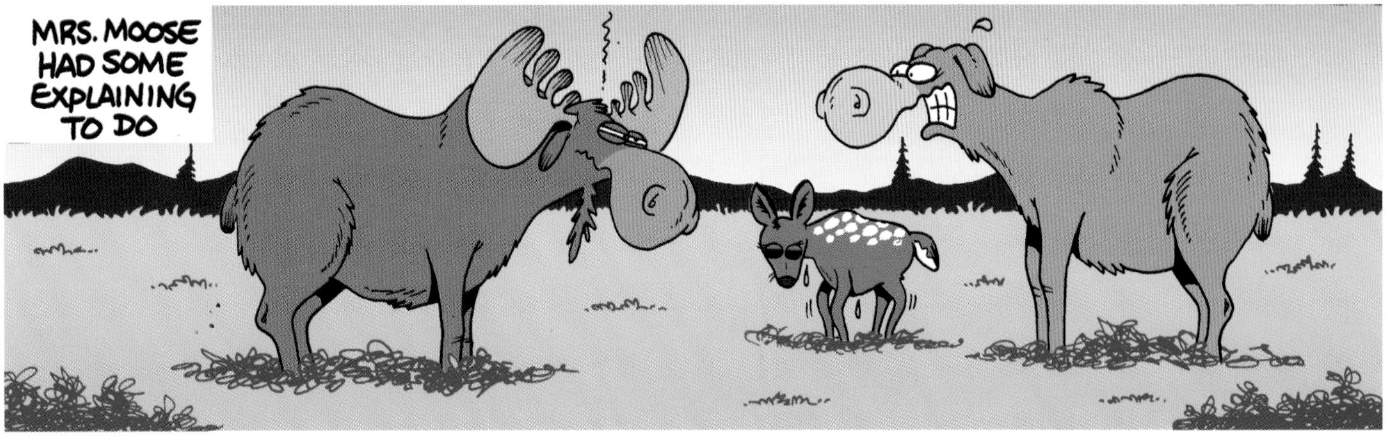
MRS. MOOSE HAD SOME EXPLAINING TO DO

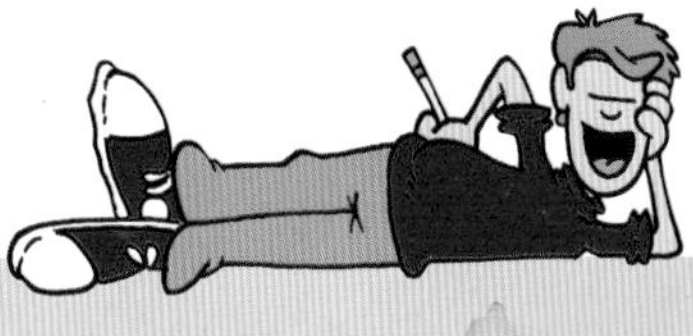

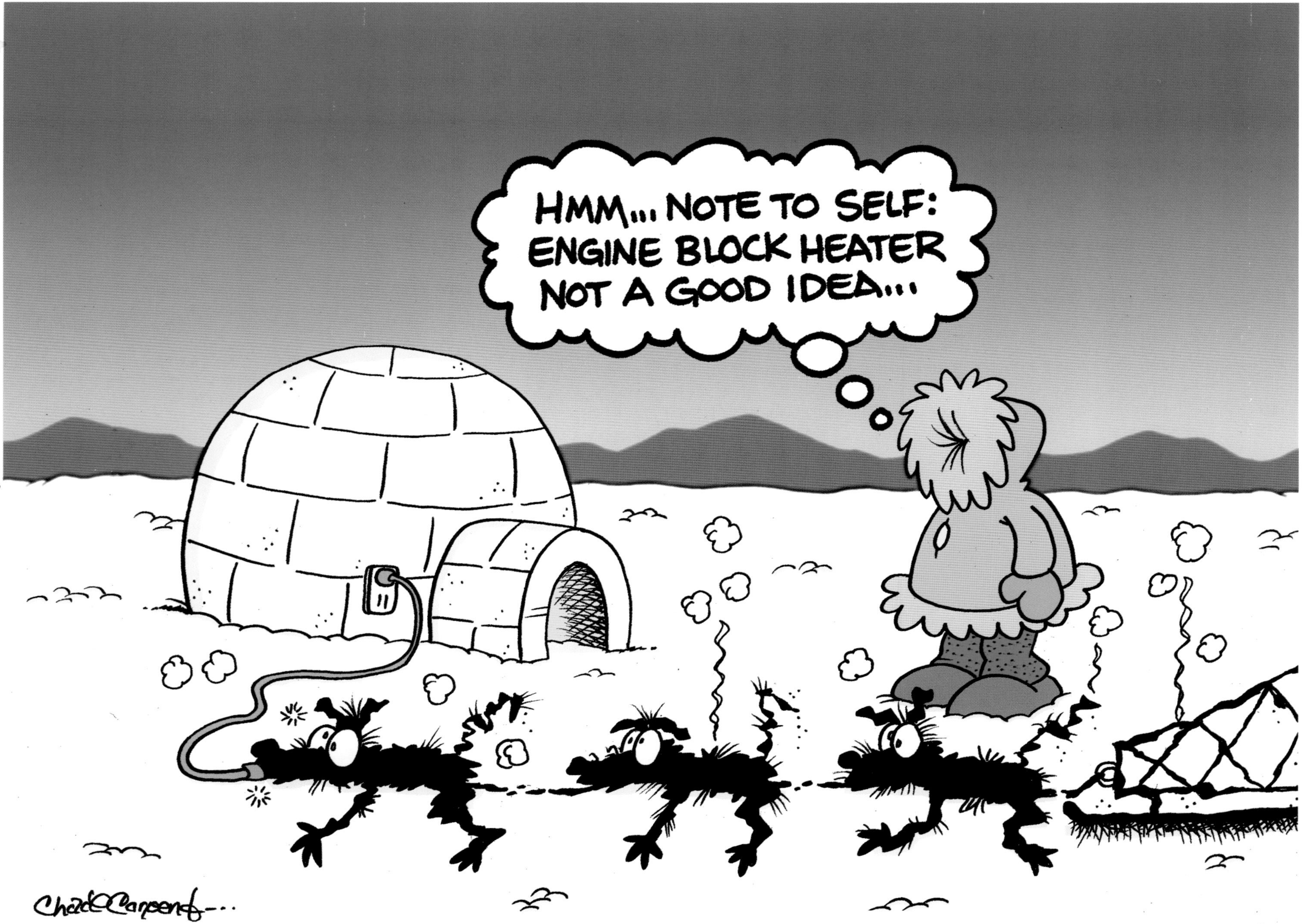
HMM... NOTE TO SELF: ENGINE BLOCK HEATER NOT A GOOD IDEA...

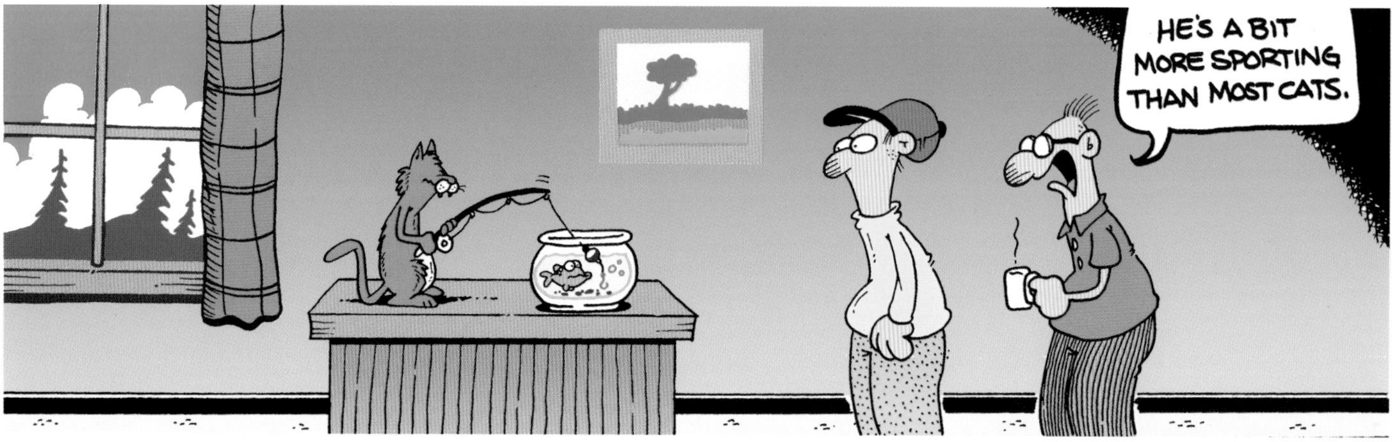
HE'S A BIT MORE SPORTING THAN MOST CATS.

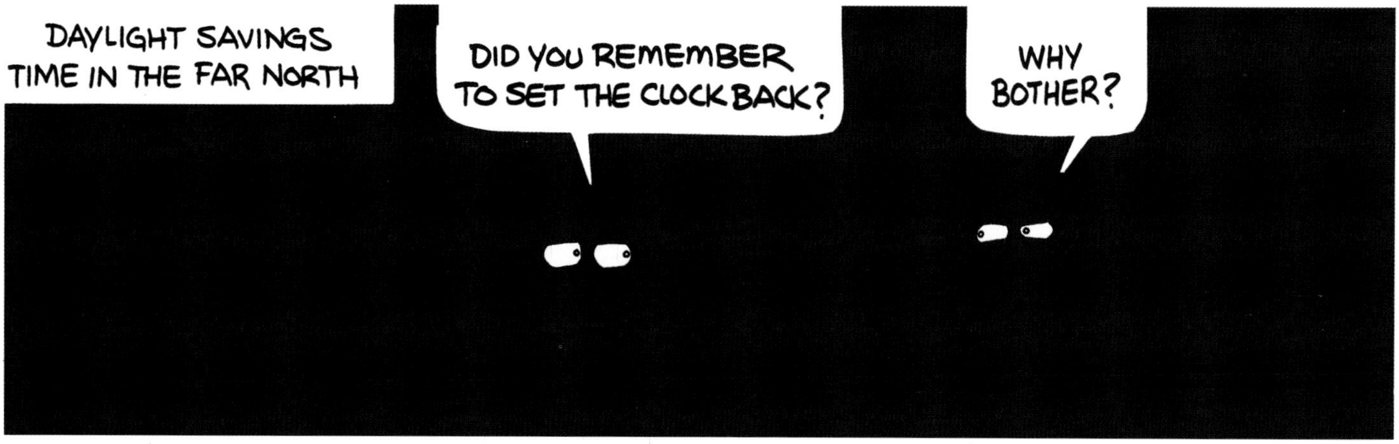
DAYLIGHT SAVINGS TIME IN THE FAR NORTH
DID YOU REMEMBER TO SET THE CLOCK BACK?
WHY BOTHER?

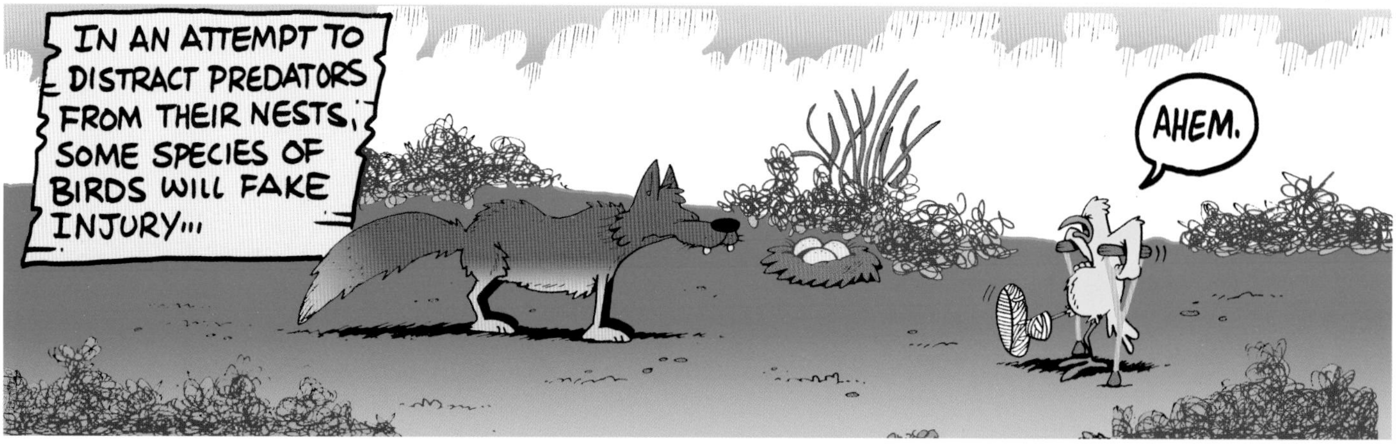
IN AN ATTEMPT TO DISTRACT PREDATORS FROM THEIR NESTS, SOME SPECIES OF BIRDS WILL FAKE INJURY...
AHEM.

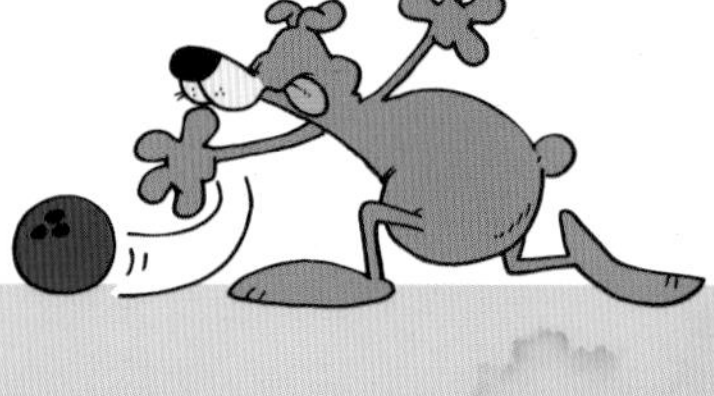

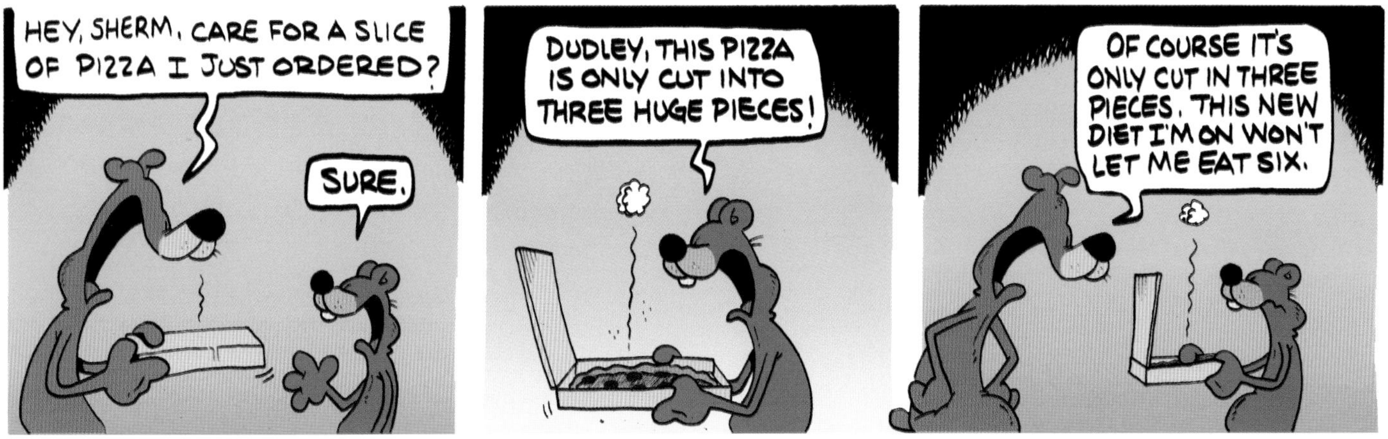
HEY, SHERM. CARE FOR A SLICE OF PIZZA I JUST ORDERED?
SURE.
DUDLEY, THIS PIZZA IS ONLY CUT INTO THREE HUGE PIECES!
OF COURSE IT'S ONLY CUT IN THREE PIECES. THIS NEW DIET I'M ON WON'T LET ME EAT SIX.

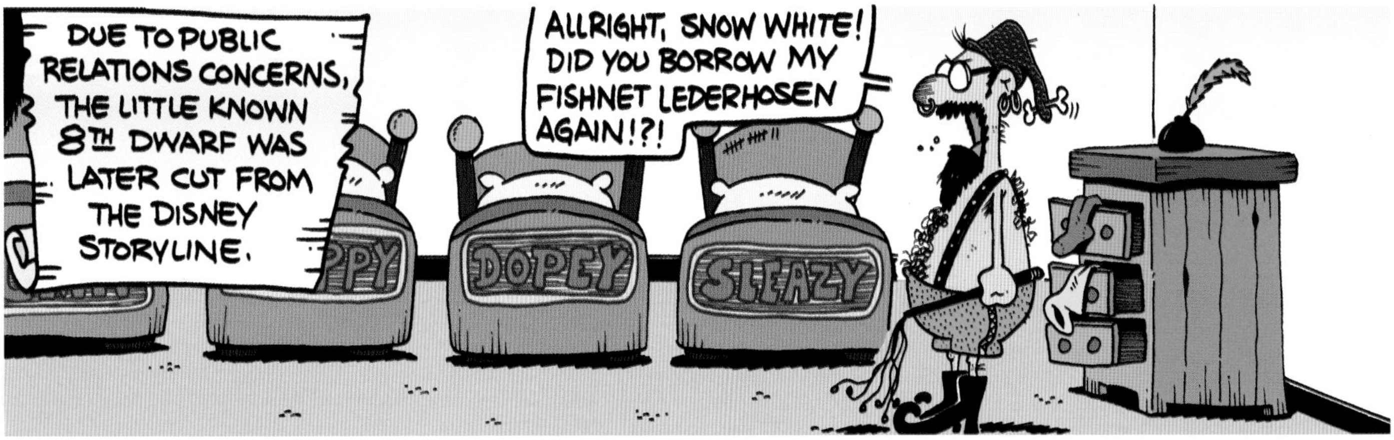
DUE TO PUBLIC RELATIONS CONCERNS, THE LITTLE KNOWN 8TH DWARF WAS LATER CUT FROM THE DISNEY STORYLINE.
ALLRIGHT, SNOW WHITE! DID YOU BORROW MY FISHNET LEDERHOSEN AGAIN!?!
DOPEY
SLEAZY

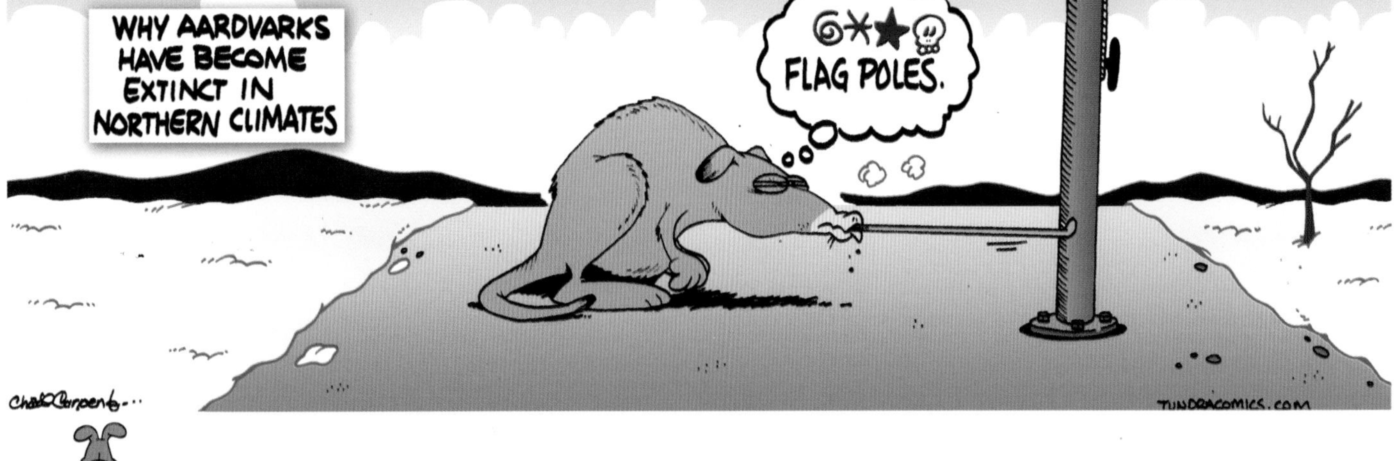
WHY AARDVARKS HAVE BECOME EXTINCT IN NORTHERN CLIMATES
FLAG POLES.
TUNDRACOMICS.COM

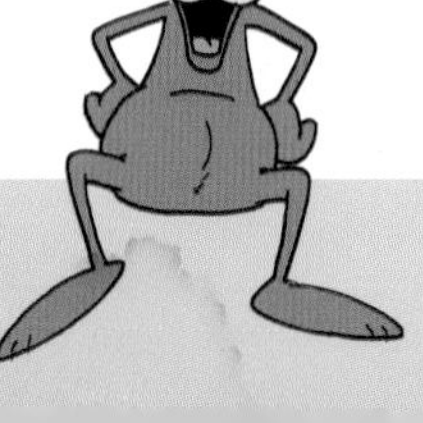

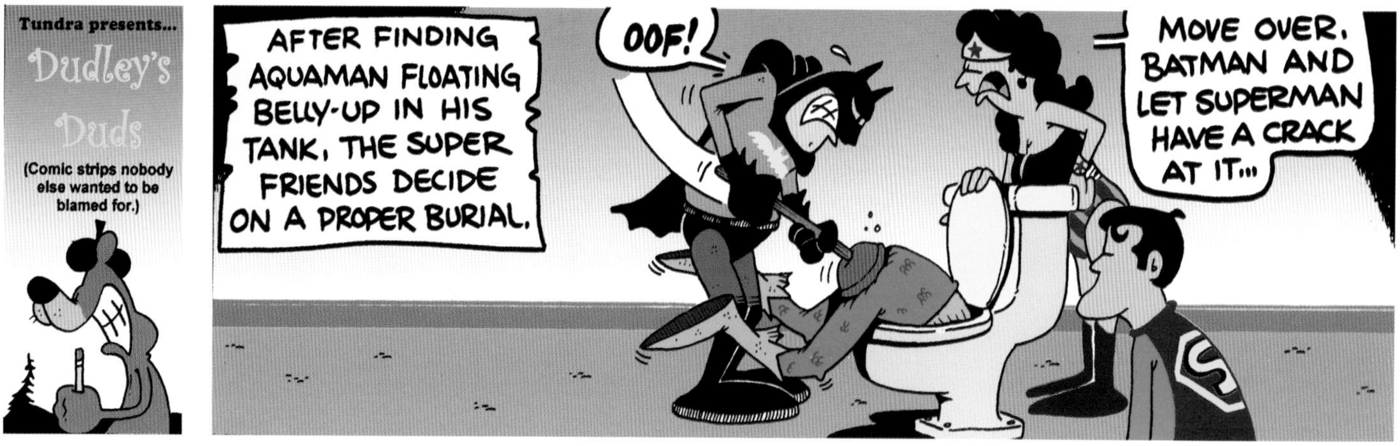
Tundra presents...
Dudley's Duds
(Comic strips nobody else wanted to be blamed for.)
AFTER FINDING AQUAMAN FLOATING BELLY-UP IN HIS TANK, THE SUPER FRIENDS DECIDE ON A PROPER BURIAL.
OOF!
MOVE OVER, BATMAN AND LET SUPERMAN HAVE A CRACK AT IT...

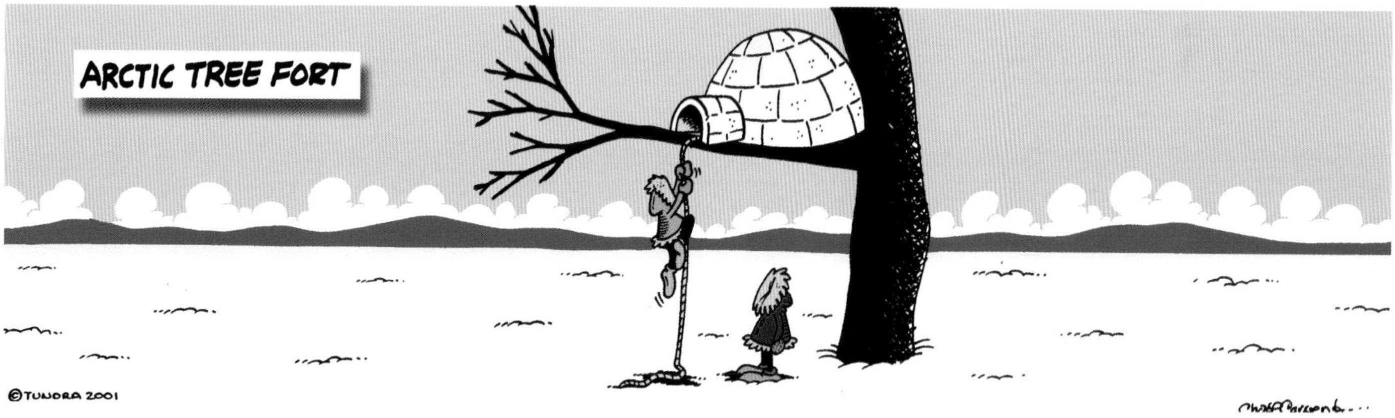
ARCTIC TREE FORT
©TUNDRA 2001

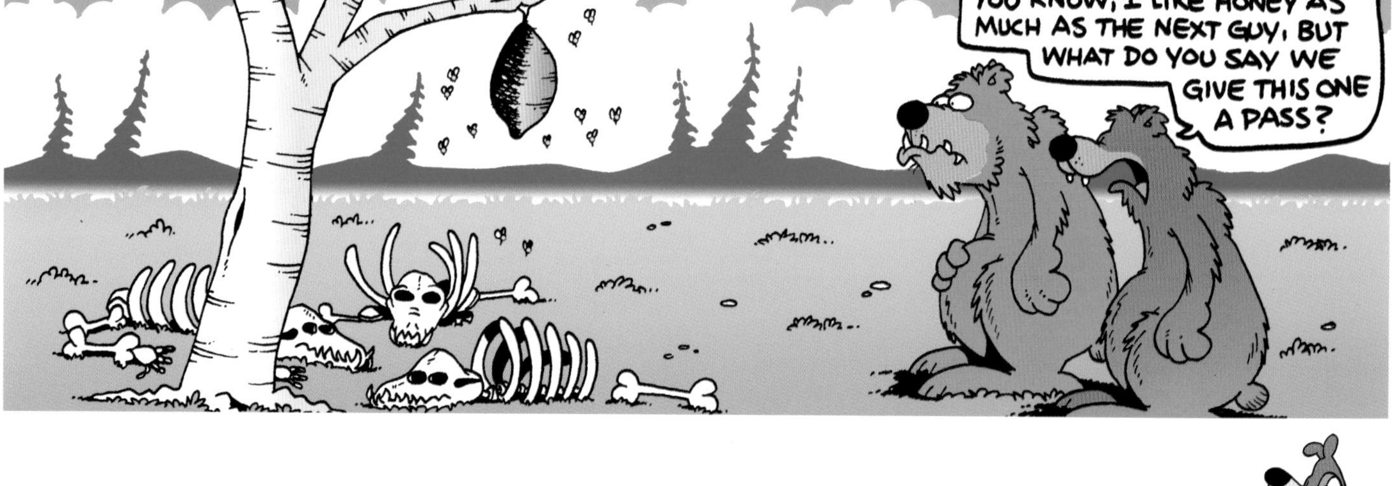
YOU KNOW, I LIKE HONEY AS MUCH AS THE NEXT GUY, BUT WHAT DO YOU SAY WE GIVE THIS ONE A PASS?

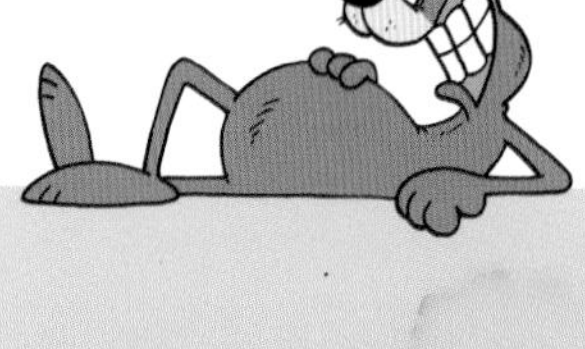

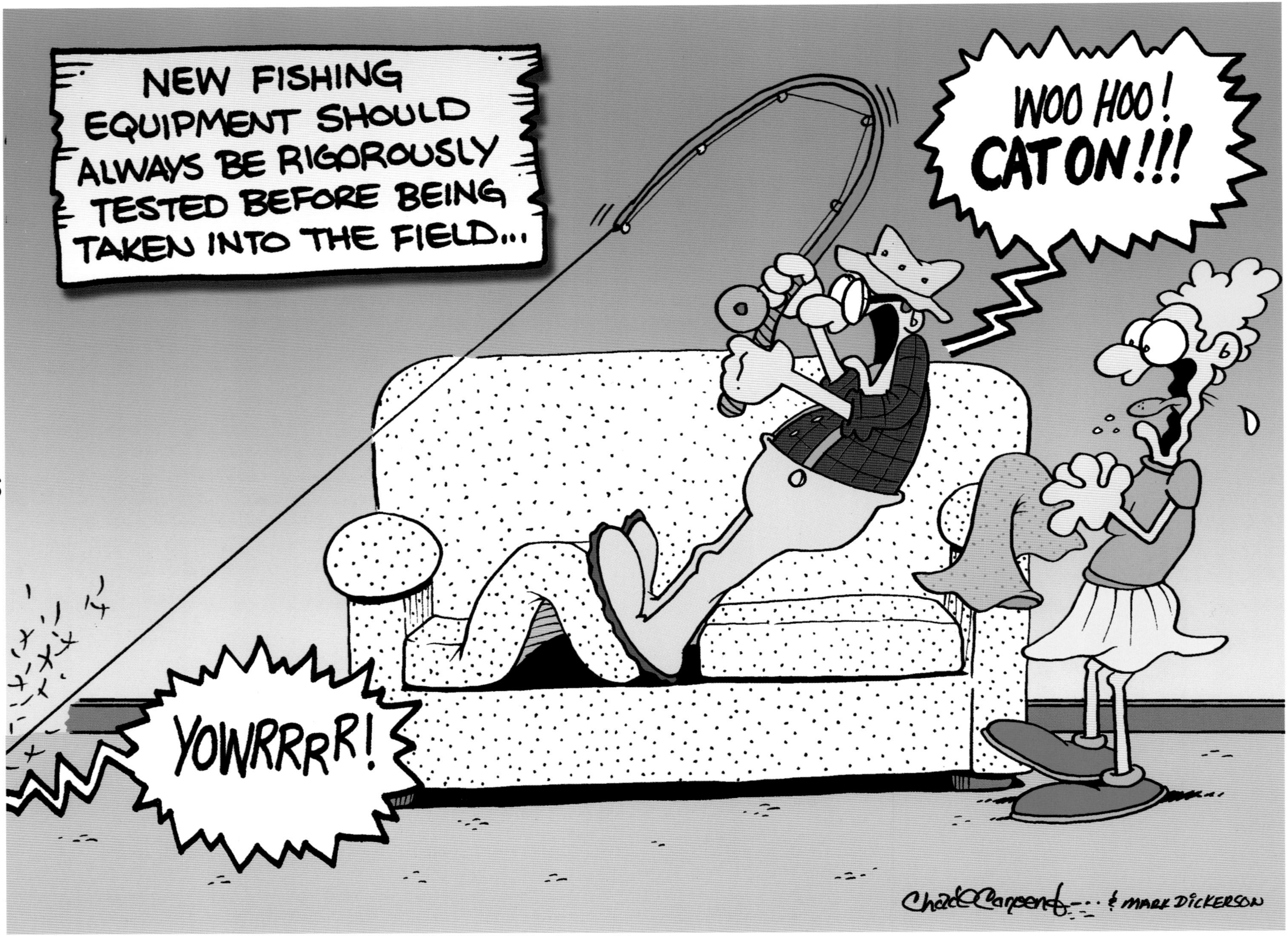
NEW FISHING EQUIPMENT SHOULD ALWAYS BE RIGOROUSLY TESTED BEFORE BEING TAKEN INTO THE FIELD...
WOO HOO! CAT ON!!!
YOWRRRR!
Chad Carpenter ... & MARK DICKERSON

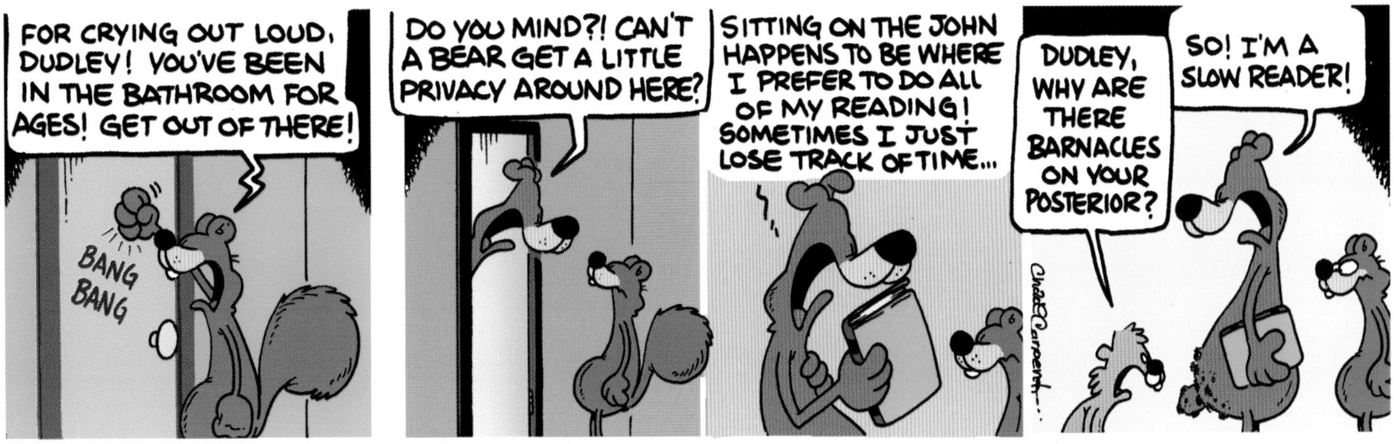
FOR CRYING OUT LOUD, DUDLEY! YOU'VE BEEN IN THE BATHROOM FOR AGES! GET OUT OF THERE!
BANG BANG
DO YOU MIND?! CAN'T A BEAR GET A LITTLE PRIVACY AROUND HERE?
SITTING ON THE JOHN HAPPENS TO BE WHERE I PREFER TO DO ALL OF MY READING! SOMETIMES I JUST LOSE TRACK OF TIME...
DUDLEY, WHY ARE THERE BARNACLES ON YOUR POSTERIOR?
SO! I'M A SLOW READER!

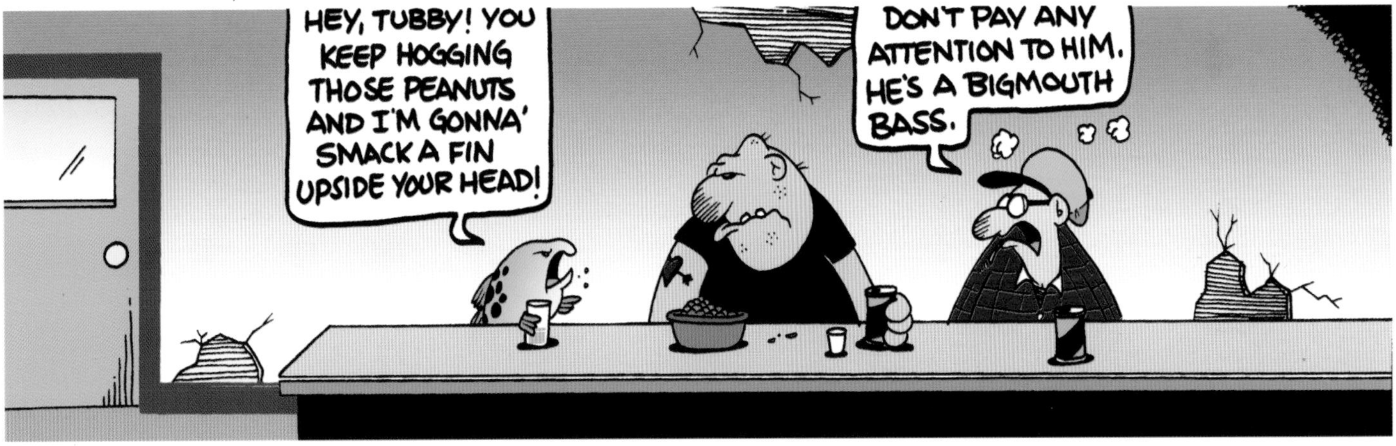
HEY, TUBBY! YOU KEEP HOGGING THOSE PEANUTS AND I'M GONNA' SMACK A FIN UPSIDE YOUR HEAD!
DON'T PAY ANY ATTENTION TO HIM. HE'S A BIGMOUTH BASS.

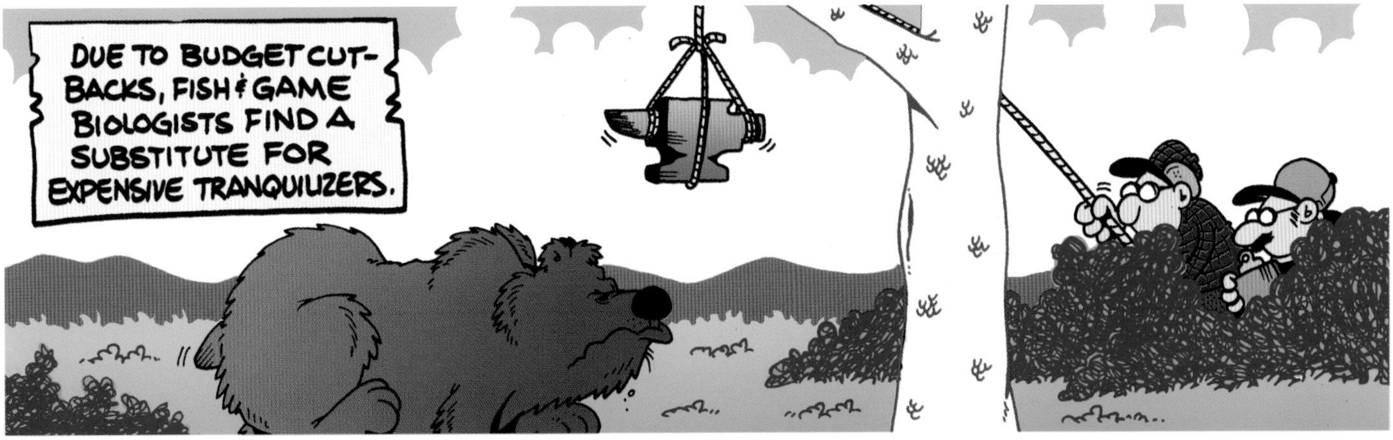
DUE TO BUDGET CUT-BACKS, FISH & GAME BIOLOGISTS FIND A SUBSTITUTE FOR EXPENSIVE TRANQUILIZERS.

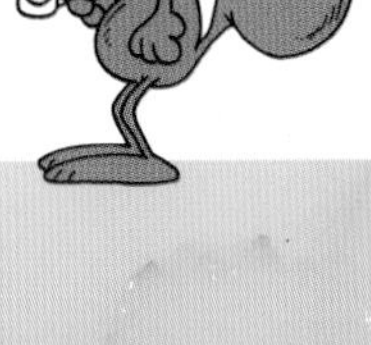

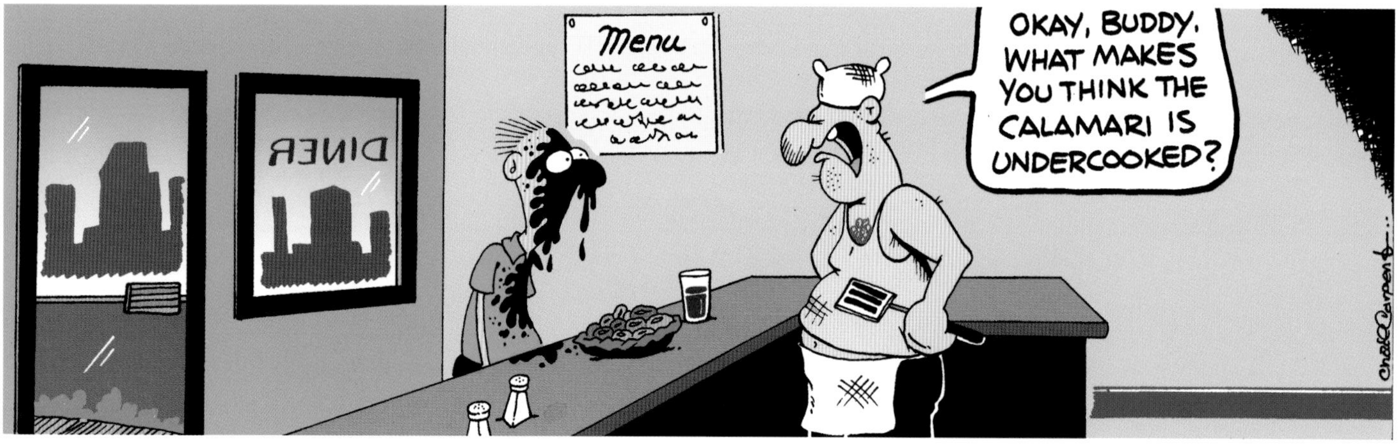
Menu
DINER
OKAY, BUDDY. WHAT MAKES YOU THINK THE CALAMARI IS UNDERCOOKED?

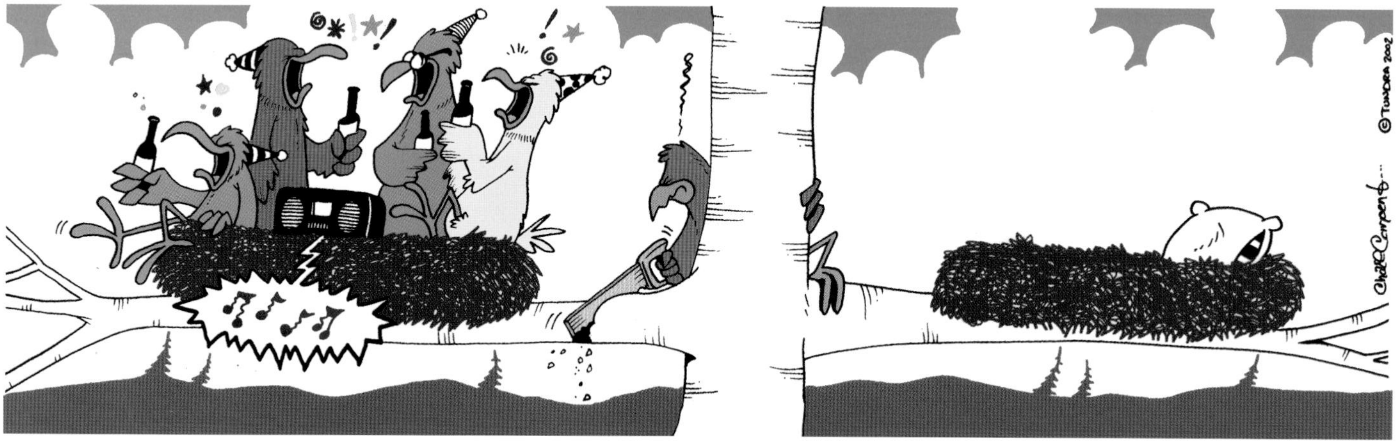

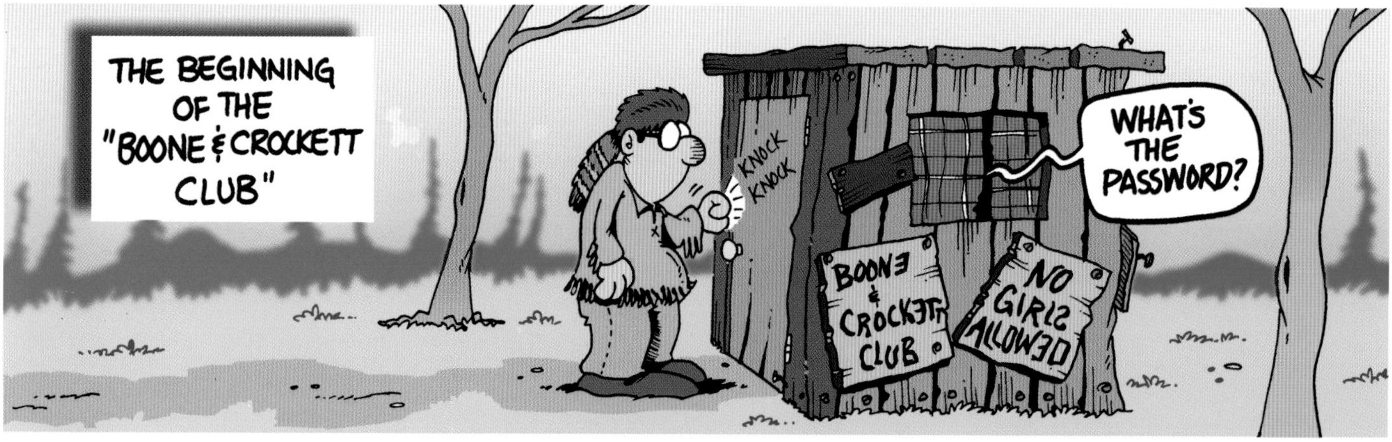
THE BEGINNING OF THE "BOONE & CROCKETT CLUB"
KNOCK KNOCK
WHAT'S THE PASSWORD?
BOONE & CROCKETT CLUB
NO GIRLS ALLOWED

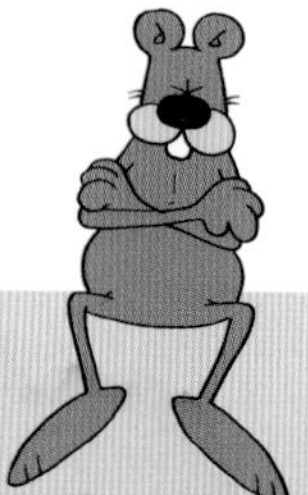

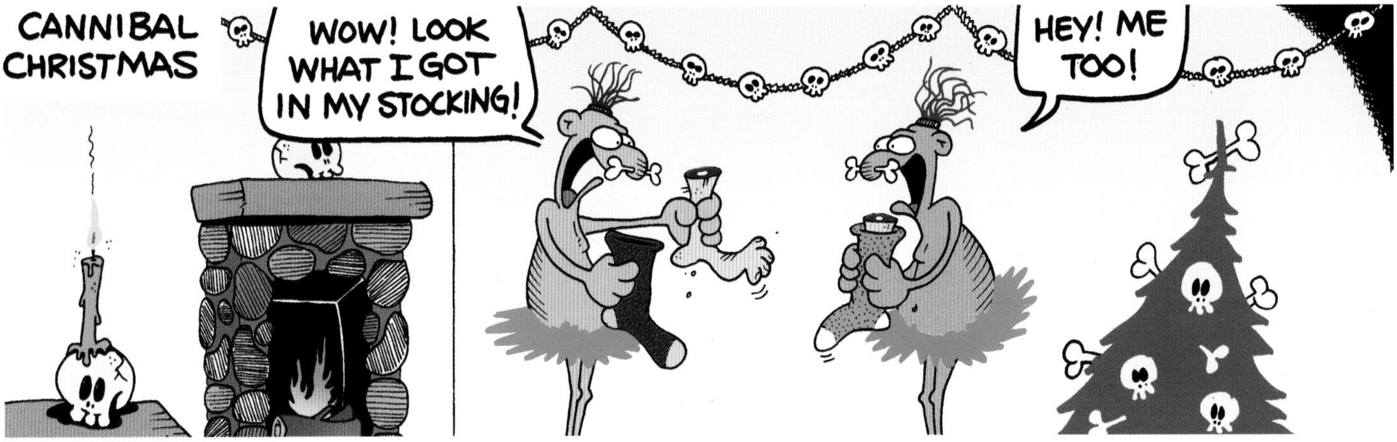
CANNIBAL CHRISTMAS
WOW! LOOK WHAT I GOT IN MY STOCKING!
HEY! ME TOO!

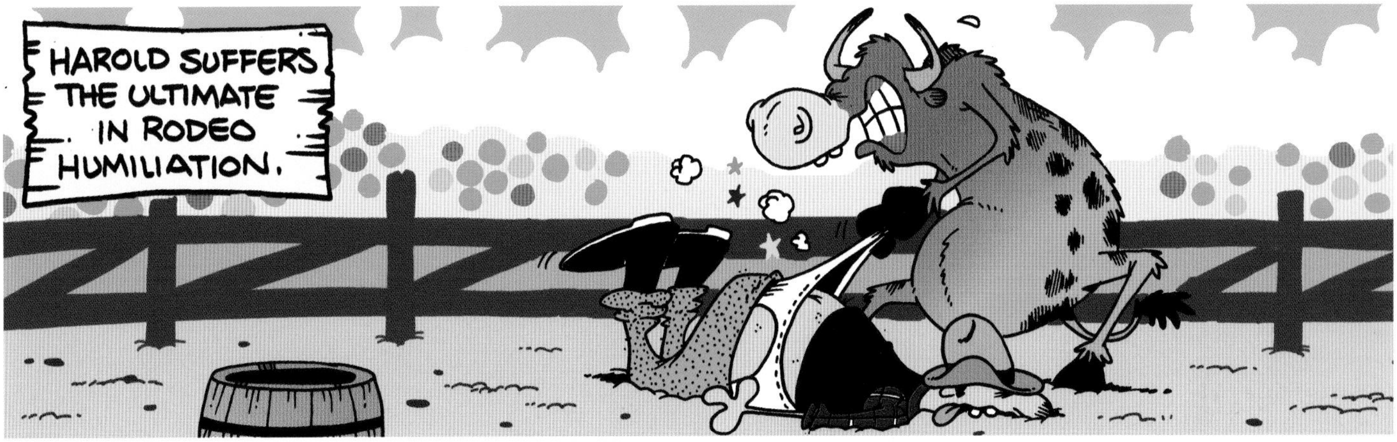
HAROLD SUFFERS THE ULTIMATE IN RODEO HUMILIATION.

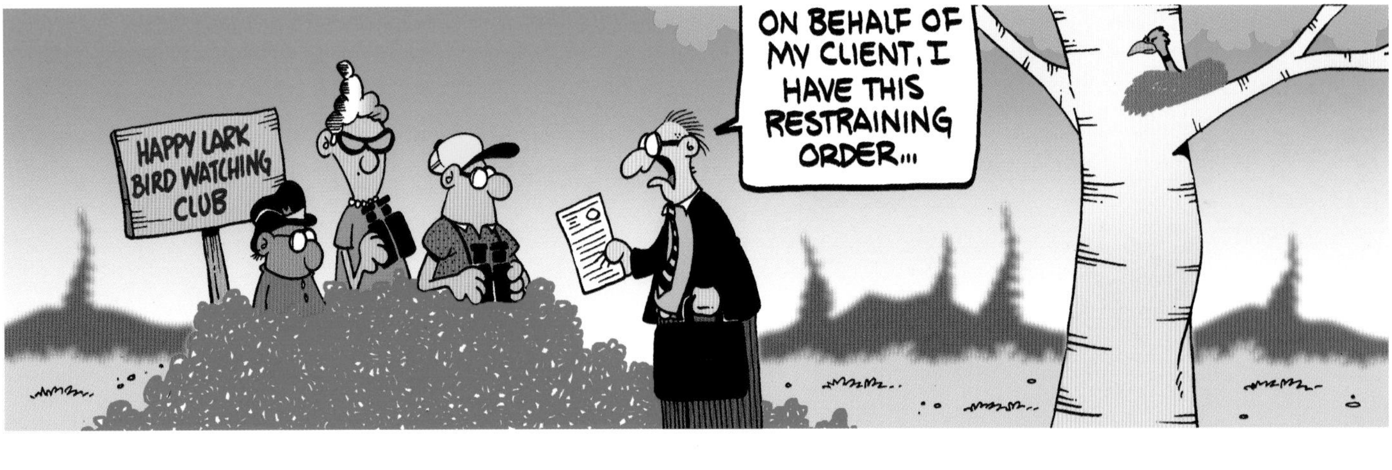
HAPPY LARK BIRD WATCHING CLUB
ON BEHALF OF MY CLIENT, I HAVE THIS RESTRAINING ORDER...

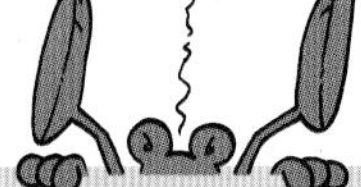

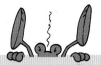

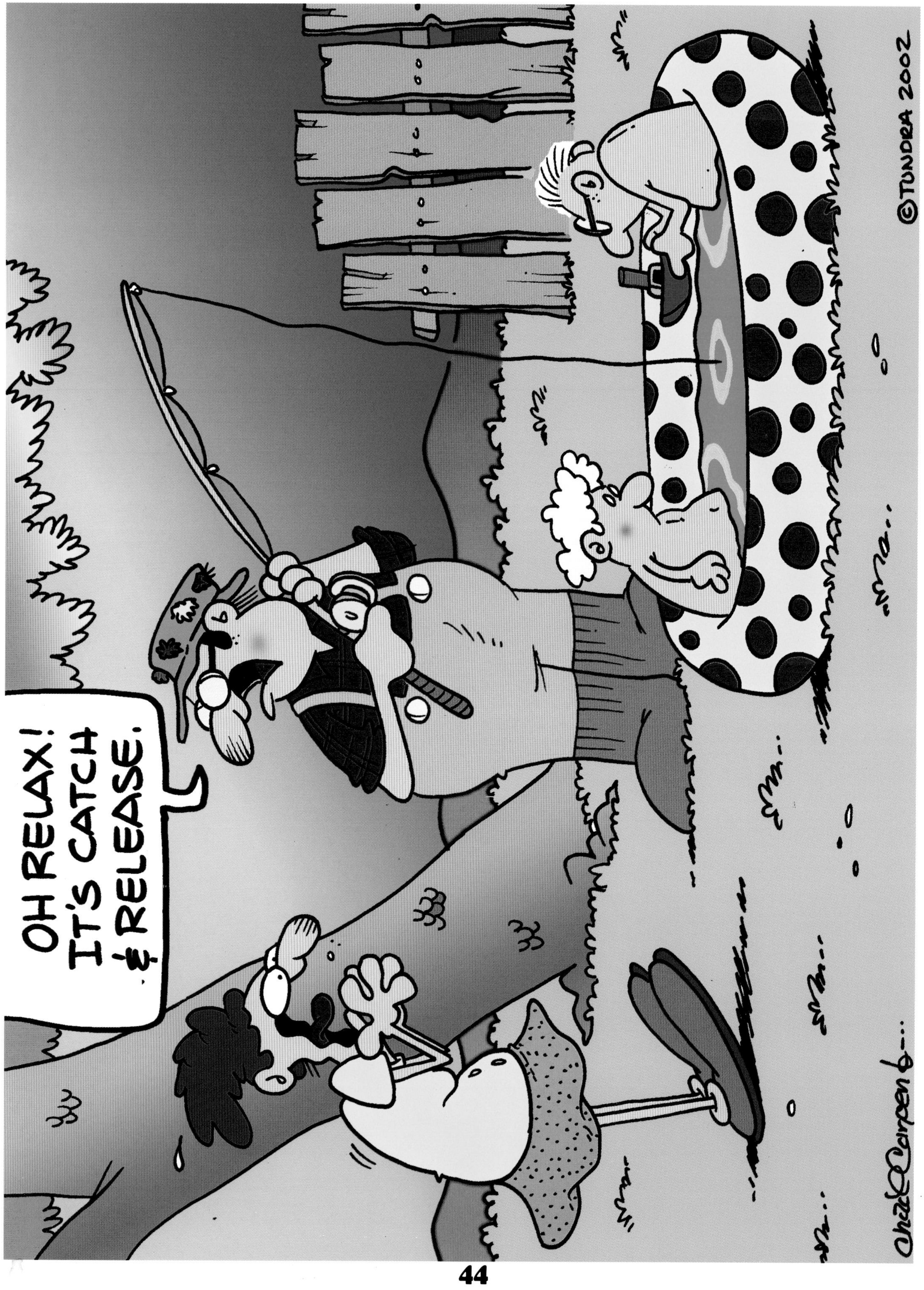
OH RELAX! IT'S CATCH & RELEASE.
©TUNDRA 2002

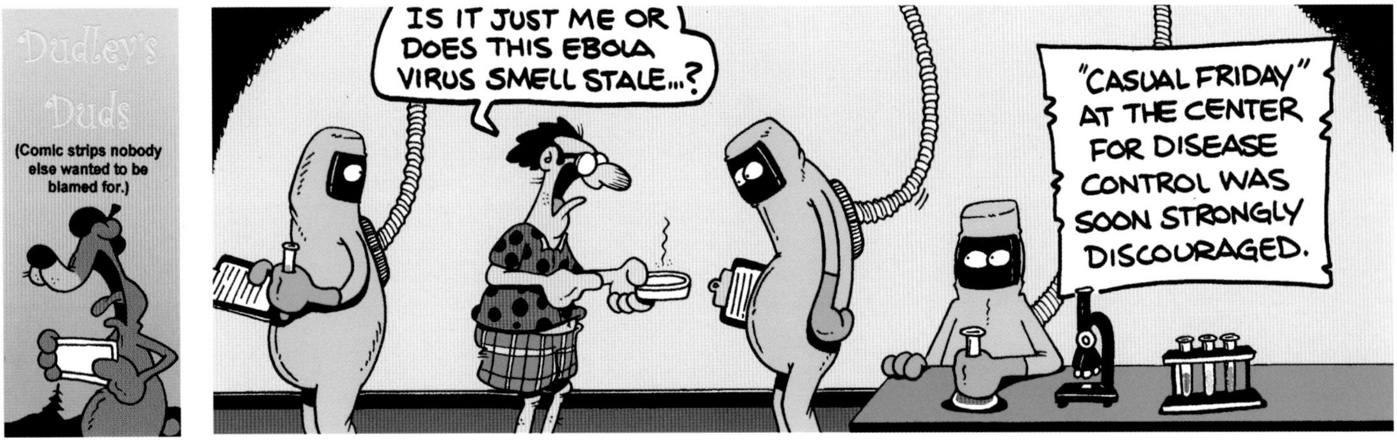
Dudley's Duds
(Comic strips nobody else wanted to be blamed for.)
IS IT JUST ME OR DOES THIS EBOLA VIRUS SMELL STALE...?
"CASUAL FRIDAY" AT THE CENTER FOR DISEASE CONTROL WAS SOON STRONGLY DISCOURAGED.

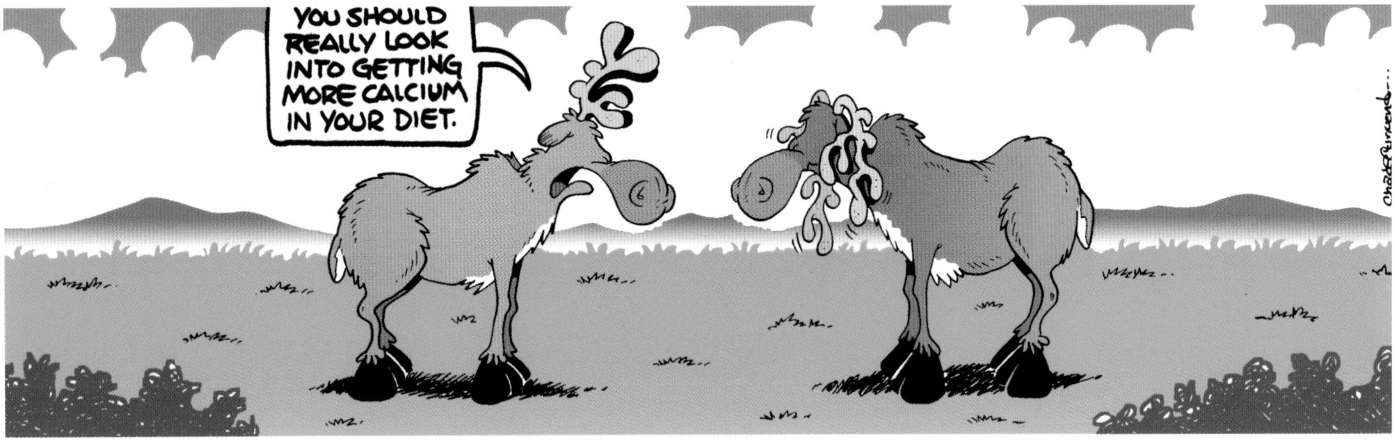
YOU SHOULD REALLY LOOK INTO GETTING MORE CALCIUM IN YOUR DIET.

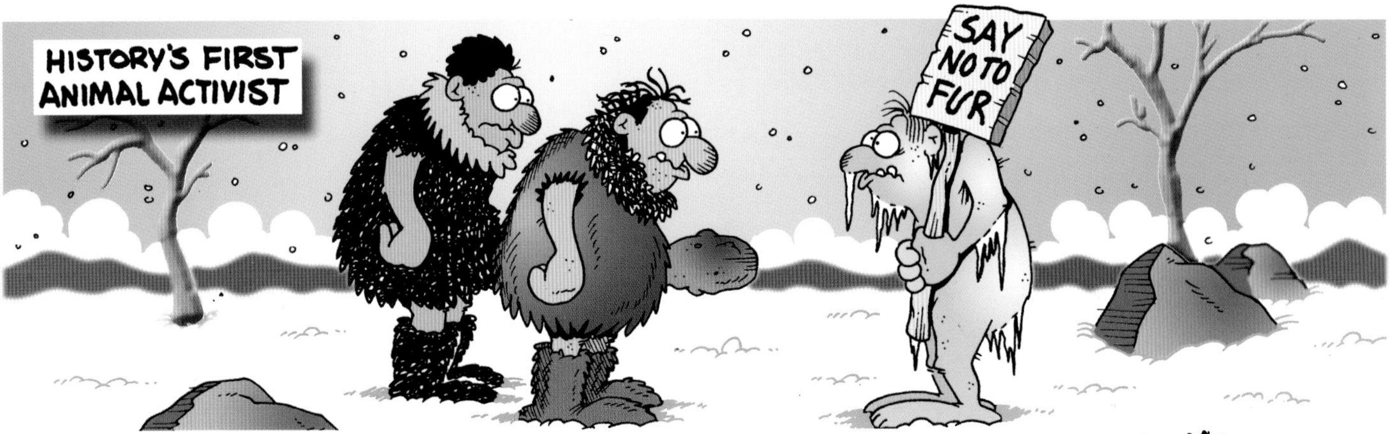
HISTORY'S FIRST ANIMAL ACTIVIST
SAY NO TO FUR

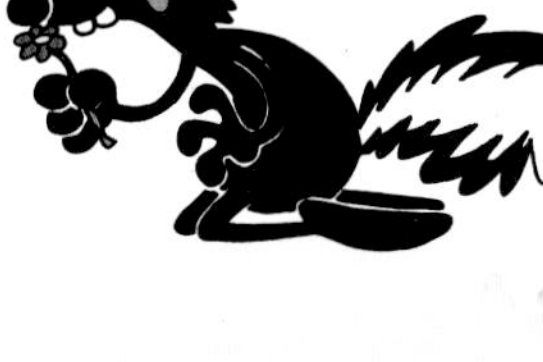

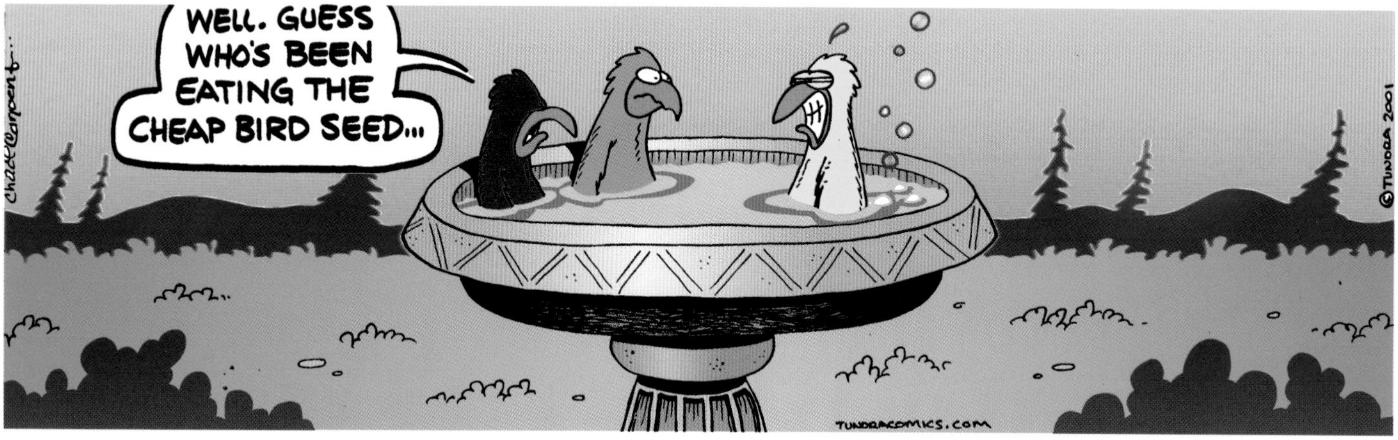
WELL. GUESS WHO'S BEEN EATING THE CHEAP BIRD SEED...
©TUNDRA 2001
TUNDRACOMICS.COM

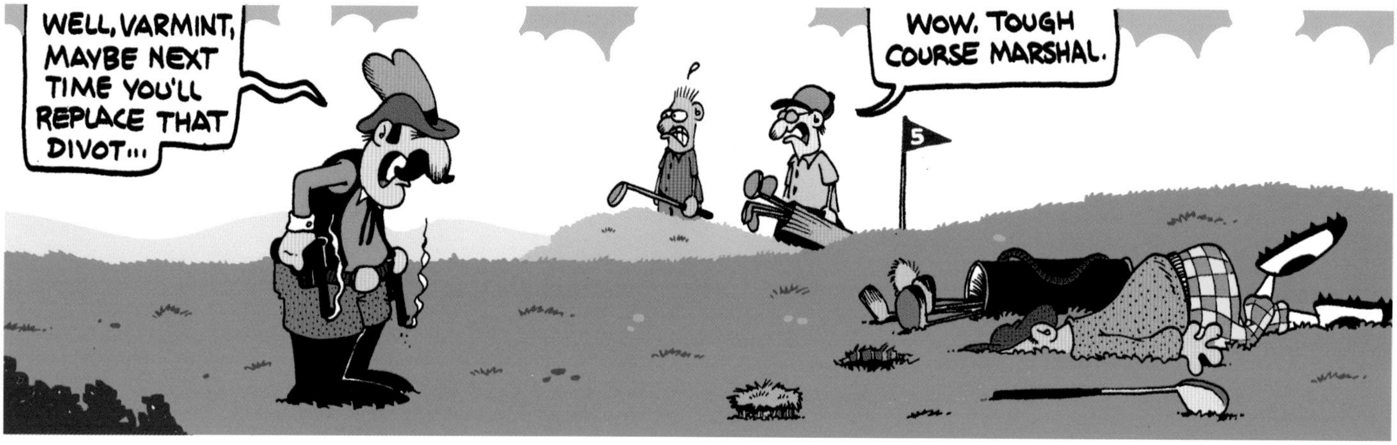
WELL, VARMINT, MAYBE NEXT TIME YOU'LL REPLACE THAT DIVOT...
WOW. TOUGH COURSE MARSHAL.
5

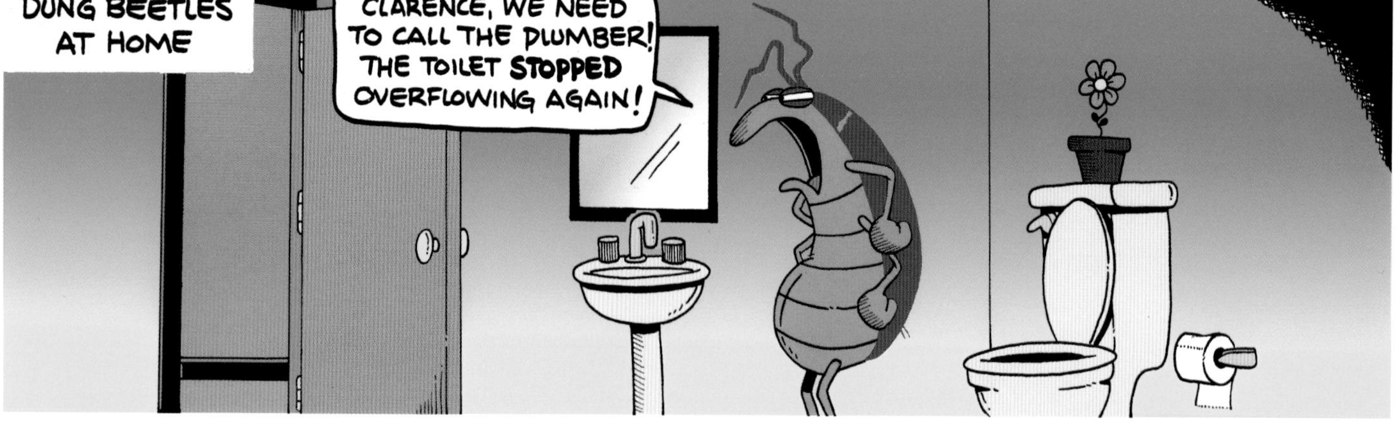
DUNG BEETLES AT HOME
CLARENCE, WE NEED TO CALL THE PLUMBER! THE TOILET STOPPED OVERFLOWING AGAIN!

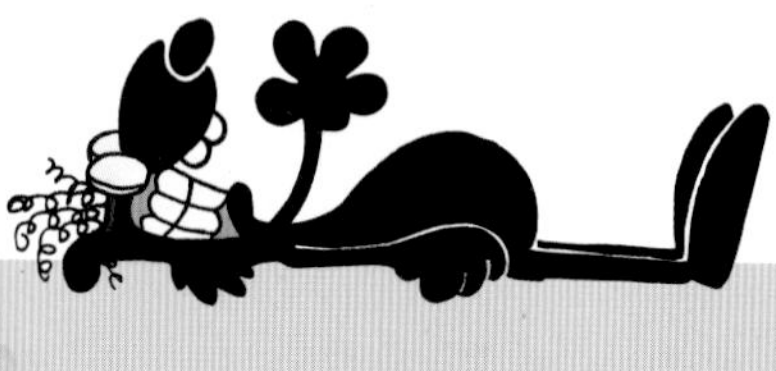

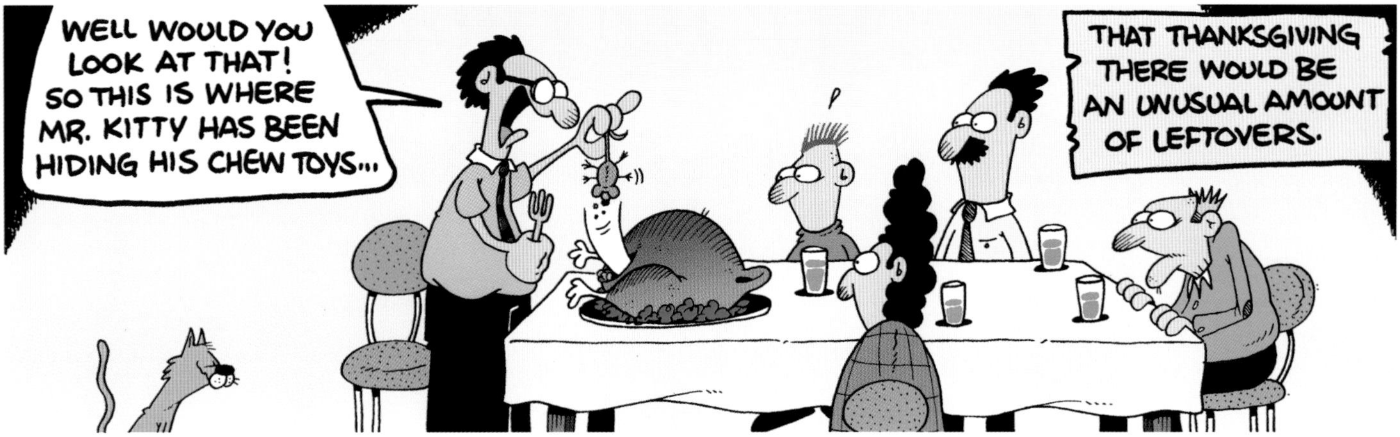
WELL WOULD YOU LOOK AT THAT! SO THIS IS WHERE MR. KITTY HAS BEEN HIDING HIS CHEW TOYS...
THAT THANKSGIVING THERE WOULD BE AN UNUSUAL AMOUNT OF LEFTOVERS.

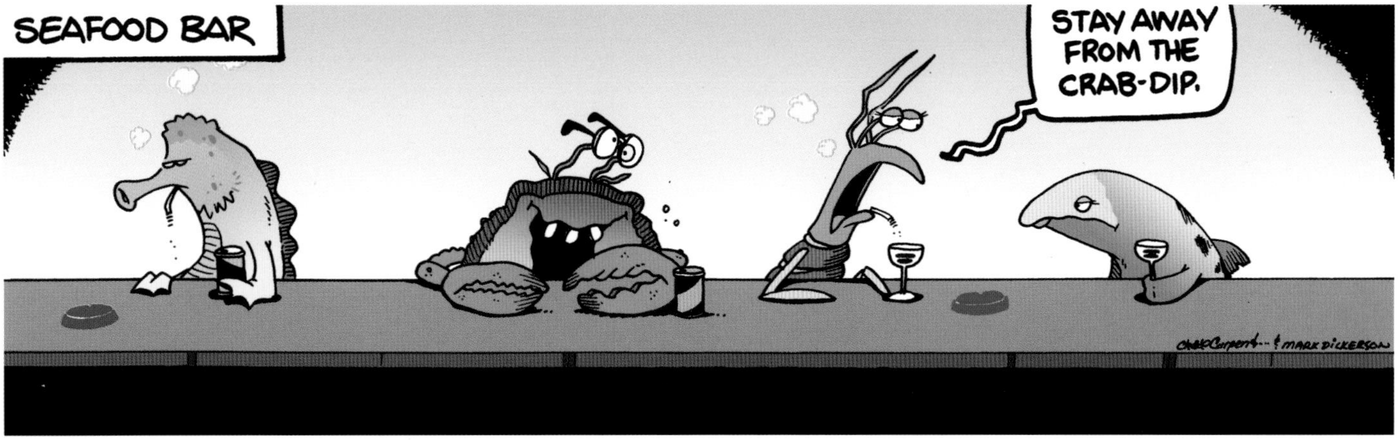
SEAFOOD BAR
STAY AWAY FROM THE CRAB-DIP.

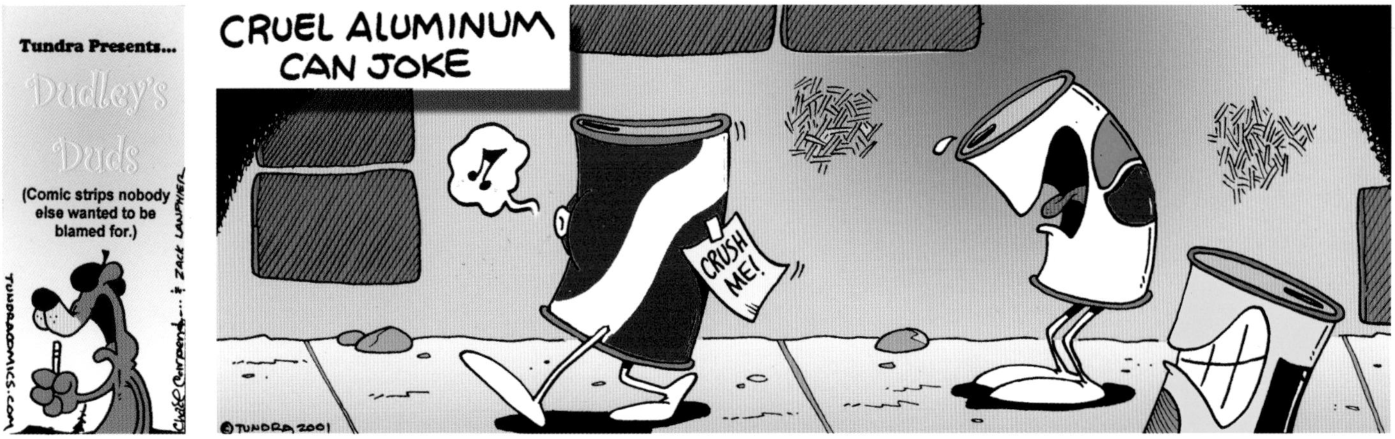
Tundra Presents...
Dudley's Duds
(Comic strips nobody else wanted to be blamed for.)
CRUEL ALUMINUM CAN JOKE
CRUSH ME!
©TUNDRA 2001

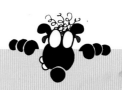

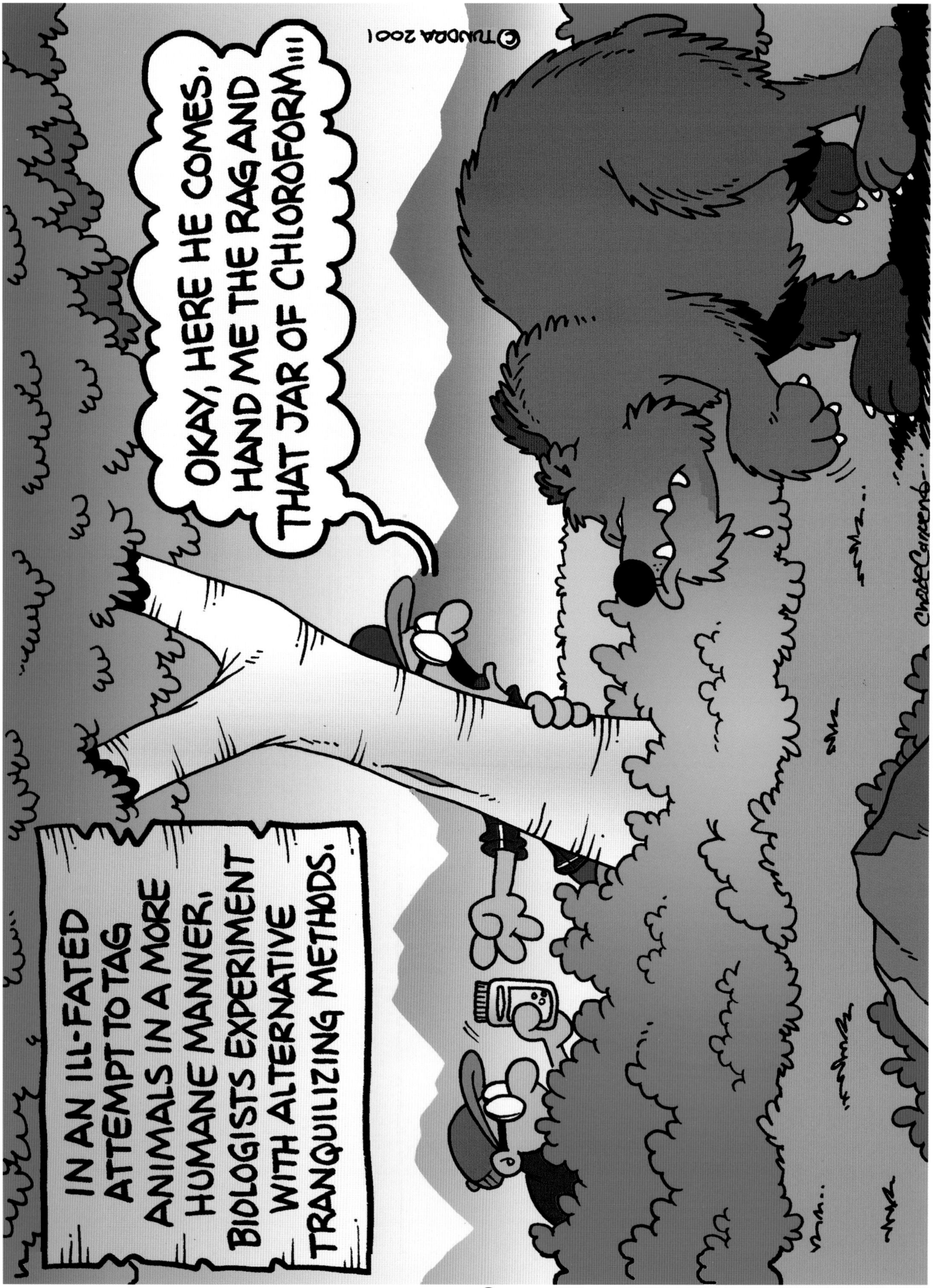
IN AN ILL-FATED ATTEMPT TO TAG ANIMALS IN A MORE HUMANE MANNER, BIOLOGISTS EXPERIMENT WITH ALTERNATIVE TRANQUILIZING METHODS.
OKAY, HERE HE COMES. HAND ME THE RAG AND THAT JAR OF CHLOROFORM!!!
© TUNDRA 2001

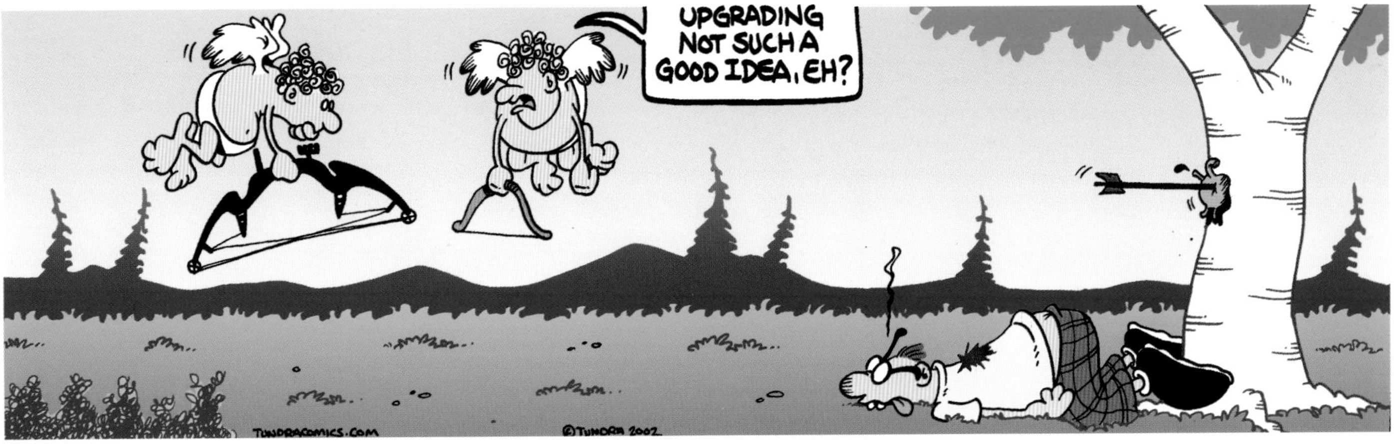
UPGRADING NOT SUCH A GOOD IDEA, EH?
TUNDRACOMICS.COM
©TUNDRA 2002

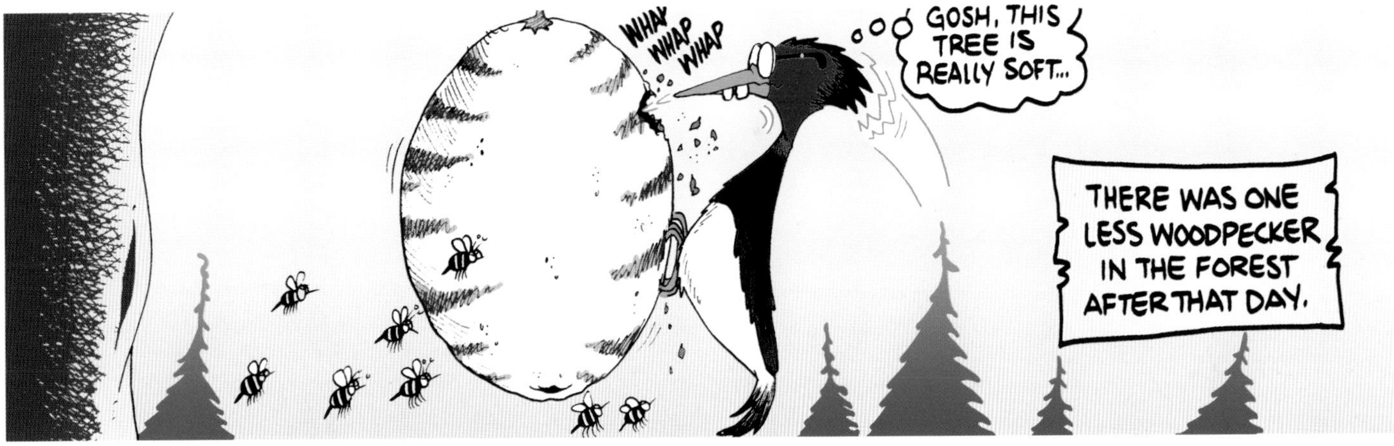
WHAP WHAP WHAP
GOSH, THIS TREE IS REALLY SOFT...
THERE WAS ONE LESS WOODPECKER IN THE FOREST AFTER THAT DAY.

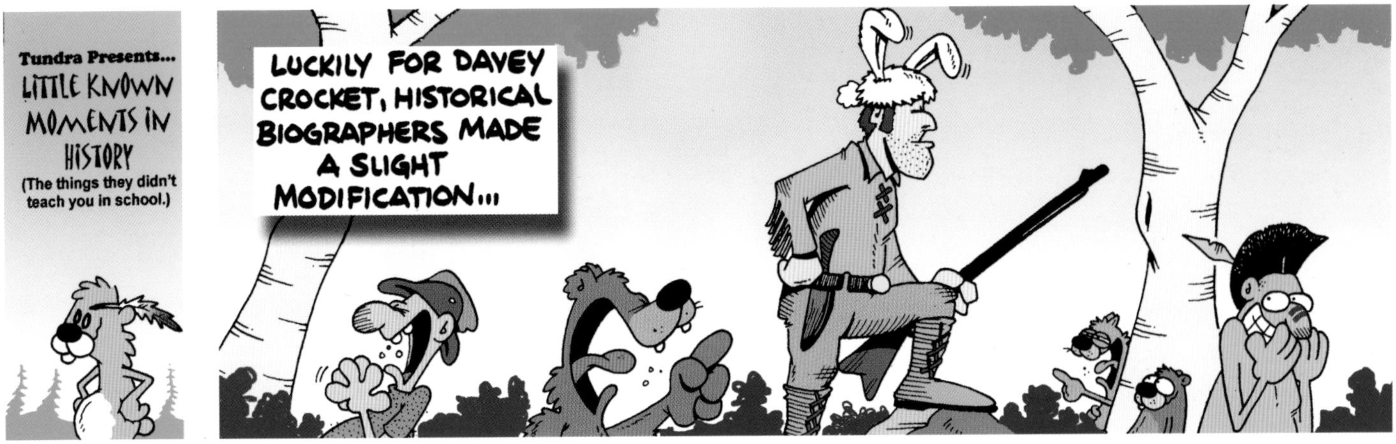
Tundra Presents...
LITTLE KNOWN MOMENTS IN HISTORY
(The things they didn't teach you in school.)
LUCKILY FOR DAVEY CROCKET, HISTORICAL BIOGRAPHERS MADE A SLIGHT MODIFICATION...

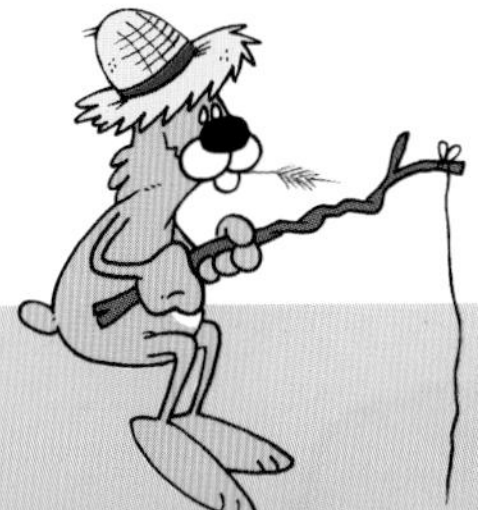

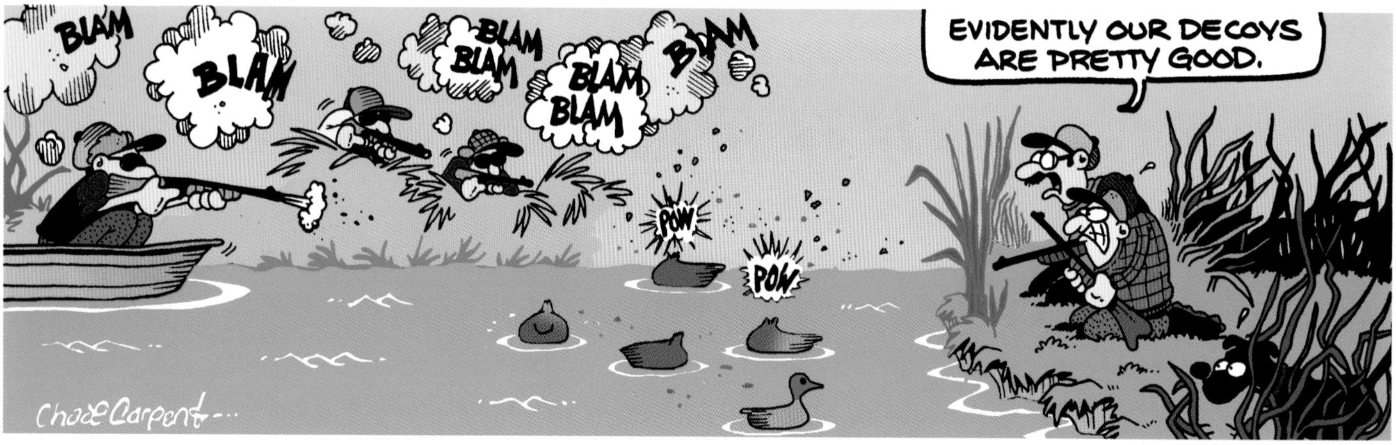
BLAM
BLAM
BLAM BLAM
BLAM BLAM
BLAM
POW
POW
EVIDENTLY OUR DECOYS ARE PRETTY GOOD.

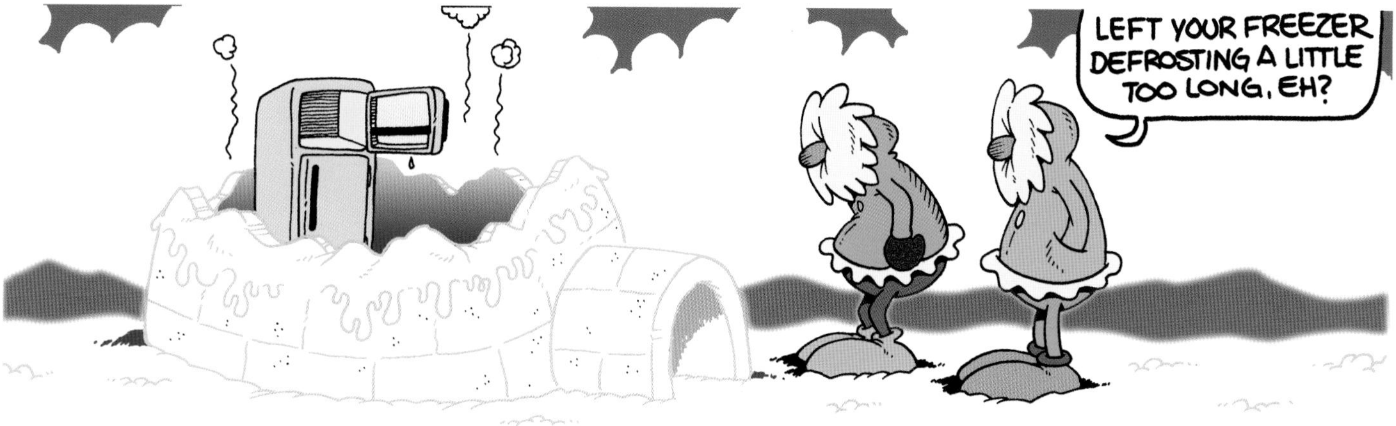
LEFT YOUR FREEZER DEFROSTING A LITTLE TOO LONG, EH?

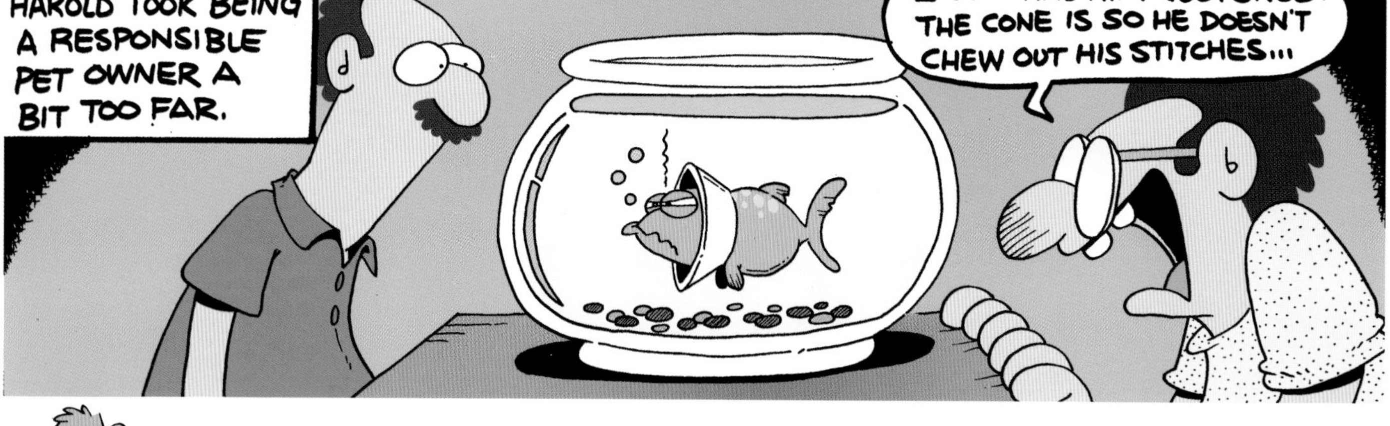
HAROLD TOOK BEING A RESPONSIBLE PET OWNER A BIT TOO FAR.
I JUST HAD HIM NEUTERED. THE CONE IS SO HE DOESN'T CHEW OUT HIS STITCHES...

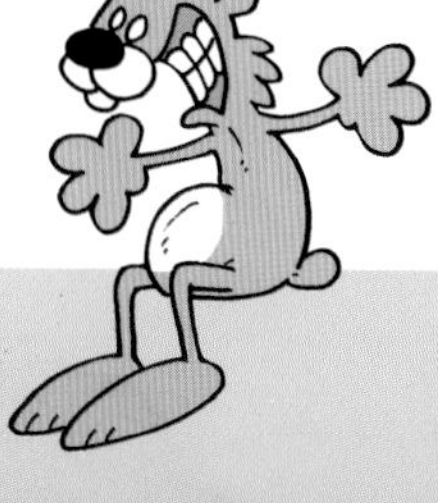

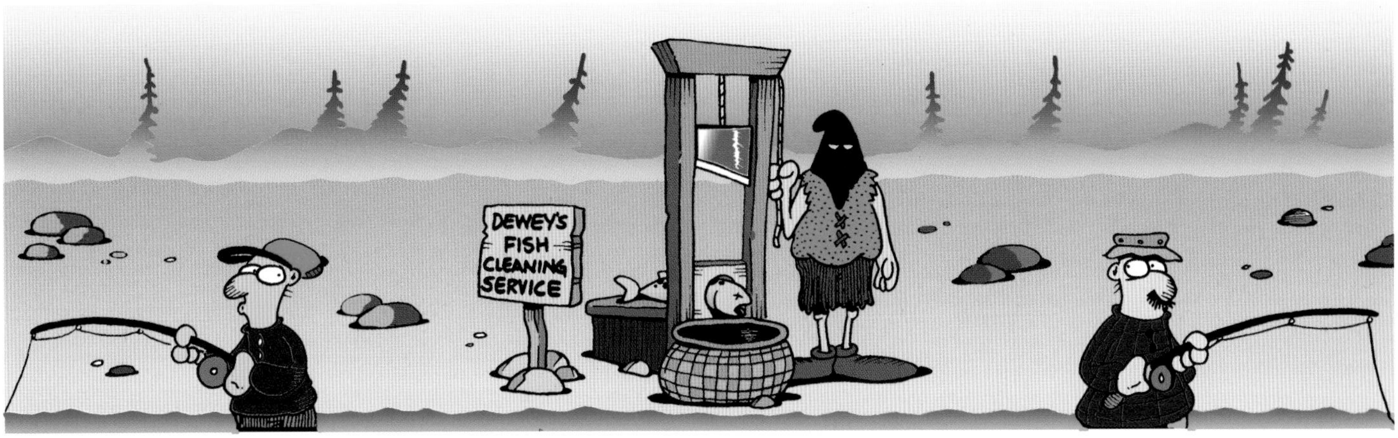
DEWEY'S FISH CLEANING SERVICE

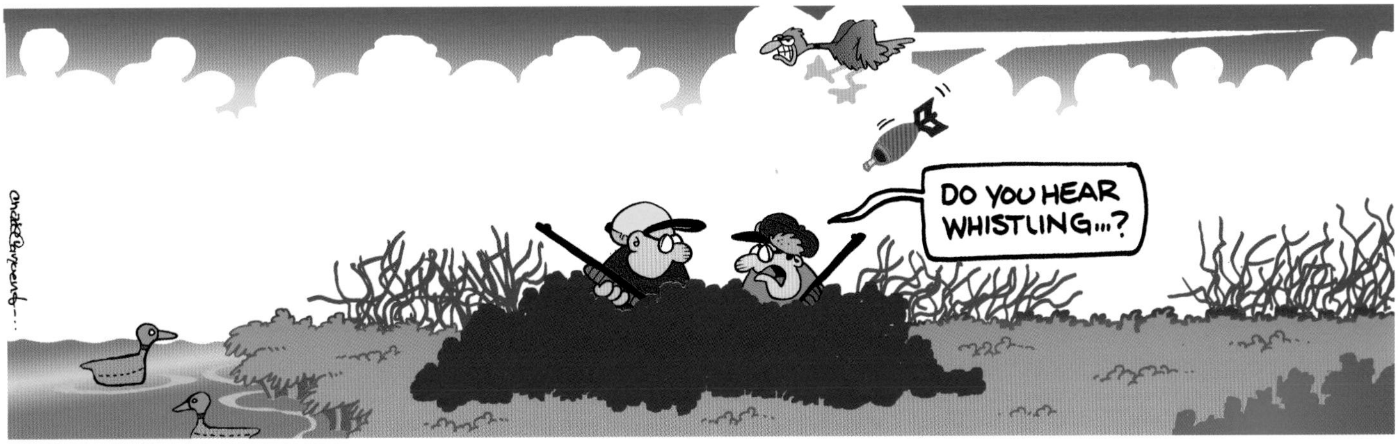
DO YOU HEAR WHISTLING...?

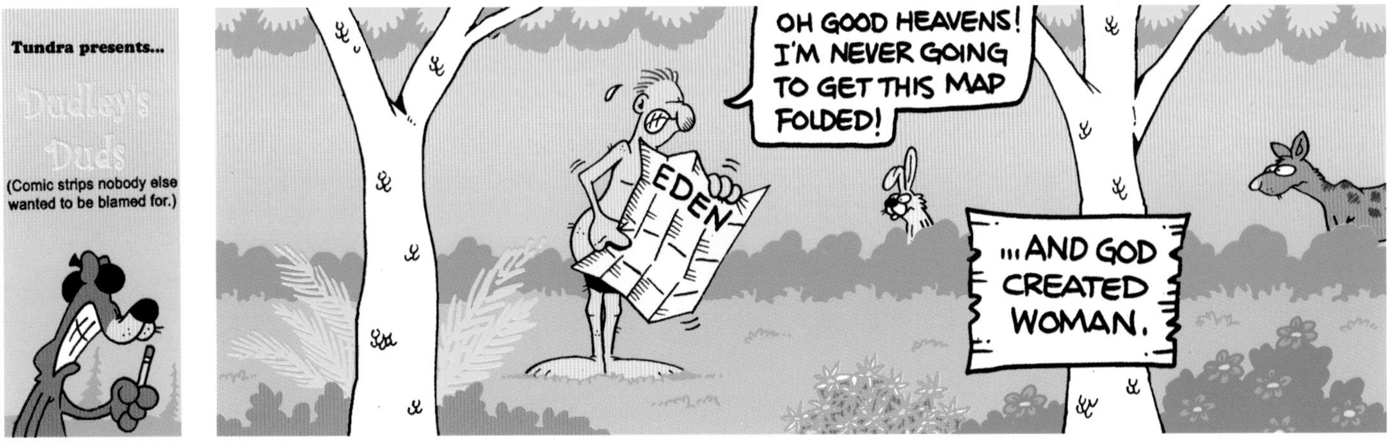
Tundra presents...
Dudley's Duds
(Comic strips nobody else wanted to be blamed for.)
OH GOOD HEAVENS! I'M NEVER GOING TO GET THIS MAP FOLDED!
EDEN
...AND GOD CREATED WOMAN.

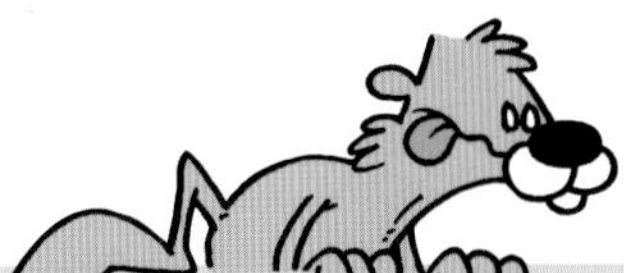

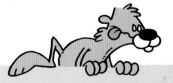

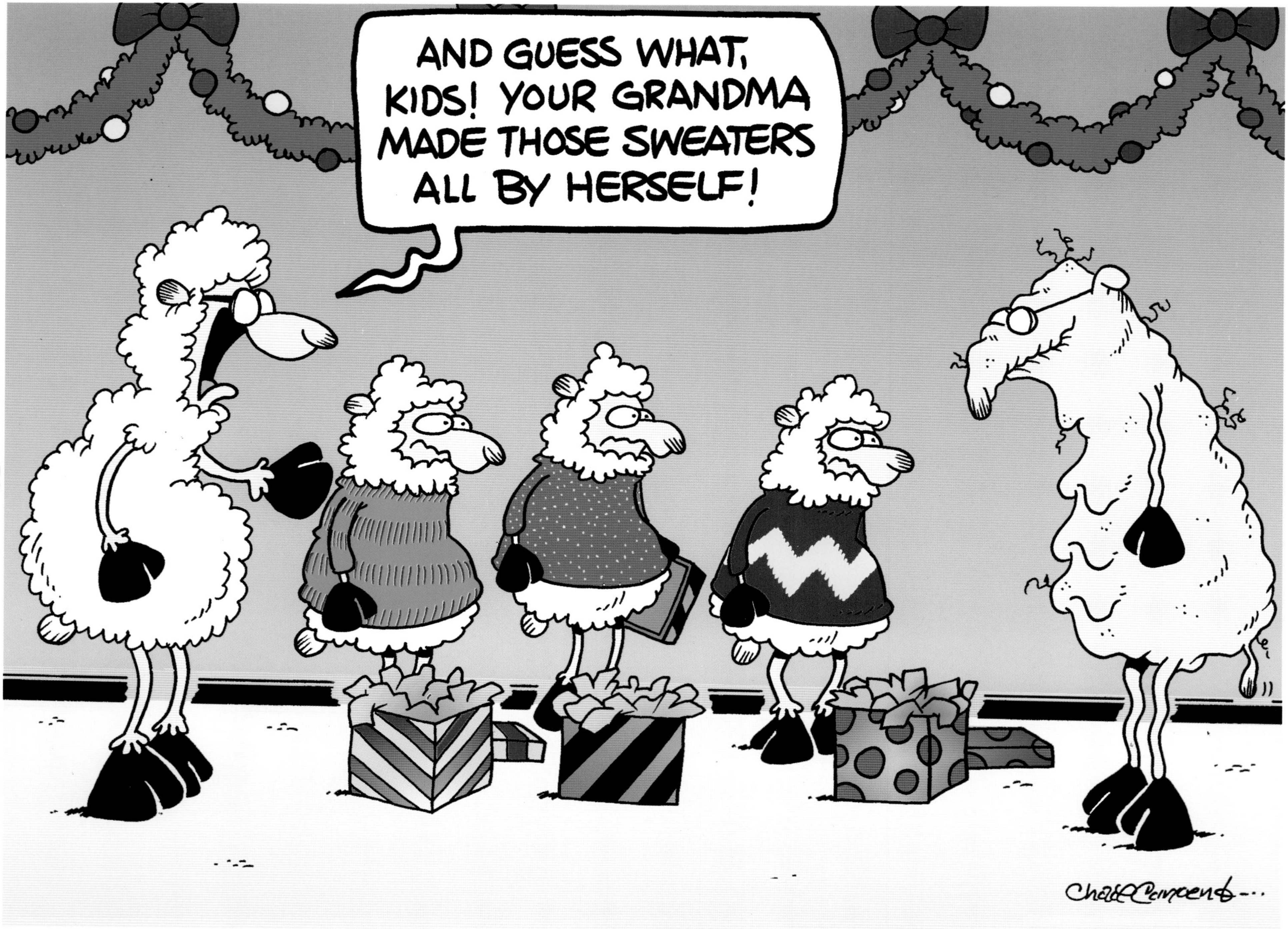
AND GUESS WHAT, KIDS! YOUR GRANDMA MADE THOSE SWEATERS ALL BY HERSELF!

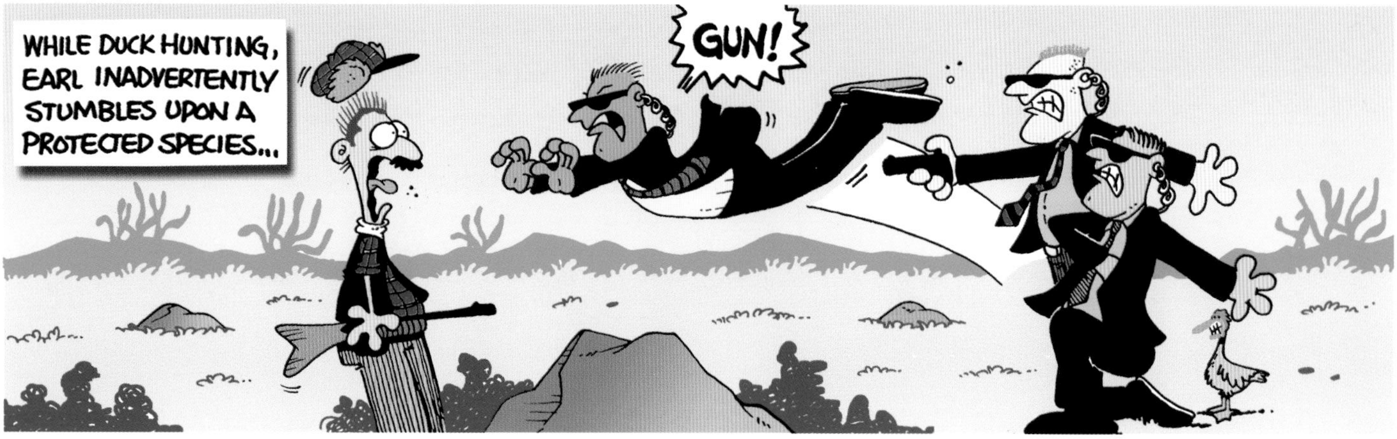
WHILE DUCK HUNTING, EARL INADVERTENTLY STUMBLES UPON A PROTECTED SPECIES...
GUN!

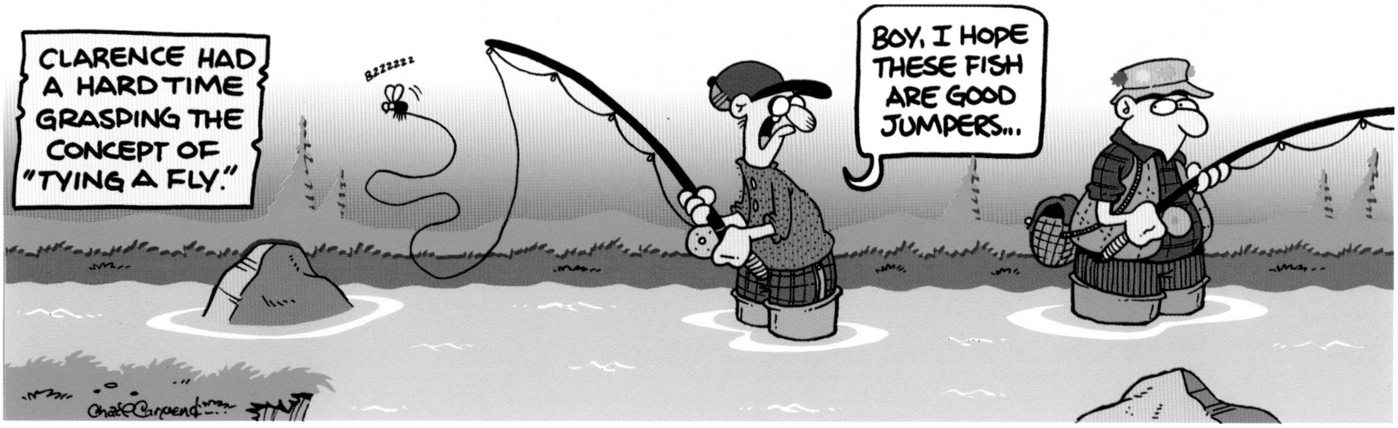
CLARENCE HAD A HARD TIME GRASPING THE CONCEPT OF "TYING A FLY."
BZZZZZZ
BOY, I HOPE THESE FISH ARE GOOD JUMPERS...

Tundra presents...

Whiffs Stinkers

(Comic strips even Dudley didn't want to be blamed for.)

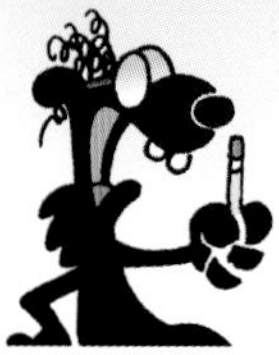

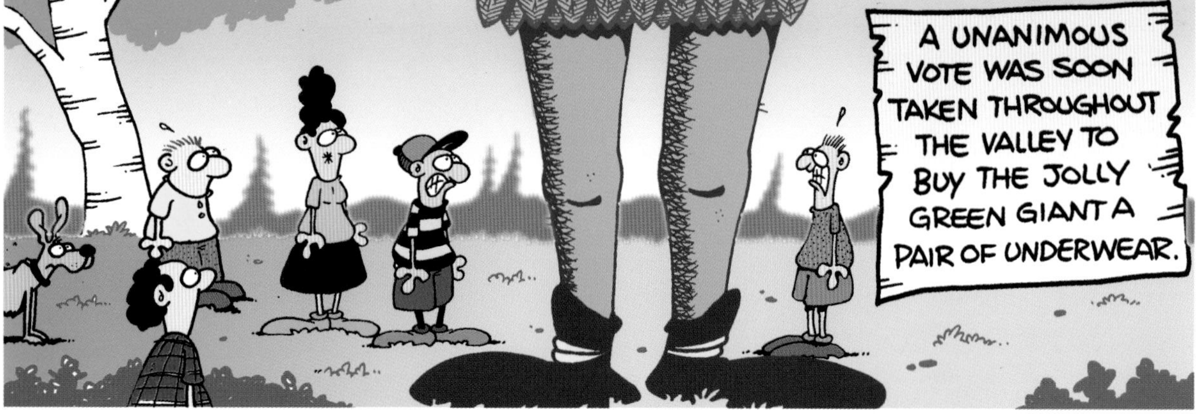
A UNANIMOUS VOTE WAS SOON TAKEN THROUGHOUT THE VALLEY TO BUY THE JOLLY GREEN GIANT A PAIR OF UNDERWEAR.

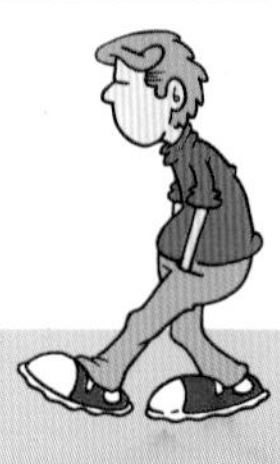

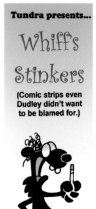

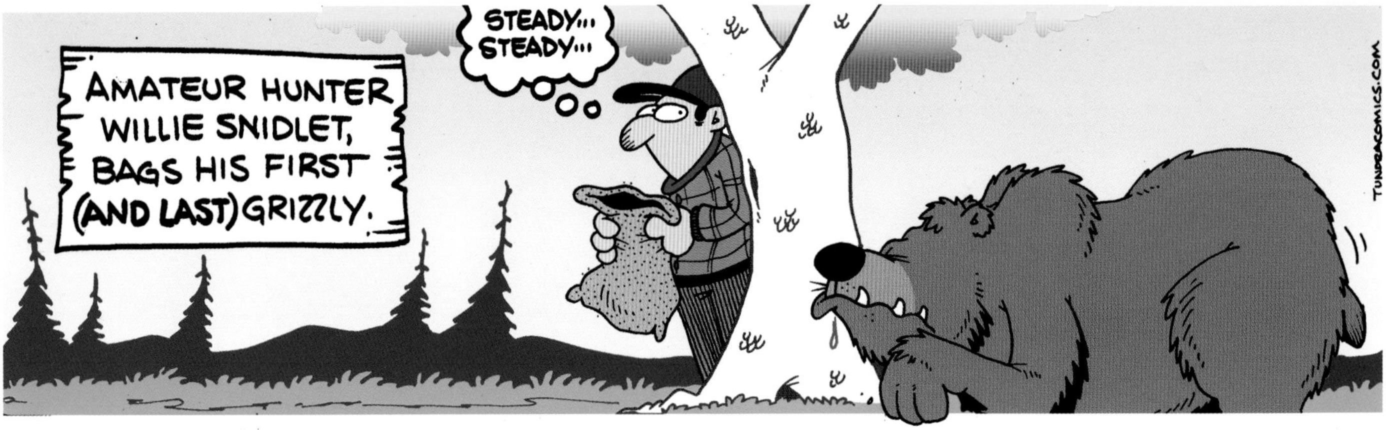
AMATEUR HUNTER WILLIE SNIDLET, BAGS HIS FIRST (AND LAST) GRIZZLY.
STEADY... STEADY...
TUNDRACOMICS.COM

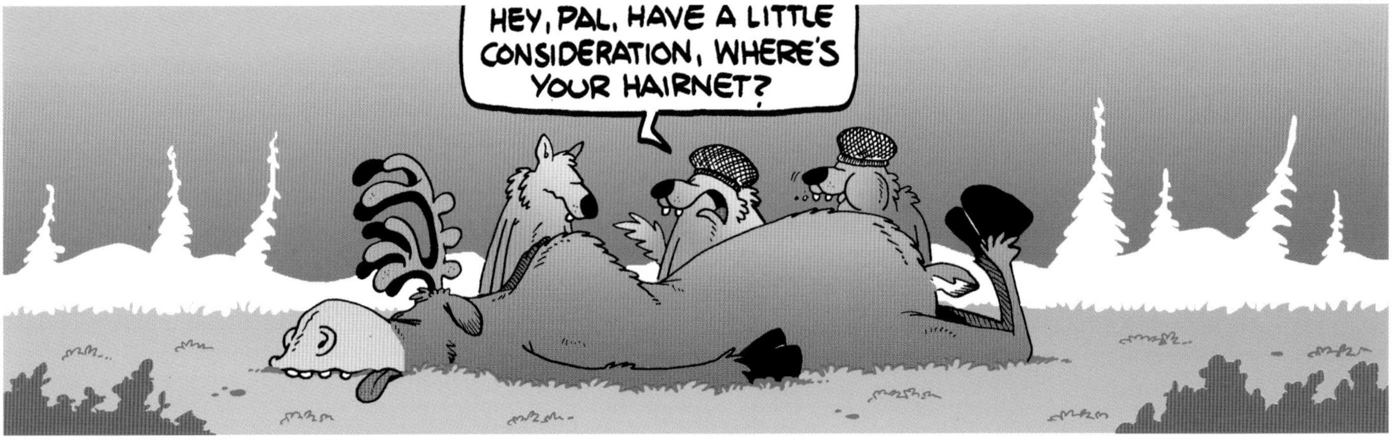
HEY, PAL, HAVE A LITTLE CONSIDERATION, WHERE'S YOUR HAIRNET?

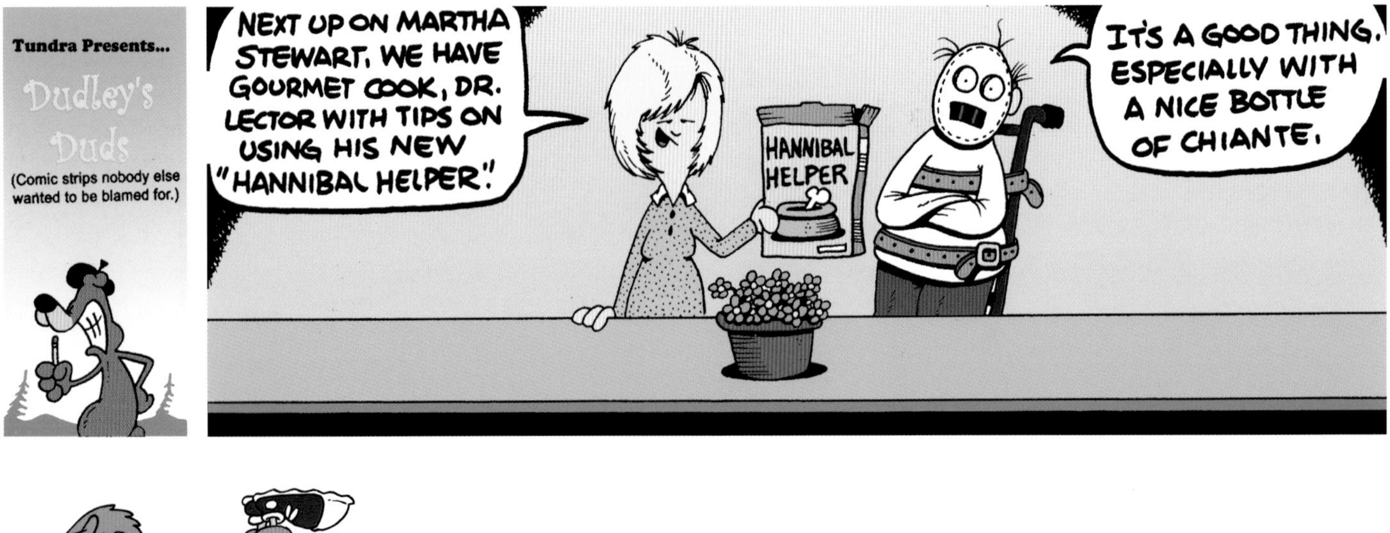
Tundra Presents...
Dudley's Duds
(Comic strips nobody else wanted to be blamed for.)
NEXT UP ON MARTHA STEWART, WE HAVE GOURMET COOK, DR. LECTOR WITH TIPS ON USING HIS NEW "HANNIBAL HELPER".
HANNIBAL HELPER
IT'S A GOOD THING, ESPECIALLY WITH A NICE BOTTLE OF CHIANTE.

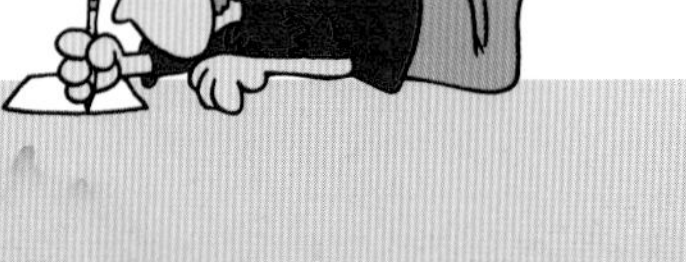

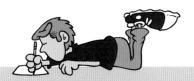

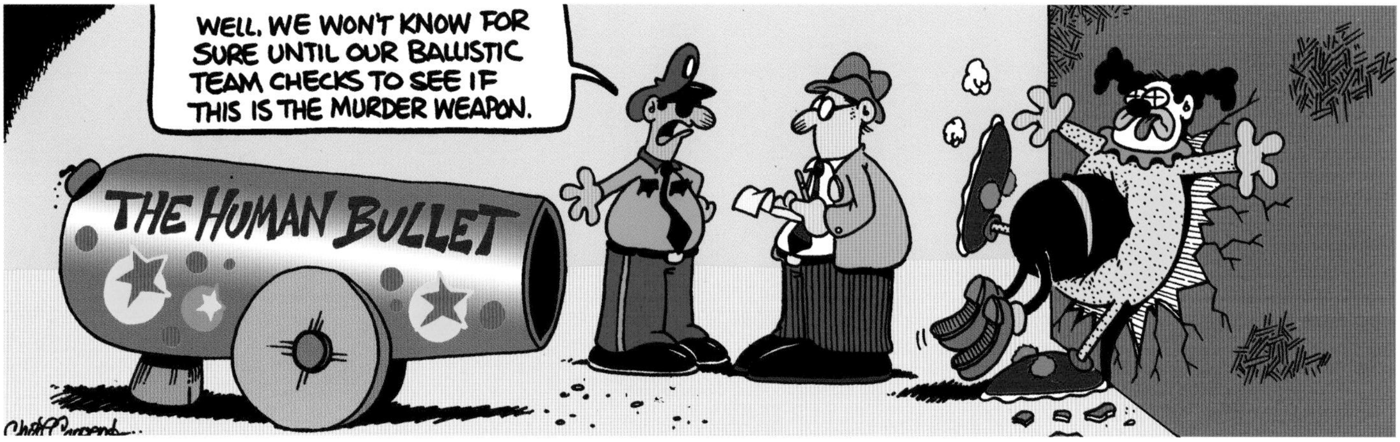
WELL, WE WON'T KNOW FOR SURE UNTIL OUR BALLISTIC TEAM CHECKS TO SEE IF THIS IS THE MURDER WEAPON.
THE HUMAN BULLET

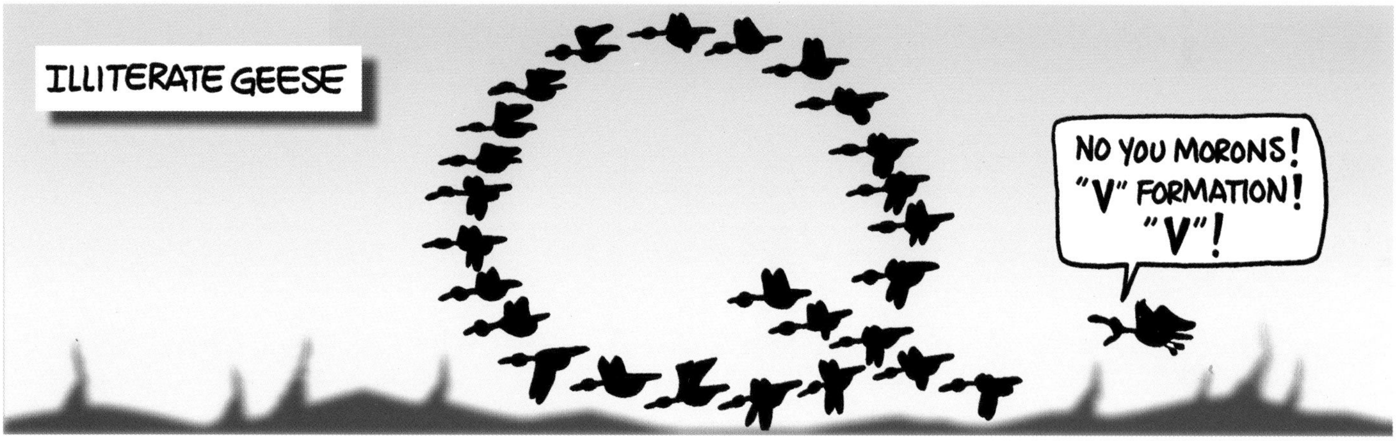
ILLITERATE GEESE
NO YOU MORONS! "V" FORMATION! "V"!

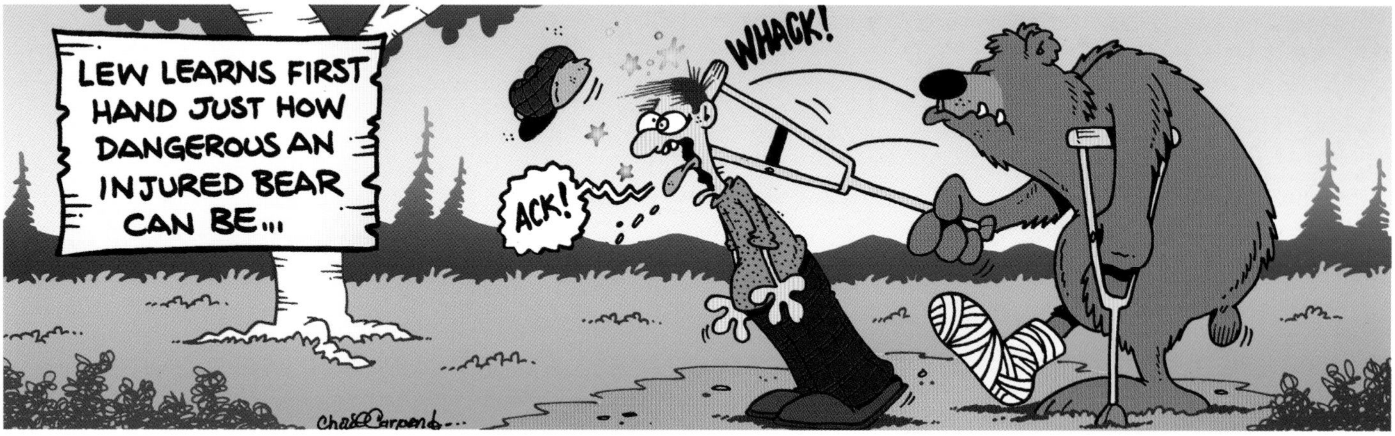
LEW LEARNS FIRST HAND JUST HOW DANGEROUS AN INJURED BEAR CAN BE...
WHACK!
ACK!

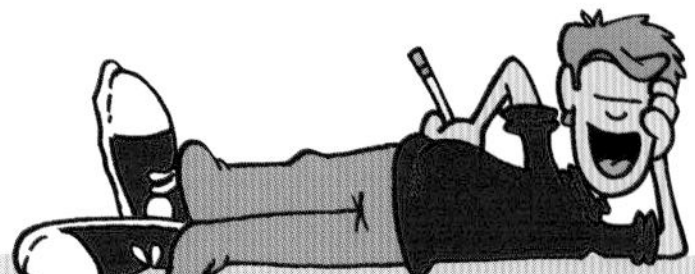

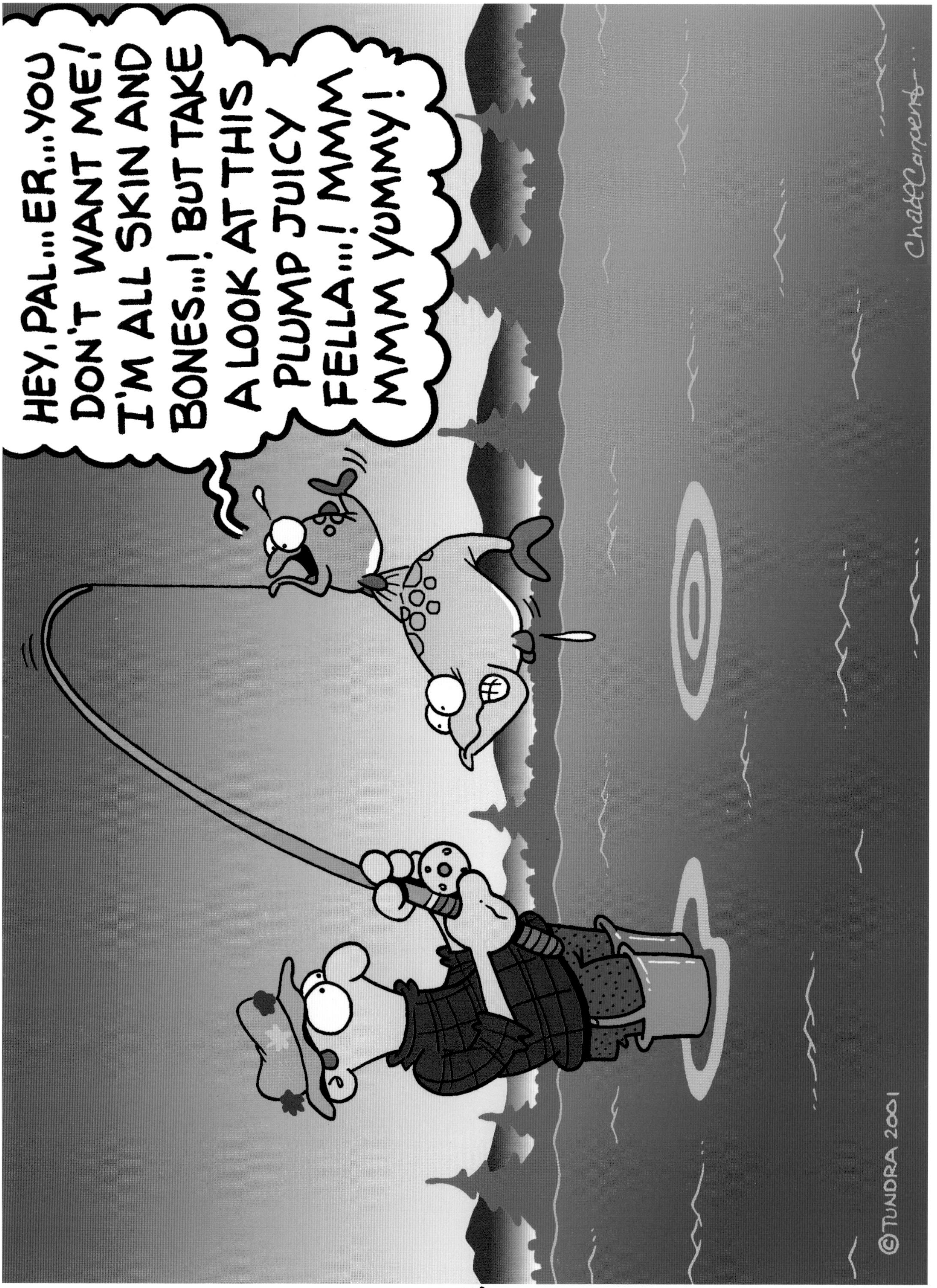
HEY, PAL...ER...YOU DON'T WANT ME! I'M ALL SKIN AND BONES...! BUT TAKE A LOOK AT THIS PLUMP JUICY FELLA...! MMM MMM YUMMY!
©TUNDRA 2001
Chad Carpenter

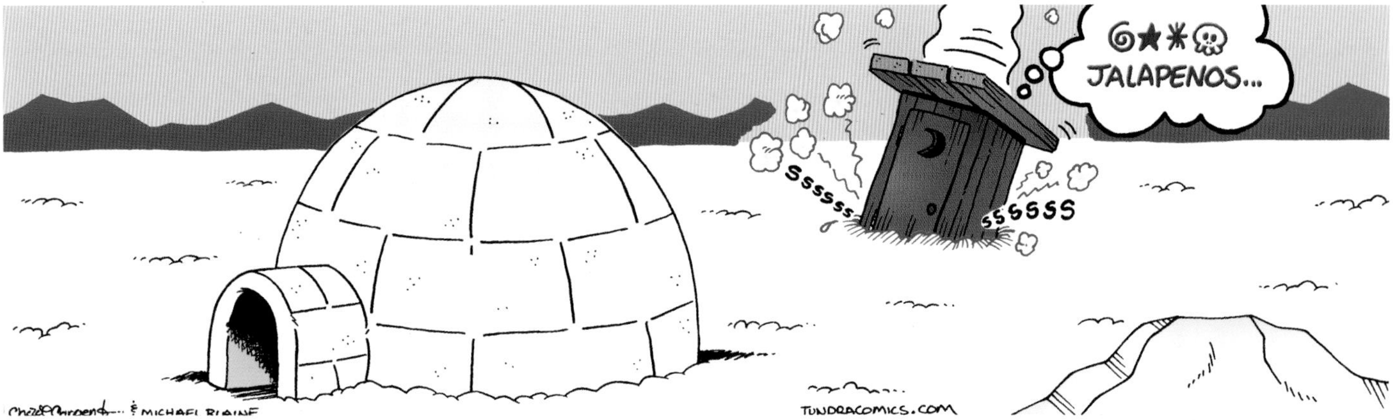
JALAPENOS...
SSSSSS
SSSSSS
TUNDRACOMICS.COM

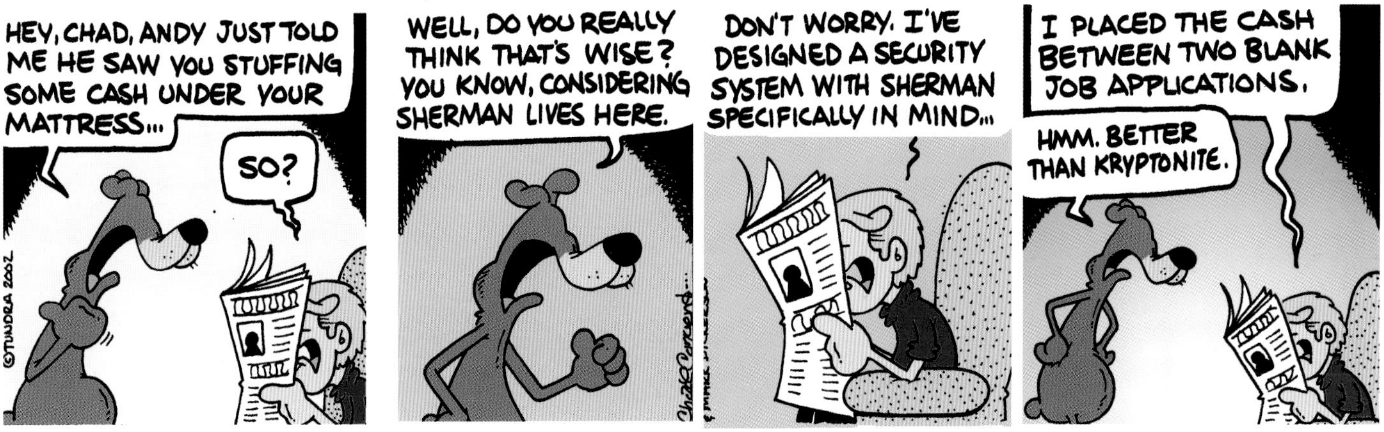
HEY, CHAD, ANDY JUST TOLD ME HE SAW YOU STUFFING SOME CASH UNDER YOUR MATTRESS...
SO?
©TUNDRA 2002
WELL, DO YOU REALLY THINK THAT'S WISE? YOU KNOW, CONSIDERING SHERMAN LIVES HERE.
DON'T WORRY. I'VE DESIGNED A SECURITY SYSTEM WITH SHERMAN SPECIFICALLY IN MIND...
I PLACED THE CASH BETWEEN TWO BLANK JOB APPLICATIONS.
HMM. BETTER THAN KRYPTONITE.

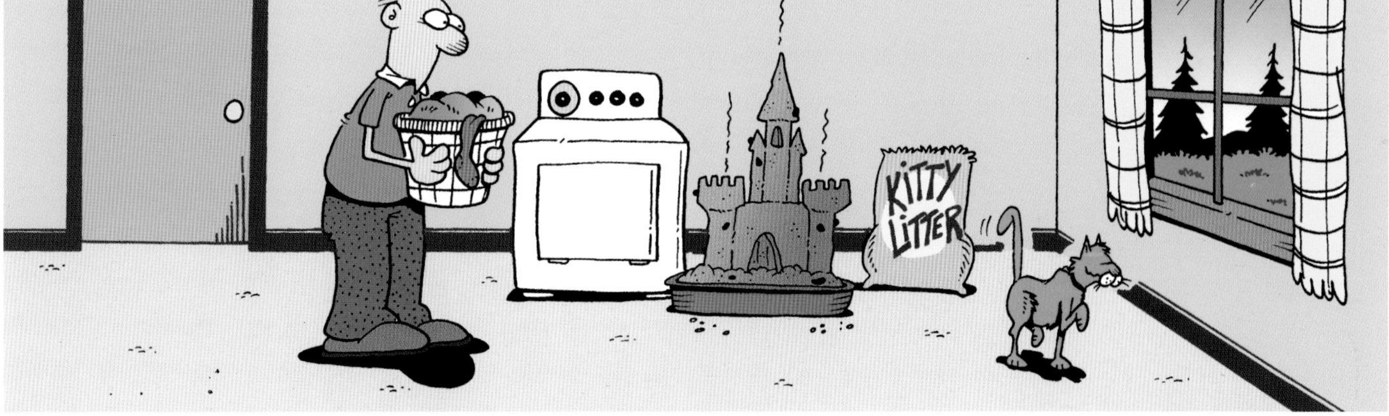
KITTY LITTER

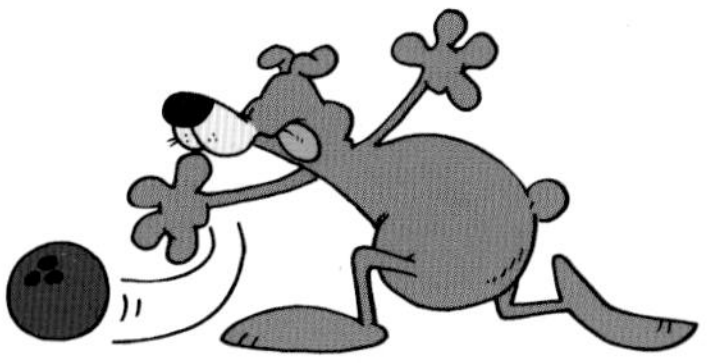

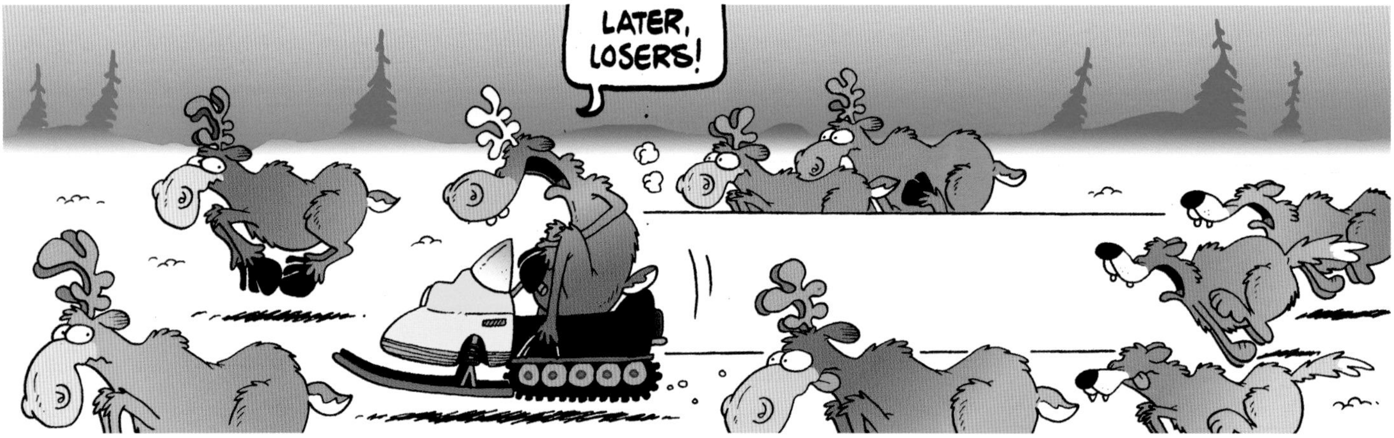
LATER, LOSERS!

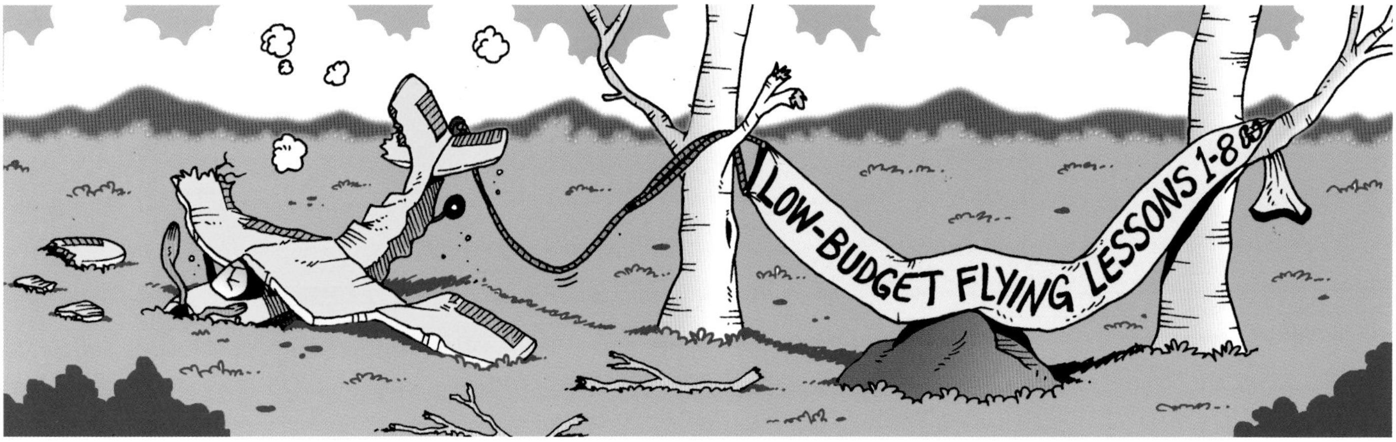
LOW-BUDGET FLYING LESSONS 1-8

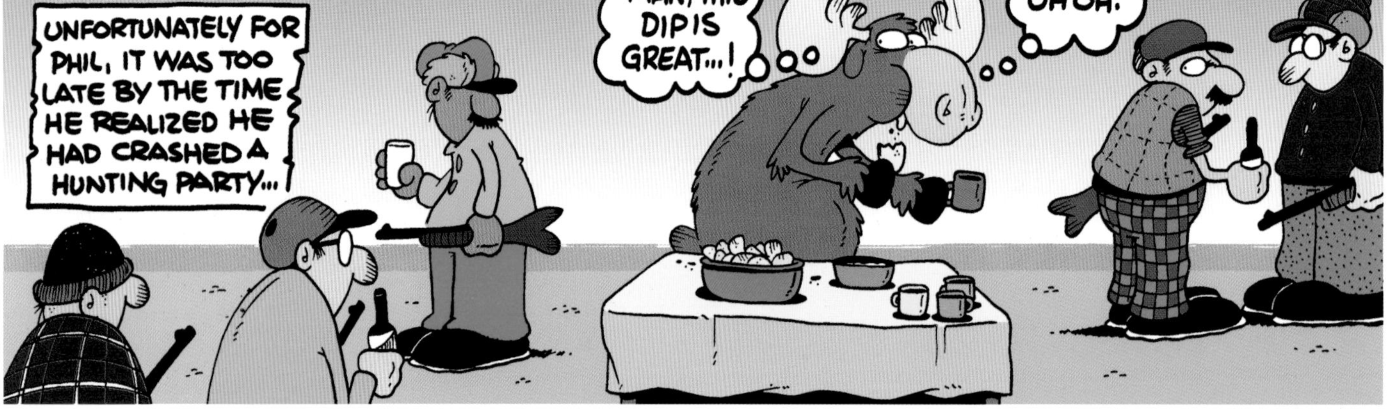
UNFORTUNATELY FOR PHIL, IT WAS TOO LATE BY THE TIME HE REALIZED HE HAD CRASHED A HUNTING PARTY...
MAN, THIS DIP IS GREAT...!
UH OH.

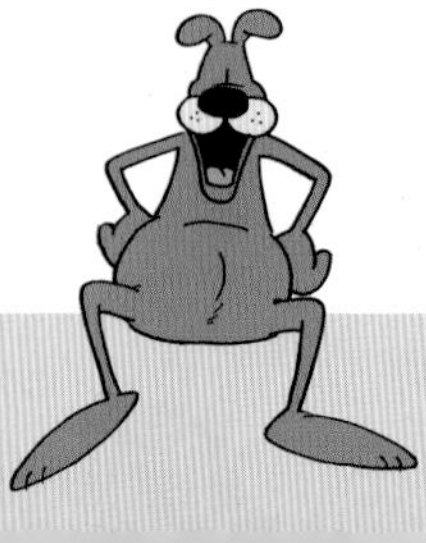

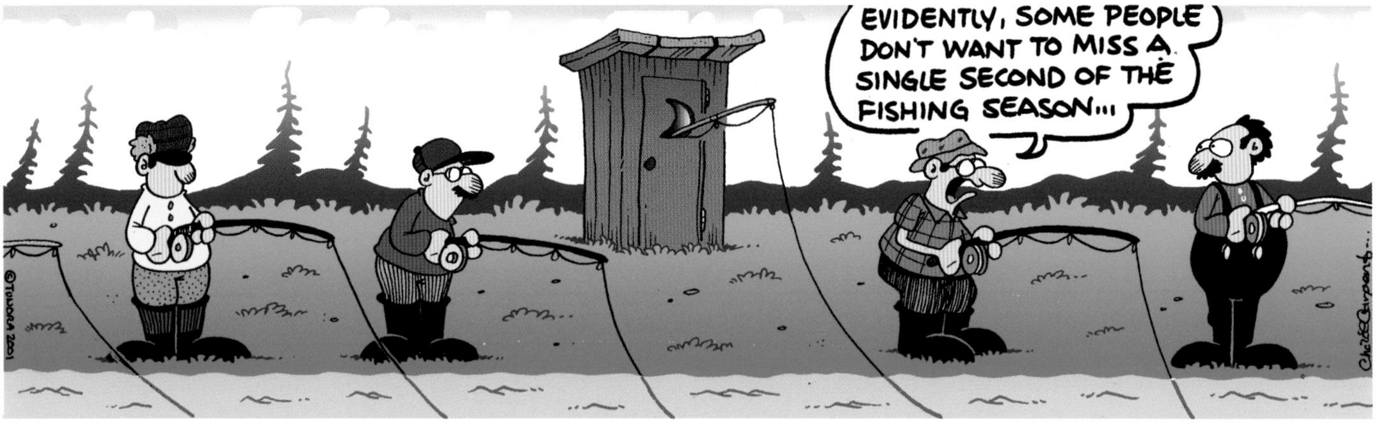
EVIDENTLY, SOME PEOPLE DON'T WANT TO MISS A SINGLE SECOND OF THE FISHING SEASON...

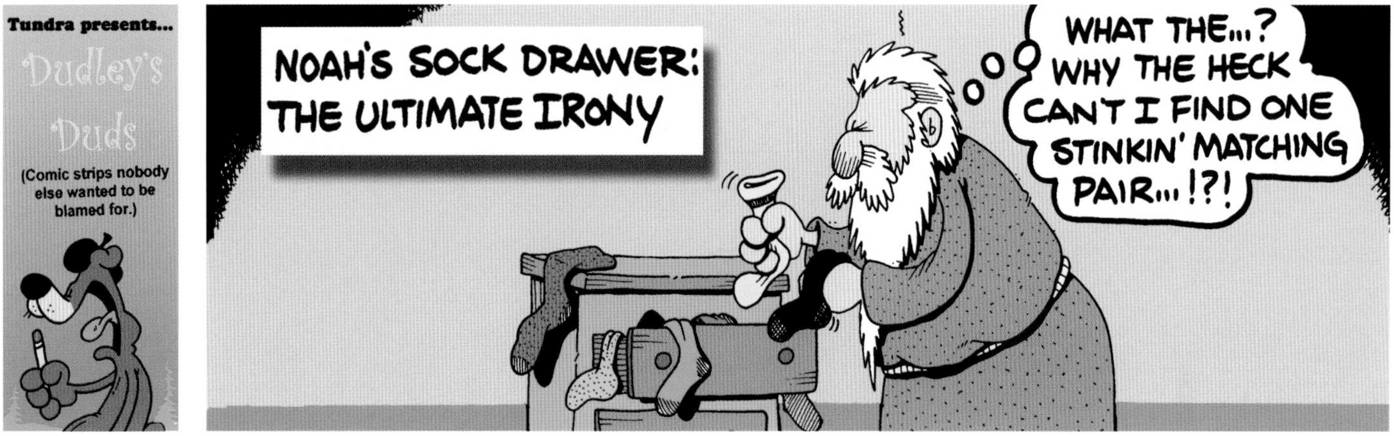
Tundra presents...
Dudley's Duds
(Comic strips nobody else wanted to be blamed for.)
NOAH'S SOCK DRAWER: THE ULTIMATE IRONY
WHAT THE...? WHY THE HECK CAN'T I FIND ONE STINKIN' MATCHING PAIR...!?!

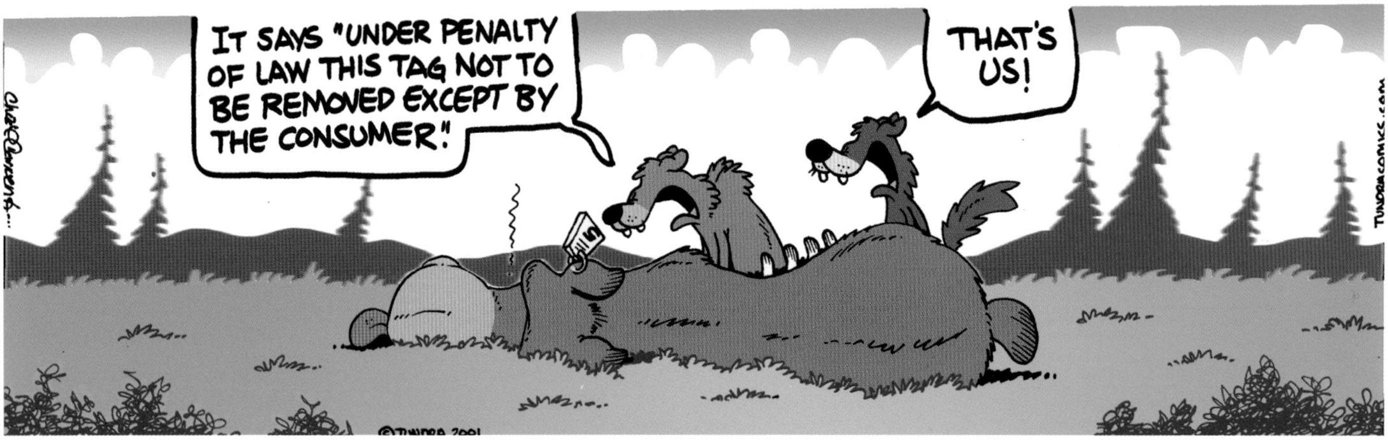
IT SAYS "UNDER PENALTY OF LAW THIS TAG NOT TO BE REMOVED EXCEPT BY THE CONSUMER."
THAT'S US!

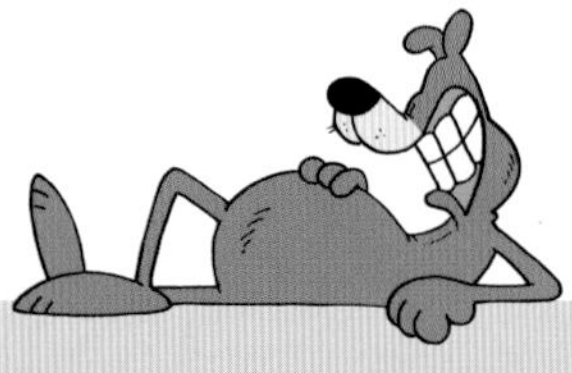

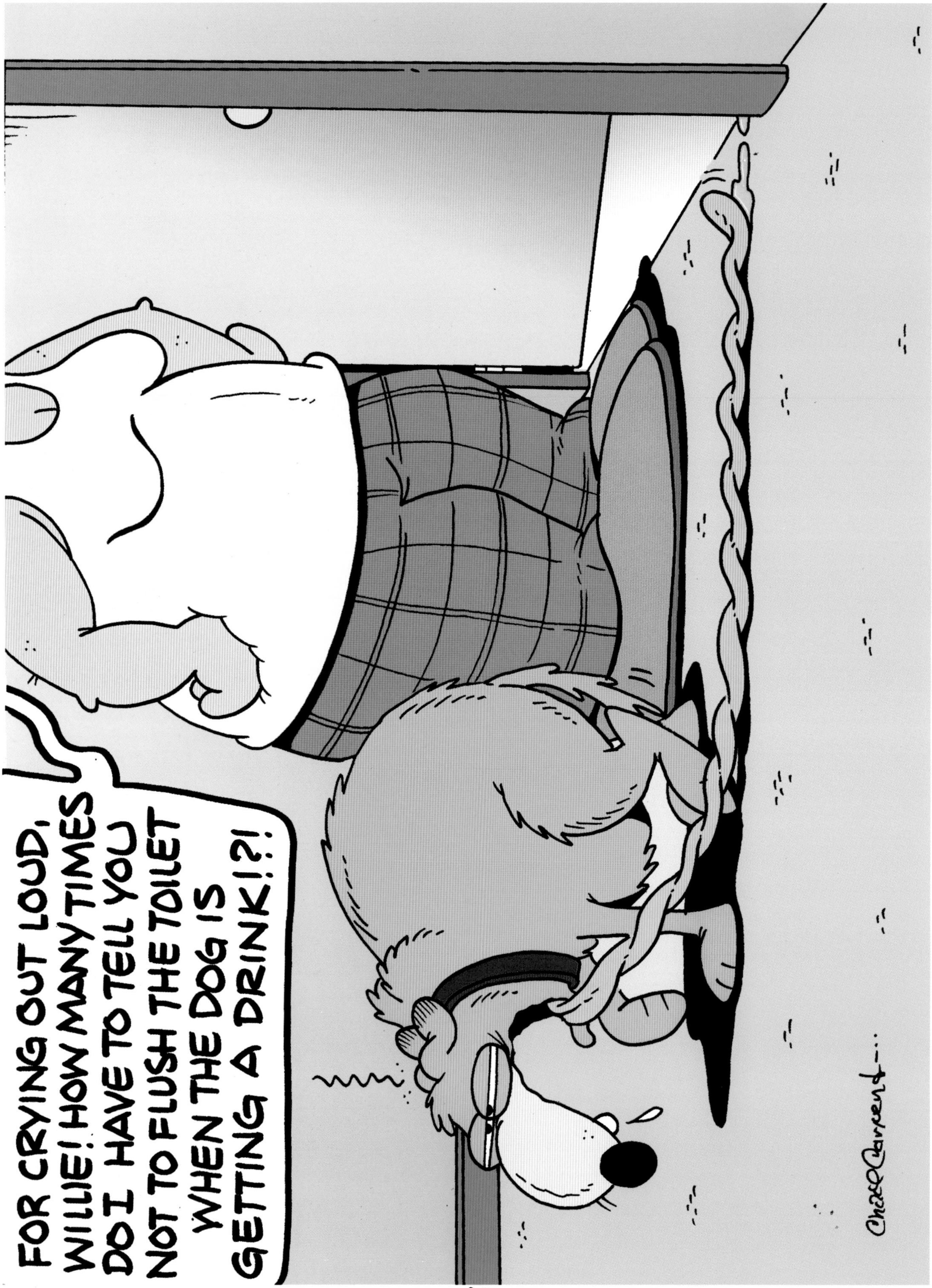
FOR CRYING OUT LOUD, WILLIE! HOW MANY TIMES DO I HAVE TO TELL YOU NOT TO FLUSH THE TOILET WHEN THE DOG IS GETTING A DRINK!?!

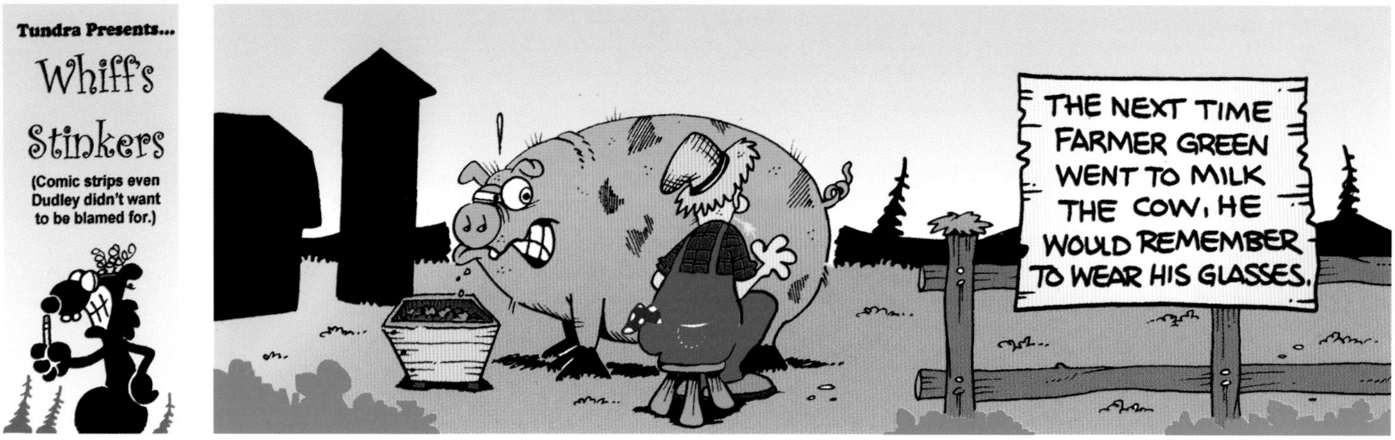
Tundra Presents...
Whiff's Stinkers
(Comic strips even Dudley didn't want to be blamed for.)
THE NEXT TIME FARMER GREEN WENT TO MILK THE COW, HE WOULD REMEMBER TO WEAR HIS GLASSES.

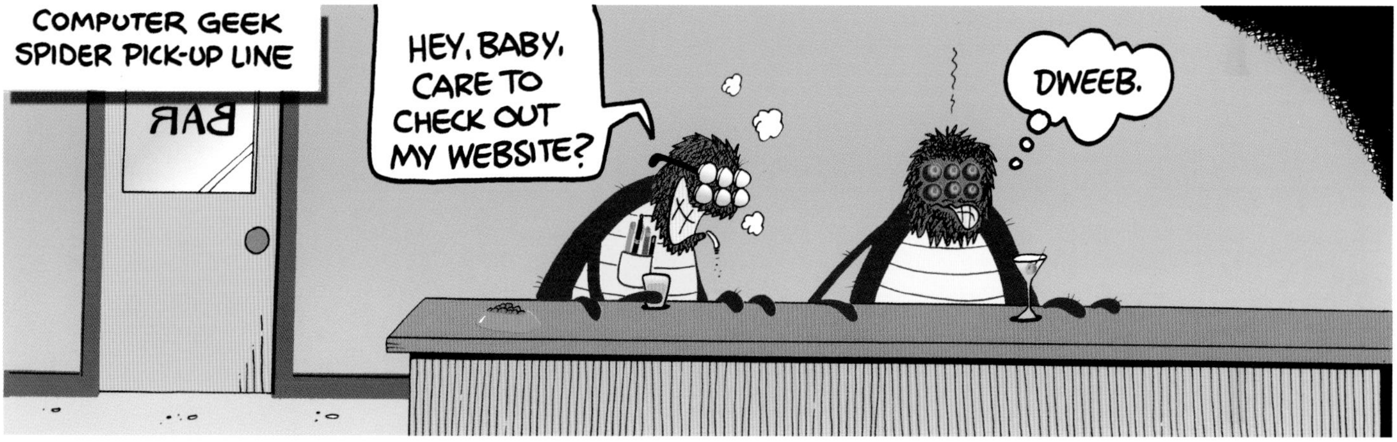
COMPUTER GEEK SPIDER PICK-UP LINE
BAR
HEY, BABY, CARE TO CHECK OUT MY WEBSITE?
DWEEB.

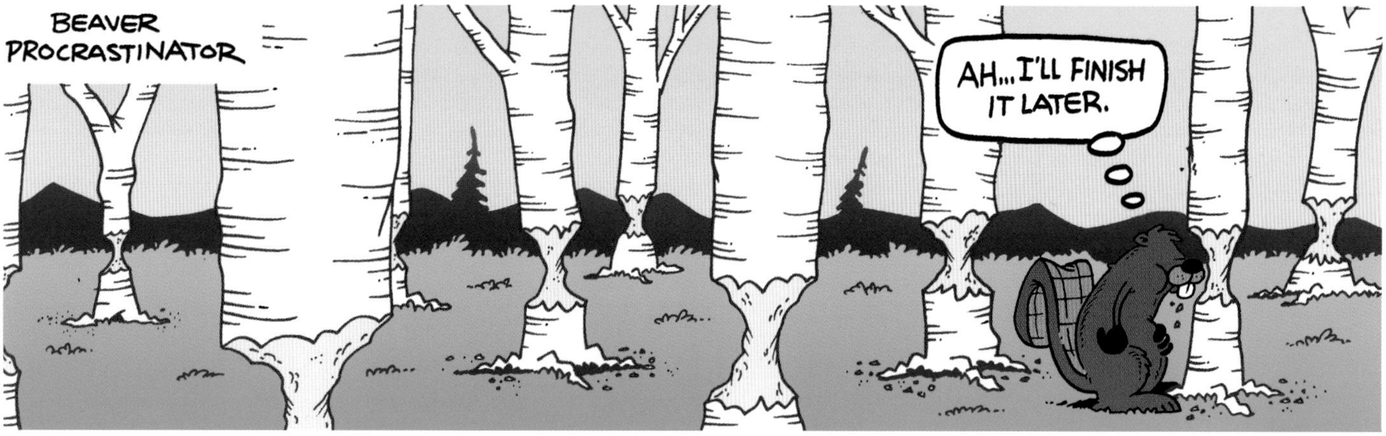
BEAVER PROCRASTINATOR
AH... I'LL FINISH IT LATER.

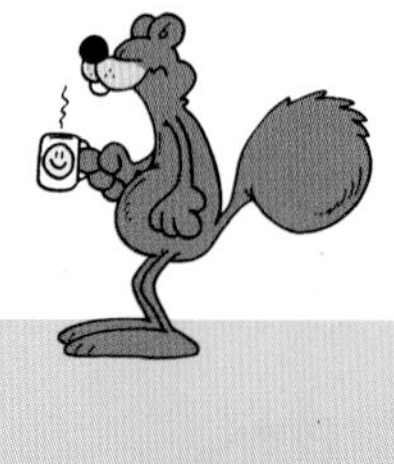

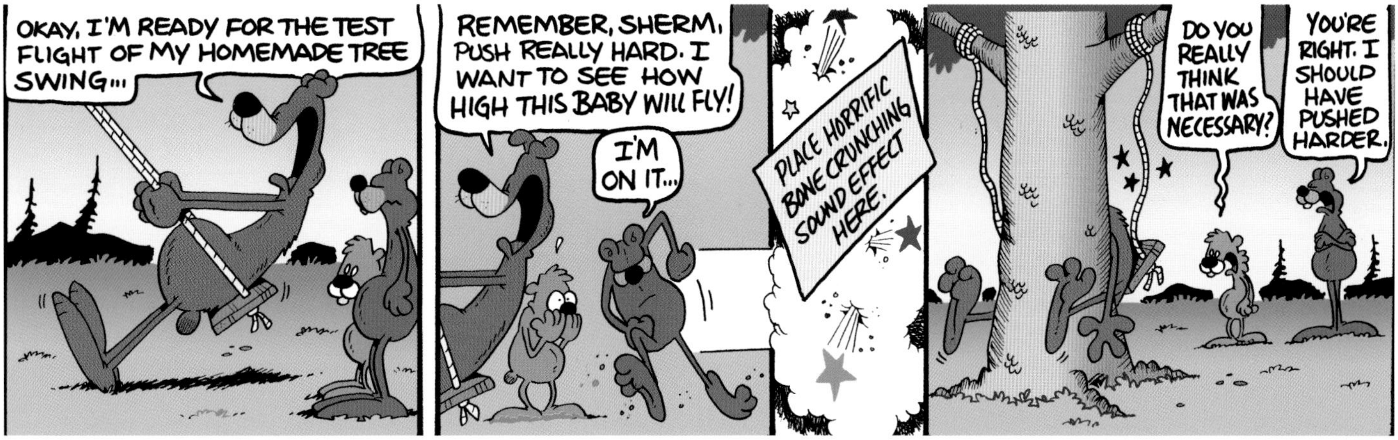
OKAY, I'M READY FOR THE TEST FLIGHT OF MY HOMEMADE TREE SWING...
REMEMBER, SHERM, PUSH REALLY HARD. I WANT TO SEE HOW HIGH THIS BABY WILL FLY!
I'M ON IT...
PLACE HORRIFIC BONE CRUNCHING SOUND EFFECT HERE.
DO YOU REALLY THINK THAT WAS NECESSARY?
YOU'RE RIGHT. I SHOULD HAVE PUSHED HARDER.

This comic strip is based on the idea of
Larry Moore
Anchorage, AK
Do you have an idea that would make a great comic strip?
Send it to:
www.tundracomics.com
or
TUNDRA IDEAS
PO BOX 770732
Eagle River, AK
99577

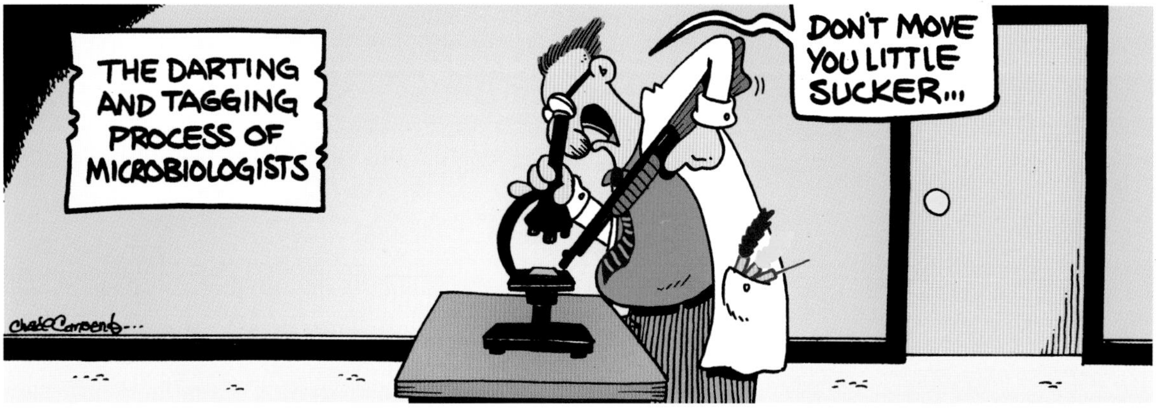
THE DARTING AND TAGGING PROCESS OF MICROBIOLOGISTS
DON'T MOVE YOU LITTLE SUCKER...

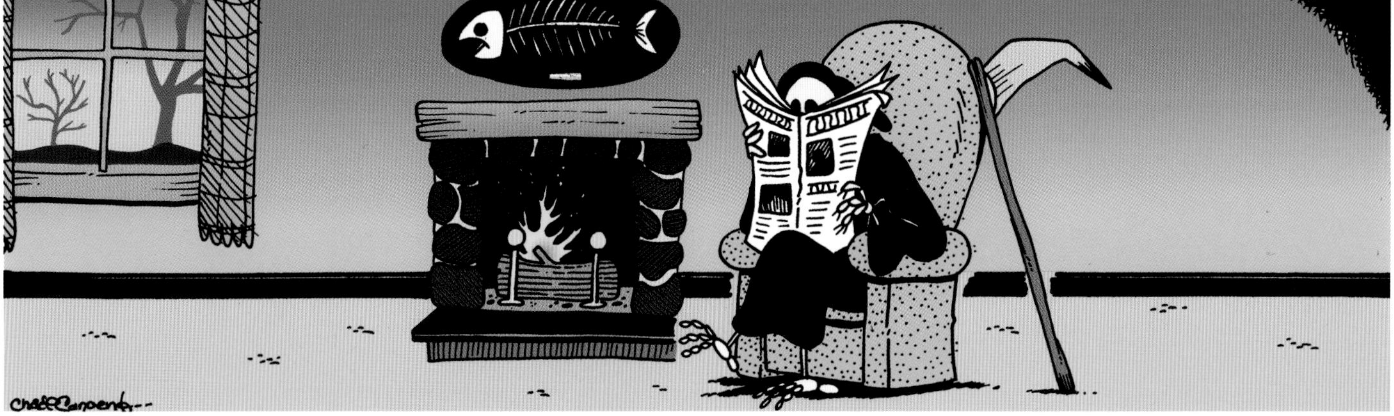

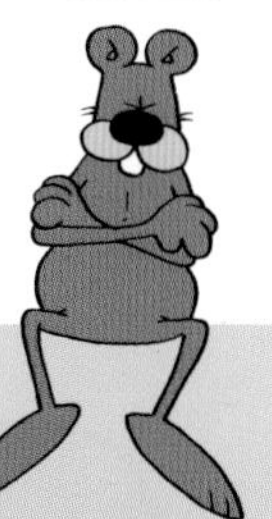

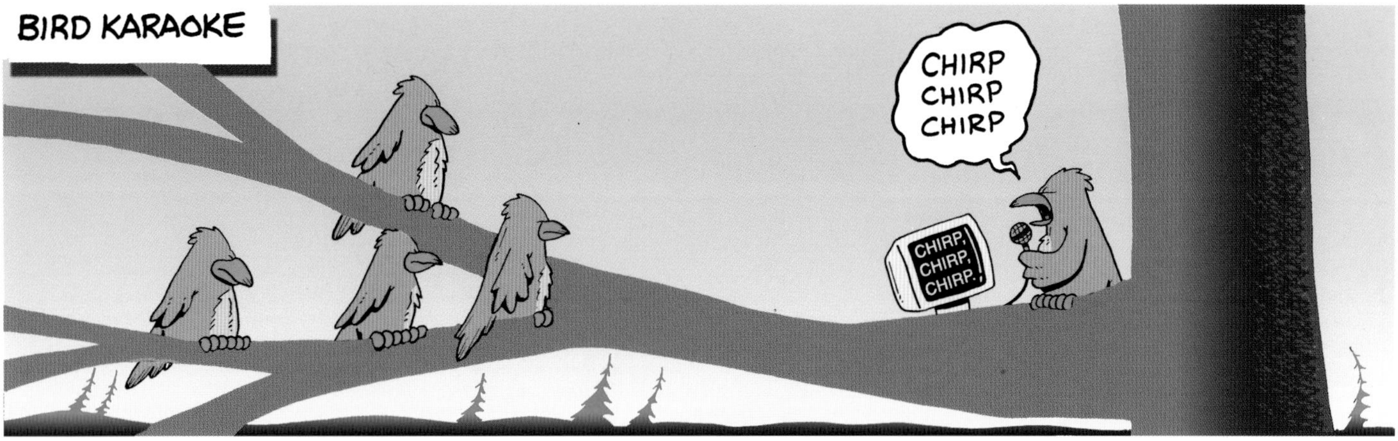
BIRD KARAOKE
CHIRP CHIRP CHIRP
CHIRP, CHIRP, CHIRP.

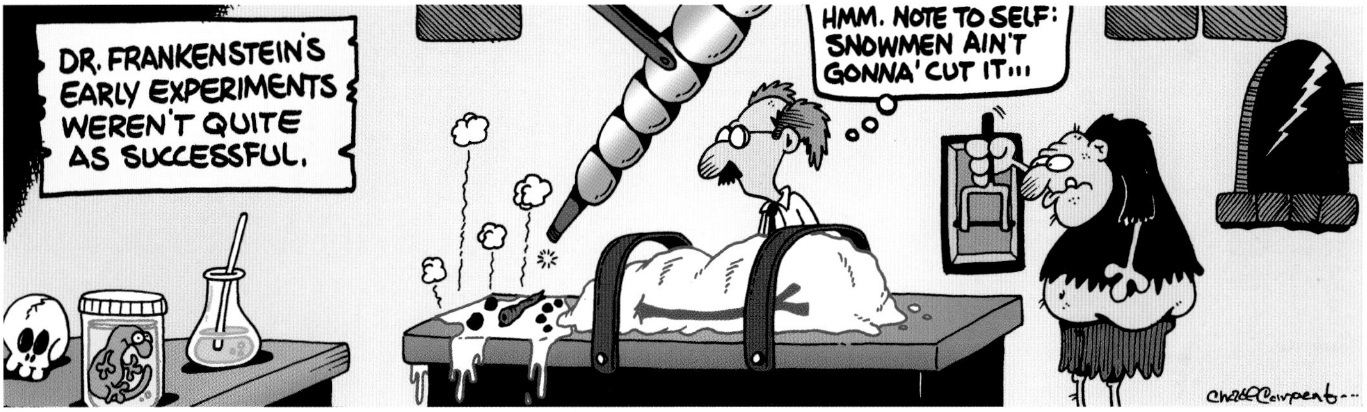
DR. FRANKENSTEIN'S EARLY EXPERIMENTS WEREN'T QUITE AS SUCCESSFUL.
HMM. NOTE TO SELF: SNOWMEN AIN'T GONNA' CUT IT...

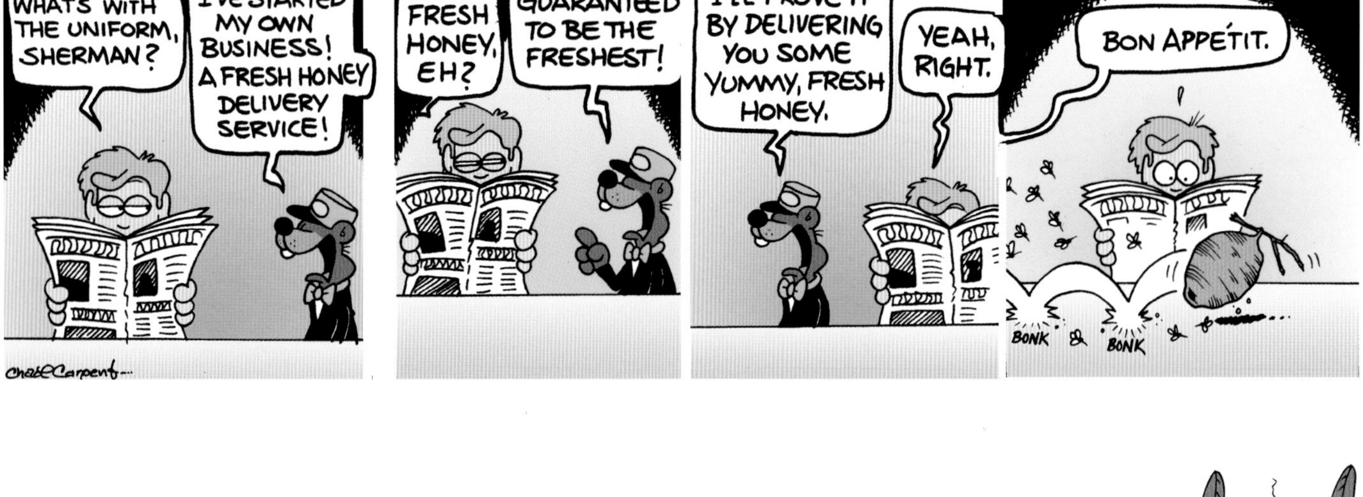
WHAT'S WITH THE UNIFORM, SHERMAN?
I'VE STARTED MY OWN BUSINESS! A FRESH HONEY DELIVERY SERVICE!
UH HUH. FRESH HONEY, EH?
GUARANTEED TO BE THE FRESHEST!
I'LL PROVE IT BY DELIVERING YOU SOME YUMMY, FRESH HONEY.
YEAH, RIGHT.
BON APPÉTIT.
BONK
BONK

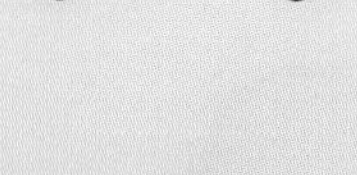

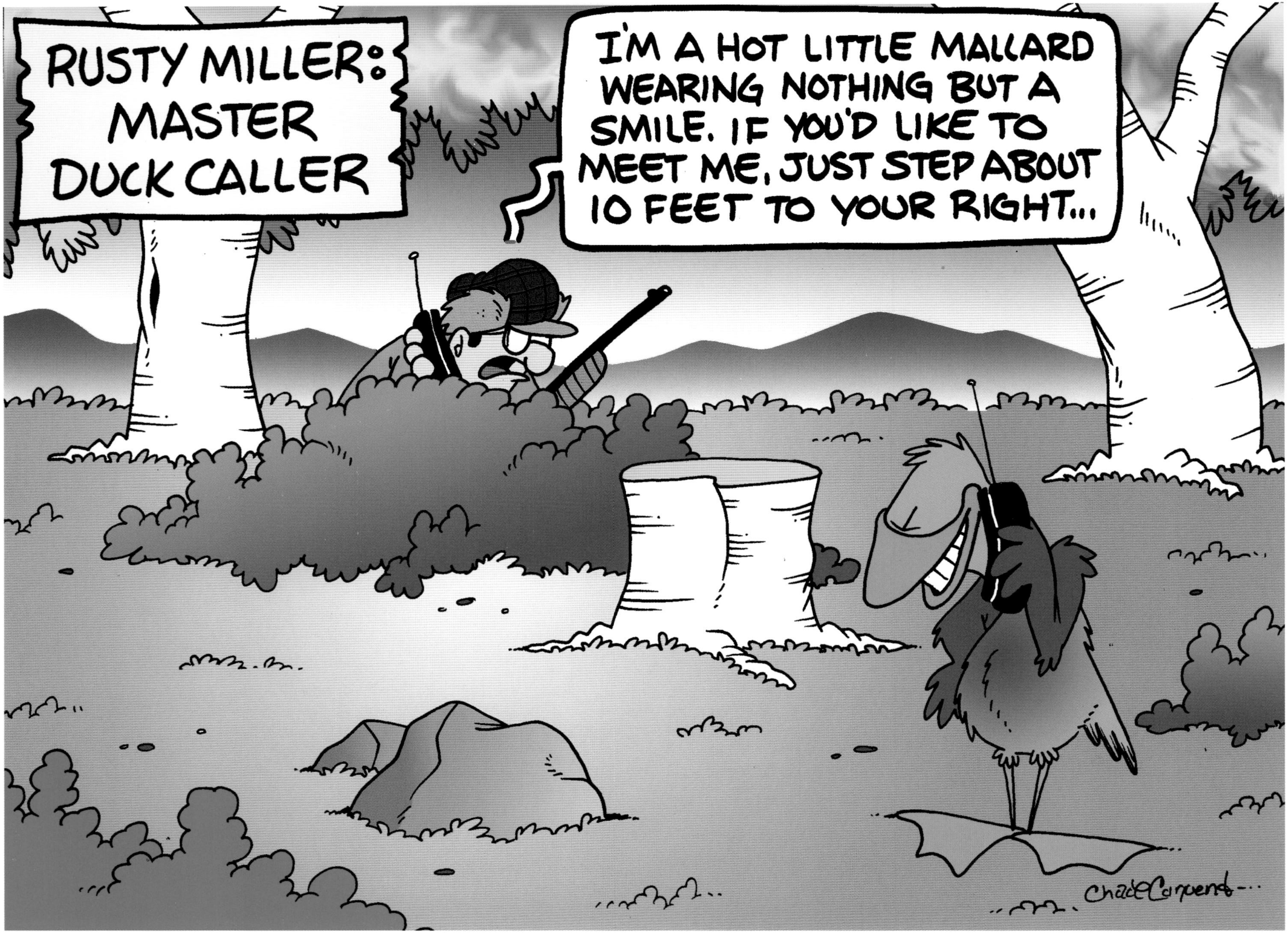
RUSTY MILLER: MASTER DUCK CALLER
I'M A HOT LITTLE MALLARD WEARING NOTHING BUT A SMILE. IF YOU'D LIKE TO MEET ME, JUST STEP ABOUT 10 FEET TO YOUR RIGHT...
Chad Carpenter

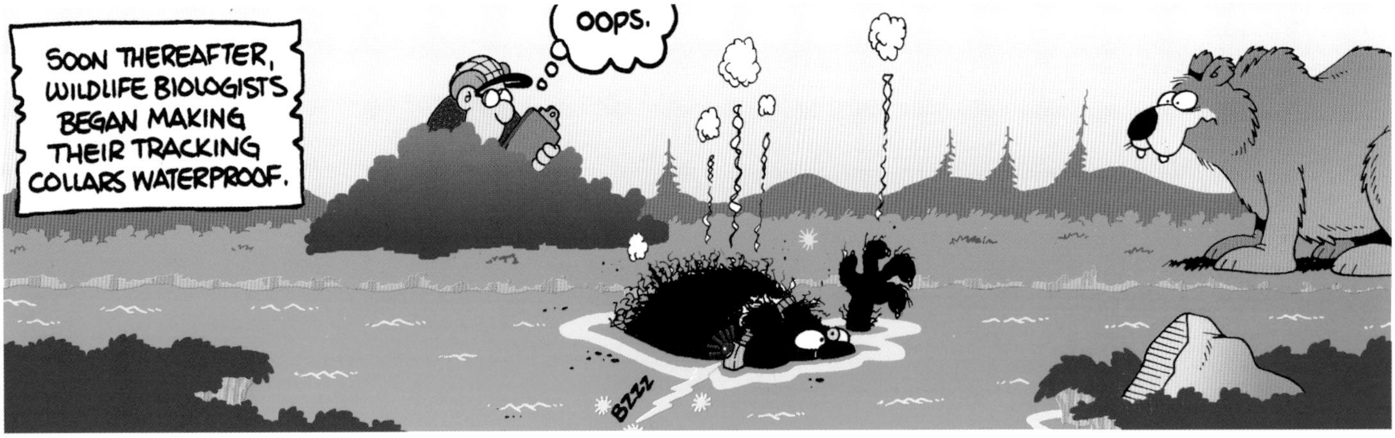
SOON THEREAFTER, WILDLIFE BIOLOGISTS BEGAN MAKING THEIR TRACKING COLLARS WATERPROOF.
OOPS.
BZZZ

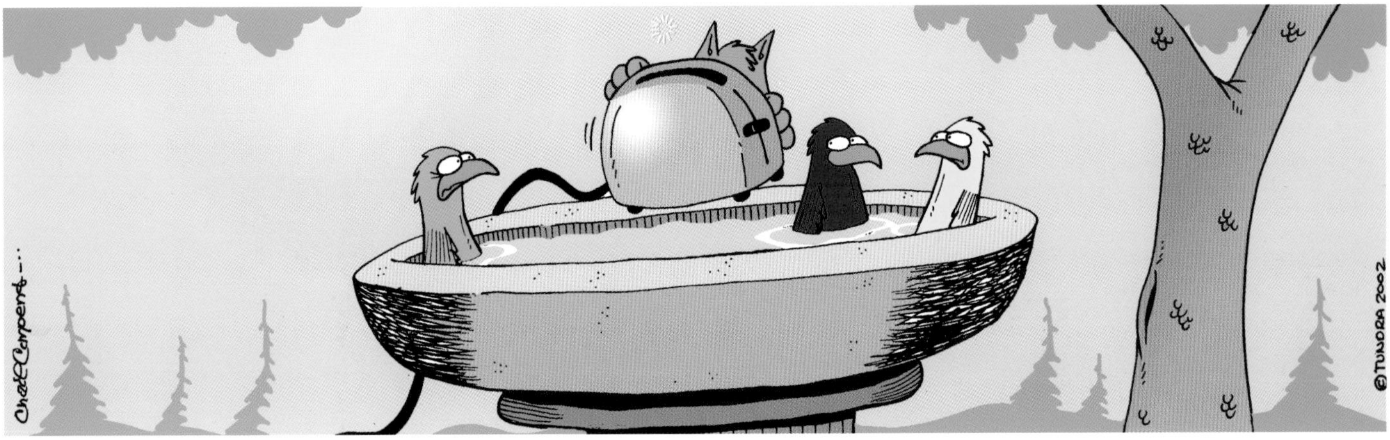
©TUNDRA 2002

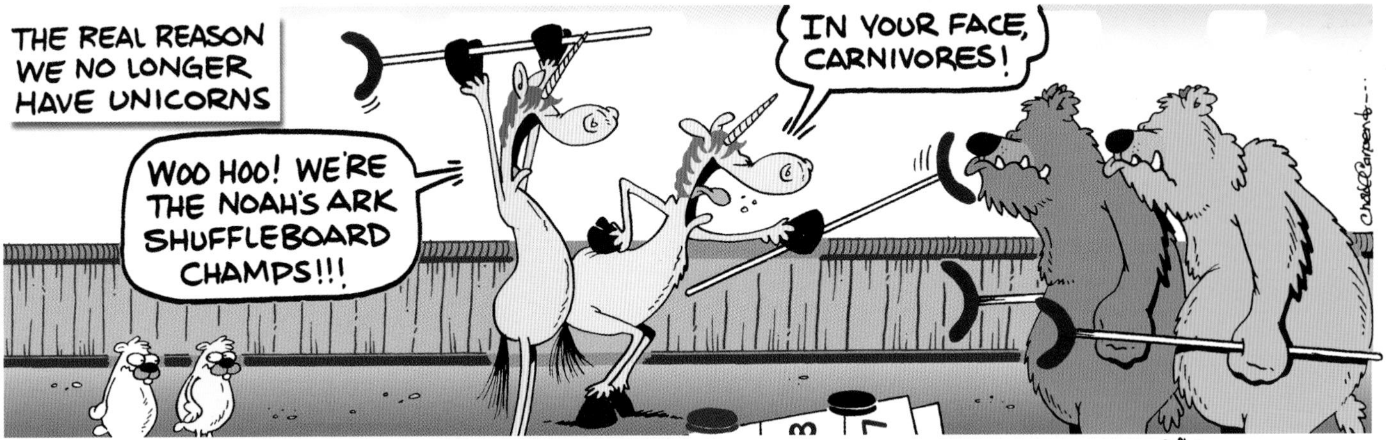
THE REAL REASON WE NO LONGER HAVE UNICORNS
WOO HOO! WE'RE THE NOAH'S ARK SHUFFLEBOARD CHAMPS!!!
IN YOUR FACE, CARNIVORES!

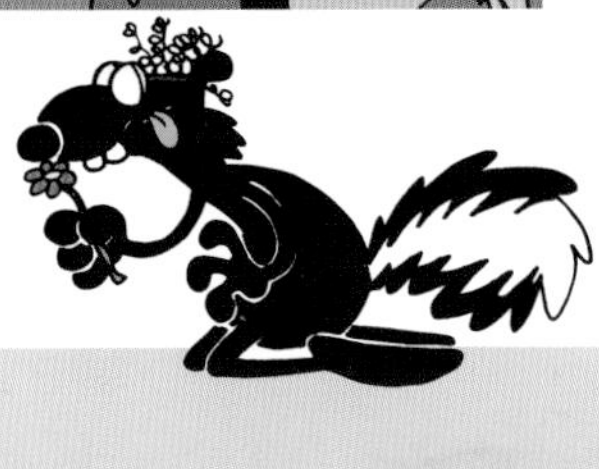

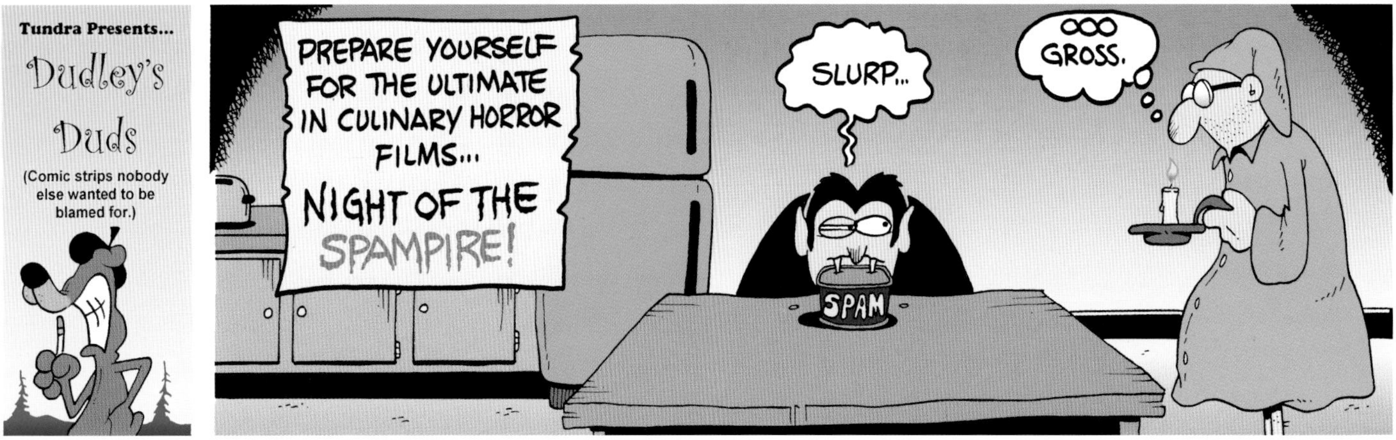
Tundra Presents...
Dudley's Duds
(Comic strips nobody else wanted to be blamed for.)
PREPARE YOURSELF FOR THE ULTIMATE IN CULINARY HORROR FILMS... NIGHT OF THE SPAMPIRE!
SLURP...
OOO GROSS.
SPAM

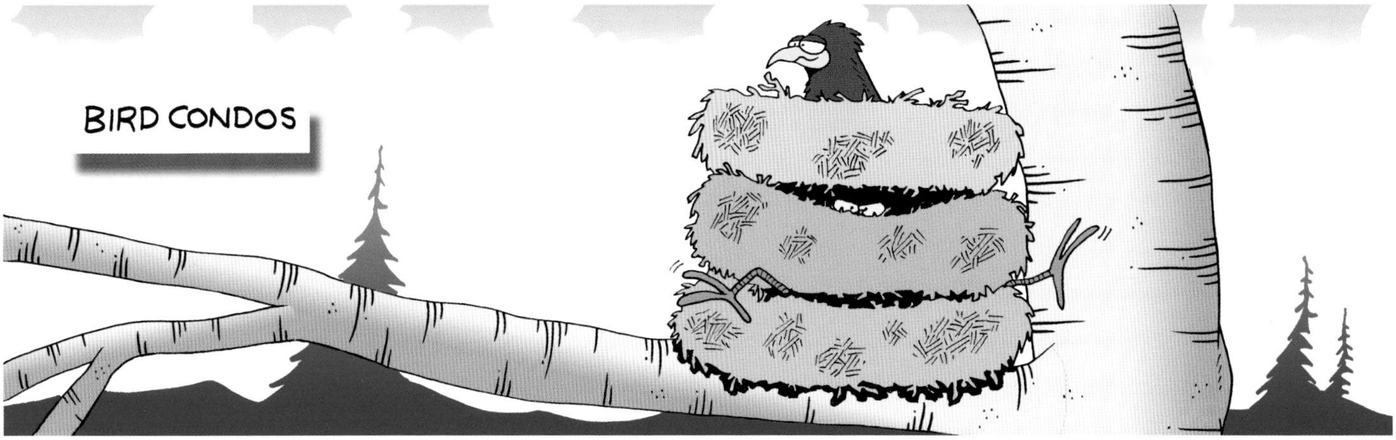
BIRD CONDOS

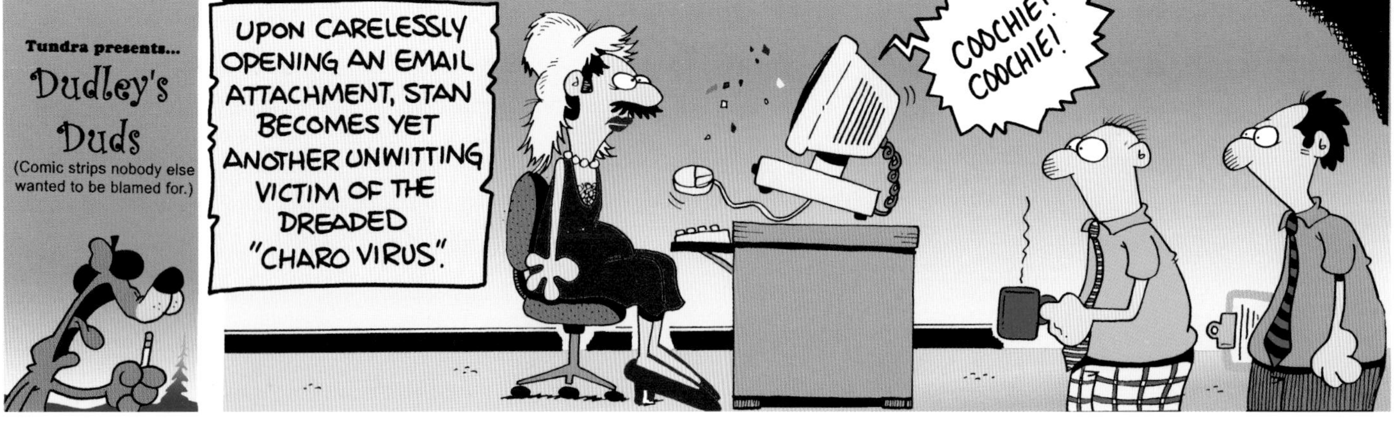
Tundra presents...
Dudley's Duds
(Comic strips nobody else wanted to be blamed for.)
UPON CARELESSLY OPENING AN EMAIL ATTACHMENT, STAN BECOMES YET ANOTHER UNWITTING VICTIM OF THE DREADED "CHARO VIRUS".
COOCHIE! COOCHIE!

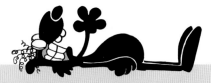

This comic strip is based on the idea of
Ted Leonard
Fairbanks, AK

Do you have an idea that would make a great comic strip? Send it to:
www.tundracomics.com
or
TUNDRA IDEAS
PO BOX 770732
Eagle River, AK
99577

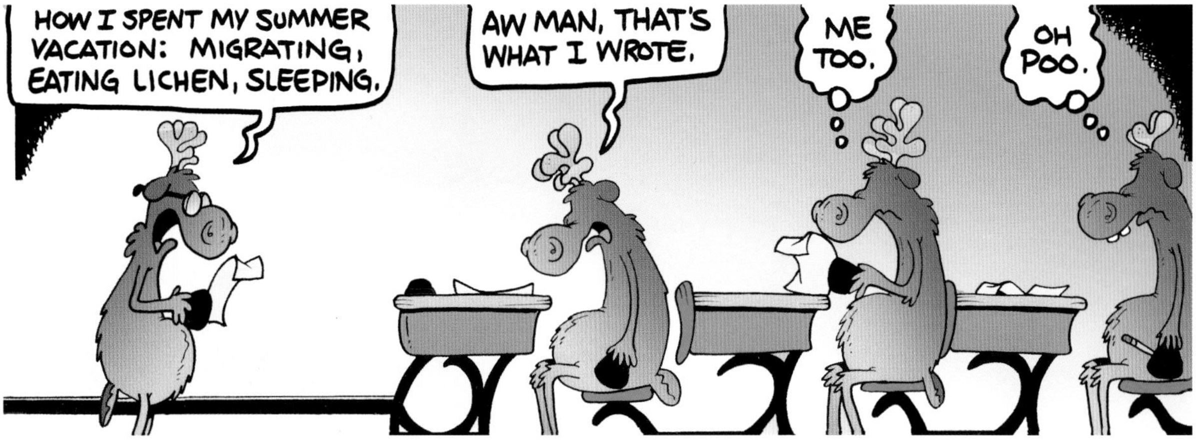
HOW I SPENT MY SUMMER VACATION: MIGRATING, EATING LICHEN, SLEEPING.
AW MAN, THAT'S WHAT I WROTE.
ME TOO.
OH POO.

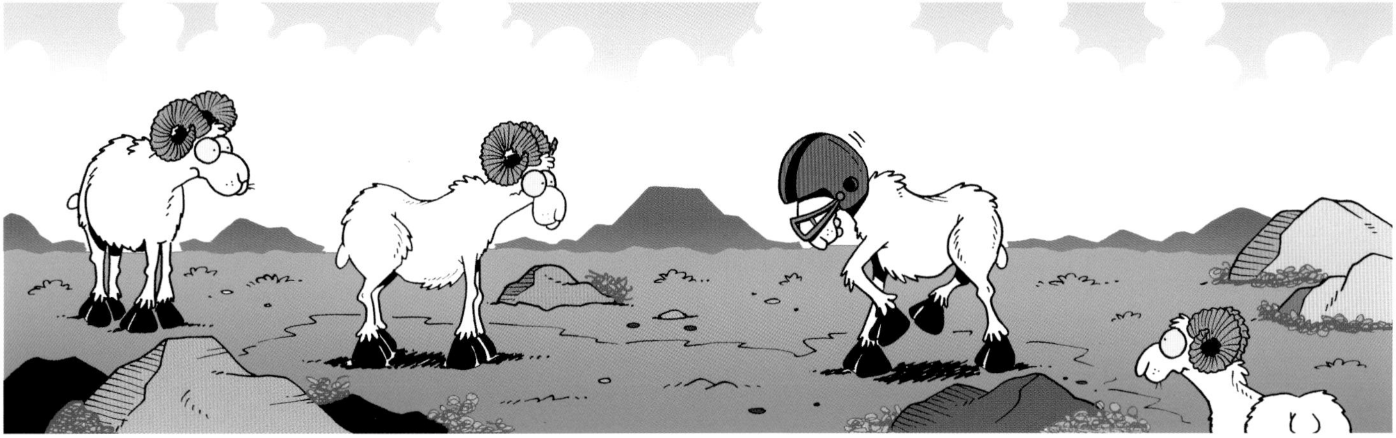

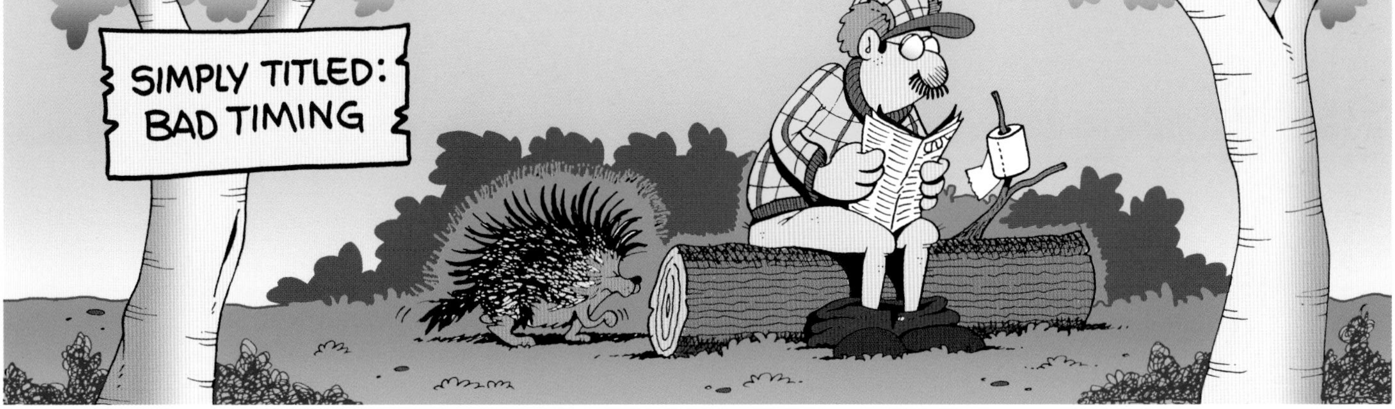
SIMPLY TITLED: BAD TIMING

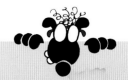

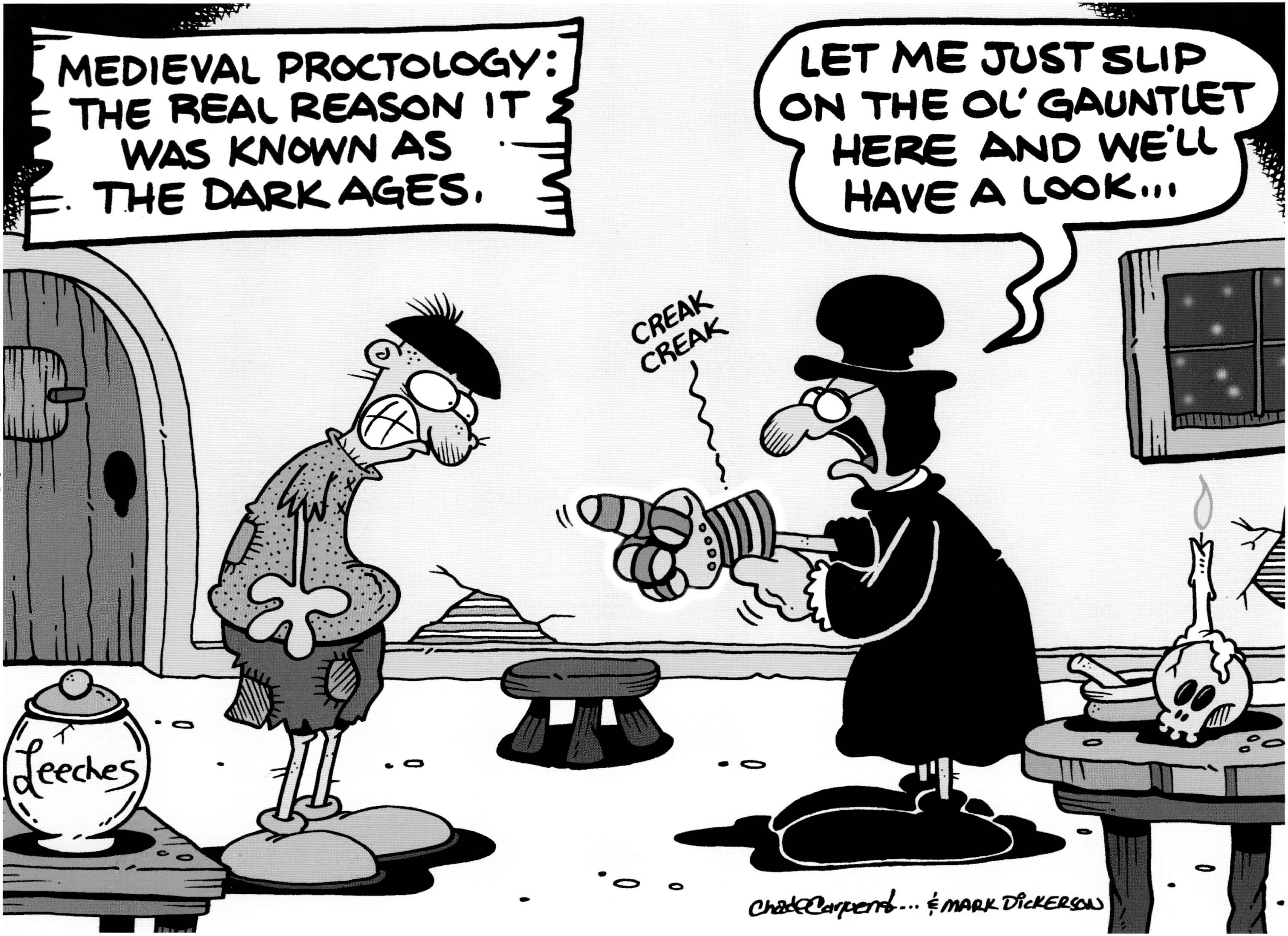
MEDIEVAL PROCTOLOGY: THE REAL REASON IT WAS KNOWN AS THE DARK AGES.
LET ME JUST SLIP ON THE OL' GAUNTLET HERE AND WE'LL HAVE A LOOK...
CREAK CREAK
Leeches
Chad Carpenter... & MARK DICKERSON

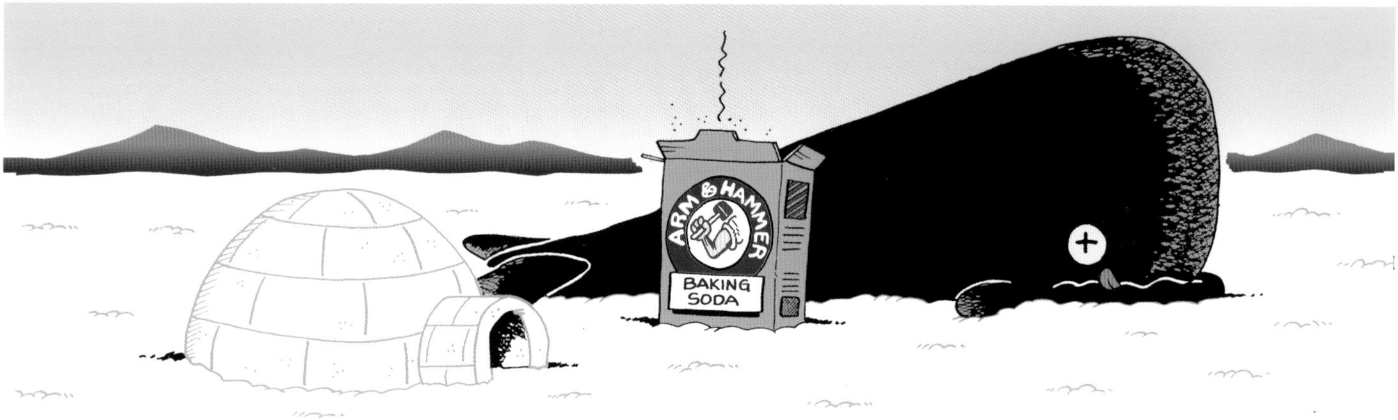
ARM & HAMMER
BAKING SODA

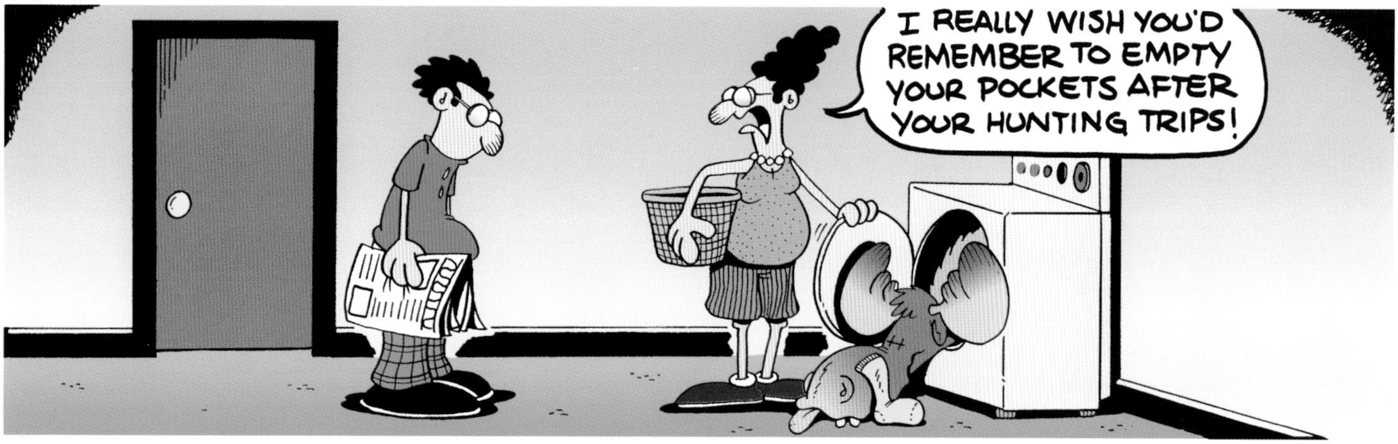
I REALLY WISH YOU'D REMEMBER TO EMPTY YOUR POCKETS AFTER YOUR HUNTING TRIPS!

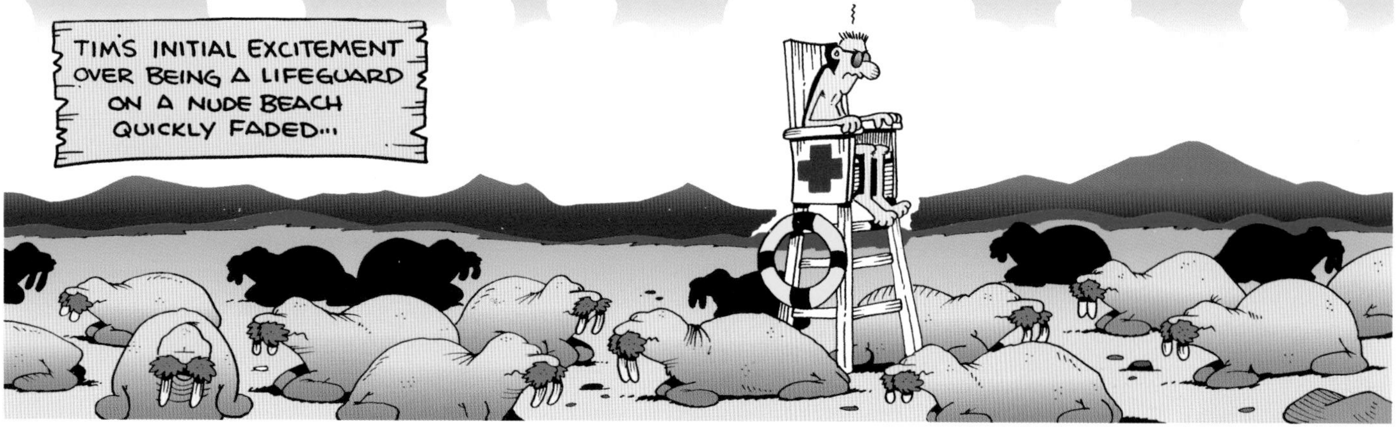
TIM'S INITIAL EXCITEMENT OVER BEING A LIFEGUARD ON A NUDE BEACH QUICKLY FADED...

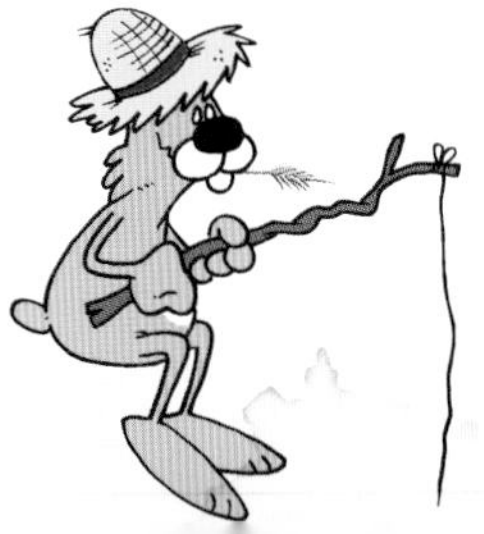

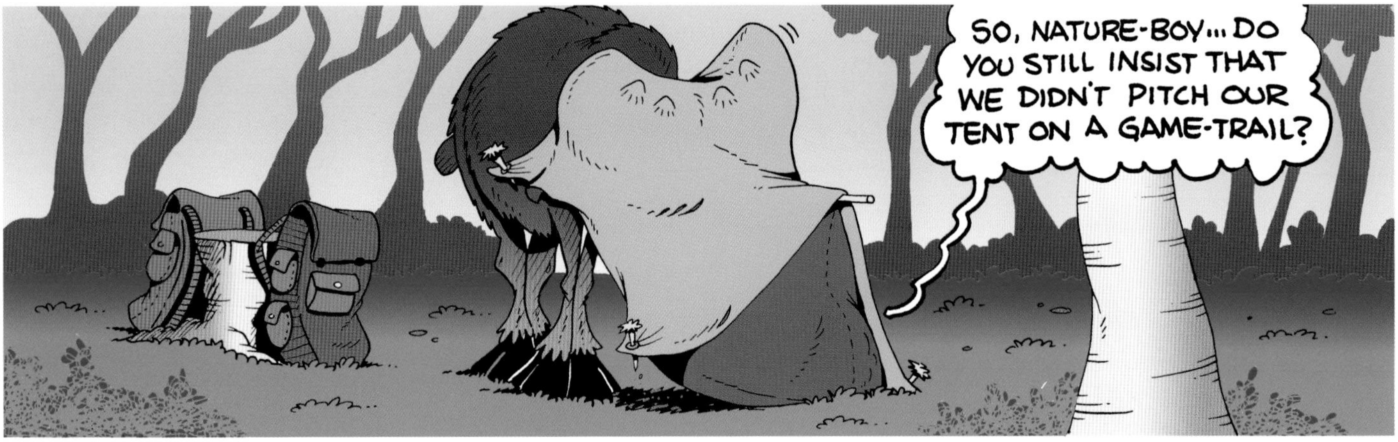
SO, NATURE-BOY... DO YOU STILL INSIST THAT WE DIDN'T PITCH OUR TENT ON A GAME-TRAIL?

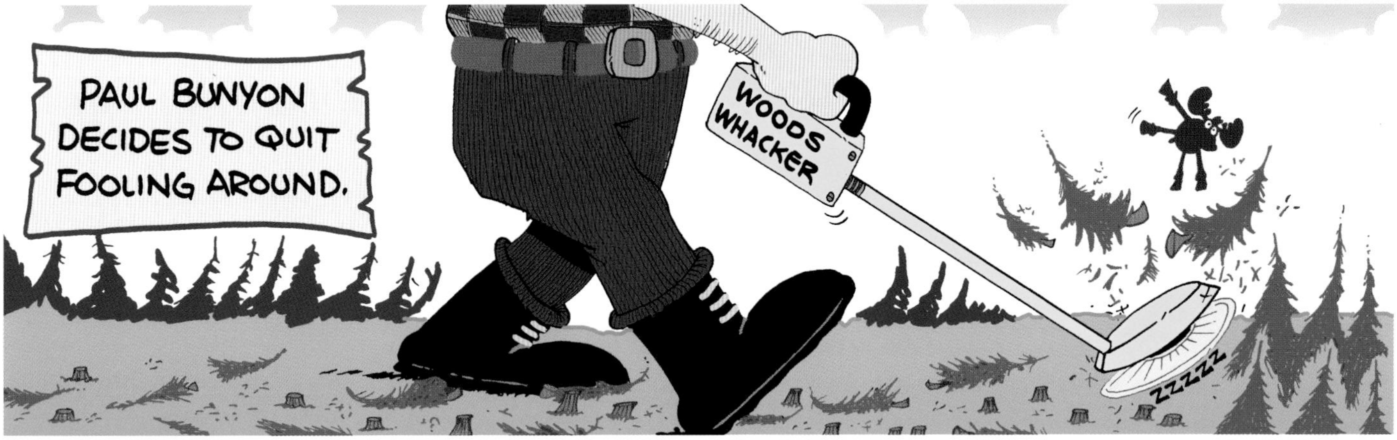
PAUL BUNYON DECIDES TO QUIT FOOLING AROUND.
WOODS WHACKER
ZZZZZ

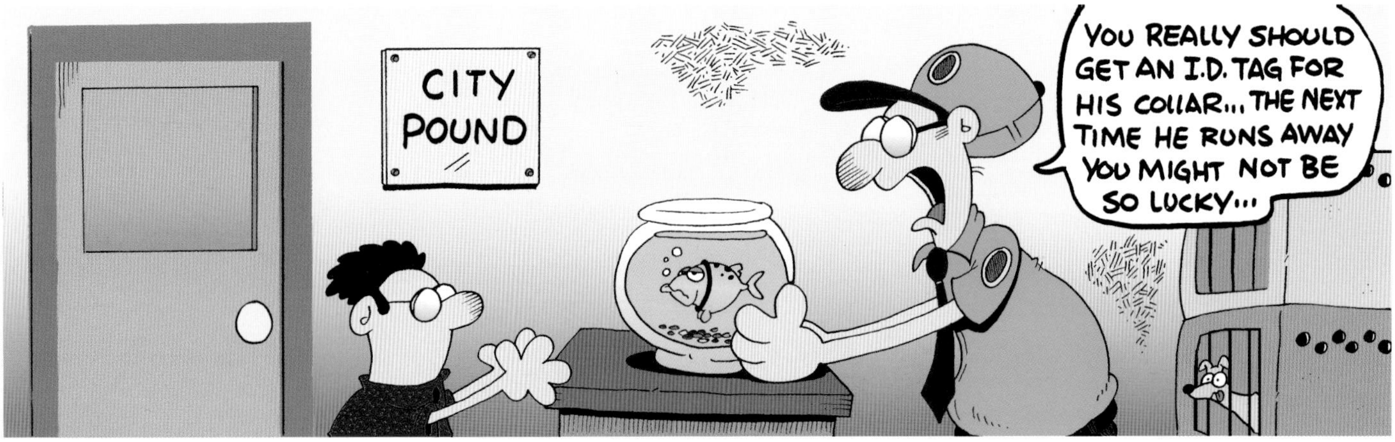
CITY POUND
YOU REALLY SHOULD GET AN I.D. TAG FOR HIS COLLAR... THE NEXT TIME HE RUNS AWAY YOU MIGHT NOT BE SO LUCKY...

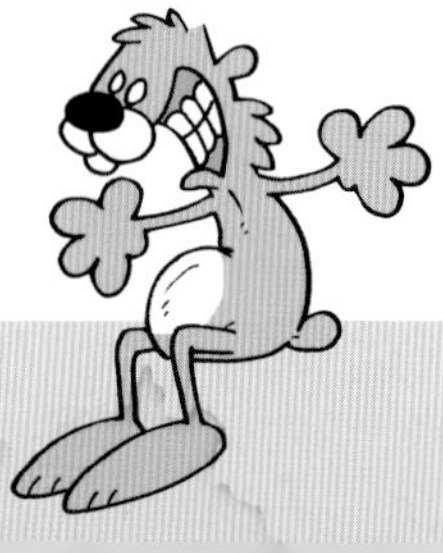

Tundra presents...

Dudley's Duds

(Comic strips nobody else wanted to be blamed for.)

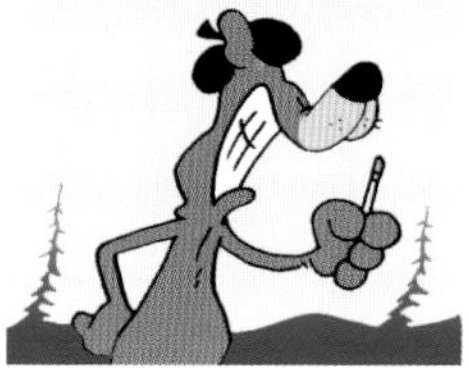

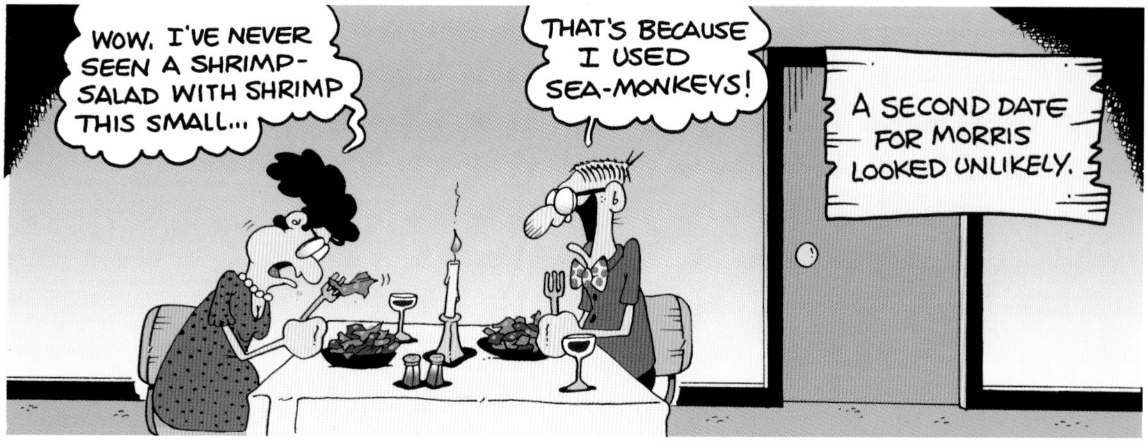
WOW. I'VE NEVER SEEN A SHRIMP-SALAD WITH SHRIMP THIS SMALL...
THAT'S BECAUSE I USED SEA-MONKEYS!
A SECOND DATE FOR MORRIS LOOKED UNLIKELY.

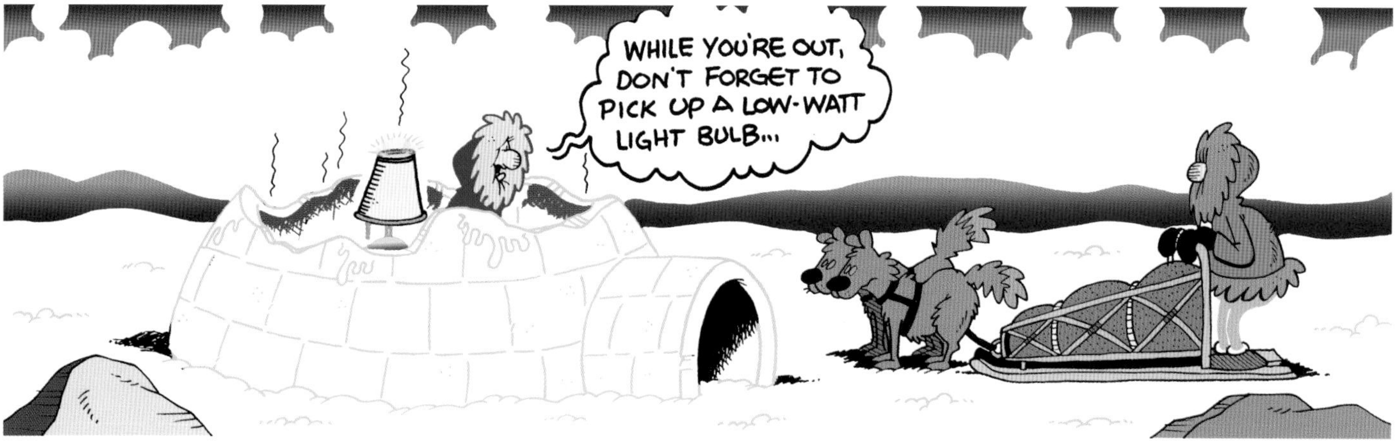
WHILE YOU'RE OUT, DON'T FORGET TO PICK UP A LOW-WATT LIGHT BULB...

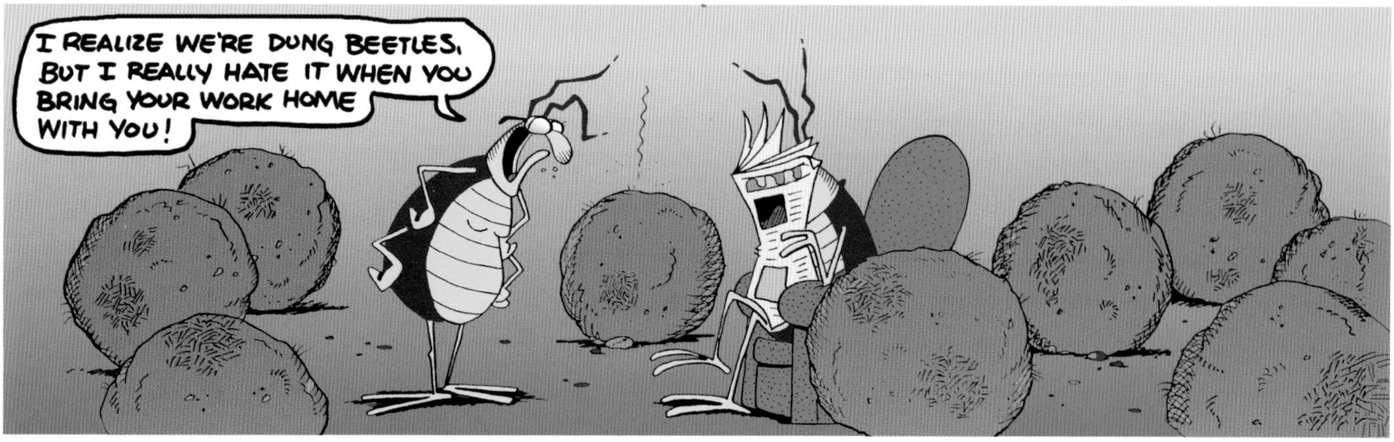
I REALIZE WE'RE DUNG BEETLES, BUT I REALLY HATE IT WHEN YOU BRING YOUR WORK HOME WITH YOU!

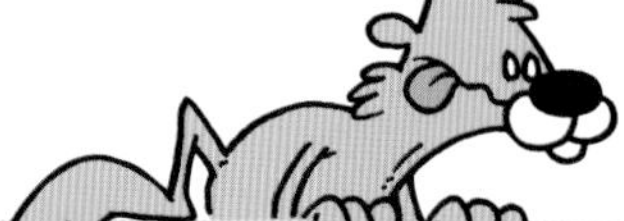

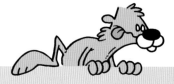

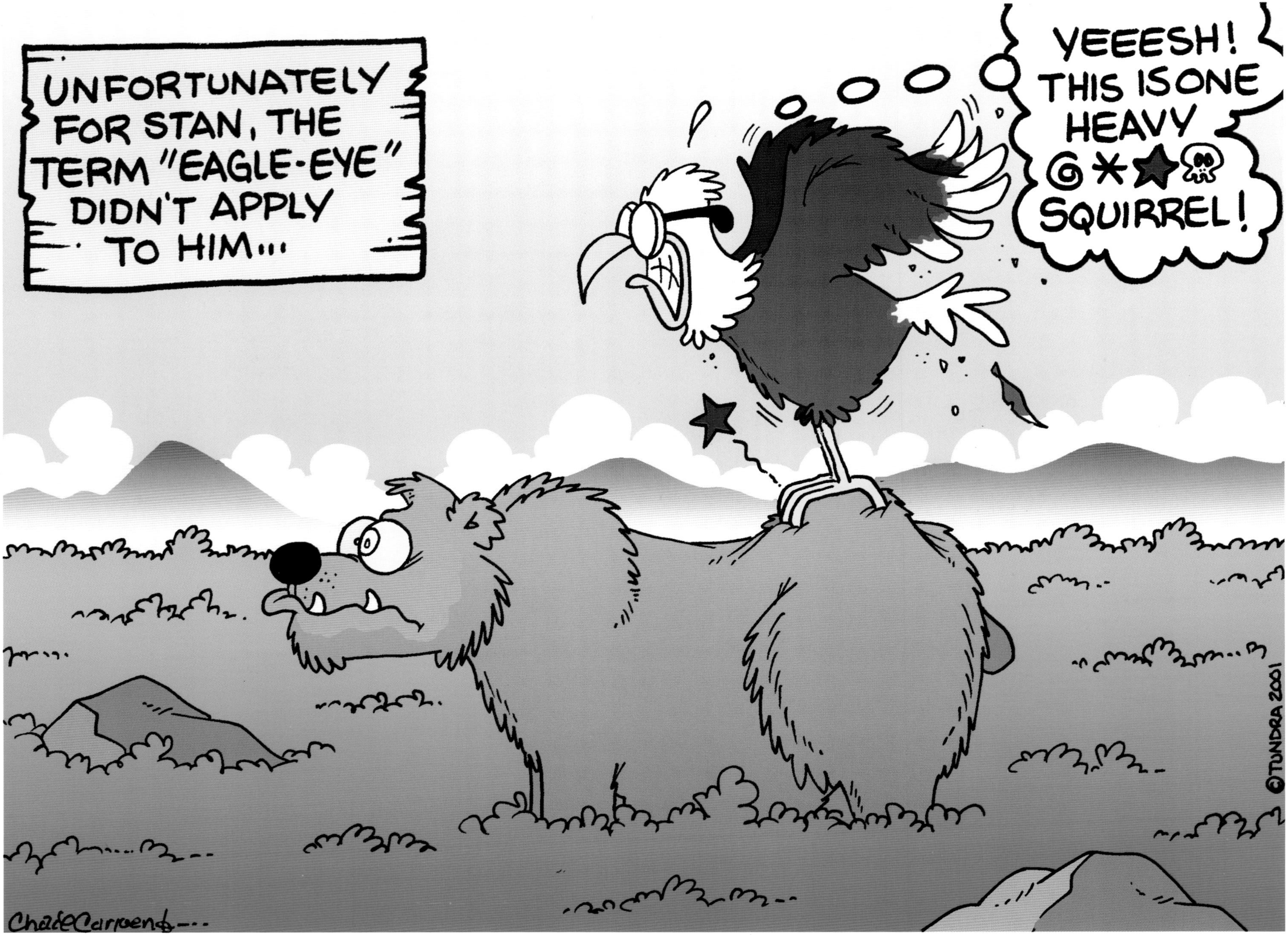
UNFORTUNATELY FOR STAN, THE TERM "EAGLE-EYE" DIDN'T APPLY TO HIM...
YEEEESH! THIS IS ONE HEAVY @*★☠ SQUIRREL!
©TUNDRA 2001
ChadeCarroens...

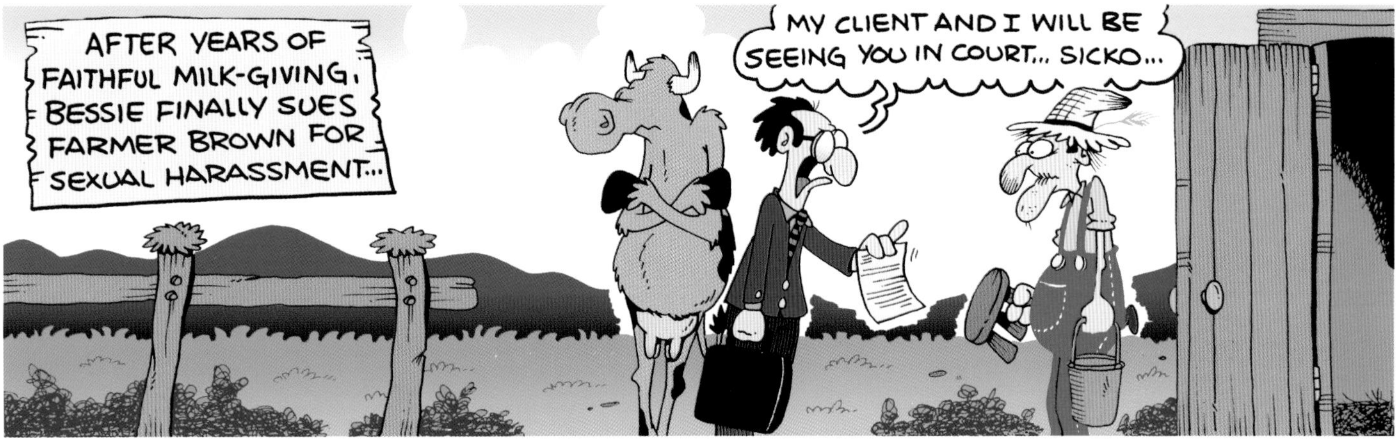
AFTER YEARS OF FAITHFUL MILK-GIVING, BESSIE FINALLY SUES FARMER BROWN FOR SEXUAL HARASSMENT...
MY CLIENT AND I WILL BE SEEING YOU IN COURT... SICKO...

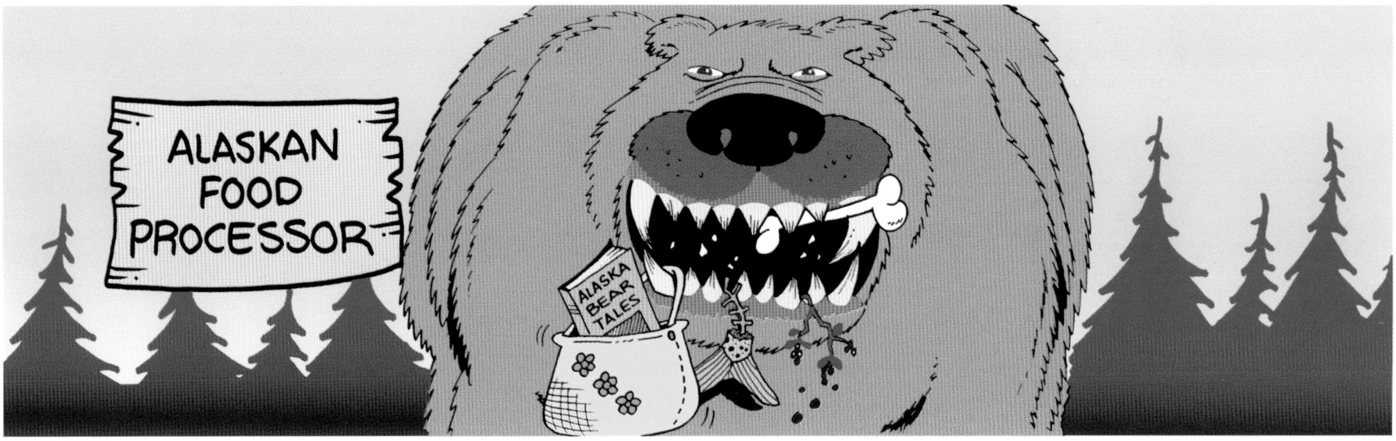
ALASKAN FOOD PROCESSOR
ALASKA BEAR TALES

This comic strip is based on the idea of

Laura Haddad
Anchorage, AK

Do you have an idea that would make a great comic strip? Send it to:

www.tundracomics.com
or
TUNDRA IDEAS
PO BOX 770732
Eagle River, AK
99577

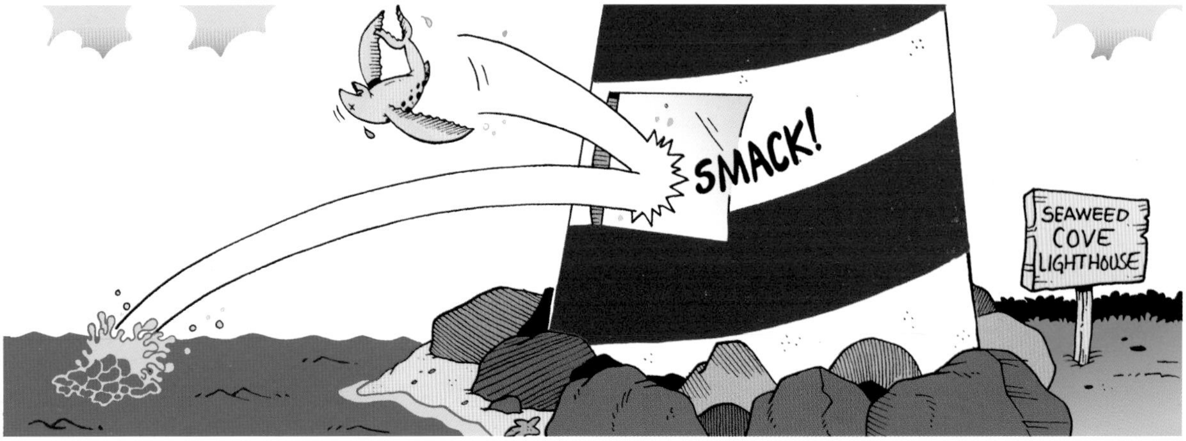
SMACK!
SEAWEED COVE LIGHTHOUSE

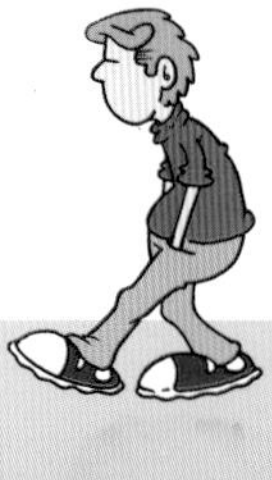

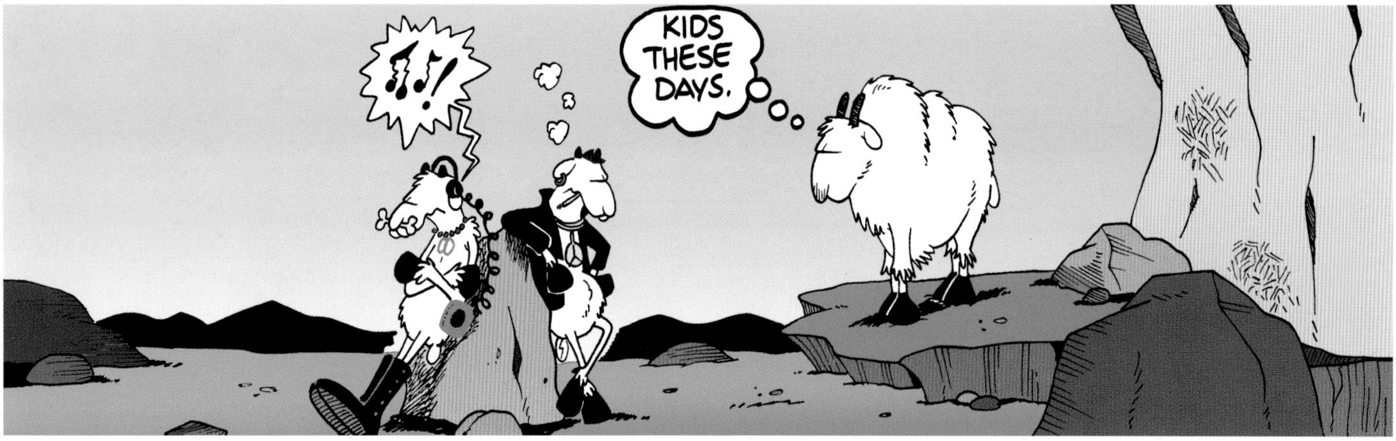
KIDS THESE DAYS.

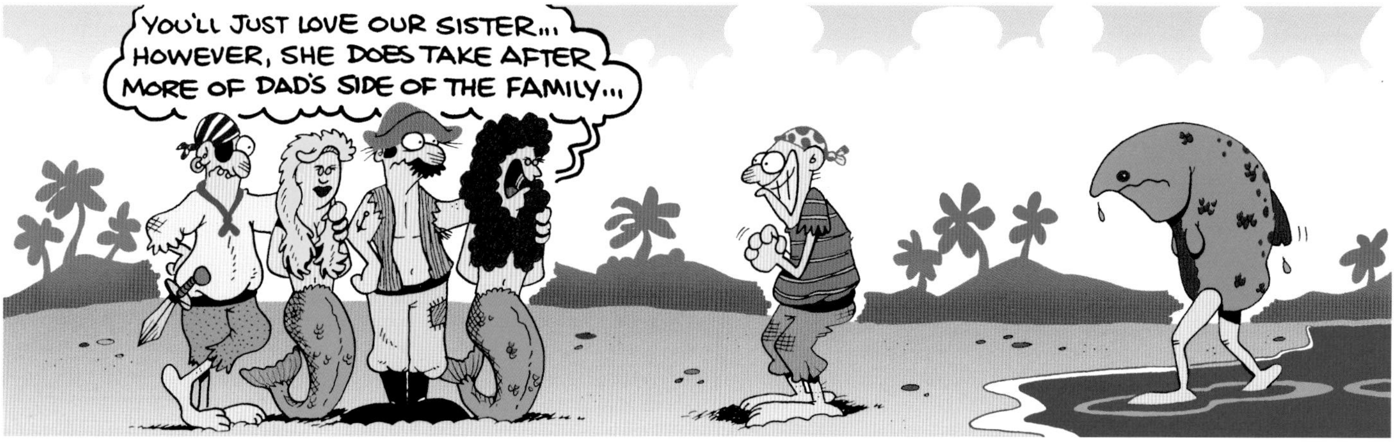
YOU'LL JUST LOVE OUR SISTER... HOWEVER, SHE DOES TAKE AFTER MORE OF DAD'S SIDE OF THE FAMILY...

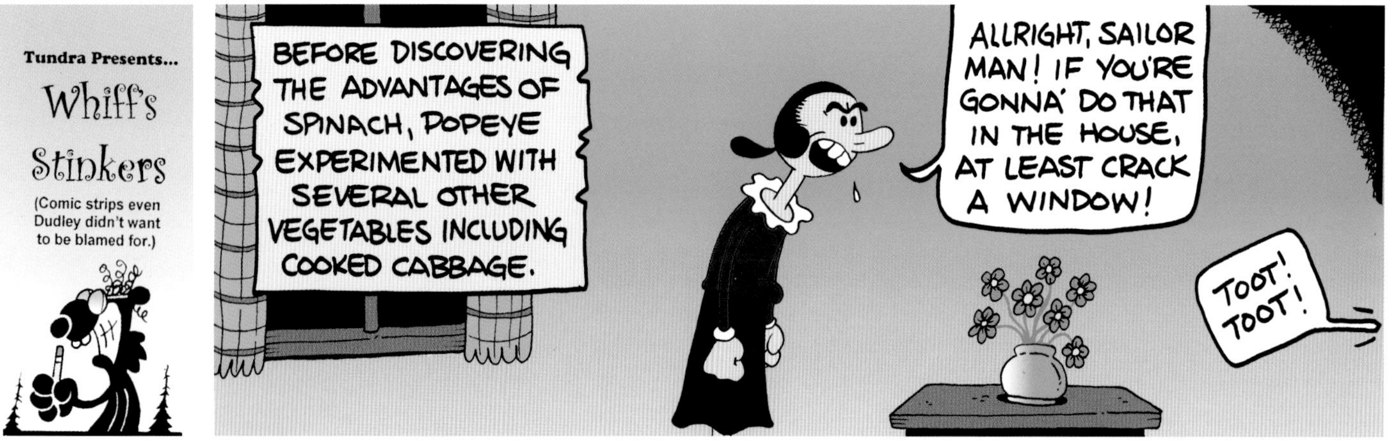
Tundra Presents...
Whiff's Stinkers
(Comic strips even Dudley didn't want to be blamed for.)
BEFORE DISCOVERING THE ADVANTAGES OF SPINACH, POPEYE EXPERIMENTED WITH SEVERAL OTHER VEGETABLES INCLUDING COOKED CABBAGE.
ALLRIGHT, SAILOR MAN! IF YOU'RE GONNA' DO THAT IN THE HOUSE, AT LEAST CRACK A WINDOW!
TOOT! TOOT!

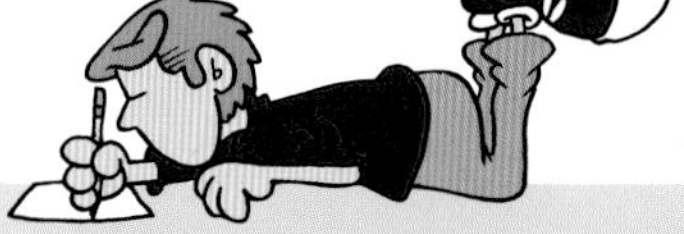

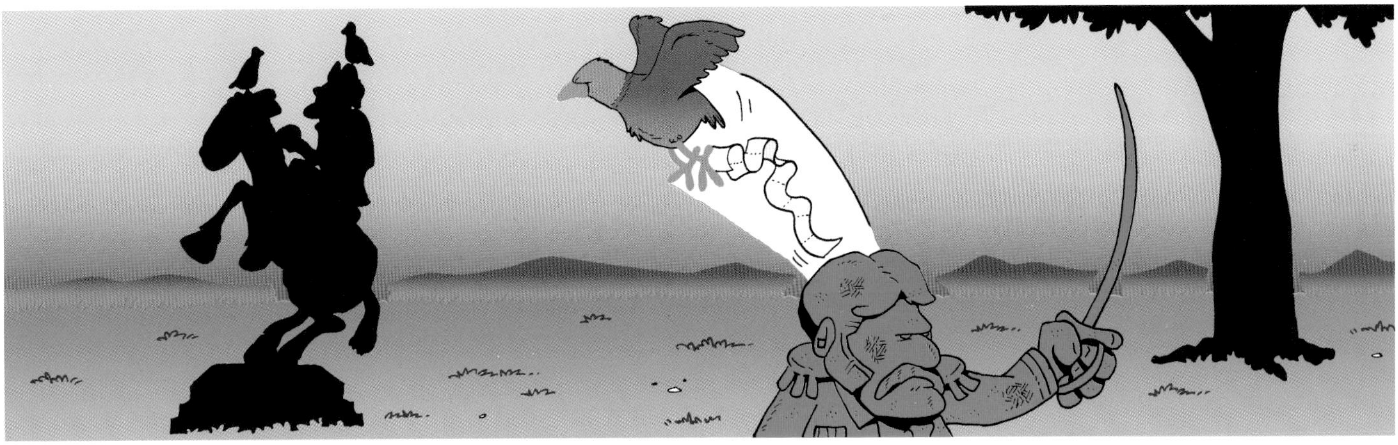

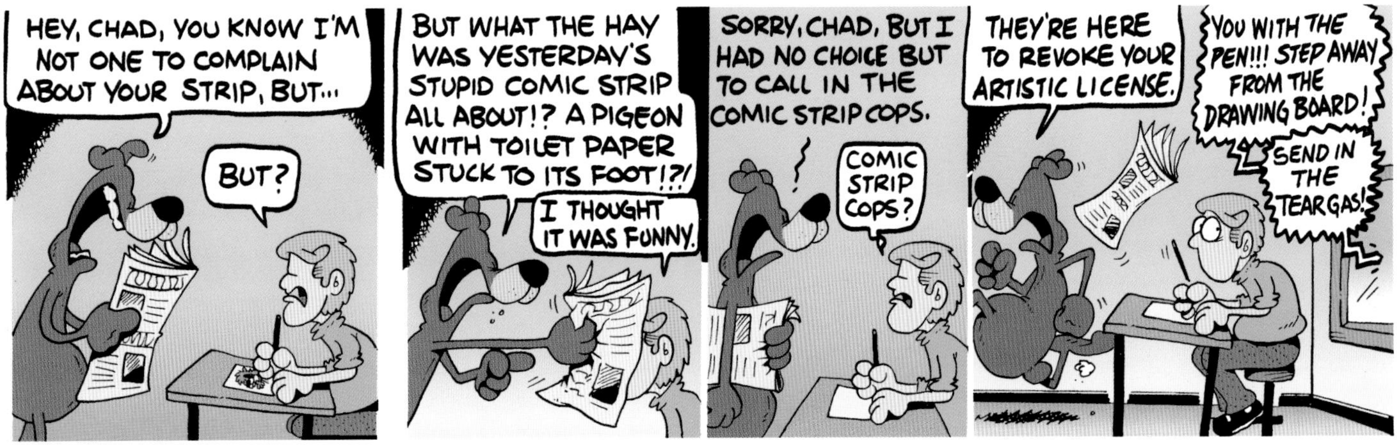

HEY, CHAD, YOU KNOW I'M NOT ONE TO COMPLAIN ABOUT YOUR STRIP, BUT...
BUT?
BUT WHAT THE HAY WAS YESTERDAY'S STUPID COMIC STRIP ALL ABOUT!? A PIGEON WITH TOILET PAPER STUCK TO ITS FOOT!?!
I THOUGHT IT WAS FUNNY.
SORRY, CHAD, BUT I HAD NO CHOICE BUT TO CALL IN THE COMIC STRIP COPS.
COMIC STRIP COPS?
THEY'RE HERE TO REVOKE YOUR ARTISTIC LICENSE.
YOU WITH THE PEN!!! STEP AWAY FROM THE DRAWING BOARD!
SEND IN THE TEAR GAS!

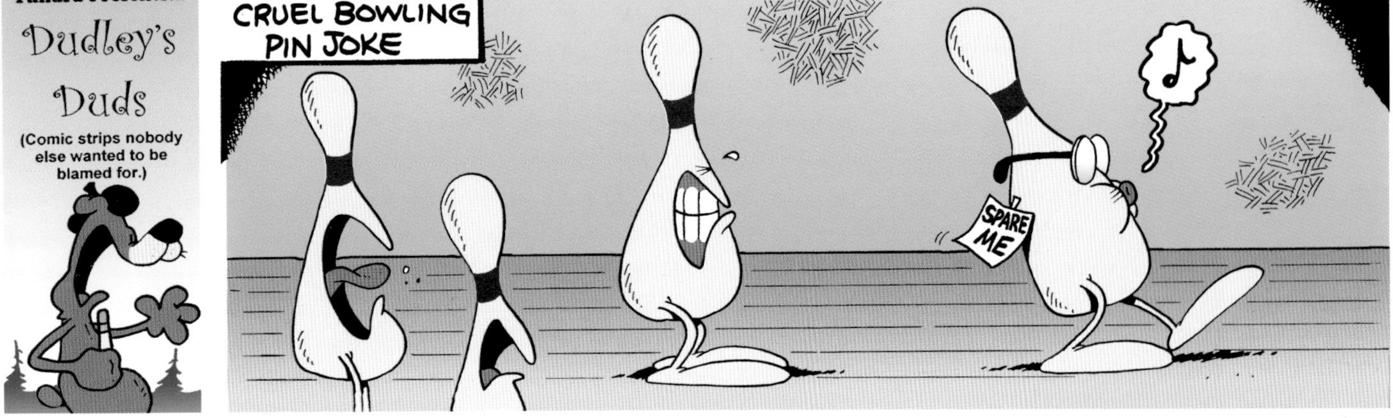

Tundra Presents...
Dudley's Duds
(Comic strips nobody else wanted to be blamed for.)
CRUEL BOWLING PIN JOKE
SPARE ME

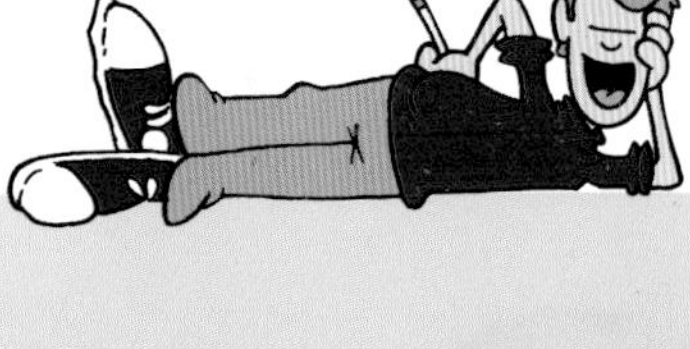

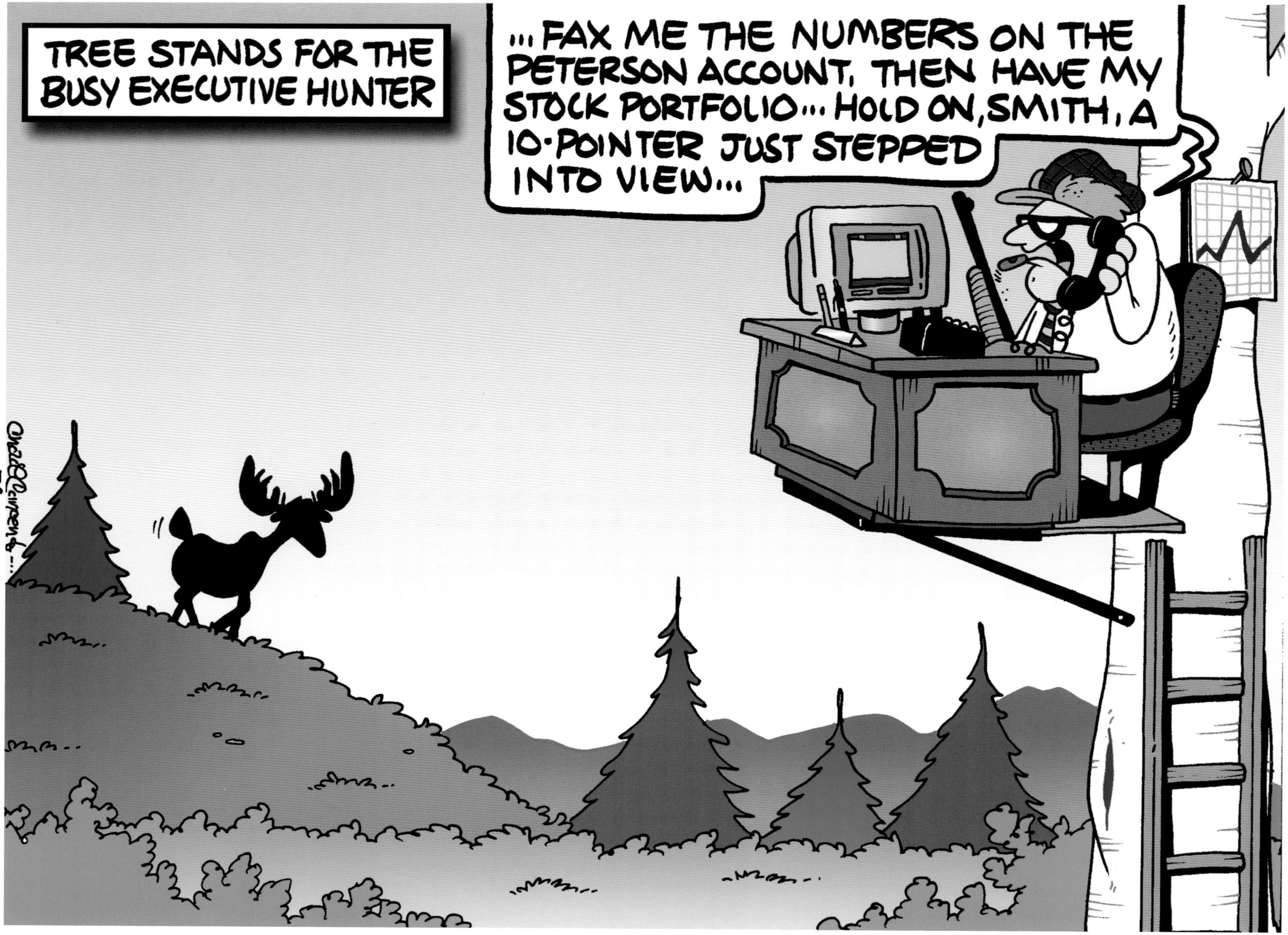
TREE STANDS FOR THE BUSY EXECUTIVE HUNTER
...FAX ME THE NUMBERS ON THE PETERSON ACCOUNT, THEN HAVE MY STOCK PORTFOLIO... HOLD ON, SMITH, A 10-POINTER JUST STEPPED INTO VIEW...

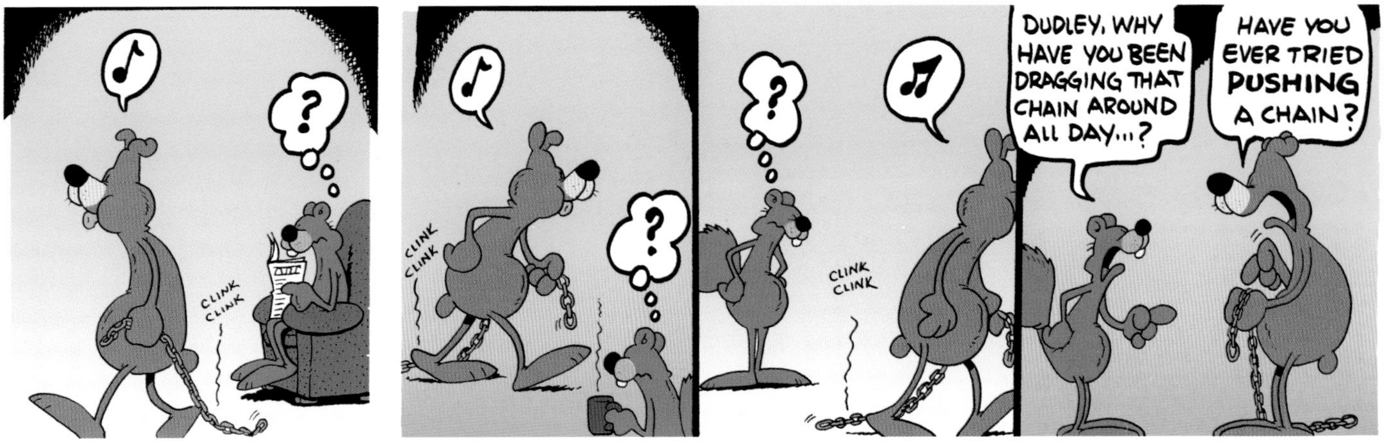
CLINK
CLINK
CLINK
CLINK
CLINK
CLINK
DUDLEY, WHY HAVE YOU BEEN DRAGGING THAT CHAIN AROUND ALL DAY...?
HAVE YOU EVER TRIED **PUSHING** A CHAIN?

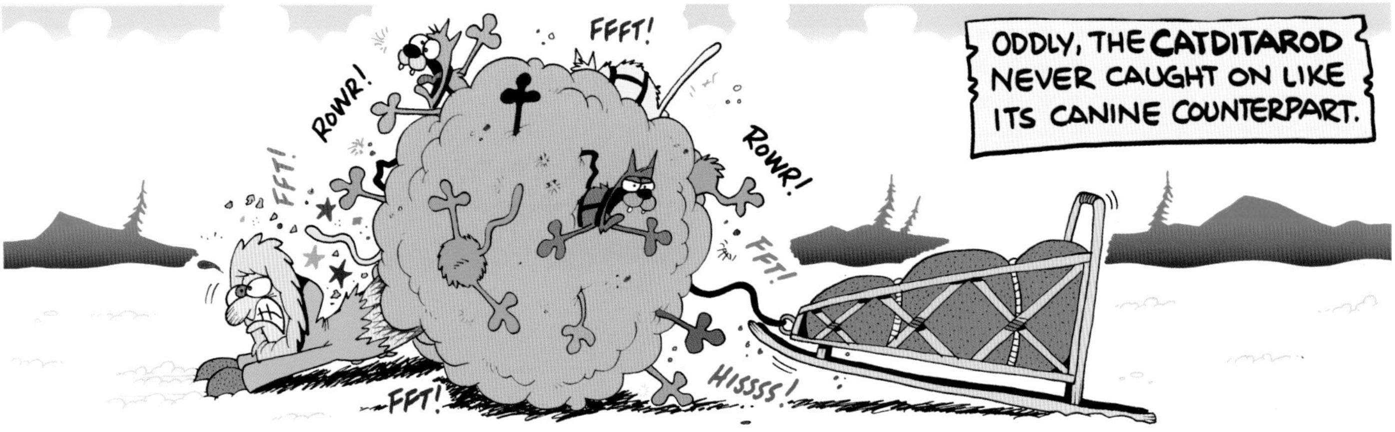
ODDLY, THE **CATDITAROD** NEVER CAUGHT ON LIKE ITS CANINE COUNTERPART.
FFFT!
ROWR!
FFT!
ROWR!
FFT!
HISSSS!
FFT!

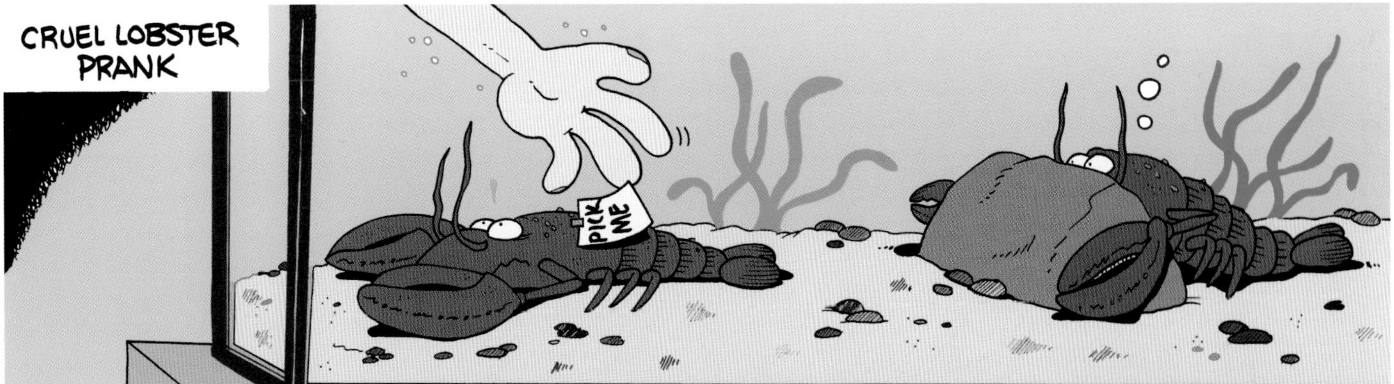
CRUEL LOBSTER PRANK
PICK ME

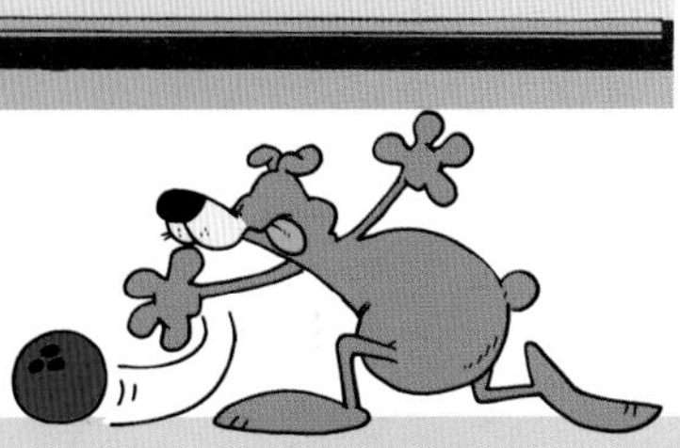

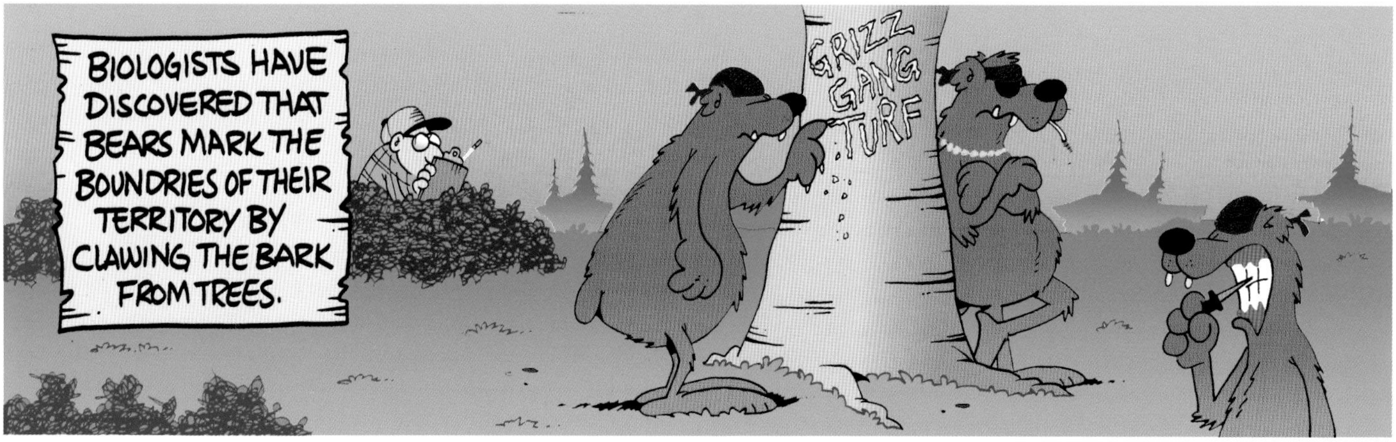
BIOLOGISTS HAVE DISCOVERED THAT BEARS MARK THE BOUNDRIES OF THEIR TERRITORY BY CLAWING THE BARK FROM TREES.
GRIZZ GANG TURF

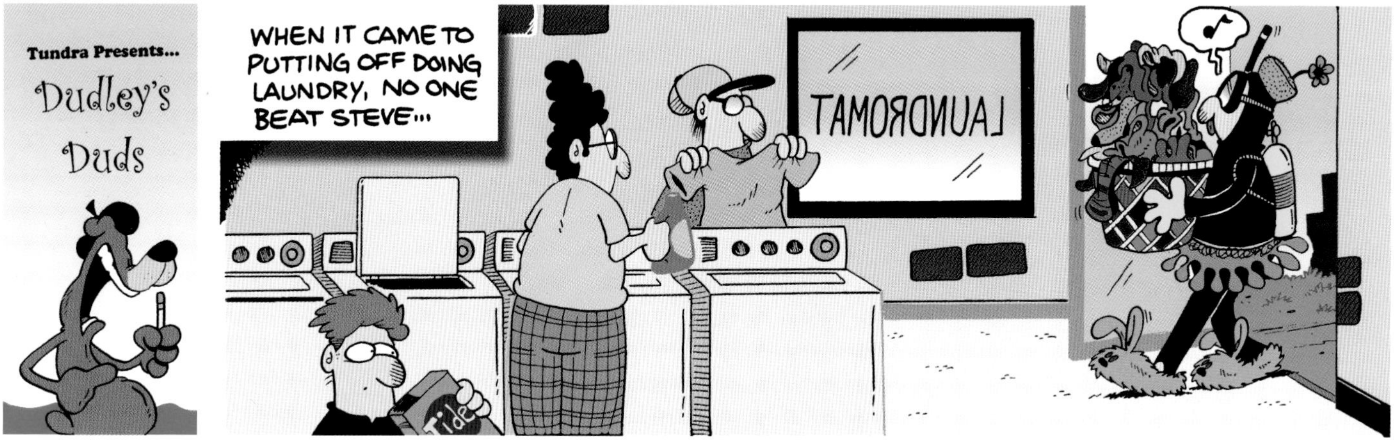
Tundra Presents...
Dudley's Duds
WHEN IT CAME TO PUTTING OFF DOING LAUNDRY, NO ONE BEAT STEVE...
LAUNDROMAT
Tide

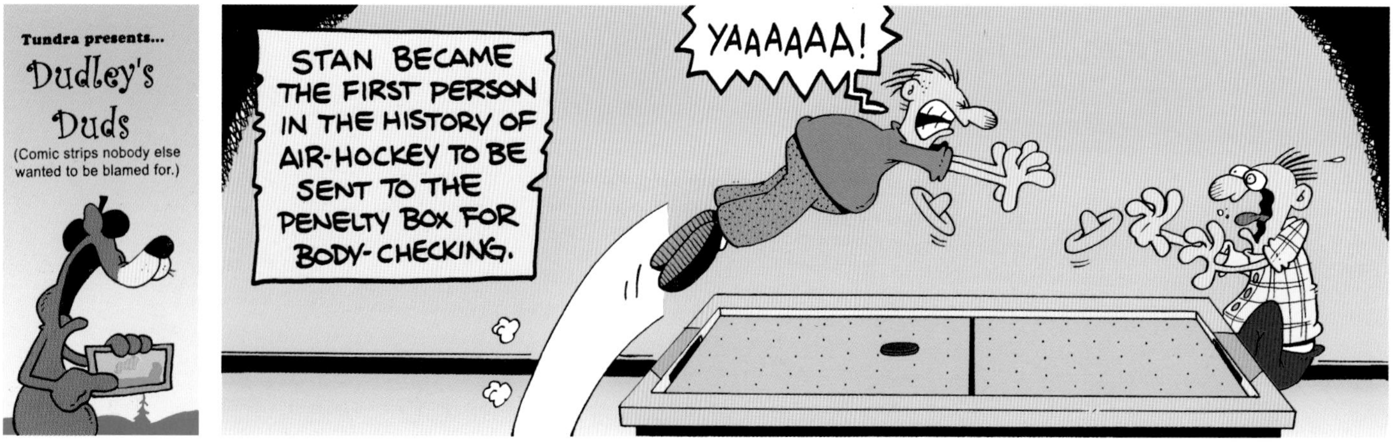
Tundra presents...
Dudley's Duds
(Comic strips nobody else wanted to be blamed for.)
STAN BECAME THE FIRST PERSON IN THE HISTORY OF AIR-HOCKEY TO BE SENT TO THE PENELTY BOX FOR BODY-CHECKING.
YAAAAAA!

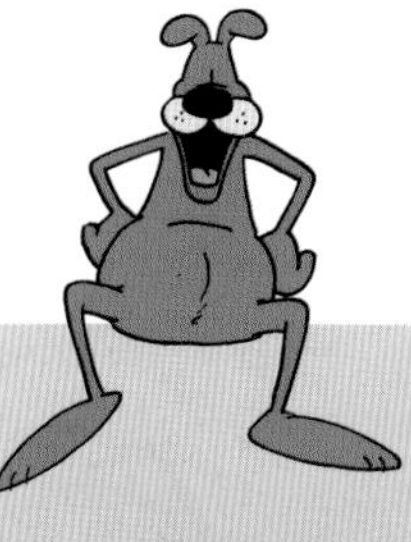

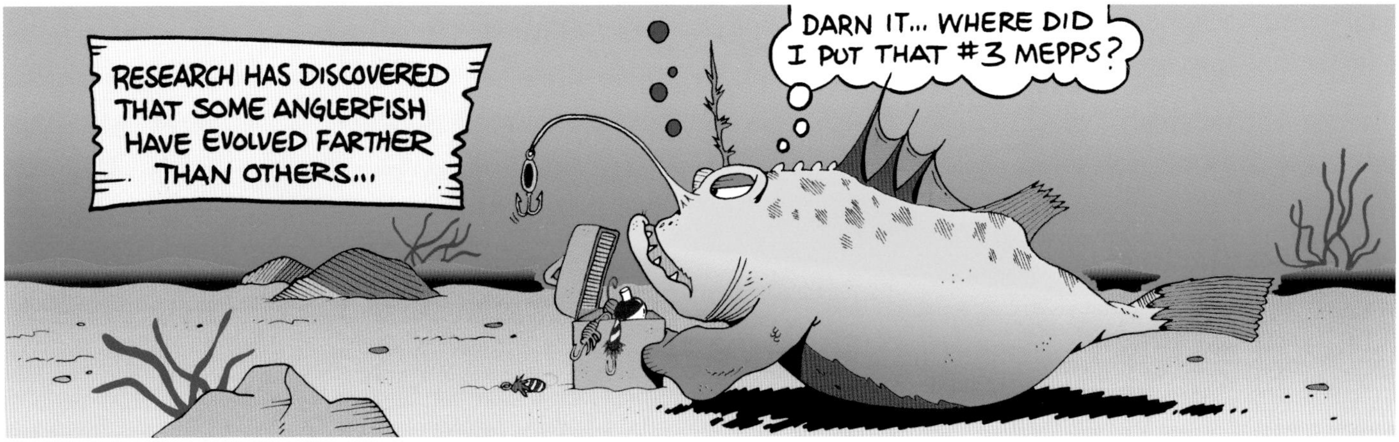
RESEARCH HAS DISCOVERED THAT SOME ANGLERFISH HAVE EVOLVED FARTHER THAN OTHERS...
DARN IT... WHERE DID I PUT THAT #3 MEPPS?

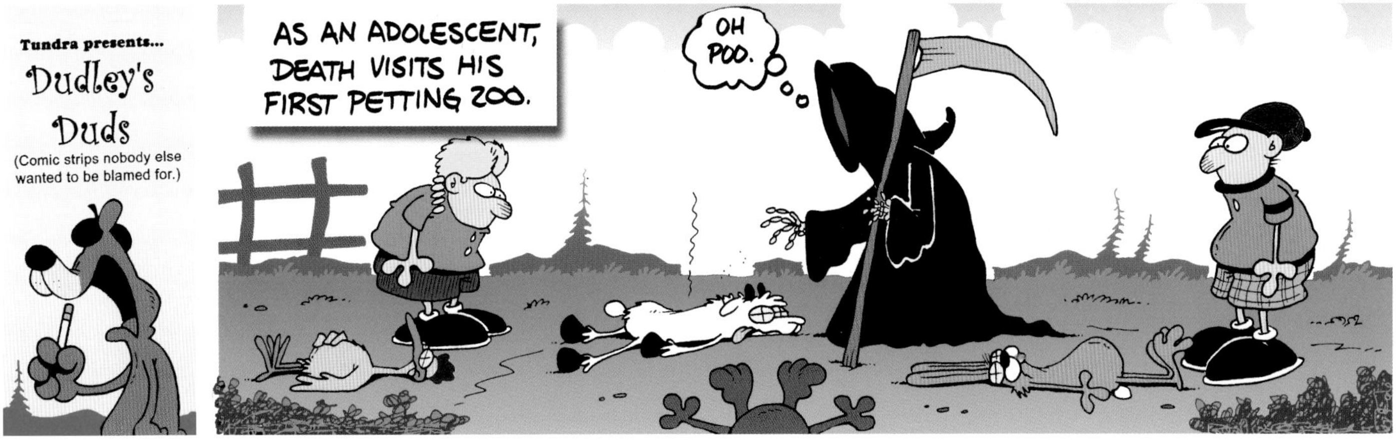
Tundra presents...
Dudley's Duds
(Comic strips nobody else wanted to be blamed for.)
AS AN ADOLESCENT, DEATH VISITS HIS FIRST PETTING ZOO.
OH POO.

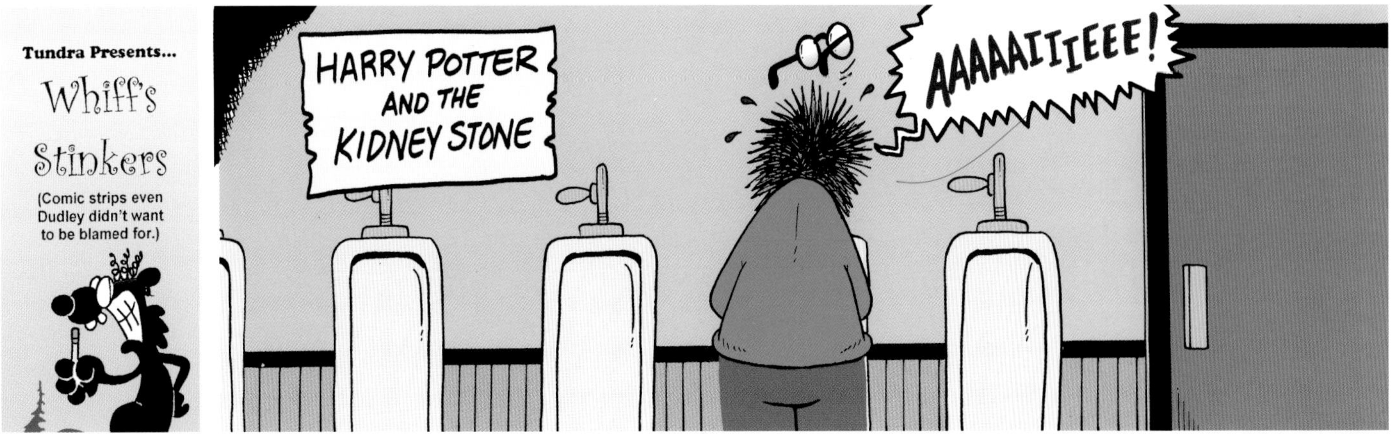
Tundra Presents...
Whiff's Stinkers
(Comic strips even Dudley didn't want to be blamed for.)
HARRY POTTER AND THE KIDNEY STONE
AAAAAIIIEEE!

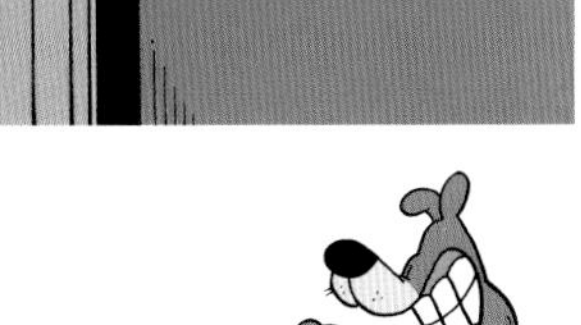

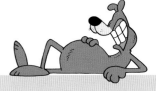

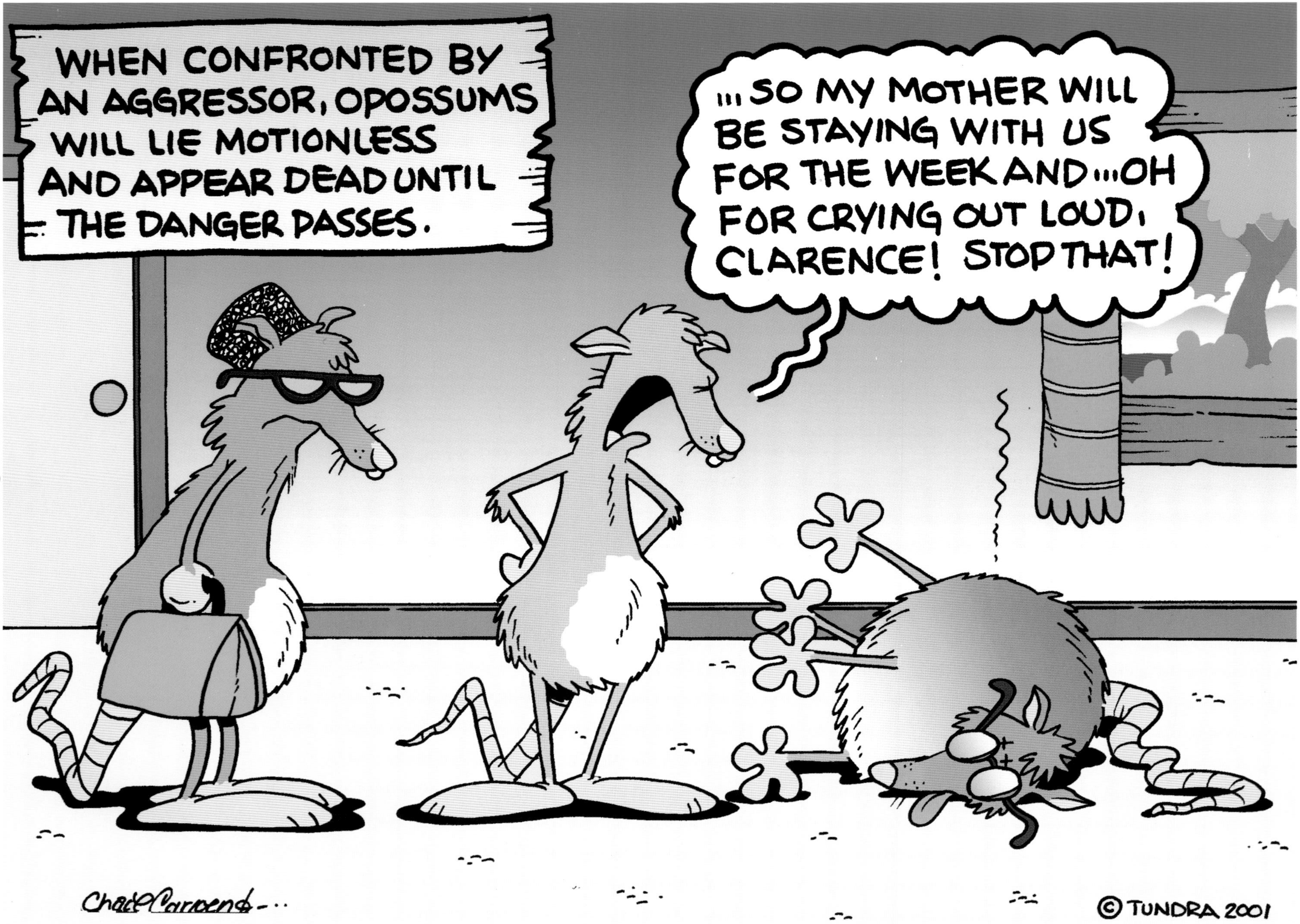
WHEN CONFRONTED BY AN AGGRESSOR, OPOSSUMS WILL LIE MOTIONLESS AND APPEAR DEAD UNTIL THE DANGER PASSES.
...SO MY MOTHER WILL BE STAYING WITH US FOR THE WEEK AND...OH FOR CRYING OUT LOUD, CLARENCE! STOP THAT!
© TUNDRA 2001

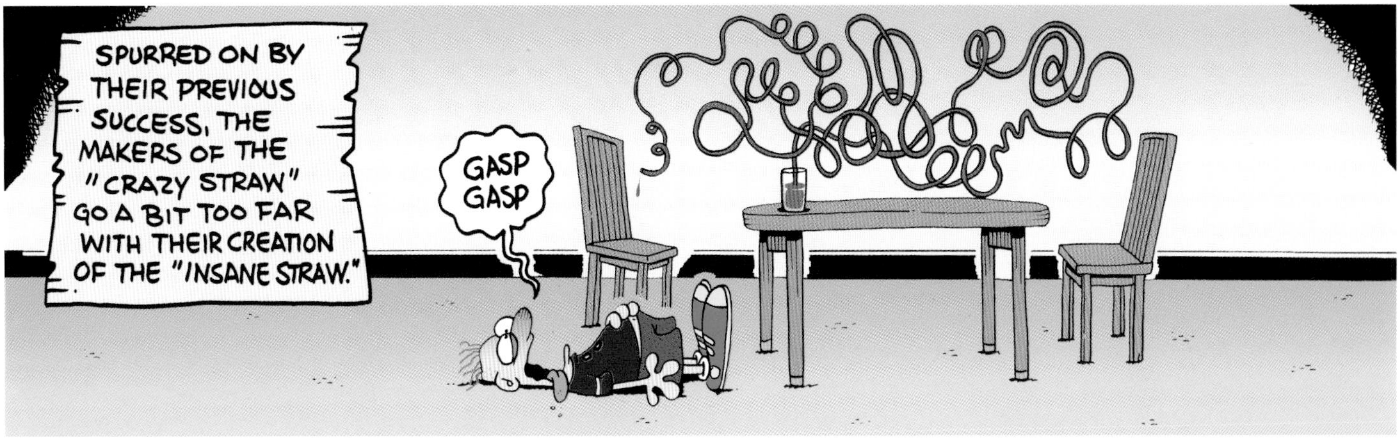
SPURRED ON BY THEIR PREVIOUS SUCCESS, THE MAKERS OF THE "CRAZY STRAW" GO A BIT TOO FAR WITH THEIR CREATION OF THE "INSANE STRAW."
GASP GASP

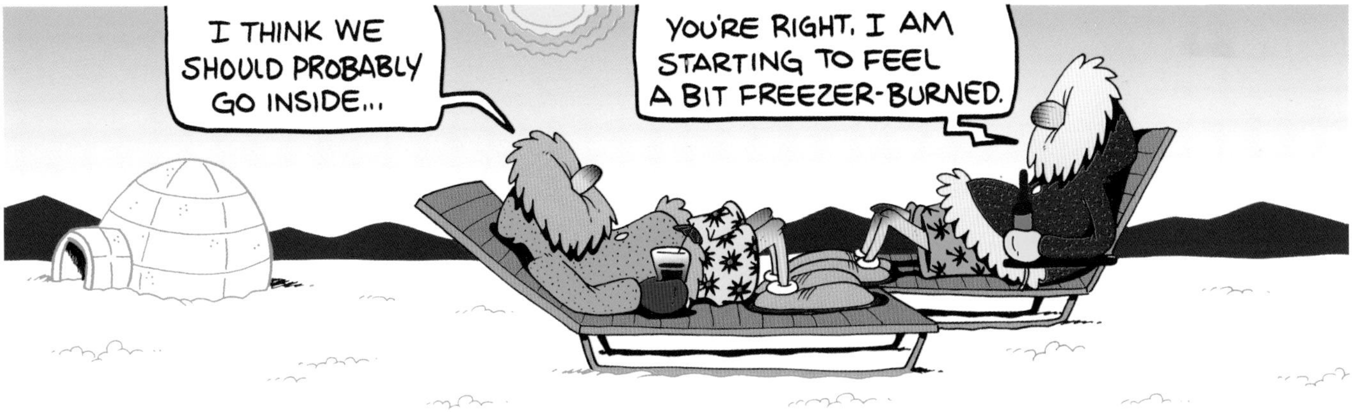
I THINK WE SHOULD PROBABLY GO INSIDE...
YOU'RE RIGHT. I AM STARTING TO FEEL A BIT FREEZER-BURNED.

This comic strip is based on the idea of
Alex Kornilov
Moscow, Russia

Do you have an idea that would make a great comic strip? Send it to:
www.tundracomics.com
or
TUNDRA IDEAS
PO BOX 770732
Eagle River, AK
99577

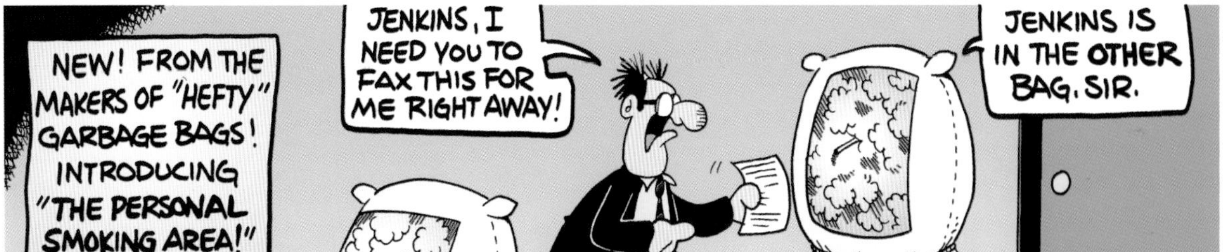
NEW! FROM THE MAKERS OF "HEFTY" GARBAGE BAGS! INTRODUCING "THE PERSONAL SMOKING AREA!"
JENKINS, I NEED YOU TO FAX THIS FOR ME RIGHT AWAY!
JENKINS IS IN THE OTHER BAG, SIR.

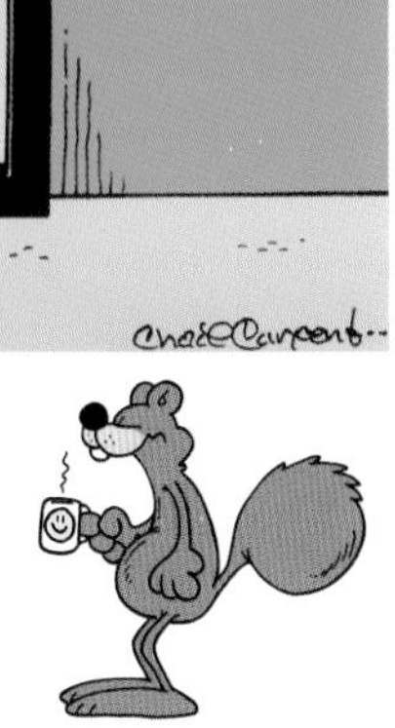

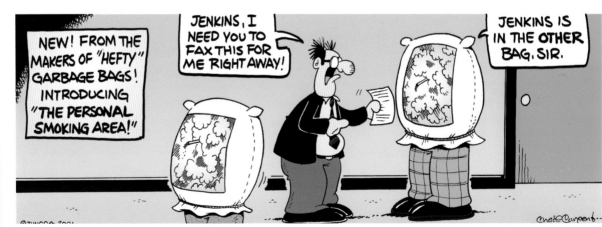

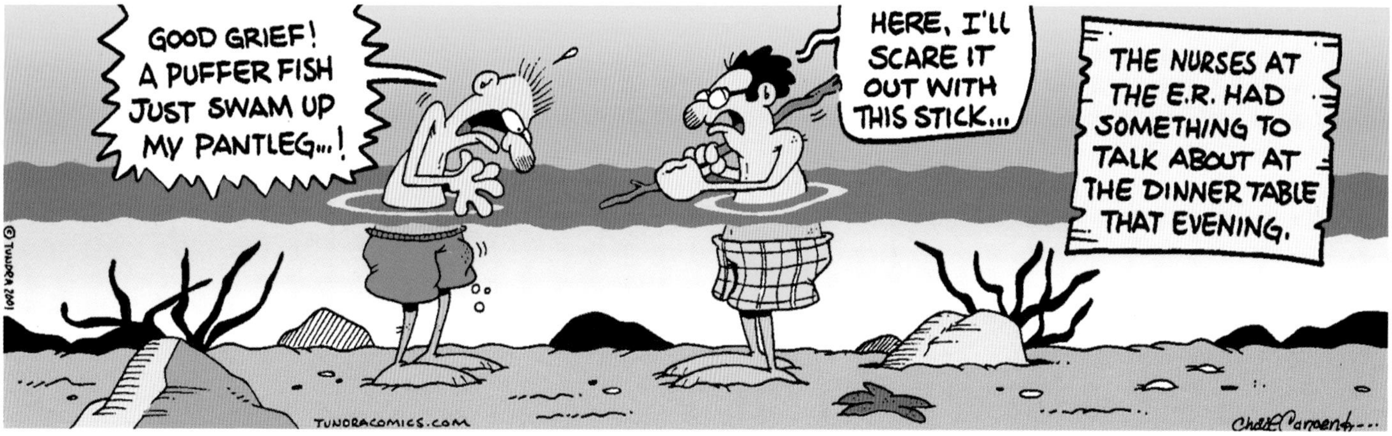
GOOD GRIEF! A PUFFER FISH JUST SWAM UP MY PANTLEG...!
HERE, I'LL SCARE IT OUT WITH THIS STICK...
THE NURSES AT THE E.R. HAD SOMETHING TO TALK ABOUT AT THE DINNER TABLE THAT EVENING.
© TUNDRA 2001
TUNDRACOMICS.COM

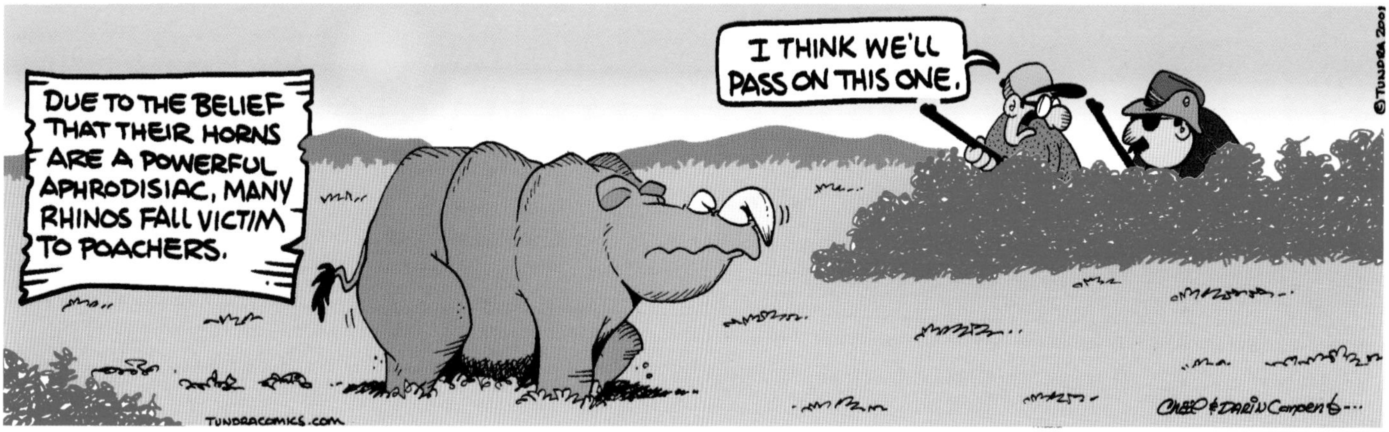
DUE TO THE BELIEF THAT THEIR HORNS ARE A POWERFUL APHRODISIAC, MANY RHINOS FALL VICTIM TO POACHERS.
I THINK WE'LL PASS ON THIS ONE.
© TUNDRA 2001
TUNDRACOMICS.COM

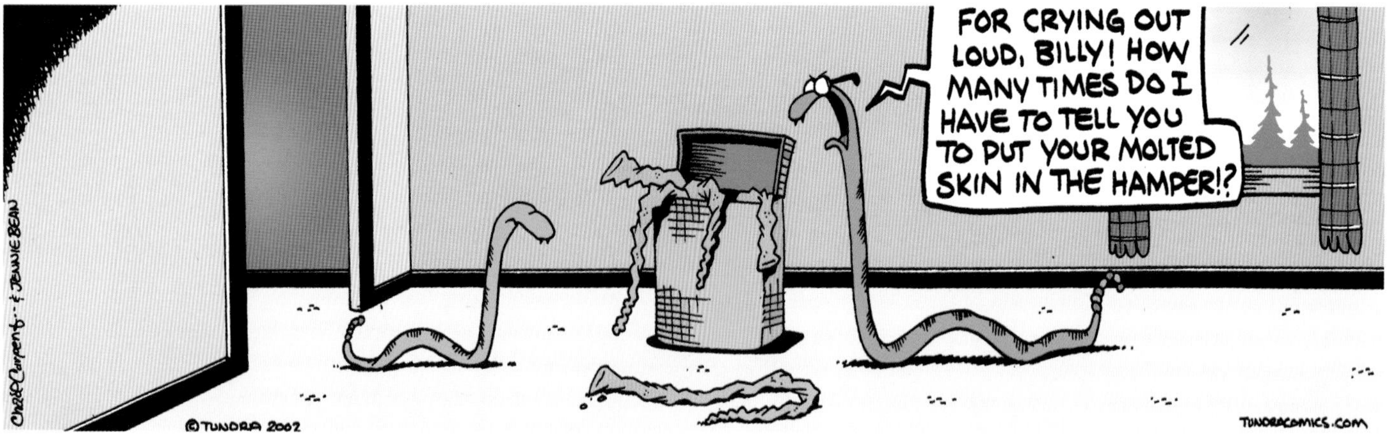
FOR CRYING OUT LOUD, BILLY! HOW MANY TIMES DO I HAVE TO TELL YOU TO PUT YOUR MOLTED SKIN IN THE HAMPER!?
©TUNDRA 2002
TUNDRACOMICS.COM

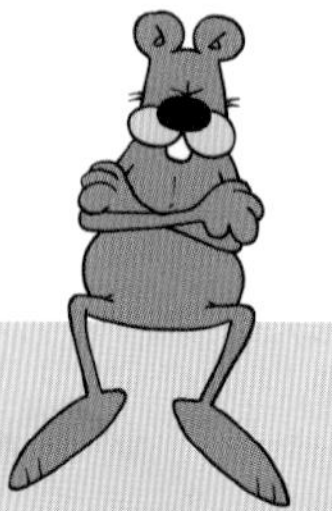

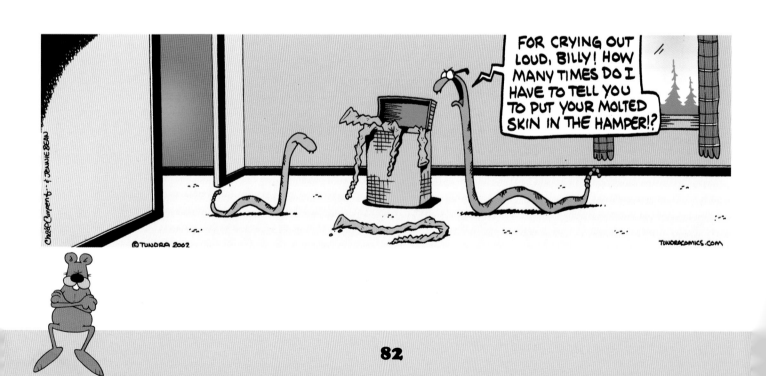

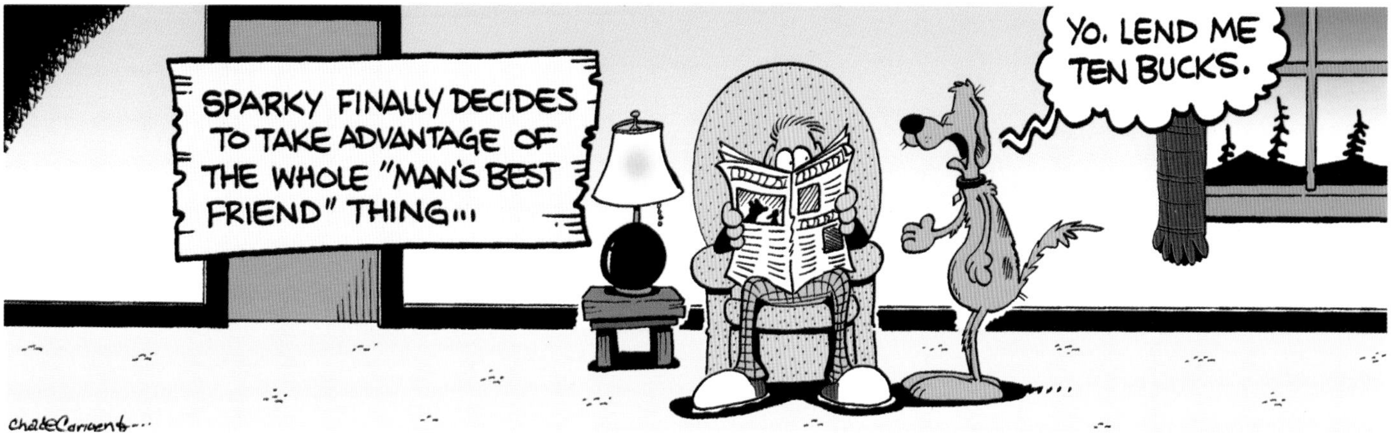
SPARKY FINALLY DECIDES TO TAKE ADVANTAGE OF THE WHOLE "MAN'S BEST FRIEND" THING...
YO. LEND ME TEN BUCKS.

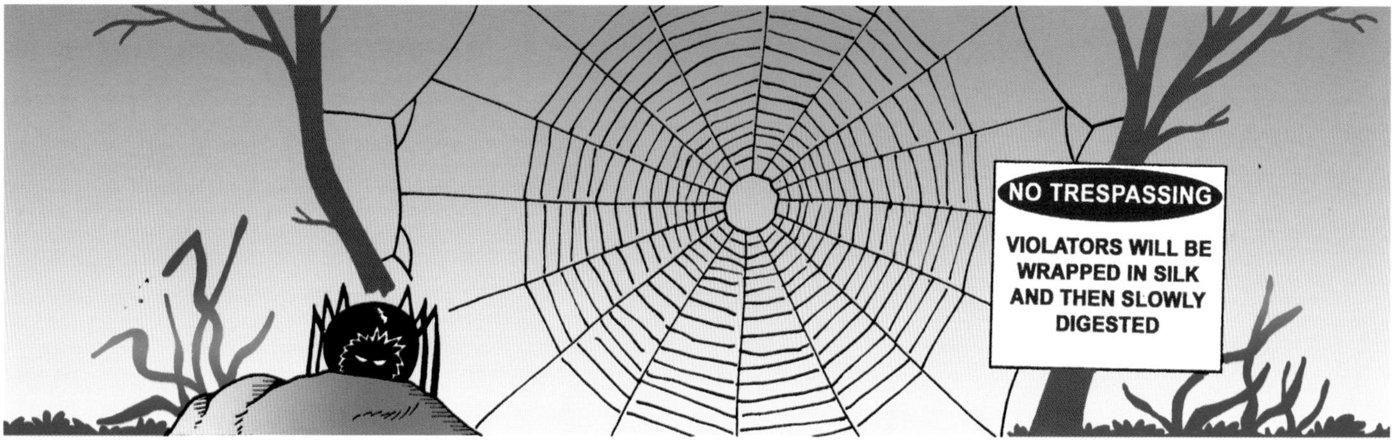
NO TRESPASSING
VIOLATORS WILL BE WRAPPED IN SILK AND THEN SLOWLY DIGESTED

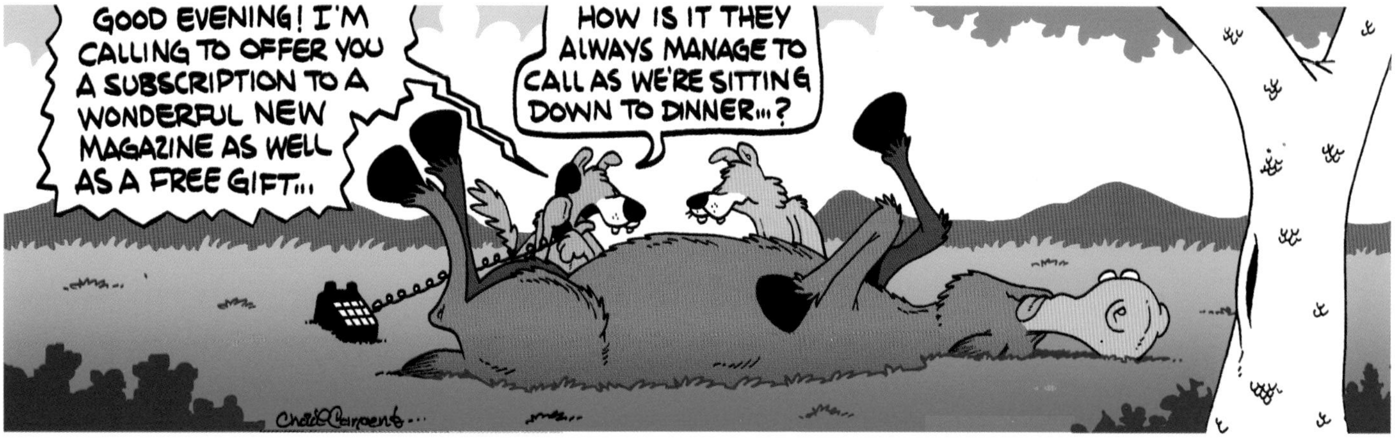
GOOD EVENING! I'M CALLING TO OFFER YOU A SUBSCRIPTION TO A WONDERFUL NEW MAGAZINE AS WELL AS A FREE GIFT...
HOW IS IT THEY ALWAYS MANAGE TO CALL AS WE'RE SITTING DOWN TO DINNER...?

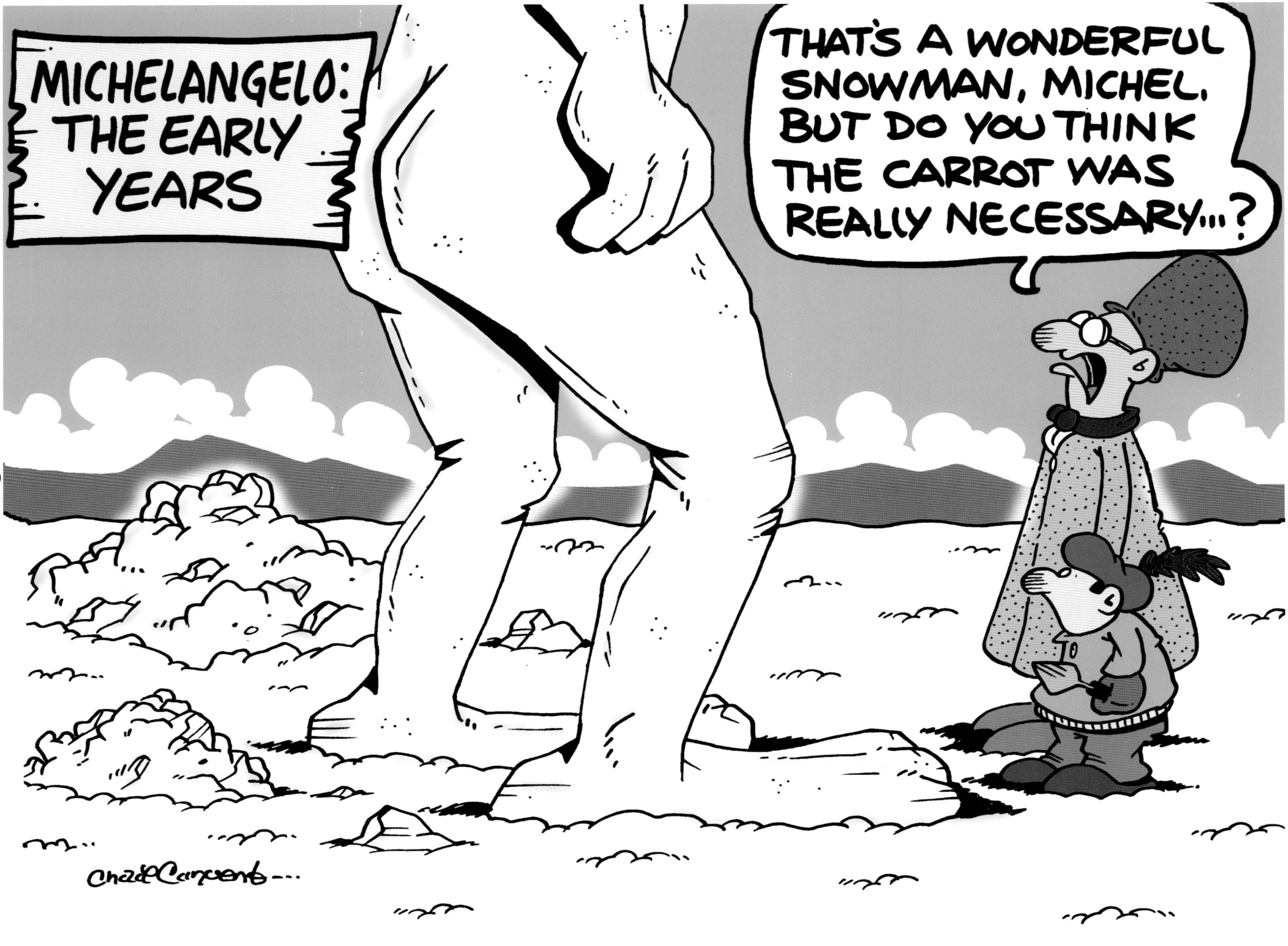
MICHELANGELO: THE EARLY YEARS
THAT'S A WONDERFUL SNOWMAN, MICHEL, BUT DO YOU THINK THE CARROT WAS REALLY NECESSARY...?
ChadCarpenter...

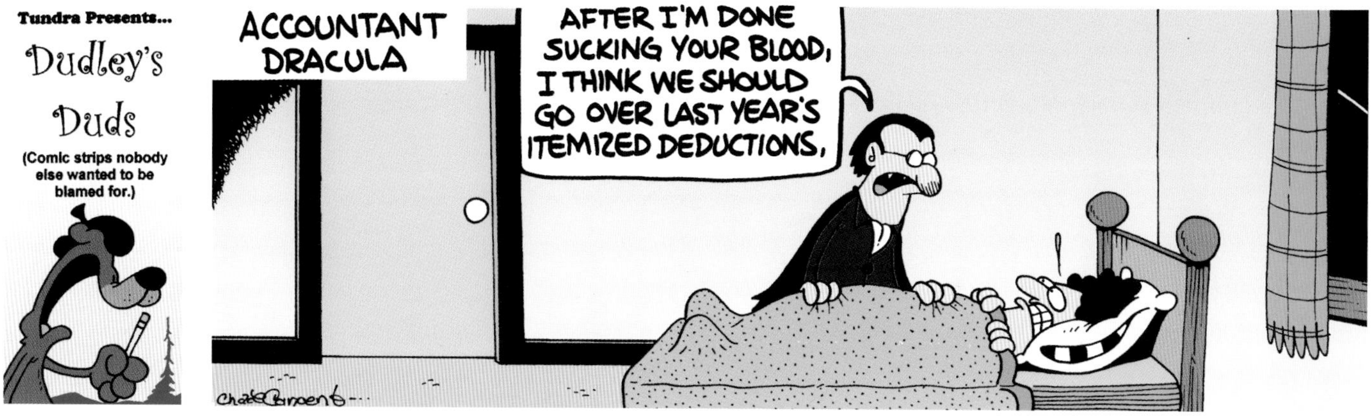
Tundra Presents...
Dudley's Duds
(Comic strips nobody else wanted to be blamed for.)
ACCOUNTANT DRACULA
AFTER I'M DONE SUCKING YOUR BLOOD, I THINK WE SHOULD GO OVER LAST YEAR'S ITEMIZED DEDUCTIONS,

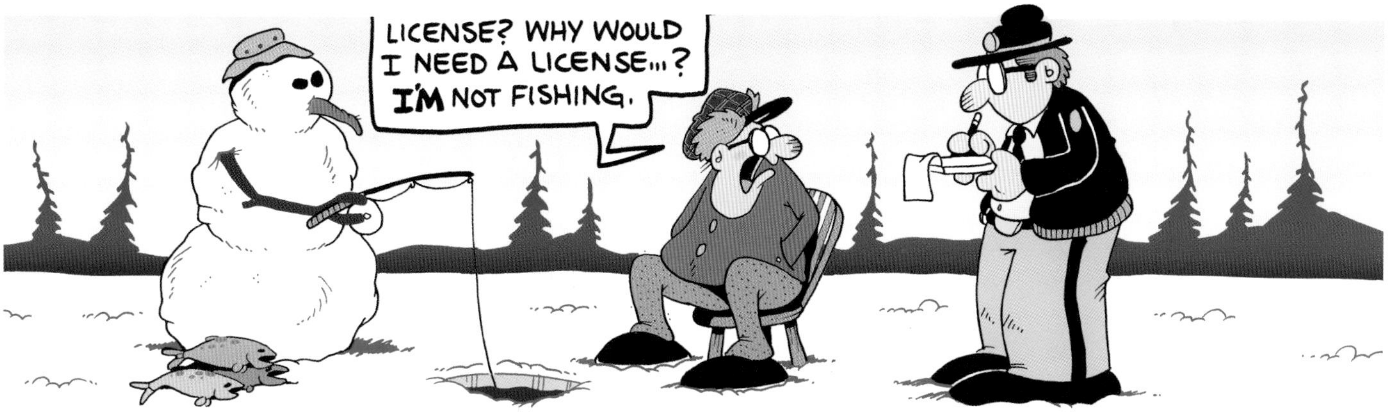
LICENSE? WHY WOULD I NEED A LICENSE...? I'M NOT FISHING.

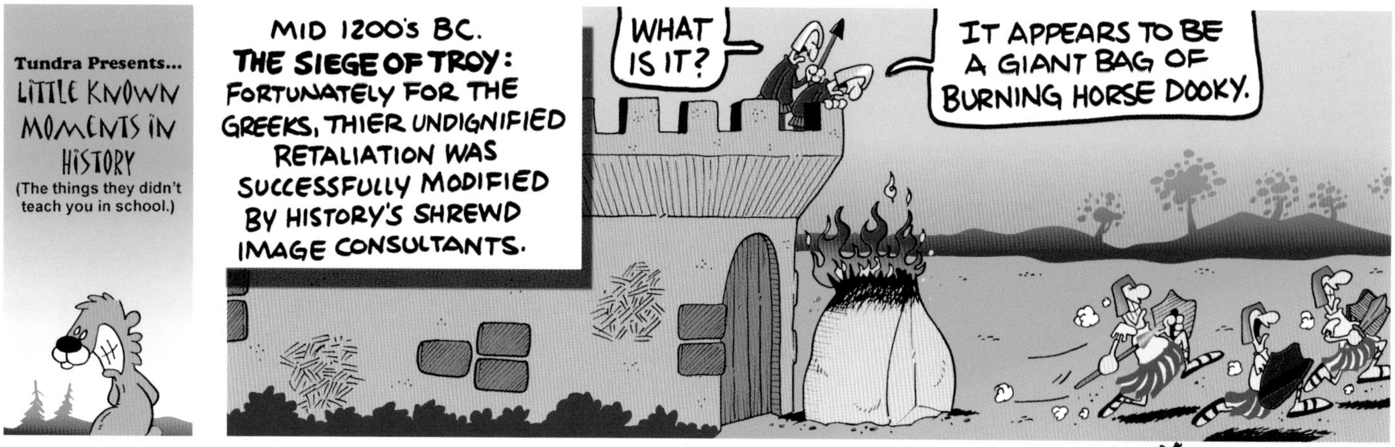
Tundra Presents...
LITTLE KNOWN MOMENTS IN HISTORY
(The things they didn't teach you in school.)
MID 1200'S BC. THE SIEGE OF TROY: FORTUNATELY FOR THE GREEKS, THIER UNDIGNIFIED RETALIATION WAS SUCCESSFULLY MODIFIED BY HISTORY'S SHREWD IMAGE CONSULTANTS.
WHAT IS IT?
IT APPEARS TO BE A GIANT BAG OF BURNING HORSE DOOKY.

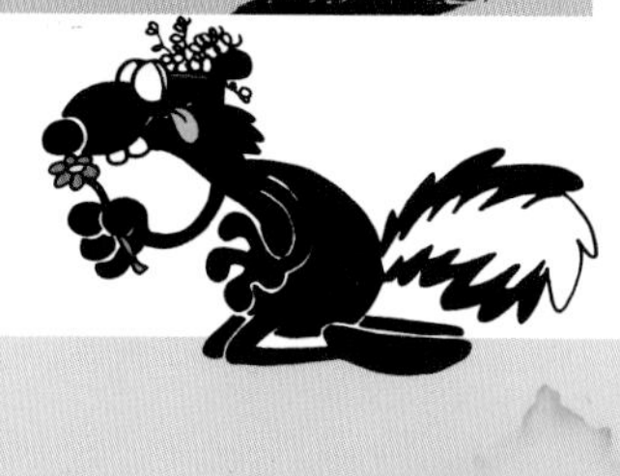

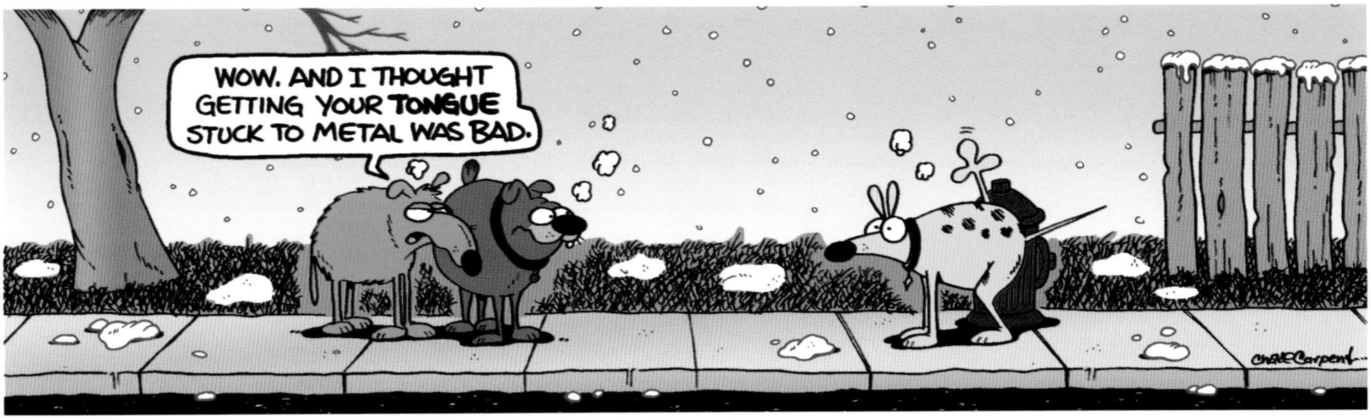
WOW. AND I THOUGHT GETTING YOUR TONGUE STUCK TO METAL WAS BAD.

This comic strip is based on the idea of

Cameron Dickerson
Anchorage, AK

Do you have an idea that would make a great comic strip? Send it to:

www.tundracomics.com

or

TUNDRA IDEAS
PO BOX 770732
Eagle River, AK
99577

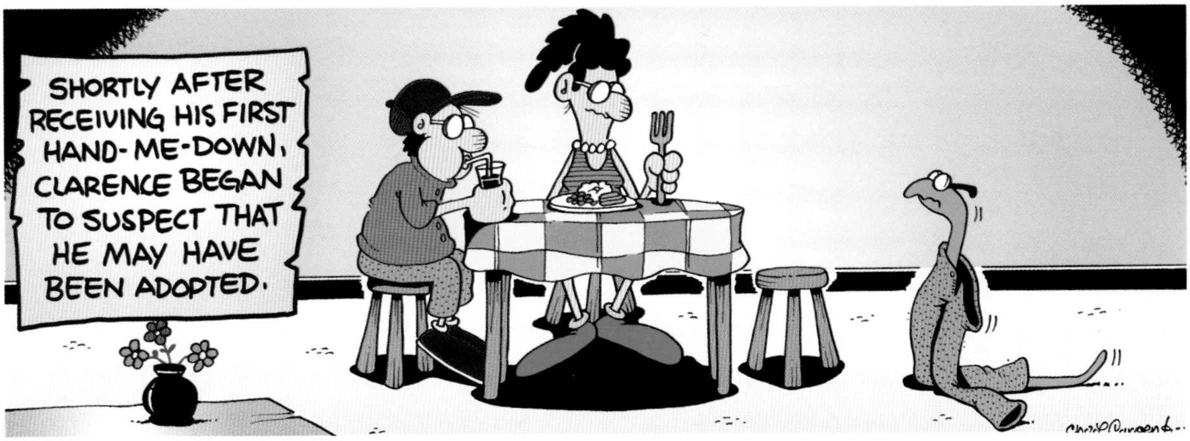
SHORTLY AFTER RECEIVING HIS FIRST HAND-ME-DOWN, CLARENCE BEGAN TO SUSPECT THAT HE MAY HAVE BEEN ADOPTED.

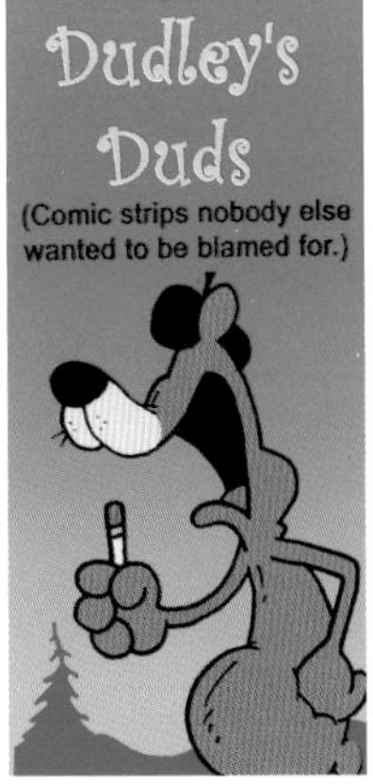
Tundra presents...
Dudley's Duds
(Comic strips nobody else wanted to be blamed for.)

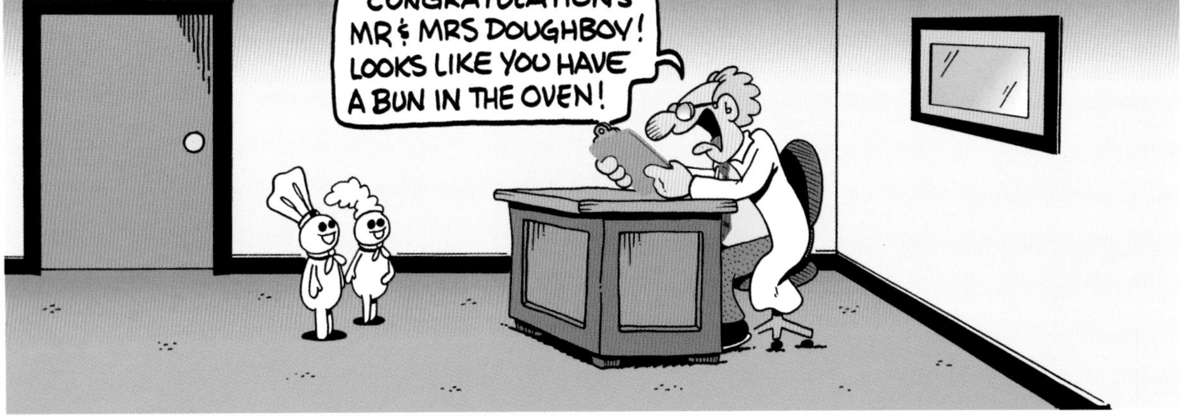
CONGRATULATIONS MR & MRS DOUGHBOY! LOOKS LIKE YOU HAVE A BUN IN THE OVEN!

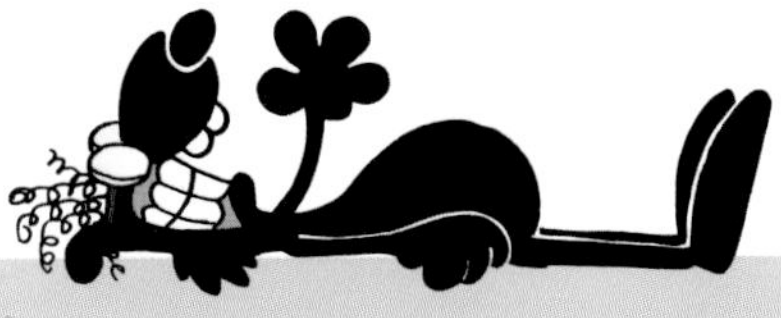

This comic strip is based on the idea of

Gary Graham
Wasilla, AK

Do you have an idea that would make a great comic strip? Send it to:

www.tundracomics.com

or

TUNDRA IDEAS
PO BOX 770732
Eagle River, AK
99577

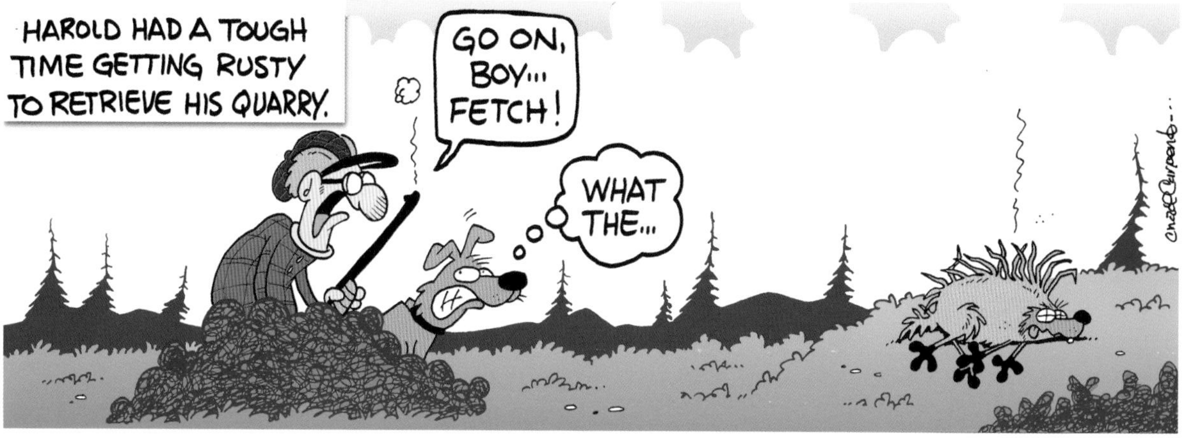
HAROLD HAD A TOUGH TIME GETTING RUSTY TO RETRIEVE HIS QUARRY.
GO ON, BOY... FETCH!
WHAT THE...

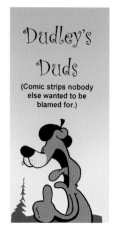

Dudley's Duds

(Comic strips nobody else wanted to be blamed for.)

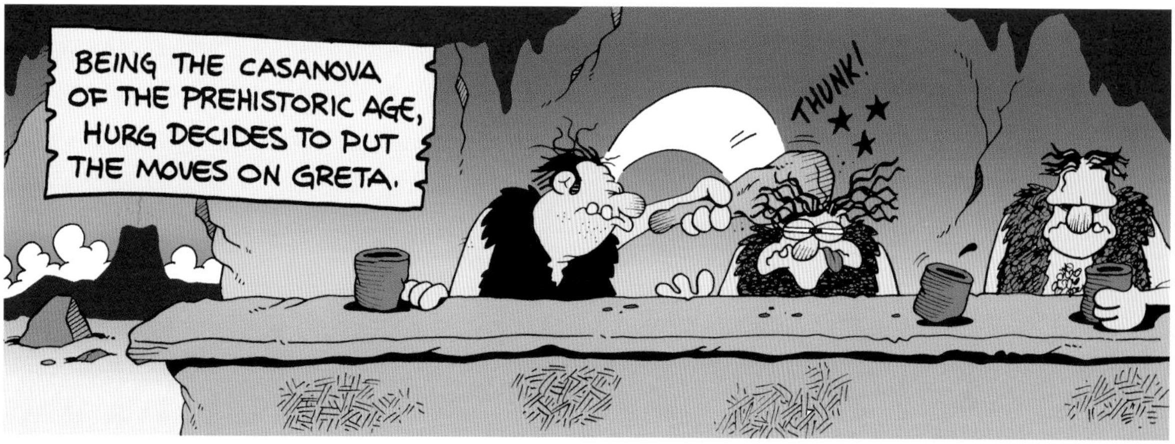
BEING THE CASANOVA OF THE PREHISTORIC AGE, HURG DECIDES TO PUT THE MOVES ON GRETA.
THUNK!

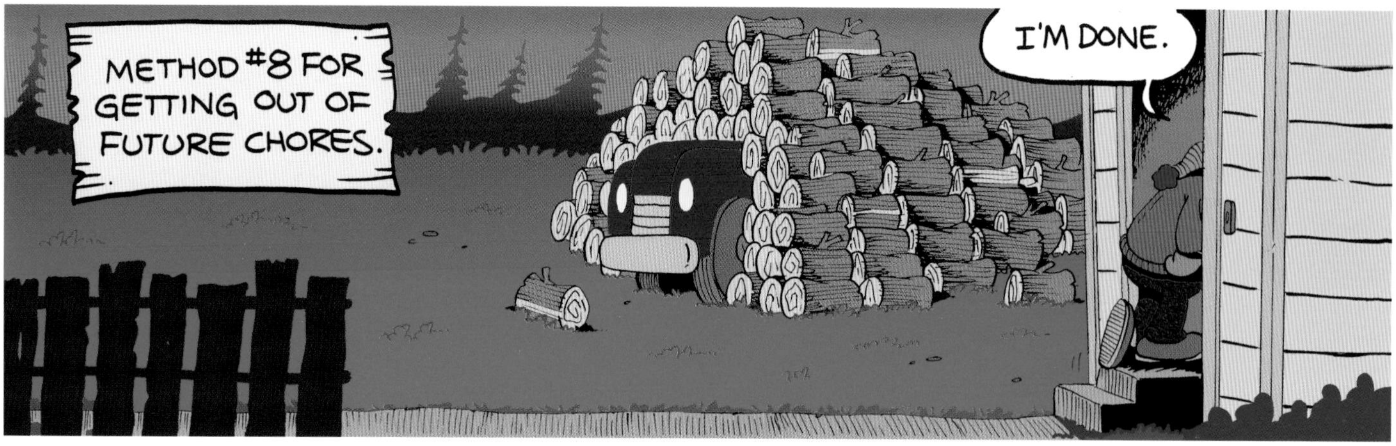
METHOD #8 FOR GETTING OUT OF FUTURE CHORES.
I'M DONE.

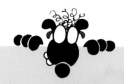

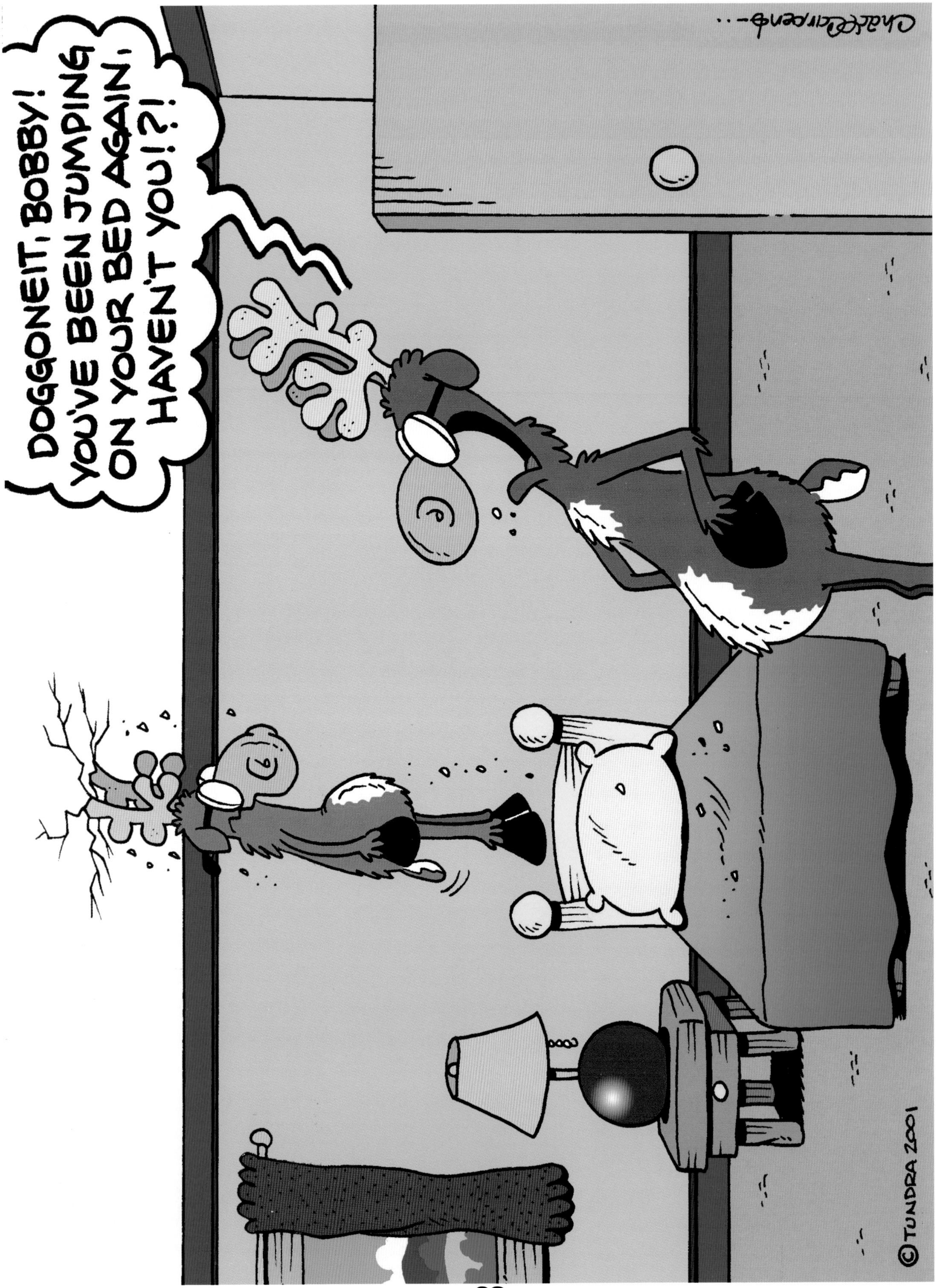
DOGGONEIT, BOBBY! YOU'VE BEEEN JUMPING ON YOUR BED AGAIN, HAVEN'T YOU!?!
©TUNDRA 2001

This comic strip is based on the idea of

Bob Decormier
Anchorage, AK

Do you have an idea that would make a great comic strip? Send it to:

www.tundracomics.com
or
TUNDRA IDEAS
PO BOX 770732
Eagle River, AK
99577

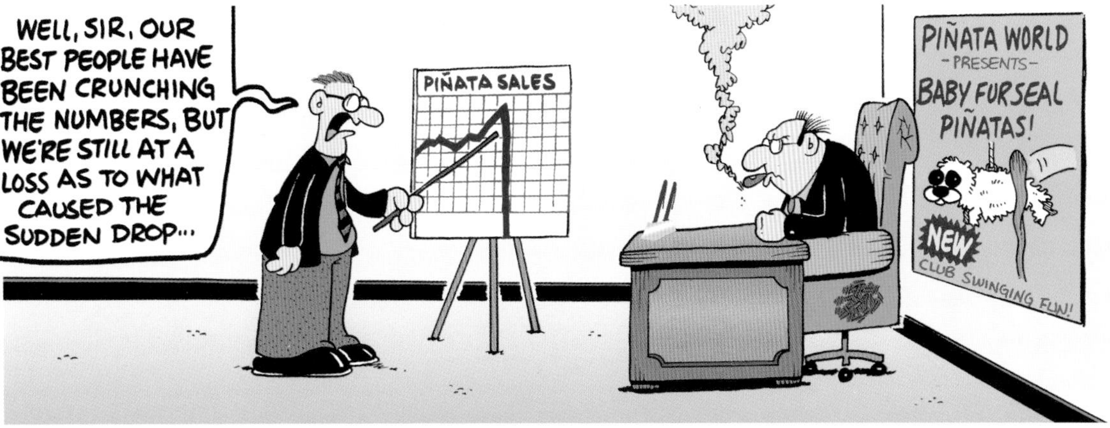
WELL, SIR, OUR BEST PEOPLE HAVE BEEN CRUNCHING THE NUMBERS, BUT WE'RE STILL AT A LOSS AS TO WHAT CAUSED THE SUDDEN DROP...
PIÑATA SALES
PIÑATA WORLD
-PRESENTS-
BABY FURSEAL PIÑATAS!
NEW
CLUB SWINGING FUN!

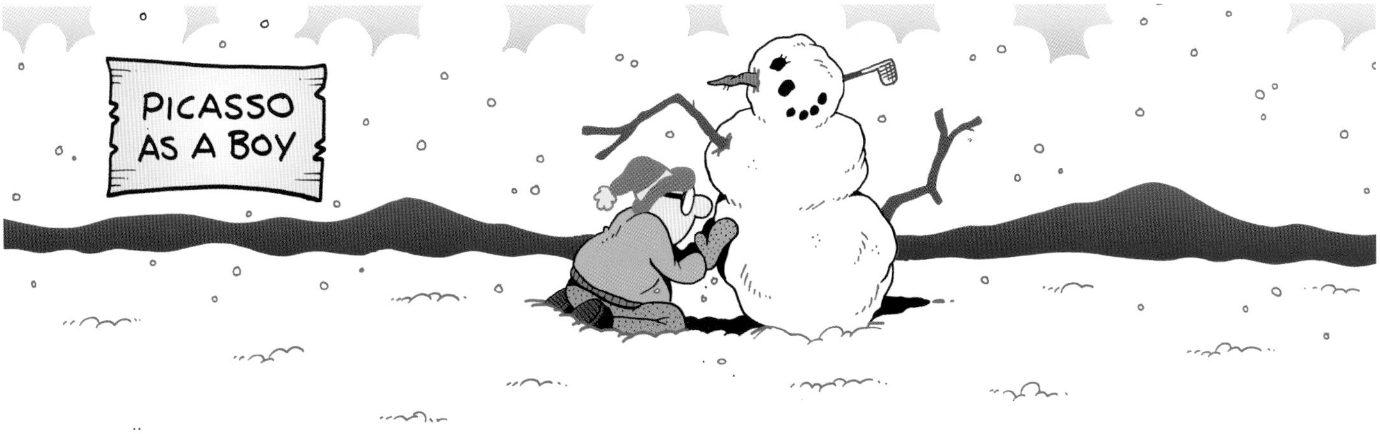
PICASSO AS A BOY

Tundra presents...

Dudley's Duds

(Comic strips nobody else wanted to be blamed for.)

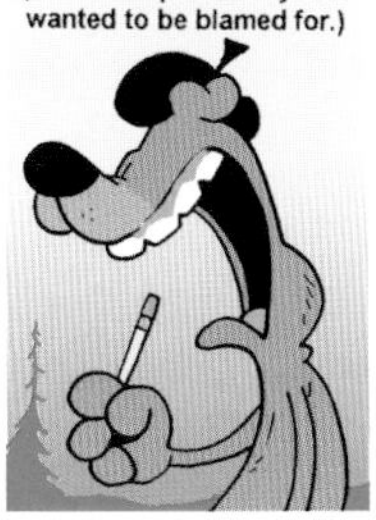

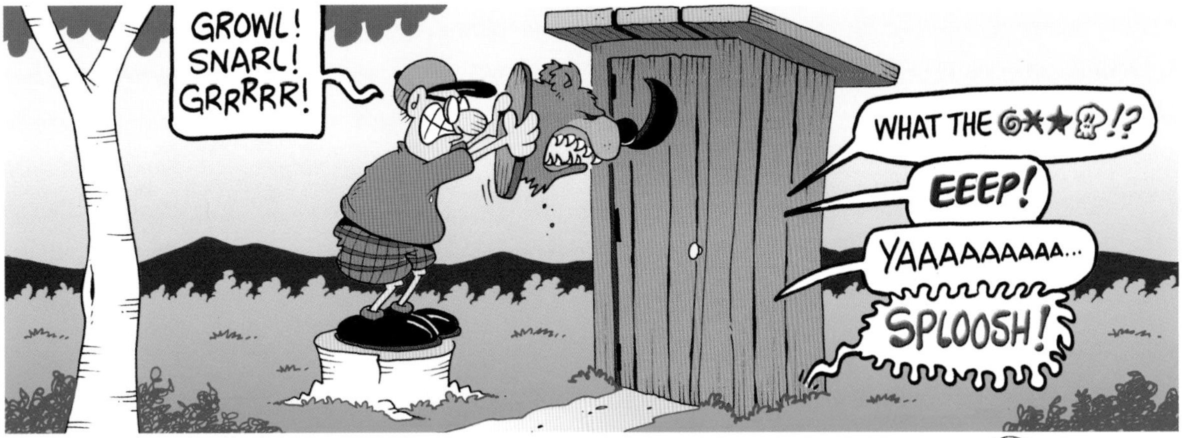
GROWL! SNARL! GRRRRR!
WHAT THE @*★!?
EEEP!
YAAAAAAAAA...
SPLOOSH!

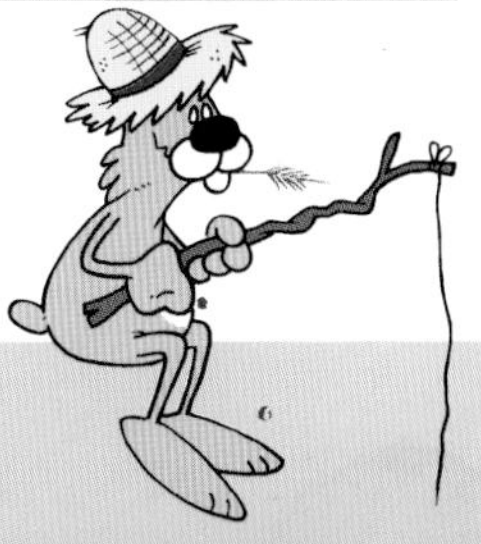

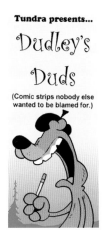

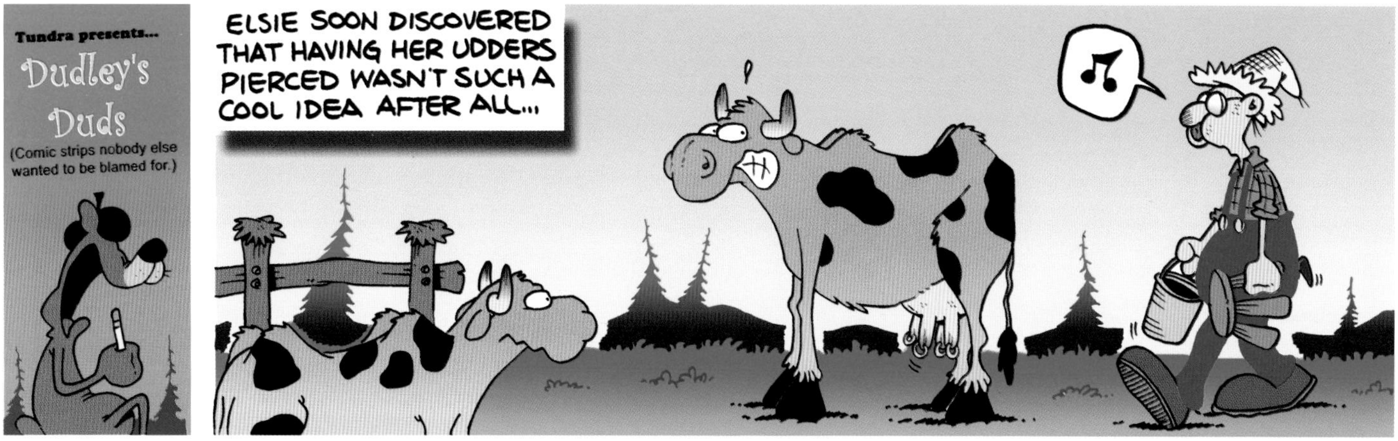
Tundra presents...
Dudley's Duds
(Comic strips nobody else wanted to be blamed for.)
ELSIE SOON DISCOVERED THAT HAVING HER UDDERS PIERCED WASN'T SUCH A COOL IDEA AFTER ALL...

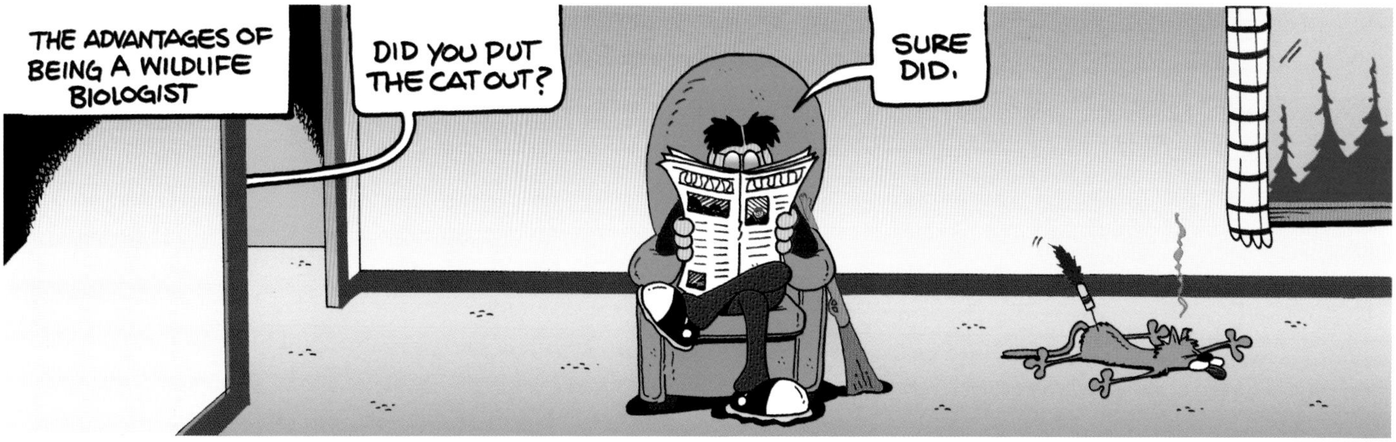
THE ADVANTAGES OF BEING A WILDLIFE BIOLOGIST
DID YOU PUT THE CAT OUT?
SURE DID.

This comic strip is based on the idea of

Michael Blaine
Peru, NY

Do you have an idea that would make a great comic strip? Send it to:
www.tundracomics .com
or
TUNDRA IDEAS
PO BOX 770732
Eagle River, AK
99577

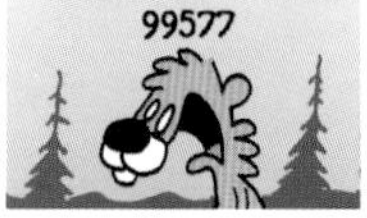

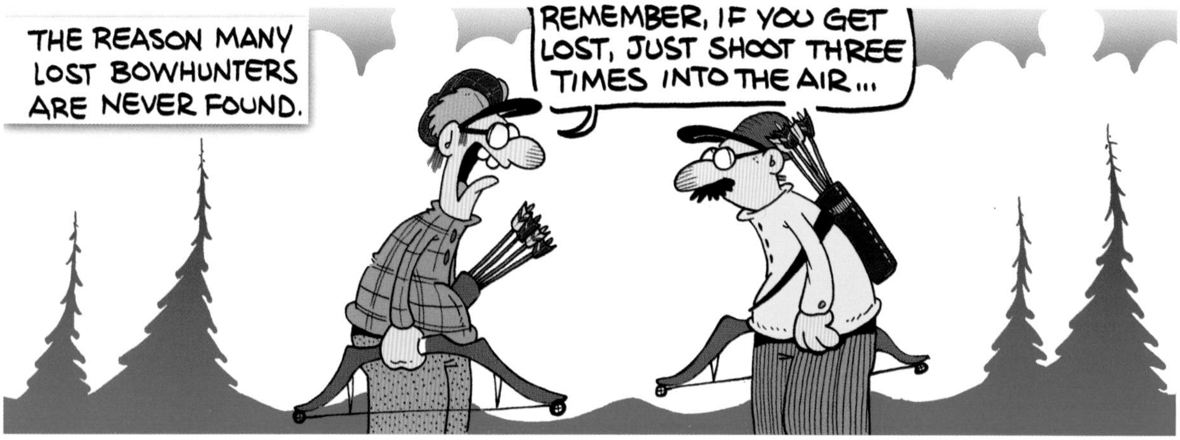
THE REASON MANY LOST BOWHUNTERS ARE NEVER FOUND.
REMEMBER, IF YOU GET LOST, JUST SHOOT THREE TIMES INTO THE AIR...

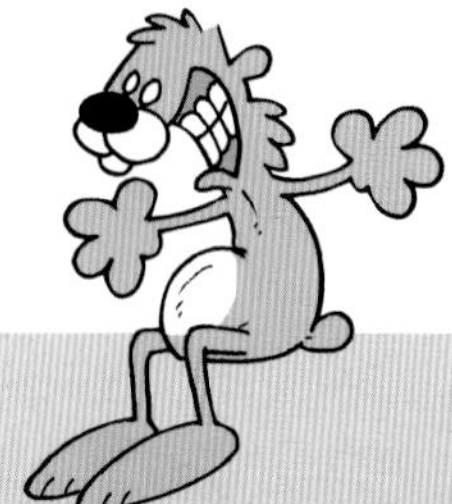

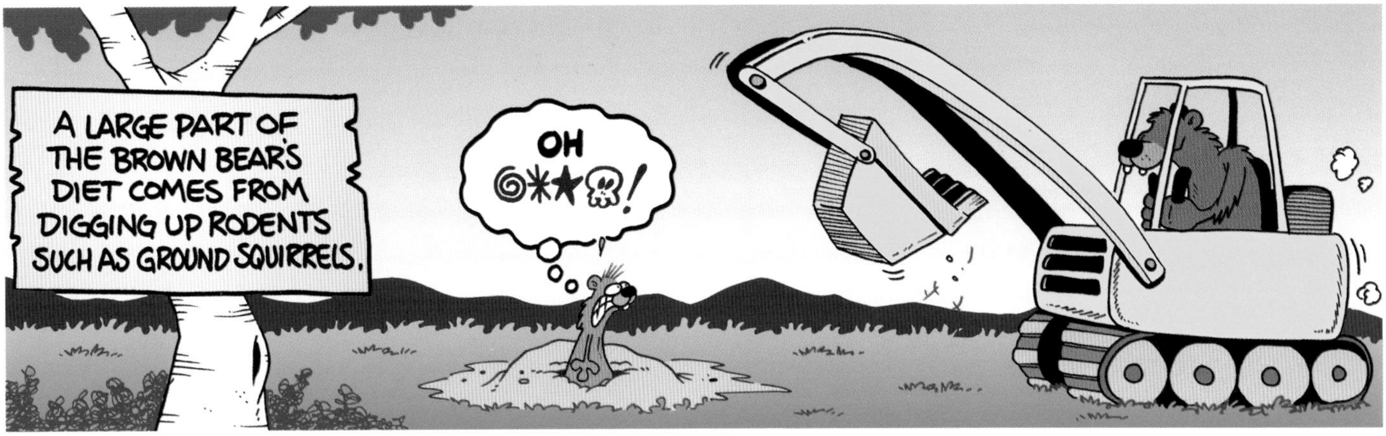
A LARGE PART OF THE BROWN BEAR'S DIET COMES FROM DIGGING UP RODENTS SUCH AS GROUND SQUIRRELS.
OH @*★☠!

This comic strip is based on the idea of

Andy Bergstrom
Delmar, NY

Do you have an idea that would make a great comic strip? Send it to:
www.tundracomics.com
or
TUNDRA IDEAS
PO BOX 770732
Eagle River, AK
99577

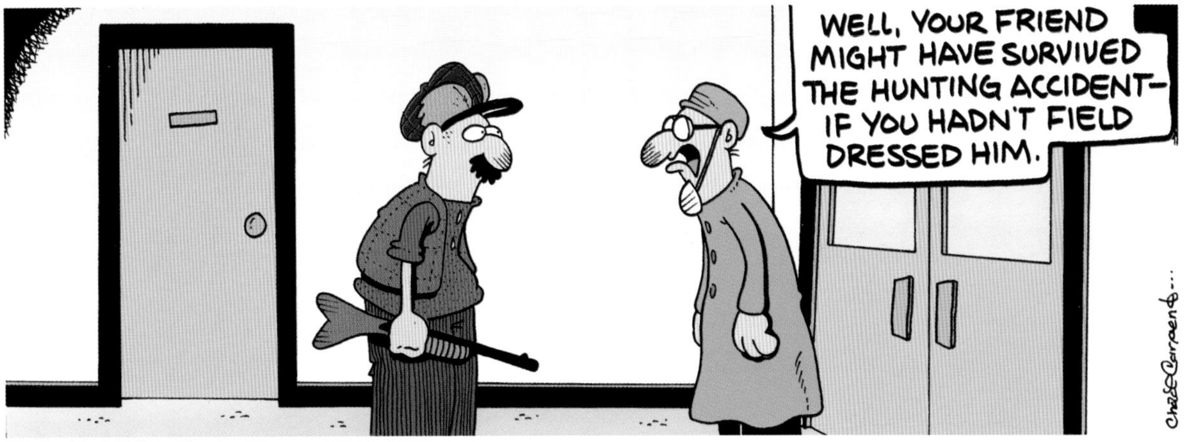
WELL, YOUR FRIEND MIGHT HAVE SURVIVED THE HUNTING ACCIDENT– IF YOU HADN'T FIELD DRESSED HIM.

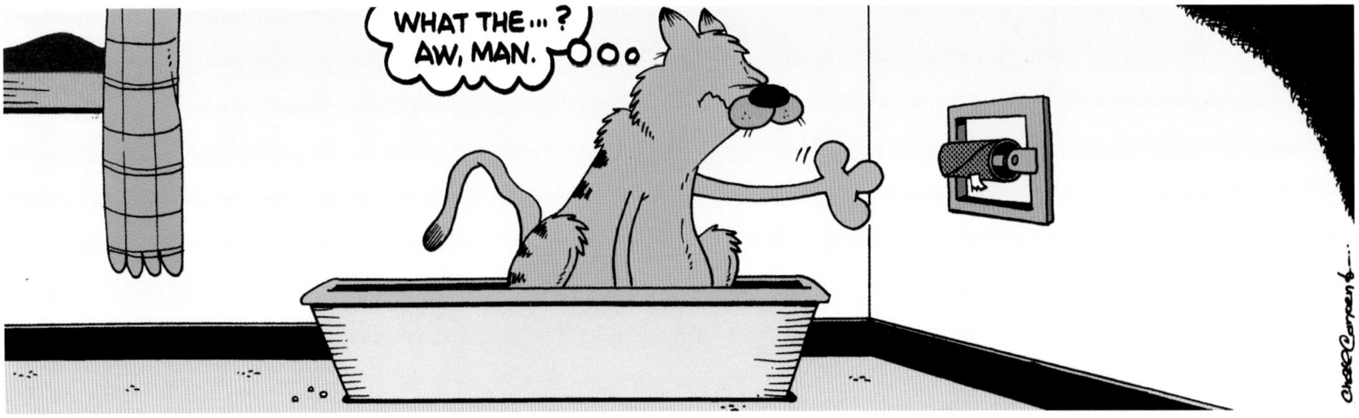
WHAT THE...? AW, MAN.

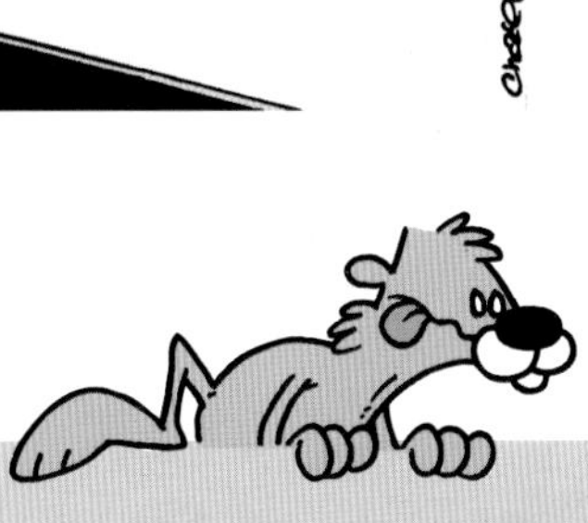

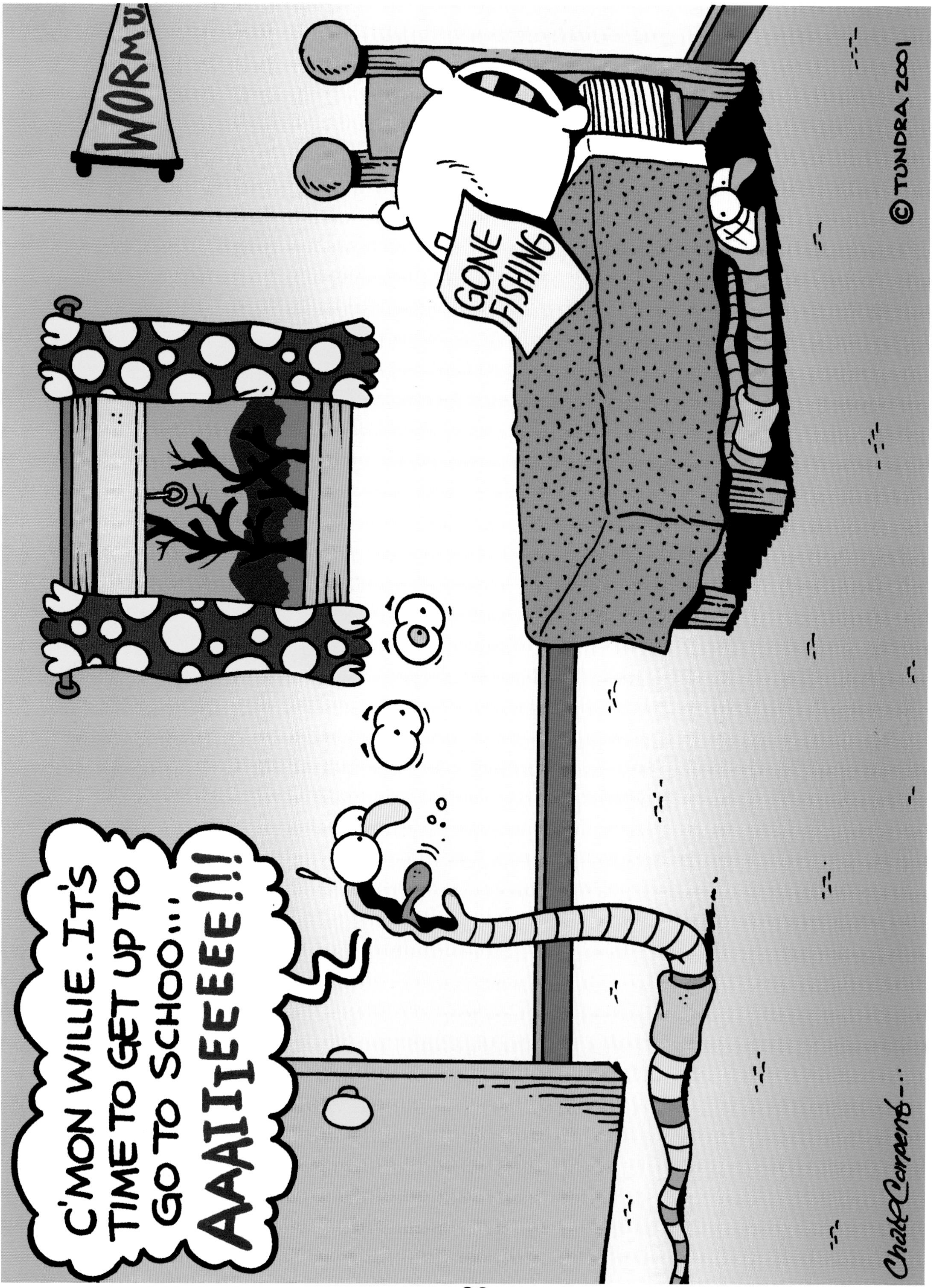
C'MON WILLIE. IT'S TIME TO GET UP TO GO TO SCHOO... AAAIIIEEEEEE!!!!
WORM U.
GONE FISHING
© TUNDRA 2001
Chad Carpenter

This comic strip is
based on the idea of
ALICIA GREENE
Anchorage, AK
Do you have an idea
that would make a
great comic strip?
Send it to:
www.tundracomics.com
or
TUNDRA IDEAS
PO BOX 770732
Eagle River, AK
99577

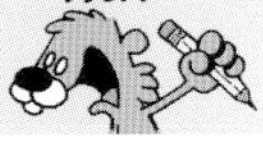

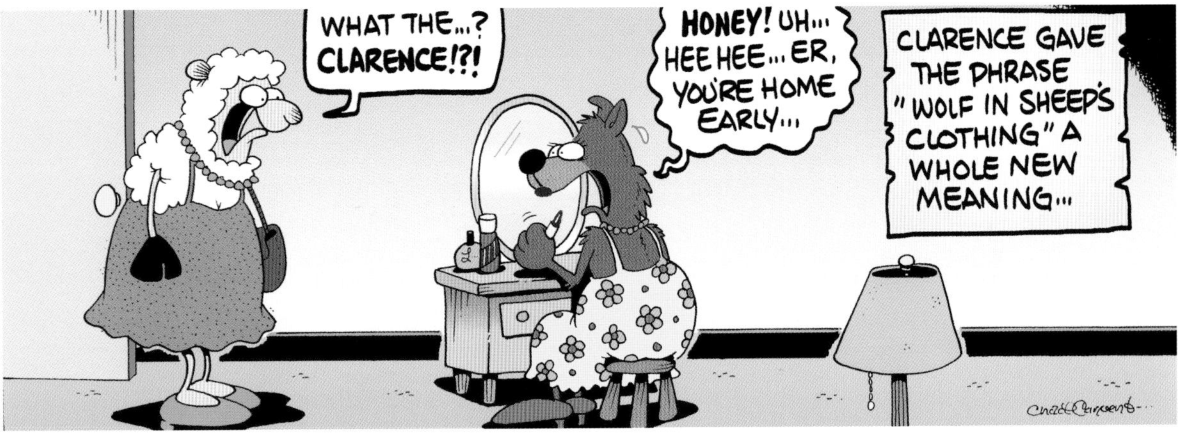
WHAT THE...? CLARENCE!?!
HONEY! UH... HEE HEE... ER, YOU'RE HOME EARLY...
CLARENCE GAVE THE PHRASE "WOLF IN SHEEP'S CLOTHING" A WHOLE NEW MEANING...

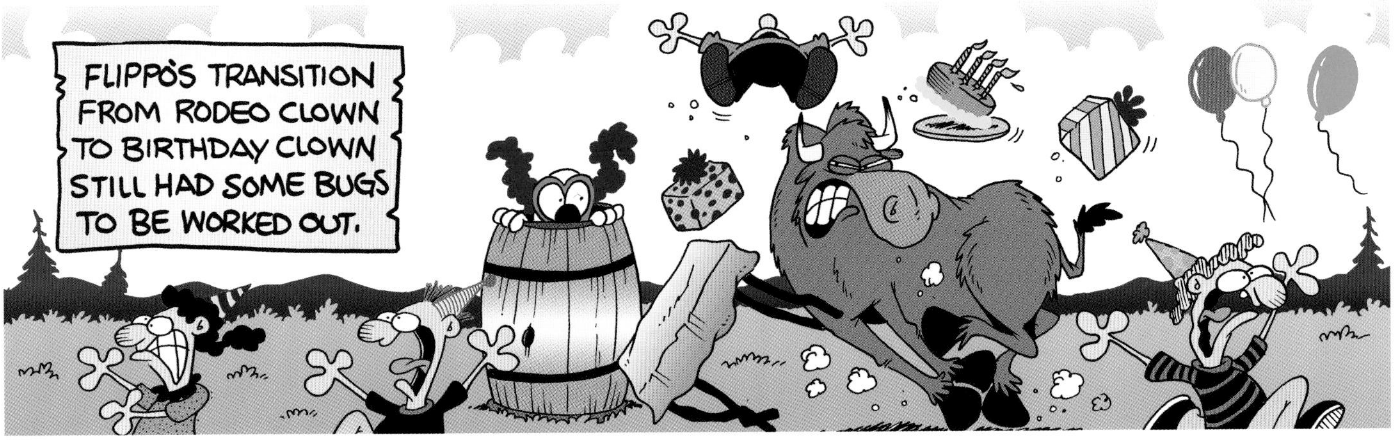
FLIPPO'S TRANSITION FROM RODEO CLOWN TO BIRTHDAY CLOWN STILL HAD SOME BUGS TO BE WORKED OUT.

This comic strip is
based on the idea of
Larry Moore
Eagle River, AK
Do you have an idea
that would make a
great comic strip?
Send it to:
www.tundracomics.com
or
TUNDRA IDEAS
PO BOX 770732
Eagle River, AK
99577

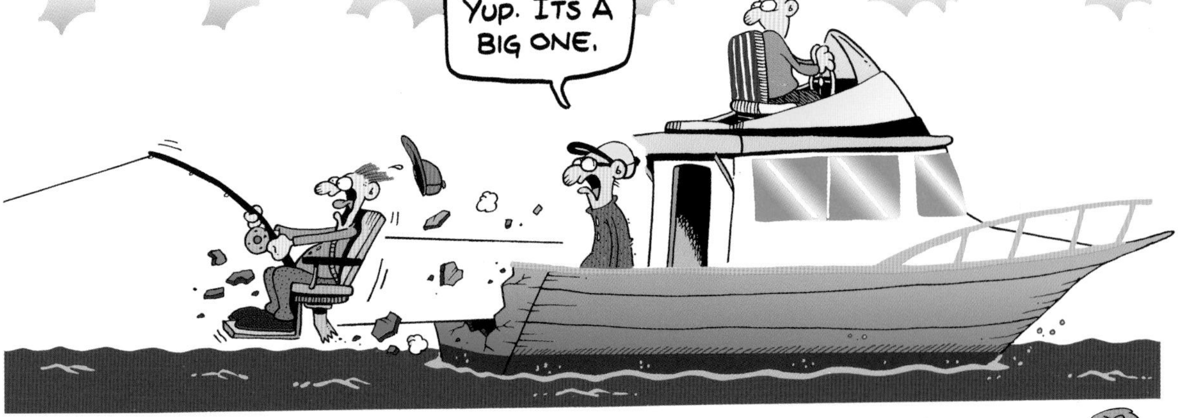
YUP. IT'S A BIG ONE.

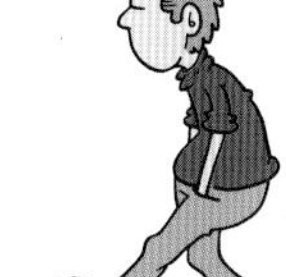

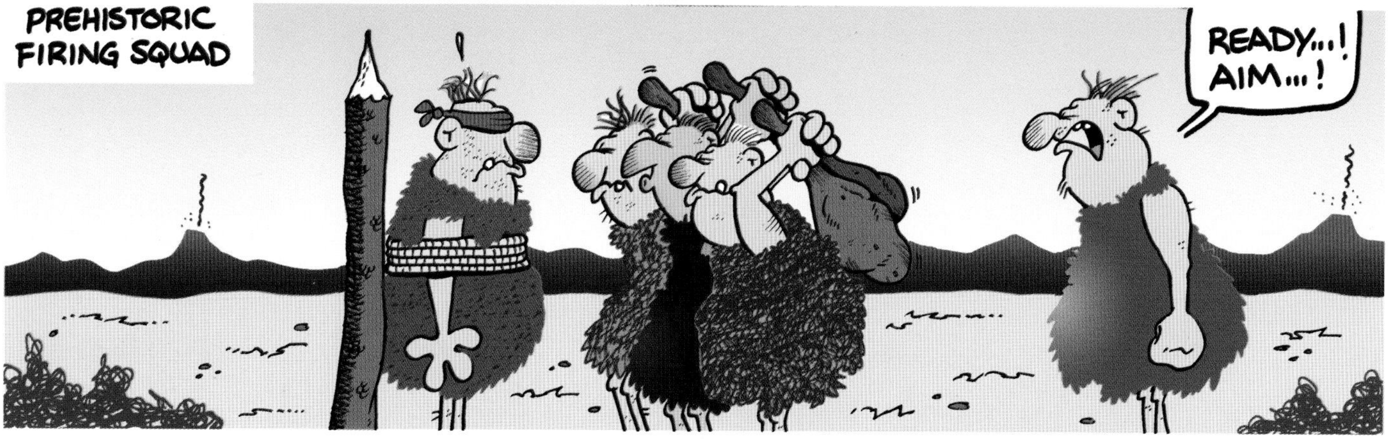
PREHISTORIC FIRING SQUAD
READY...! AIM...!

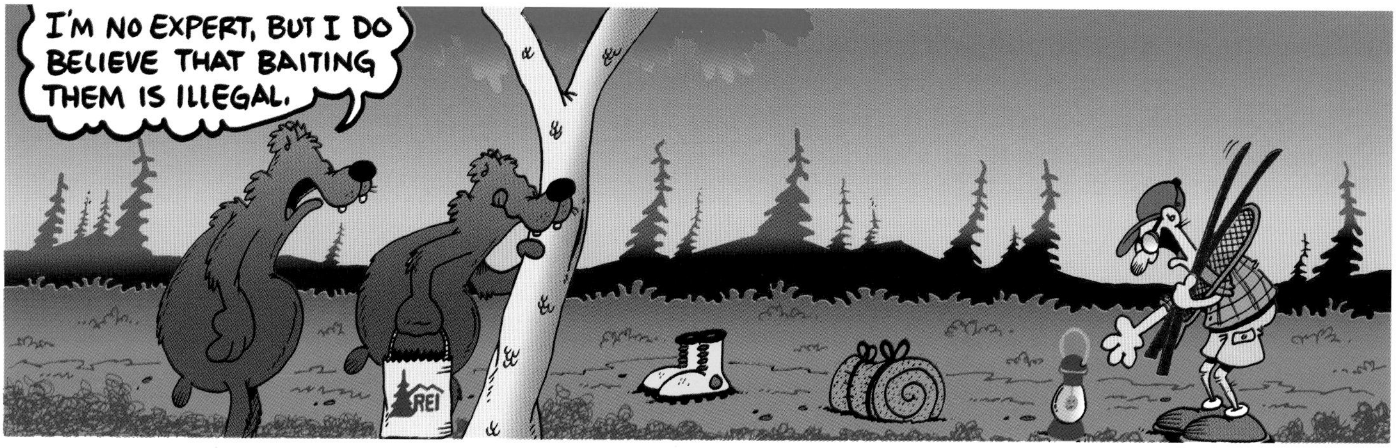
I'M NO EXPERT, BUT I DO BELIEVE THAT BAITING THEM IS ILLEGAL.
REI

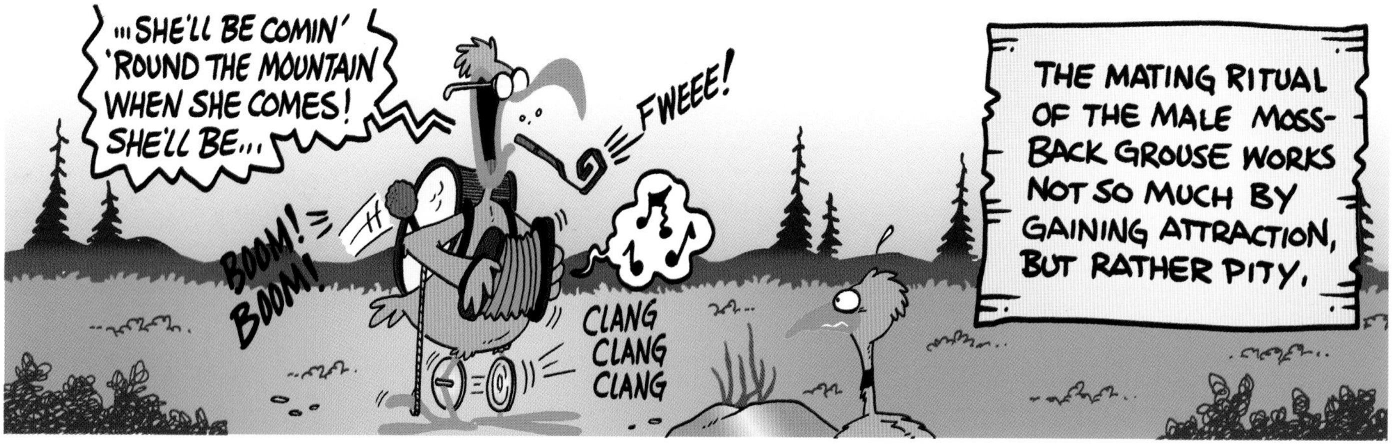
...SHE'LL BE COMIN' 'ROUND THE MOUNTAIN WHEN SHE COMES! SHE'LL BE...
FWEEE!
BOOM! BOOM!
CLANG CLANG CLANG
THE MATING RITUAL OF THE MALE MOSS-BACK GROUSE WORKS NOT SO MUCH BY GAINING ATTRACTION, BUT RATHER PITY.

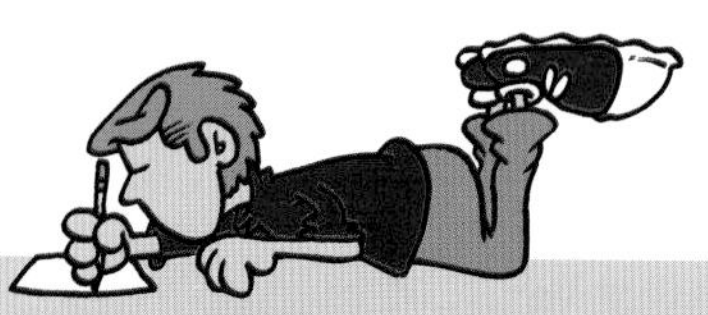

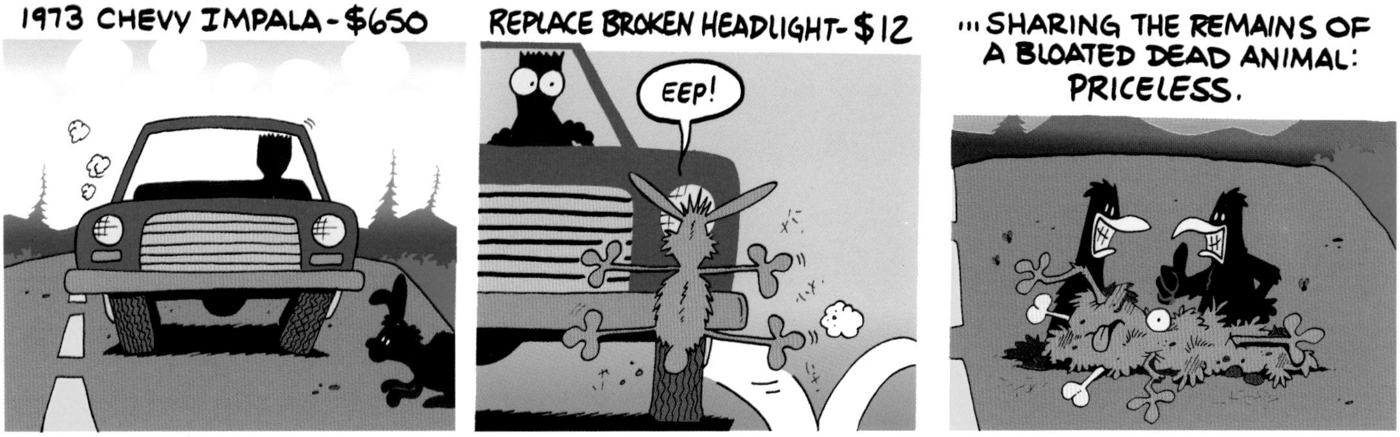
1973 CHEVY IMPALA - $650
REPLACE BROKEN HEADLIGHT - $12
EEP!
... SHARING THE REMAINS OF A BLOATED DEAD ANIMAL: PRICELESS.

This comic strip is based on the idea of

Elizabeth Roderick
Anchor Point, AK

Do you have an idea that would make a great comic strip? Send it to:

www.tundracomics.com
or
TUNDRA IDEAS
PO BOX 770732
Eagle River, AK
99577

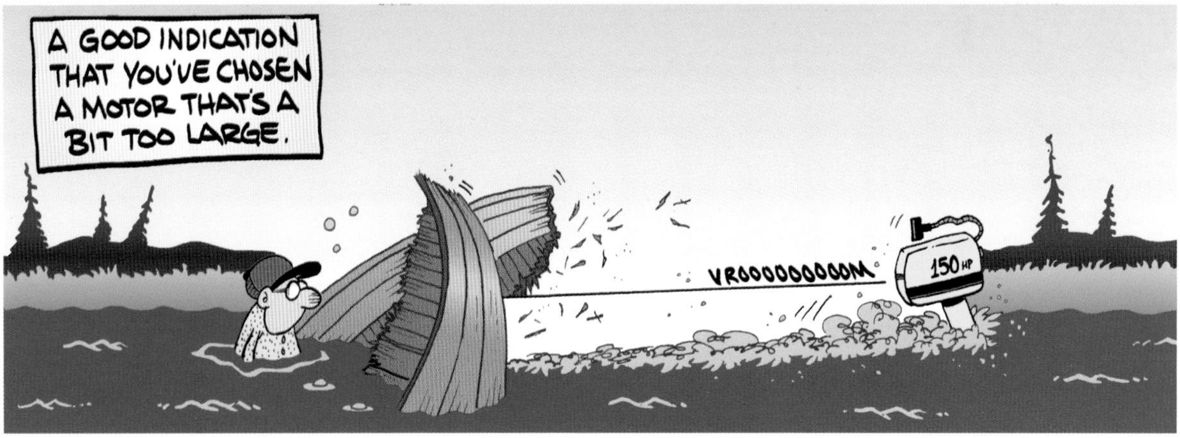
A GOOD INDICATION THAT YOU'VE CHOSEN A MOTOR THAT'S A BIT TOO LARGE.
VROOOOOOOOOM
150 HP

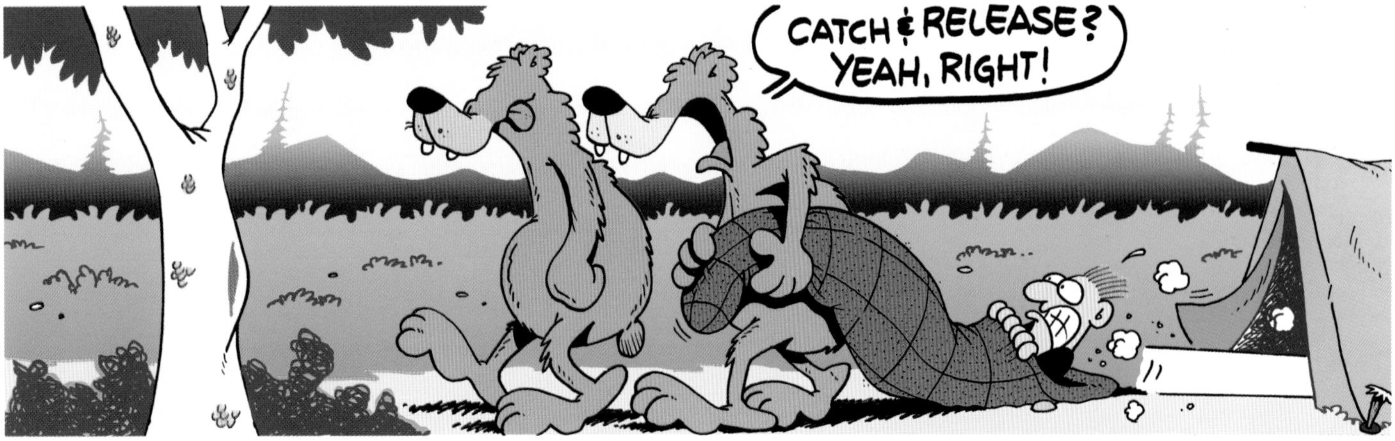
CATCH & RELEASE? YEAH, RIGHT!

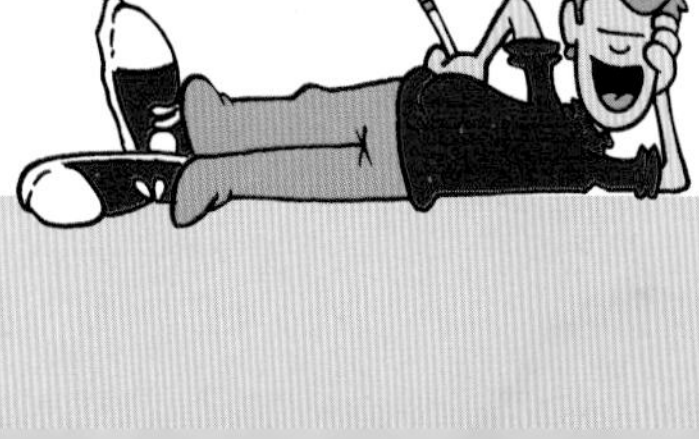

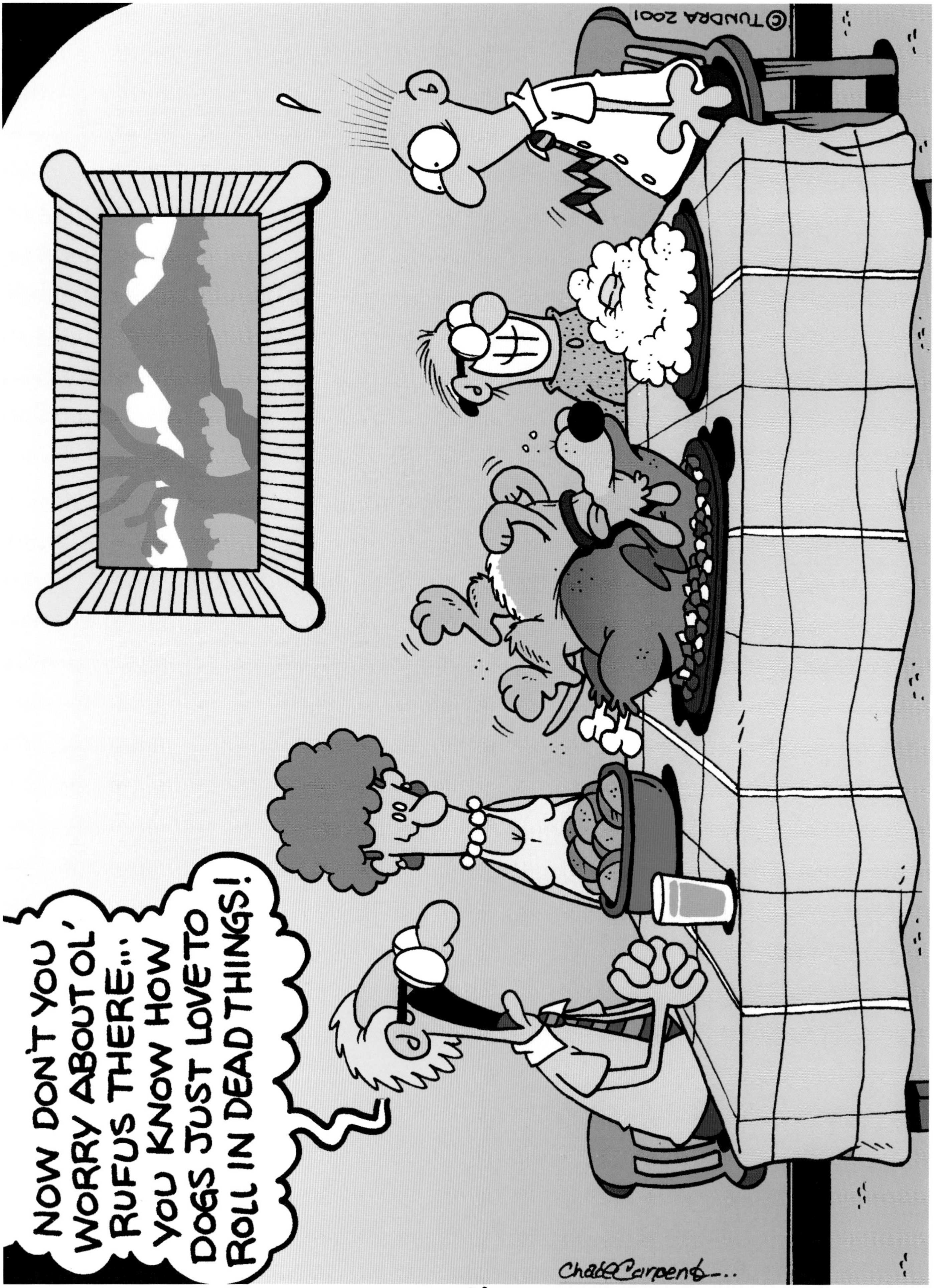
NOW DON'T YOU WORRY ABOUT OL' RUFUS THERE... YOU KNOW HOW DOGS JUST LOVE TO ROLL IN DEAD THINGS!
© TUNDRA 2001
Chad Carpenter

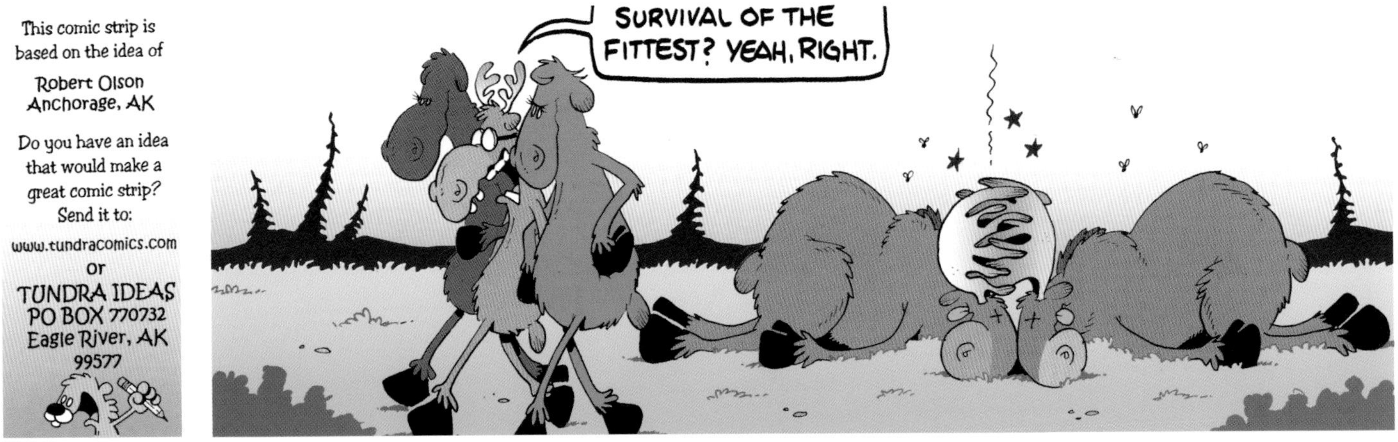
This comic strip is based on the idea of
Robert Olson Anchorage, AK
Do you have an idea that would make a great comic strip? Send it to:
www.tundracomics.com
or
TUNDRA IDEAS PO BOX 770732 Eagle River, AK 99577
SURVIVAL OF THE FITTEST? YEAH, RIGHT.

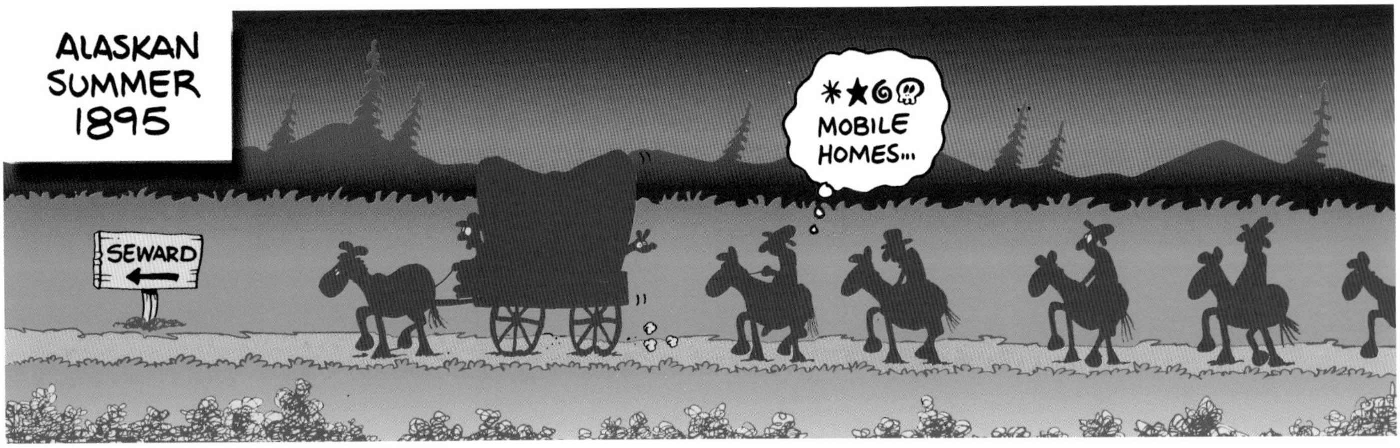
ALASKAN SUMMER 1895
SEWARD
MOBILE HOMES...

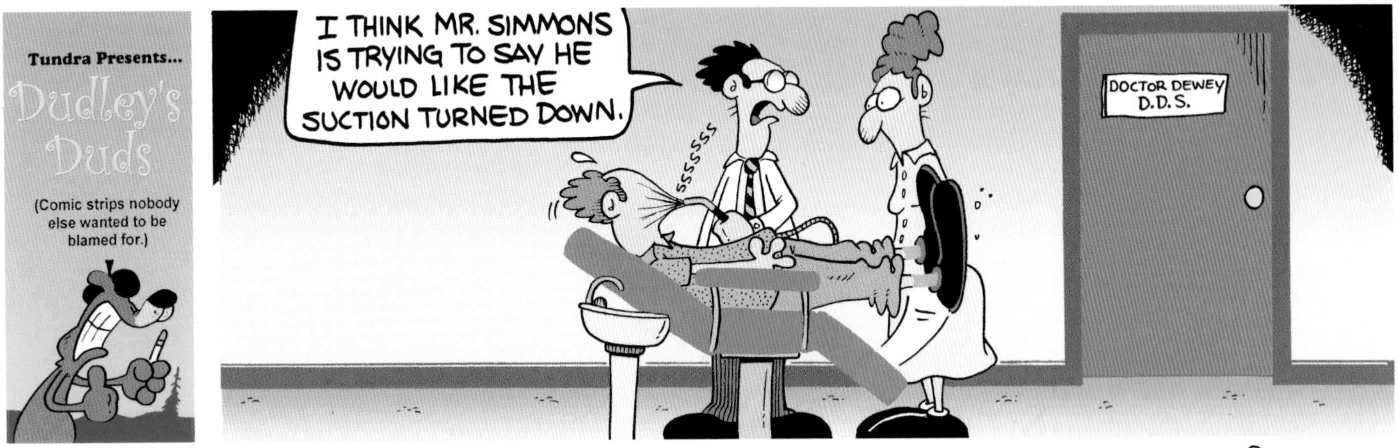
Tundra Presents...
Dudley's Duds
(Comic strips nobody else wanted to be blamed for.)
I THINK MR. SIMMONS IS TRYING TO SAY HE WOULD LIKE THE SUCTION TURNED DOWN.
SSSSSS
DOCTOR DEWEY D.D.S.

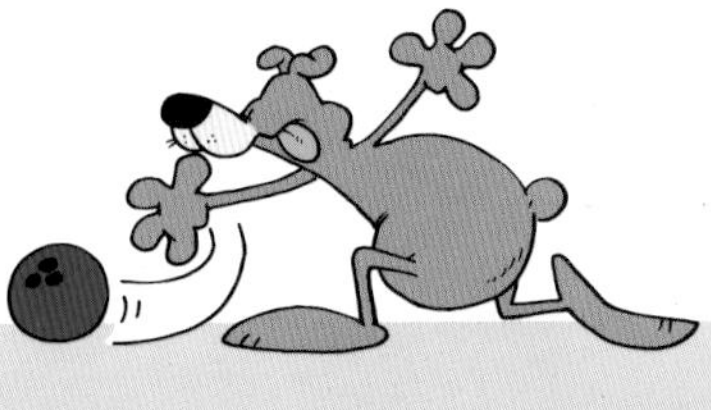

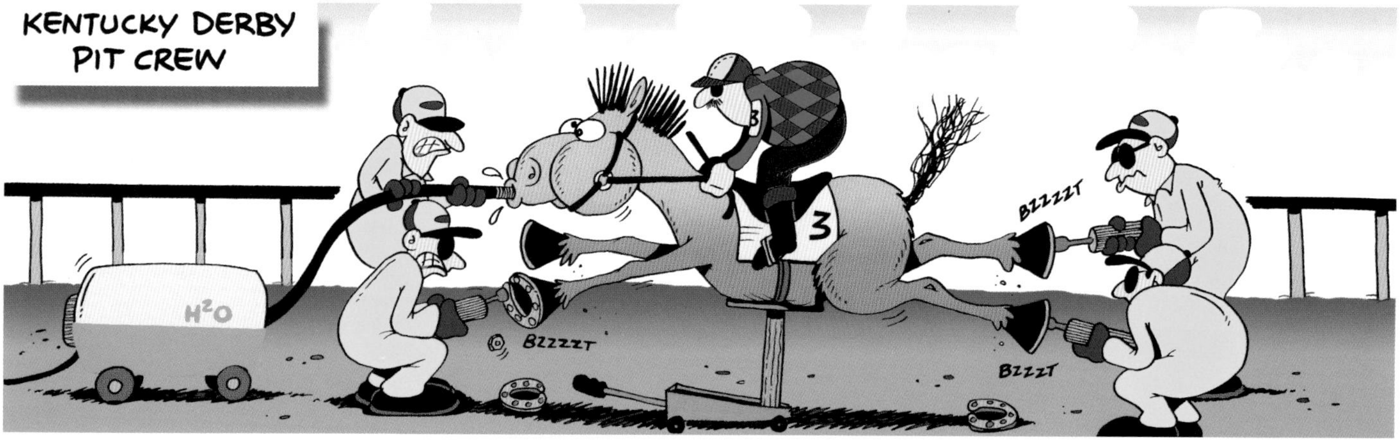
KENTUCKY DERBY
PIT CREW
H^2O
BZZZZT
BZZZZT
BZZZT

This comic strip is based on the idea of
Pam Jackson
Anchorage, AK

Do you have an idea that would make a great comic strip? Send it to:

www.tundracomics.com
or
TUNDRA IDEAS
PO BOX 770732
Eagle River, AK
99577

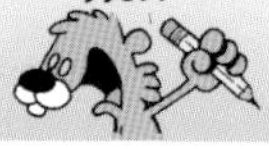

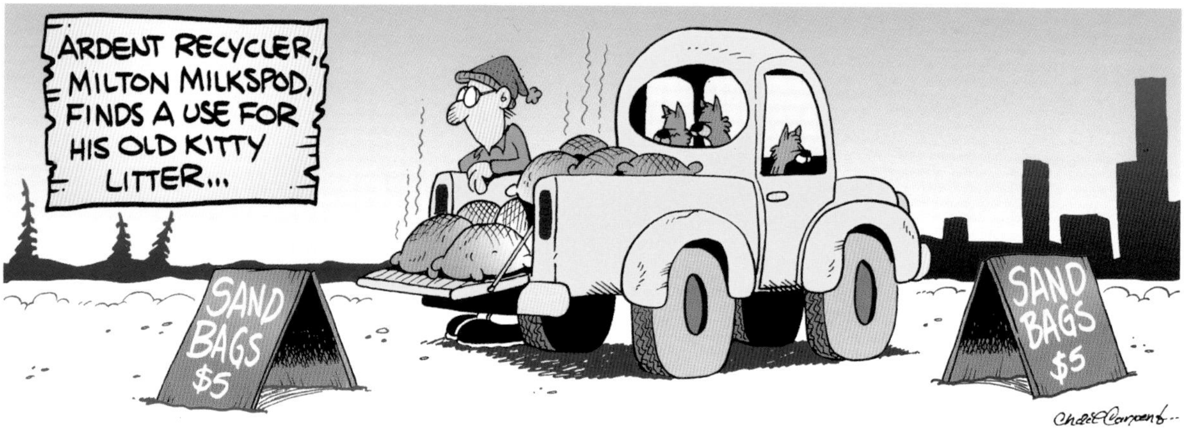
ARDENT RECYCLER, MILTON MILKSPOD, FINDS A USE FOR HIS OLD KITTY LITTER...
SAND BAGS $5
SAND BAGS $5

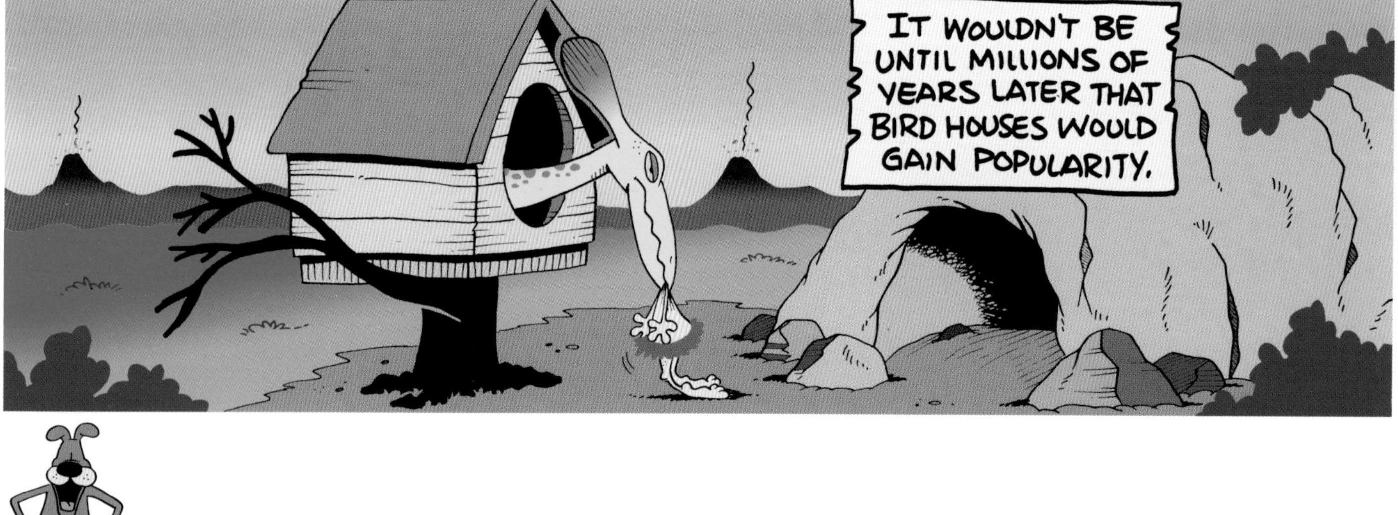
IT WOULDN'T BE UNTIL MILLIONS OF YEARS LATER THAT BIRD HOUSES WOULD GAIN POPULARITY.

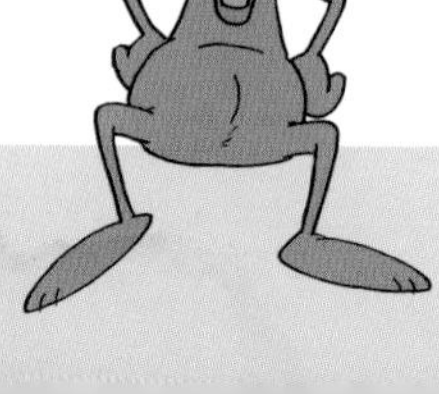

This comic strip is based on the idea of
Amy Gibson
Anchorage, AK

Do you have an idea that would make a great comic strip? Send it to:

www.tundracomics.com
or
TUNDRA IDEAS
PO BOX 770732
Eagle River, AK
99577

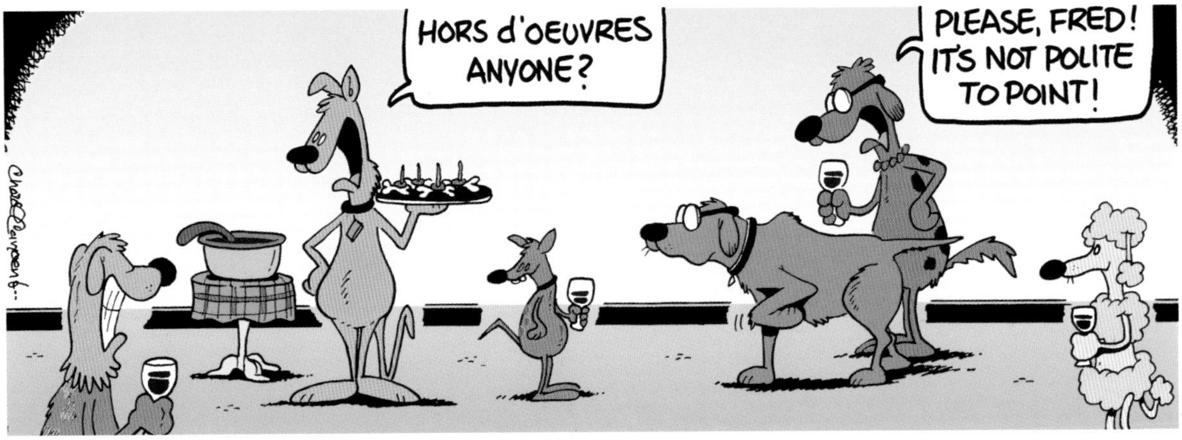
HORS d'OEUVRES ANYONE?
PLEASE, FRED! IT'S NOT POLITE TO POINT!

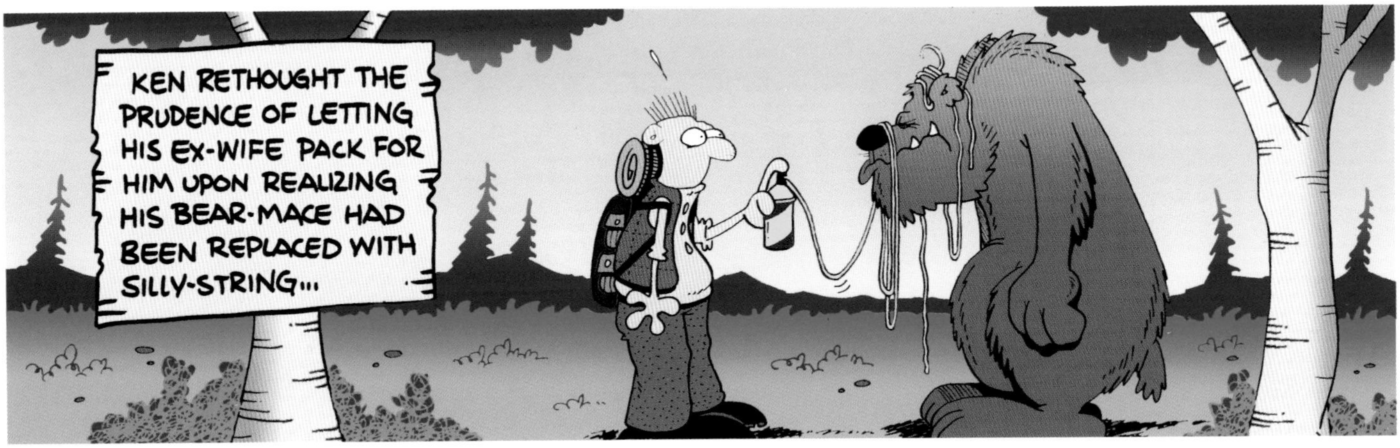
KEN RETHOUGHT THE PRUDENCE OF LETTING HIS EX-WIFE PACK FOR HIM UPON REALIZING HIS BEAR-MACE HAD BEEN REPLACED WITH SILLY-STRING...

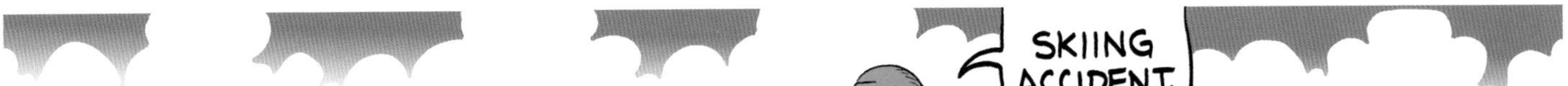
SKIING ACCIDENT.

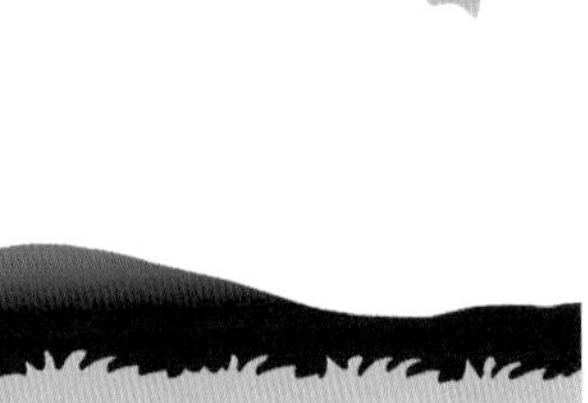

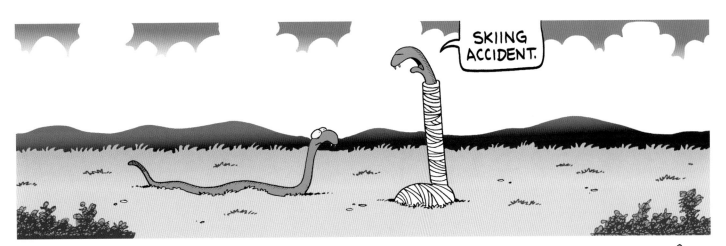

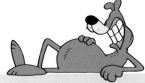

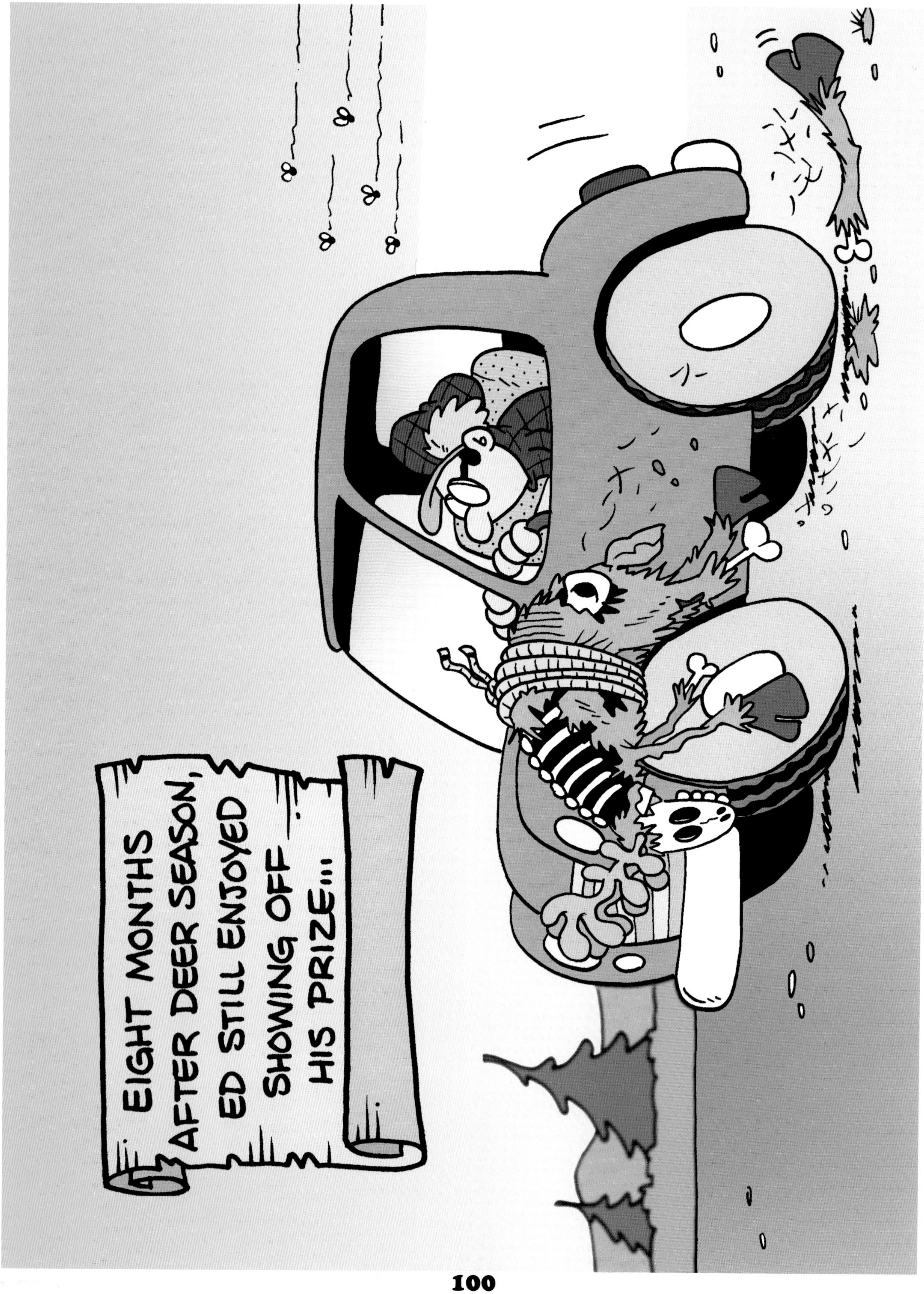
EIGHT MONTHS AFTER DEER SEASON, ED STILL ENJOYED SHOWING OFF HIS PRIZE...

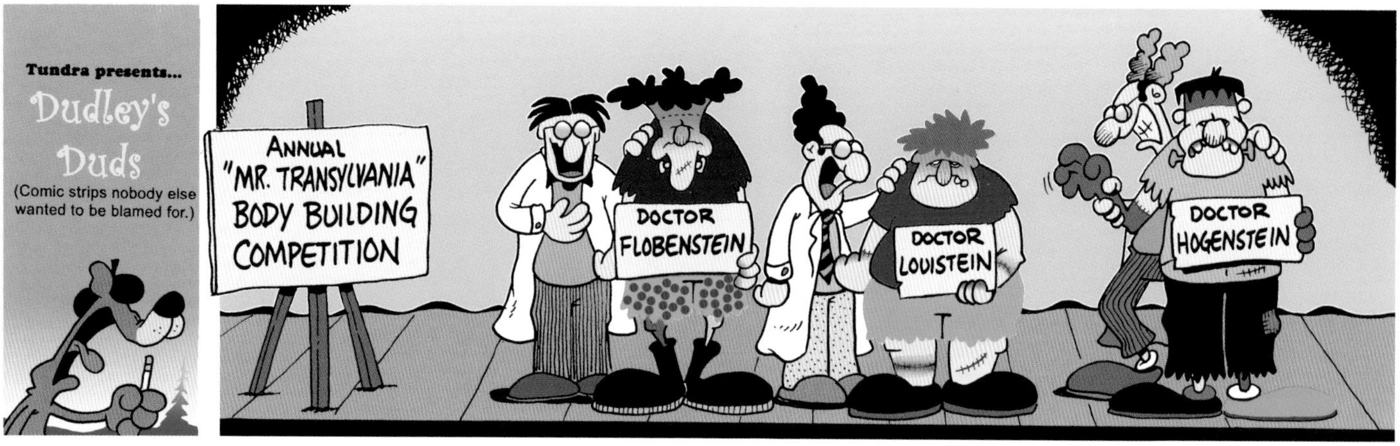
Tundra presents...
Dudley's Duds
(Comic strips nobody else wanted to be blamed for.)
ANNUAL "MR. TRANSYLVANIA" BODY BUILDING COMPETITION
DOCTOR FLOBENSTEIN
DOCTOR LOUISTEIN
DOCTOR HOGENSTEIN

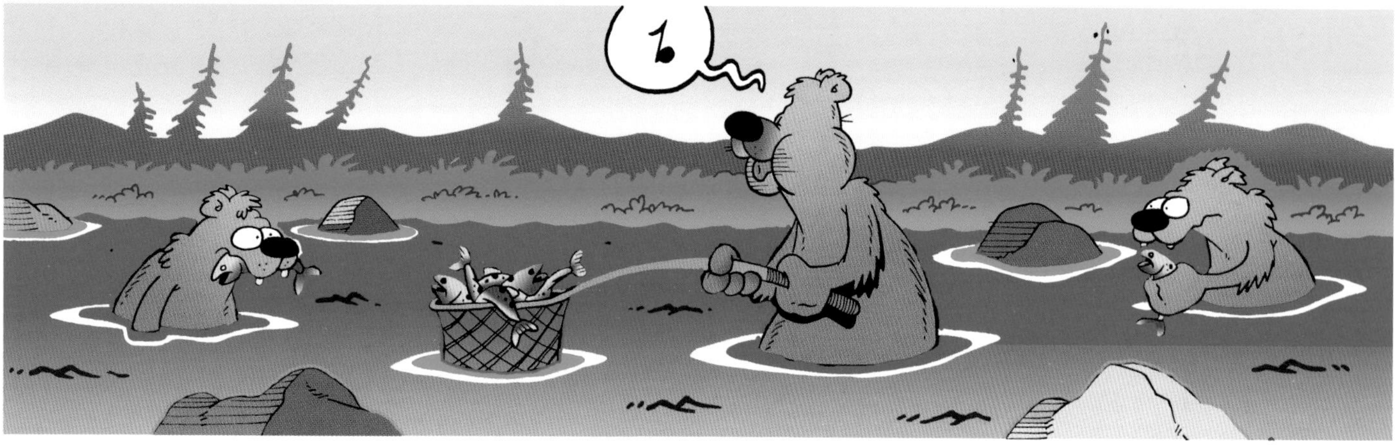

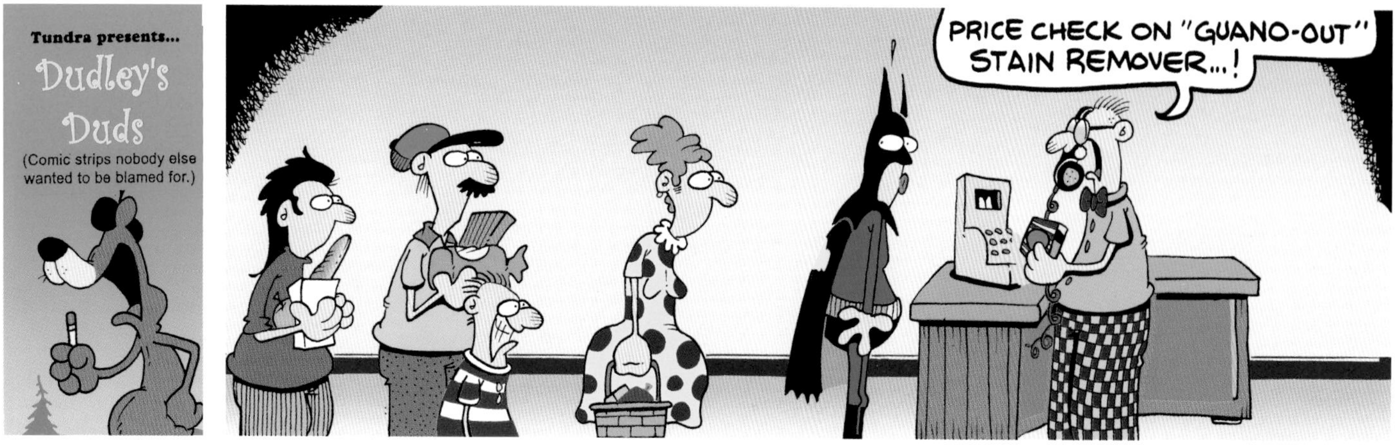
Tundra presents...
Dudley's Duds
(Comic strips nobody else wanted to be blamed for.)
PRICE CHECK ON "GUANO-OUT" STAIN REMOVER...!

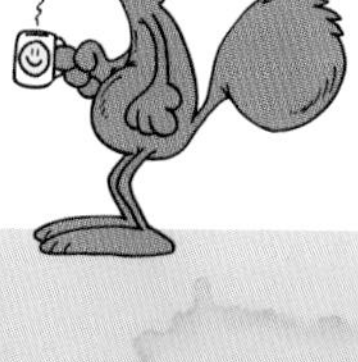

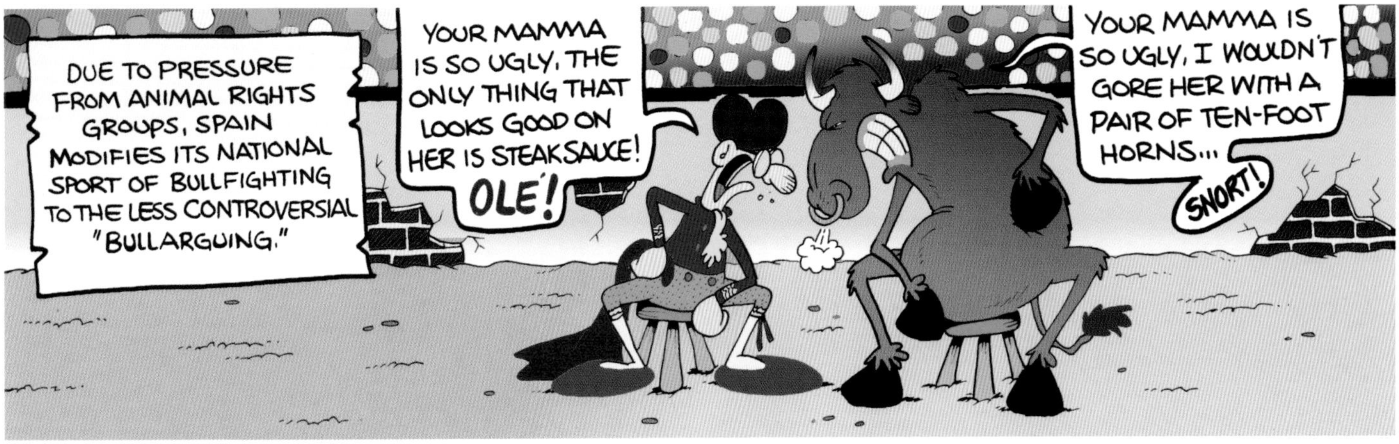
DUE TO PRESSURE FROM ANIMAL RIGHTS GROUPS, SPAIN MODIFIES ITS NATIONAL SPORT OF BULLFIGHTING TO THE LESS CONTROVERSIAL "BULLARGUING."
YOUR MAMMA IS SO UGLY, THE ONLY THING THAT LOOKS GOOD ON HER IS STEAKSAUCE!
OLÉ!
YOUR MAMMA IS SO UGLY, I WOULDN'T GORE HER WITH A PAIR OF TEN-FOOT HORNS...
SNORT!

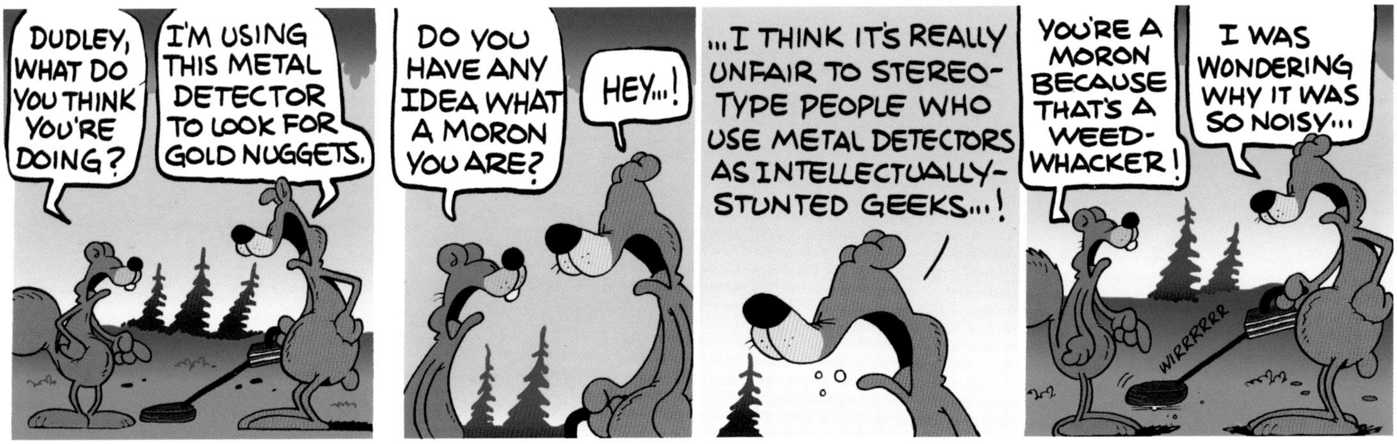
DUDLEY, WHAT DO YOU THINK YOU'RE DOING?
I'M USING THIS METAL DETECTOR TO LOOK FOR GOLD NUGGETS.
DO YOU HAVE ANY IDEA WHAT A MORON YOU ARE?
HEY...!
...I THINK IT'S REALLY UNFAIR TO STEREOTYPE PEOPLE WHO USE METAL DETECTORS AS INTELLECTUALLY-STUNTED GEEKS...!
YOU'RE A MORON BECAUSE THAT'S A WEED-WHACKER!
I WAS WONDERING WHY IT WAS SO NOISY...
WIRRRRRR

Tundra presents...

Dudley's Duds

(Comic strips nobody else wanted to be blamed for.)

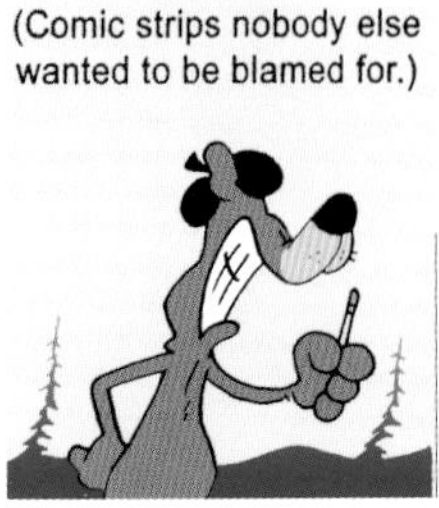

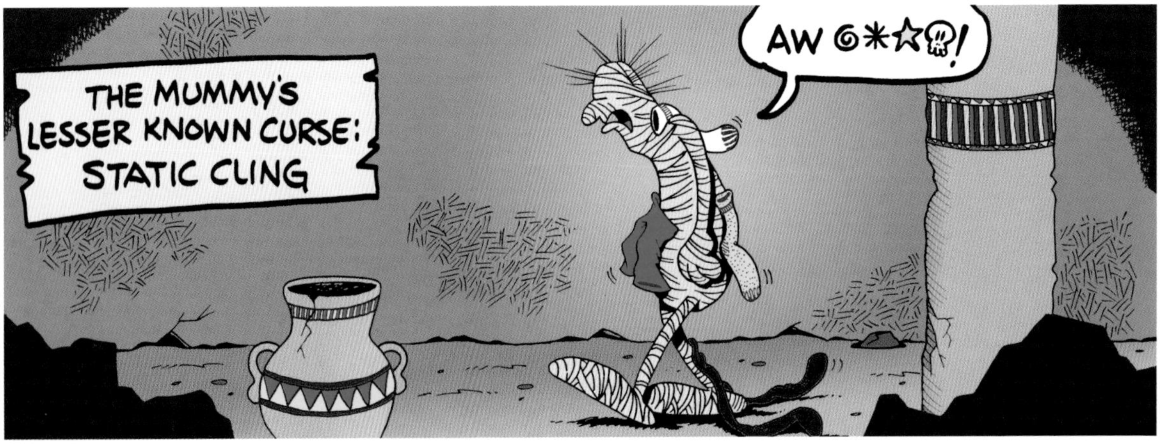
THE MUMMY'S LESSER KNOWN CURSE: STATIC CLING
AW

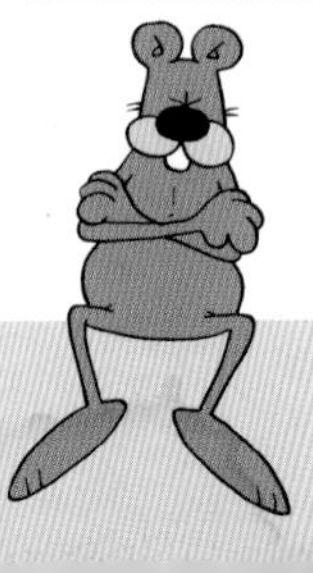

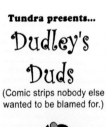

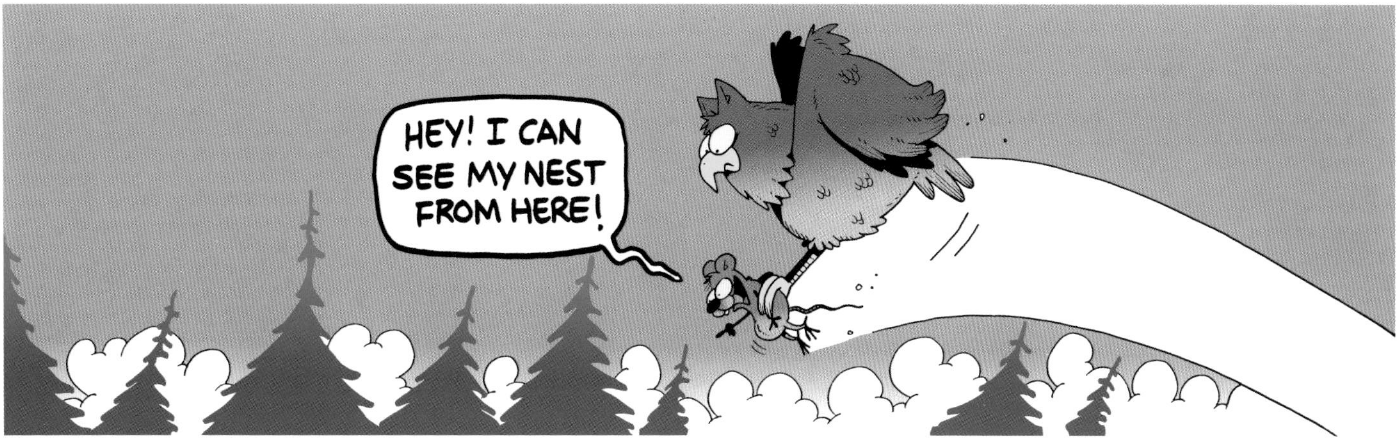
HEY! I CAN SEE MY NEST FROM HERE!

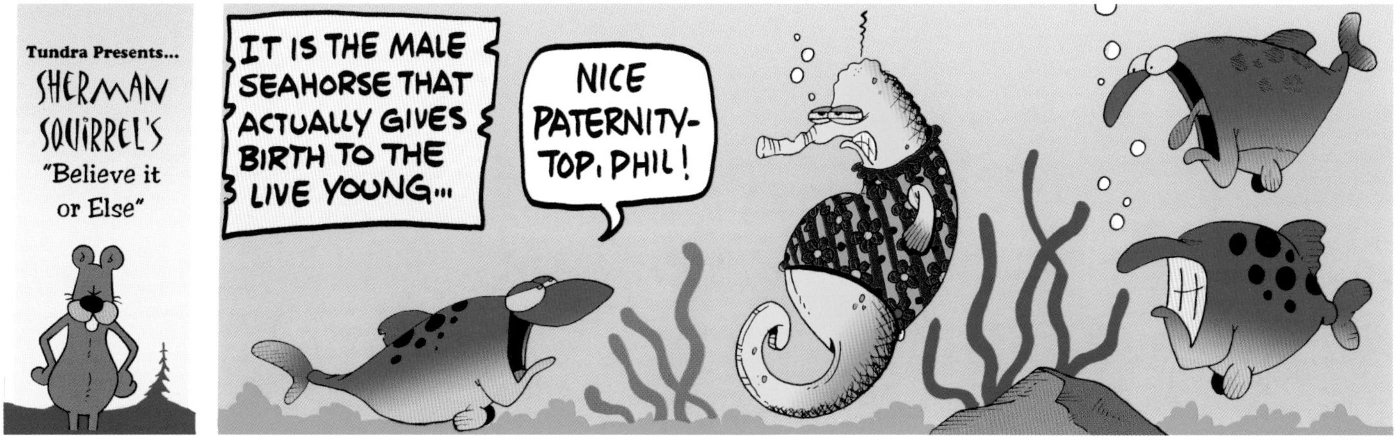
Tundra Presents...
SHERMAN SQUIRREL'S
"Believe it or Else"
IT IS THE MALE SEAHORSE THAT ACTUALLY GIVES BIRTH TO THE LIVE YOUNG...
NICE PATERNITY-TOP, PHIL!

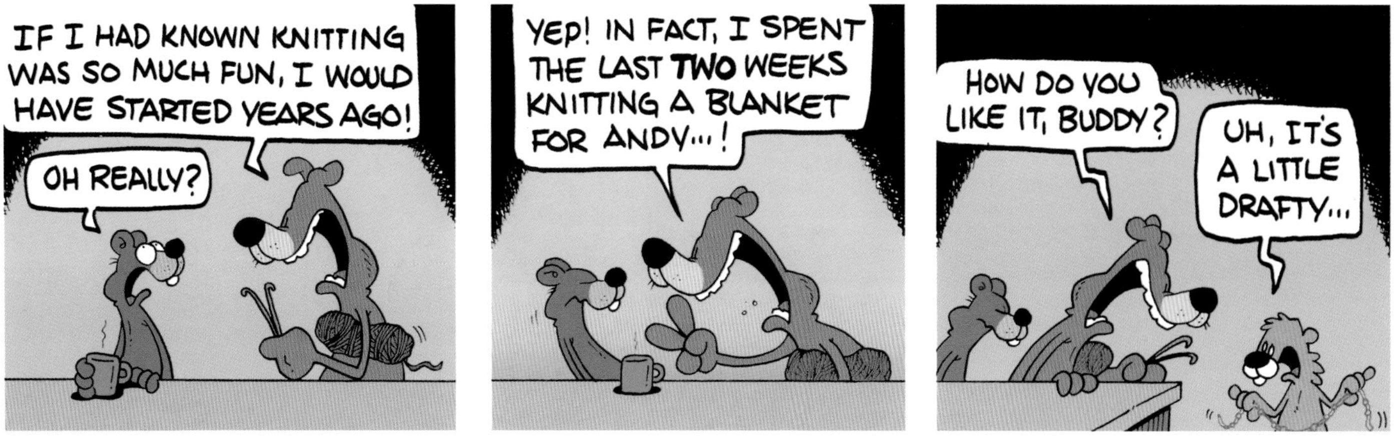
IF I HAD KNOWN KNITTING WAS SO MUCH FUN, I WOULD HAVE STARTED YEARS AGO!
OH REALLY?
YEP! IN FACT, I SPENT THE LAST TWO WEEKS KNITTING A BLANKET FOR ANDY...!
HOW DO YOU LIKE IT, BUDDY?
UH, IT'S A LITTLE DRAFTY...

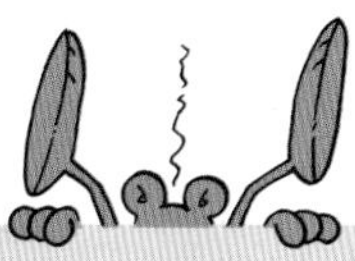

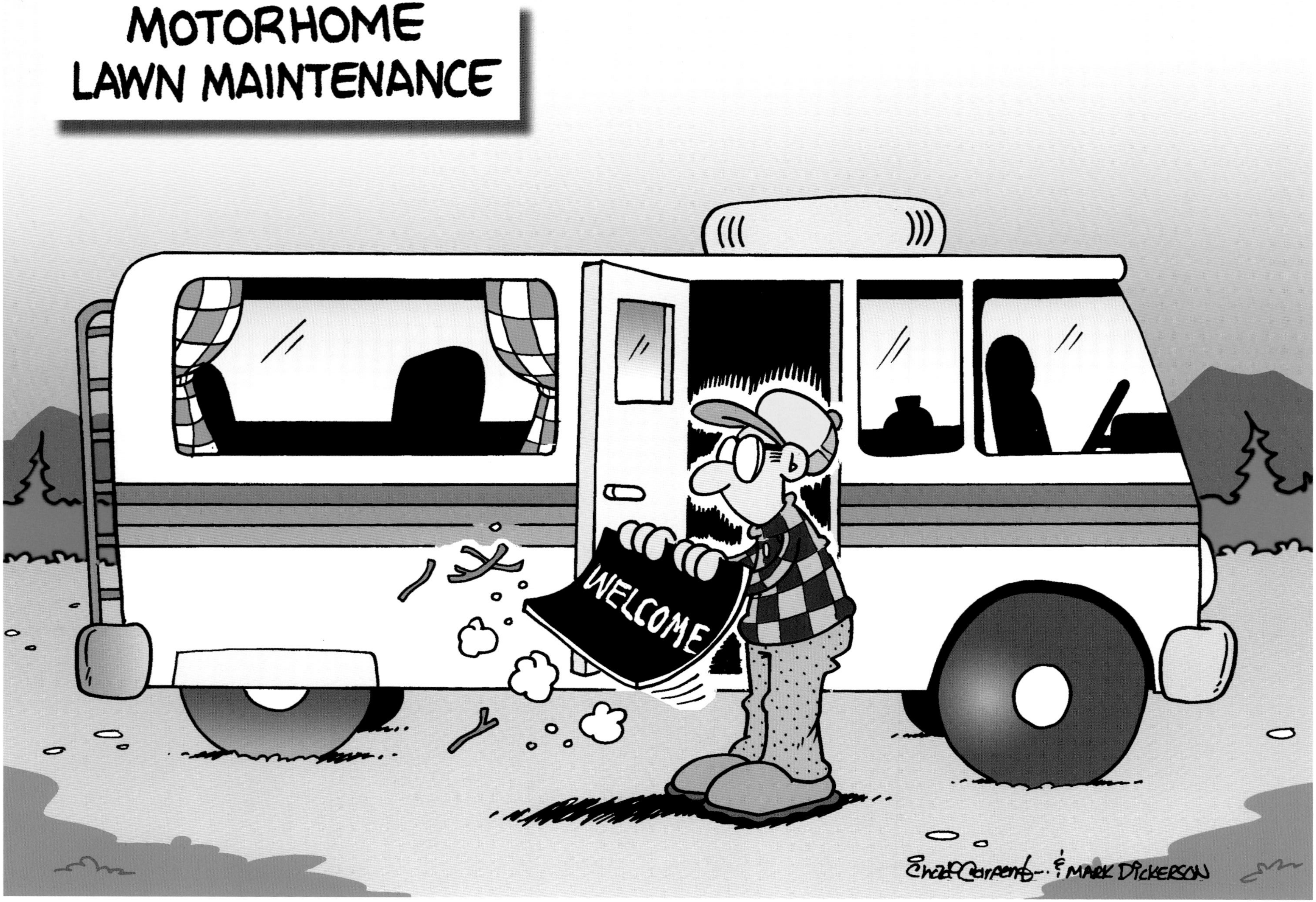
MOTORHOME
LAWN MAINTENANCE
WELCOME
Chad Carpenter & MARK DICKERSON

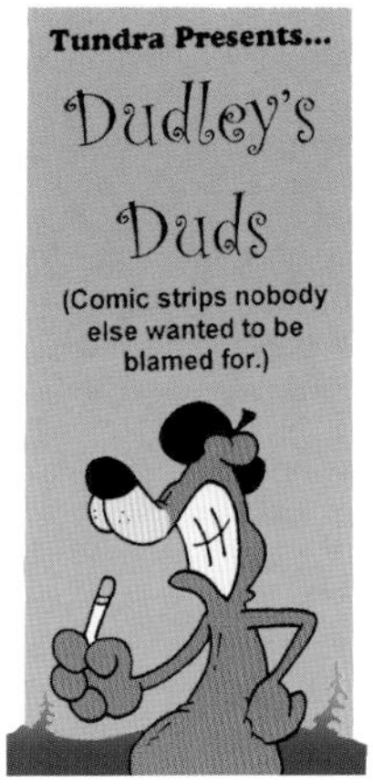
Tundra Presents...
Dudley's Duds
(Comic strips nobody else wanted to be blamed for.)

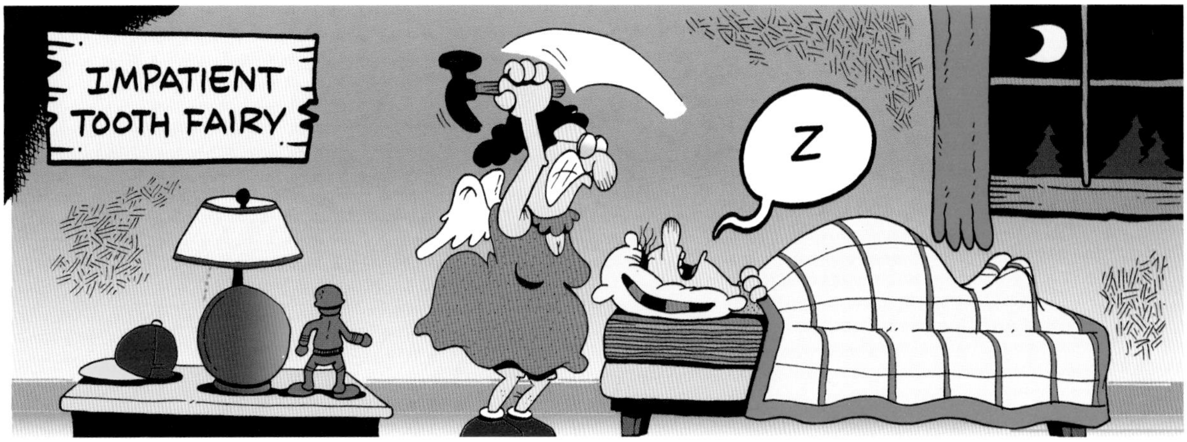
IMPATIENT TOOTH FAIRY
Z

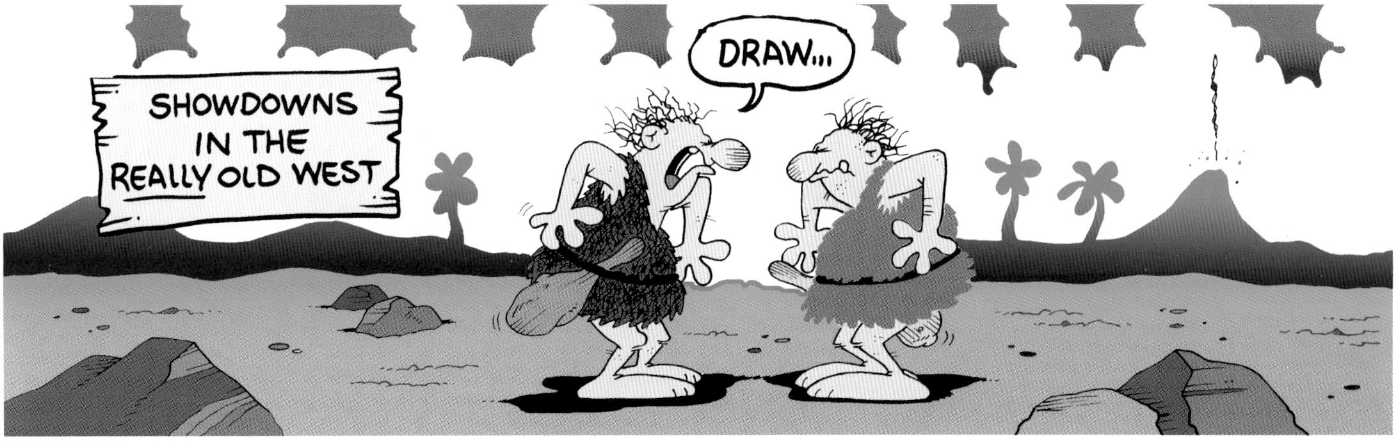
SHOWDOWNS IN THE REALLY OLD WEST
DRAW...

This comic strip is based on the idea of

Robert Wilkins
Anchorage, AK

Do you have an idea that would make a great comic strip? Send it to:

www.tundracomics.com
or
TUNDRA IDEAS
PO BOX 770732
Eagle River, AK
99577

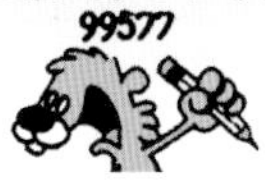

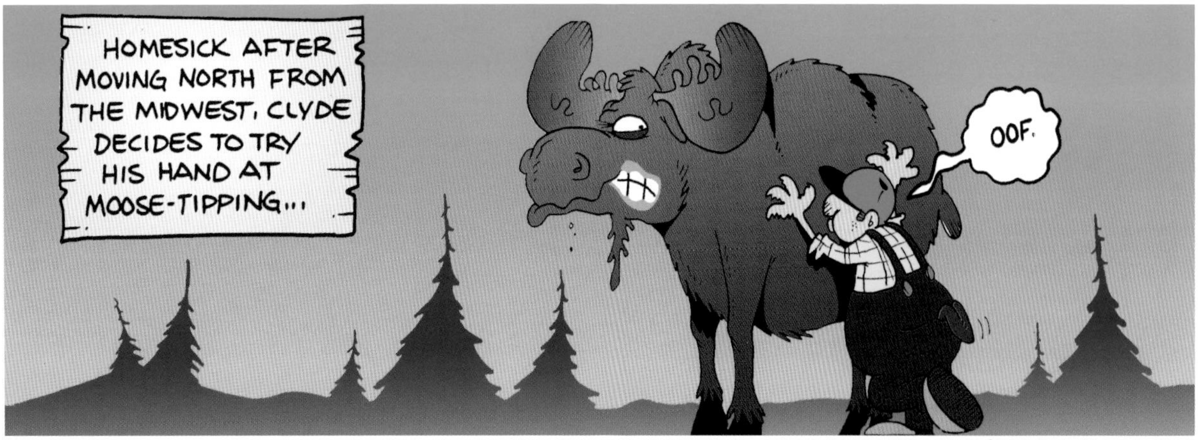
HOMESICK AFTER MOVING NORTH FROM THE MIDWEST, CLYDE DECIDES TO TRY HIS HAND AT MOOSE-TIPPING...
OOF.

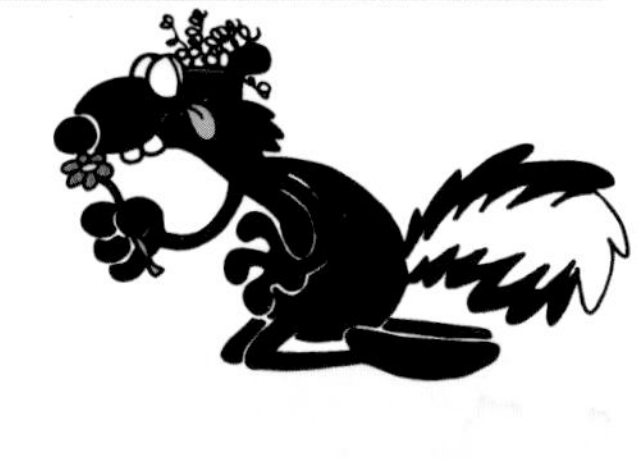

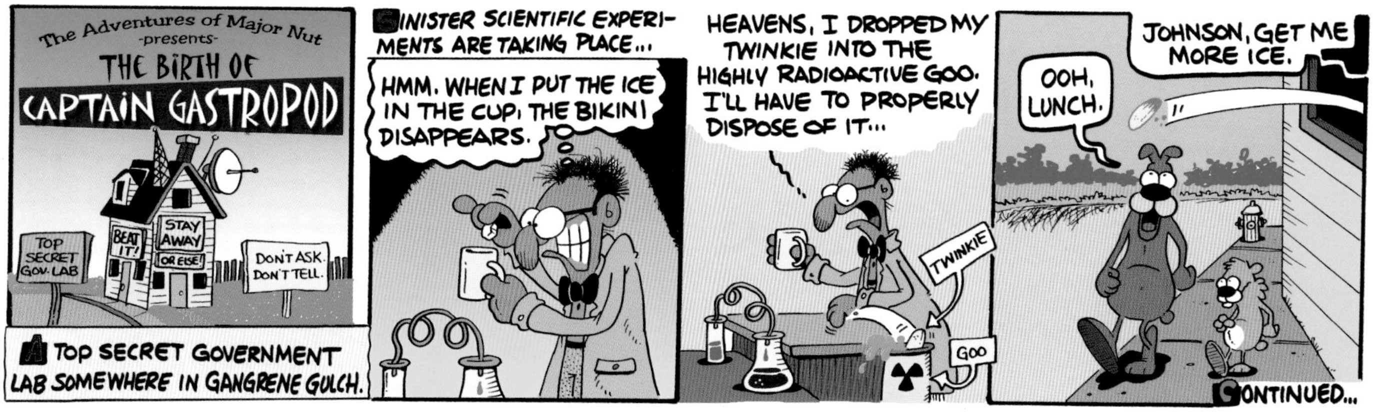
The Adventures of Major Nut
-presents-
THE BIRTH OF
CAPTAIN GASTROPOD
TOP SECRET GOV. LAB
BEAT IT!
STAY AWAY OR ELSE!
DON'T ASK. DON'T TELL.
A TOP SECRET GOVERNMENT LAB SOMEWHERE IN GANGRENE GULCH.
SINISTER SCIENTIFIC EXPERIMENTS ARE TAKING PLACE...
HMM. WHEN I PUT THE ICE IN THE CUP, THE BIKINI DISAPPEARS.
HEAVENS, I DROPPED MY TWINKIE INTO THE HIGHLY RADIOACTIVE GOO. I'LL HAVE TO PROPERLY DISPOSE OF IT...
TWINKIE
GOO
JOHNSON, GET ME MORE ICE.
OOH, LUNCH.
CONTINUED...

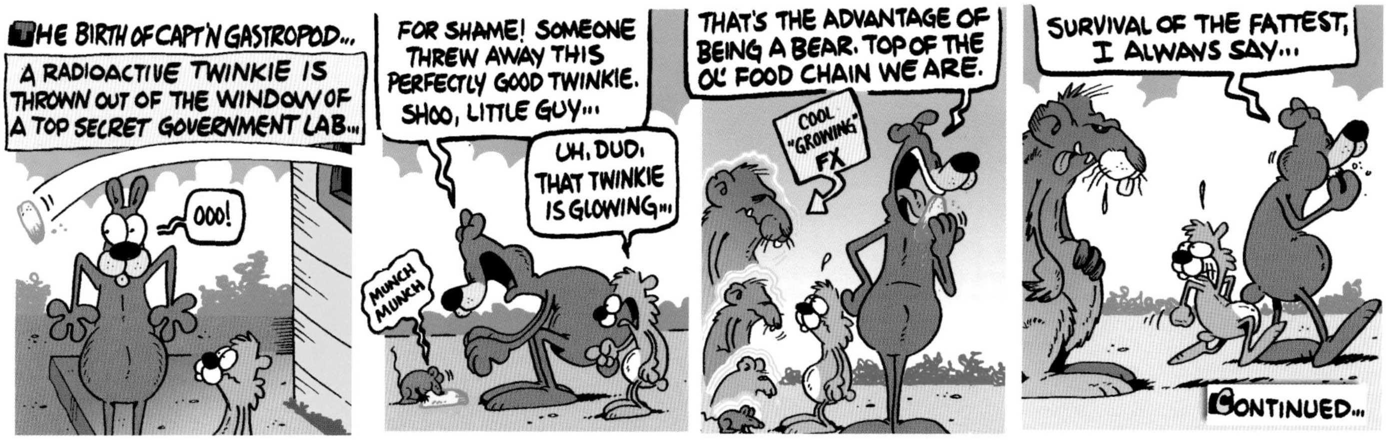
THE BIRTH OF CAPT'N GASTROPOD...
A RADIOACTIVE TWINKIE IS THROWN OUT OF THE WINDOW OF A TOP SECRET GOVERNMENT LAB...
OOO!
FOR SHAME! SOMEONE THREW AWAY THIS PERFECTLY GOOD TWINKIE. SHOO, LITTLE GUY...
UH, DUD, THAT TWINKIE IS GLOWING...
MUNCH MUNCH
THAT'S THE ADVANTAGE OF BEING A BEAR. TOP OF THE OL' FOOD CHAIN WE ARE.
COOL "GROWING" FX
SURVIVAL OF THE FATTEST, I ALWAYS SAY...
CONTINUED...

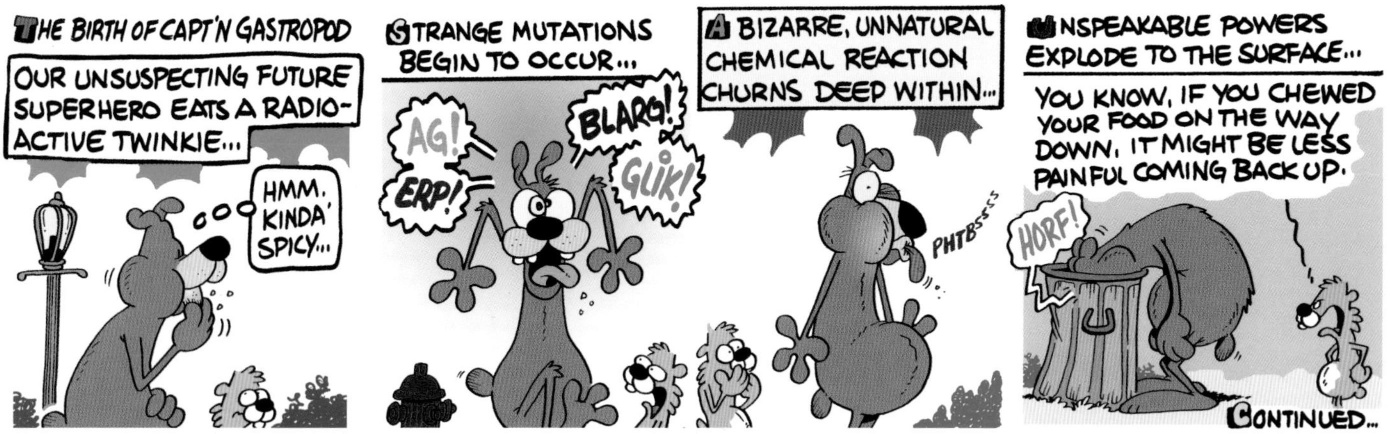
THE BIRTH OF CAPT'N GASTROPOD
OUR UNSUSPECTING FUTURE SUPERHERO EATS A RADIOACTIVE TWINKIE...
HMM. KINDA' SPICY...
STRANGE MUTATIONS BEGIN TO OCCUR...
AG!
BLARG!
ERP!
GLIK!
A BIZARRE, UNNATURAL CHEMICAL REACTION CHURNS DEEP WITHIN...
PHTBSSSS
UNSPEAKABLE POWERS EXPLODE TO THE SURFACE...
YOU KNOW, IF YOU CHEWED YOUR FOOD ON THE WAY DOWN, IT MIGHT BE LESS PAINFUL COMING BACK UP.
HORF!
CONTINUED...

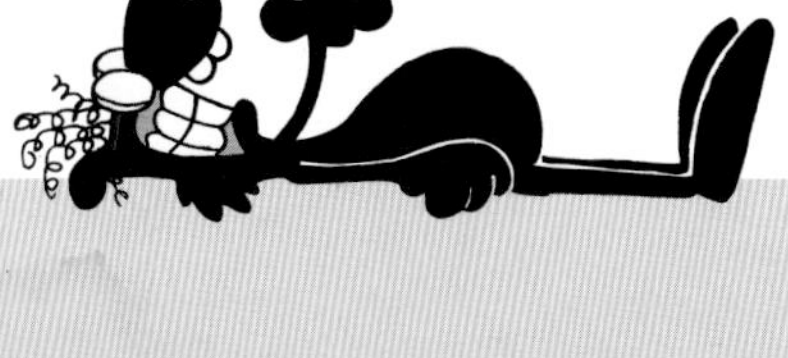

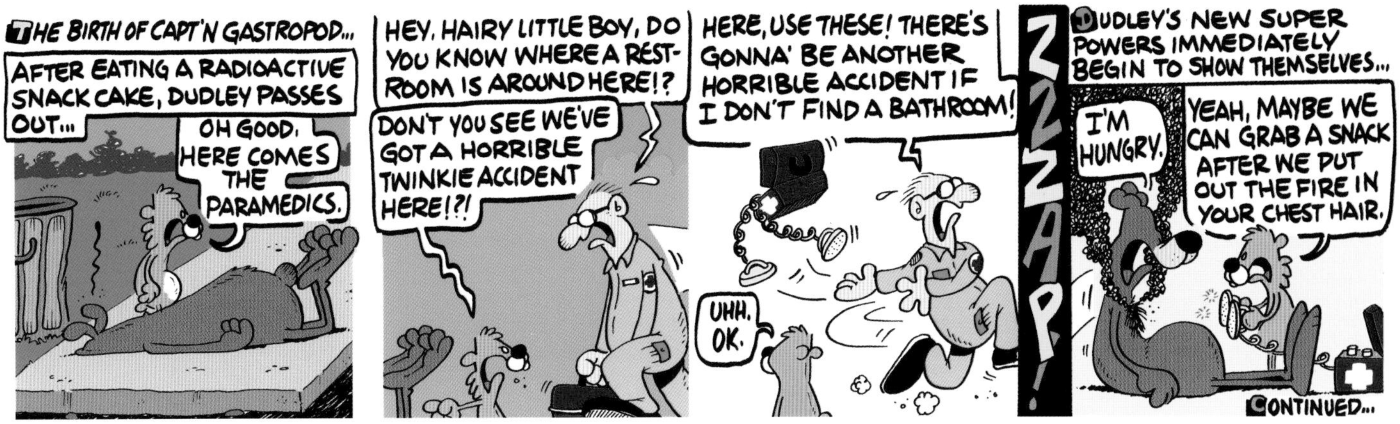
THE BIRTH OF CAPT'N GASTROPOD...
AFTER EATING A RADIOACTIVE SNACK CAKE, DUDLEY PASSES OUT...
OH GOOD, HERE COMES THE PARAMEDICS.
HEY, HAIRY LITTLE BOY, DO YOU KNOW WHERE A REST-ROOM IS AROUND HERE!?
DON'T YOU SEE WE'VE GOT A HORRIBLE TWINKIE ACCIDENT HERE!?!
HERE, USE THESE! THERE'S GONNA' BE ANOTHER HORRIBLE ACCIDENT IF I DON'T FIND A BATHROOM!
UHH, OK.
ZZZAP!
DUDLEY'S NEW SUPER POWERS IMMEDIATELY BEGIN TO SHOW THEMSELVES...
I'M HUNGRY.
YEAH, MAYBE WE CAN GRAB A SNACK AFTER WE PUT OUT THE FIRE IN YOUR CHEST HAIR.
CONTINUED...

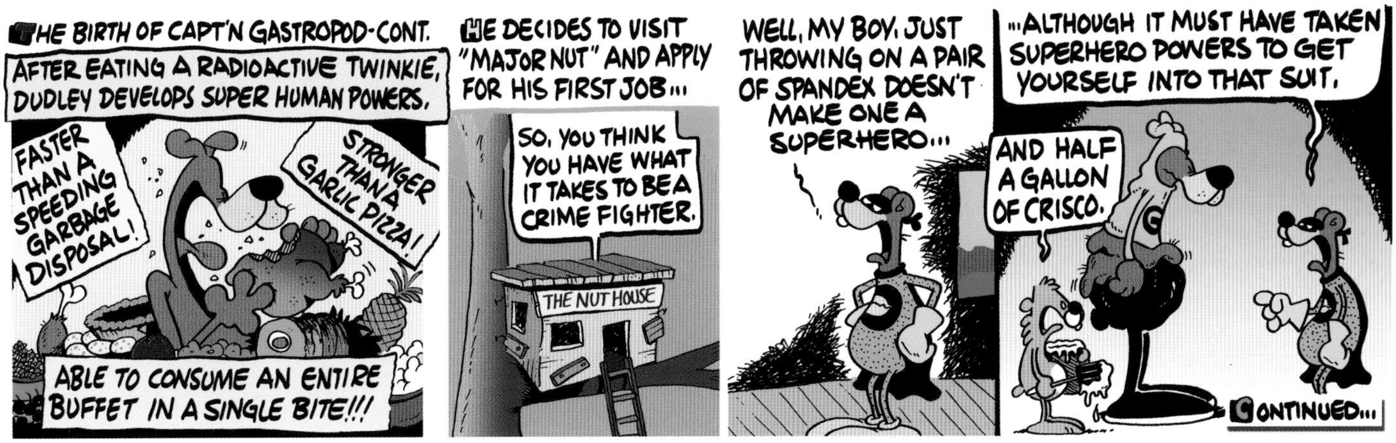
THE BIRTH OF CAPT'N GASTROPOD-CONT.
AFTER EATING A RADIOACTIVE TWINKIE, DUDLEY DEVELOPS SUPER HUMAN POWERS.
FASTER THAN A SPEEDING GARBAGE DISPOSAL!
STRONGER THAN A GARLIC PIZZA!
ABLE TO CONSUME AN ENTIRE BUFFET IN A SINGLE BITE!!!
HE DECIDES TO VISIT "MAJOR NUT" AND APPLY FOR HIS FIRST JOB...
SO, YOU THINK YOU HAVE WHAT IT TAKES TO BE A CRIME FIGHTER.
THE NUT HOUSE
WELL, MY BOY, JUST THROWING ON A PAIR OF SPANDEX DOESN'T MAKE ONE A SUPERHERO...
...ALTHOUGH IT MUST HAVE TAKEN SUPERHERO POWERS TO GET YOURSELF INTO THAT SUIT.
AND HALF A GALLON OF CRISCO.
CONTINUED...

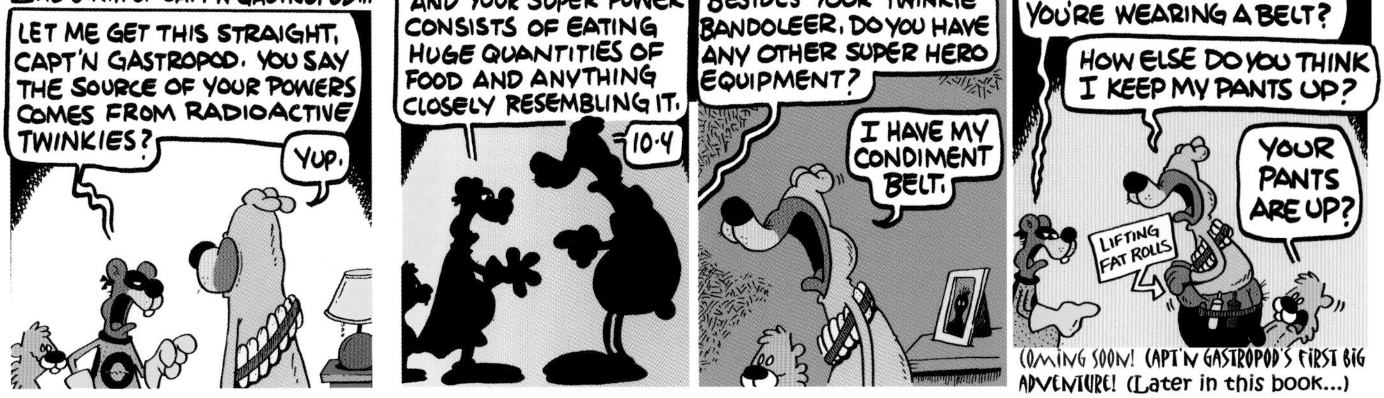
THE BIRTH OF CAPT'N GASTROPOD...
LET ME GET THIS STRAIGHT, CAPT'N GASTROPOD. YOU SAY THE SOURCE OF YOUR POWERS COMES FROM RADIOACTIVE TWINKIES?
YUP.
AND YOUR SUPER POWER CONSISTS OF EATING HUGE QUANTITIES OF FOOD AND ANYTHING CLOSELY RESEMBLING IT.
10-4
BESIDES YOUR TWINKIE BANDOLEER, DO YOU HAVE ANY OTHER SUPER HERO EQUIPMENT?
I HAVE MY CONDIMENT BELT.
YOU'RE WEARING A BELT?
HOW ELSE DO YOU THINK I KEEP MY PANTS UP?
YOUR PANTS ARE UP?
LIFTING FAT ROLLS
COMING SOON! CAPT'N GASTROPOD'S FIRST BIG ADVENTURE! (Later in this book...)

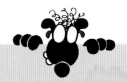

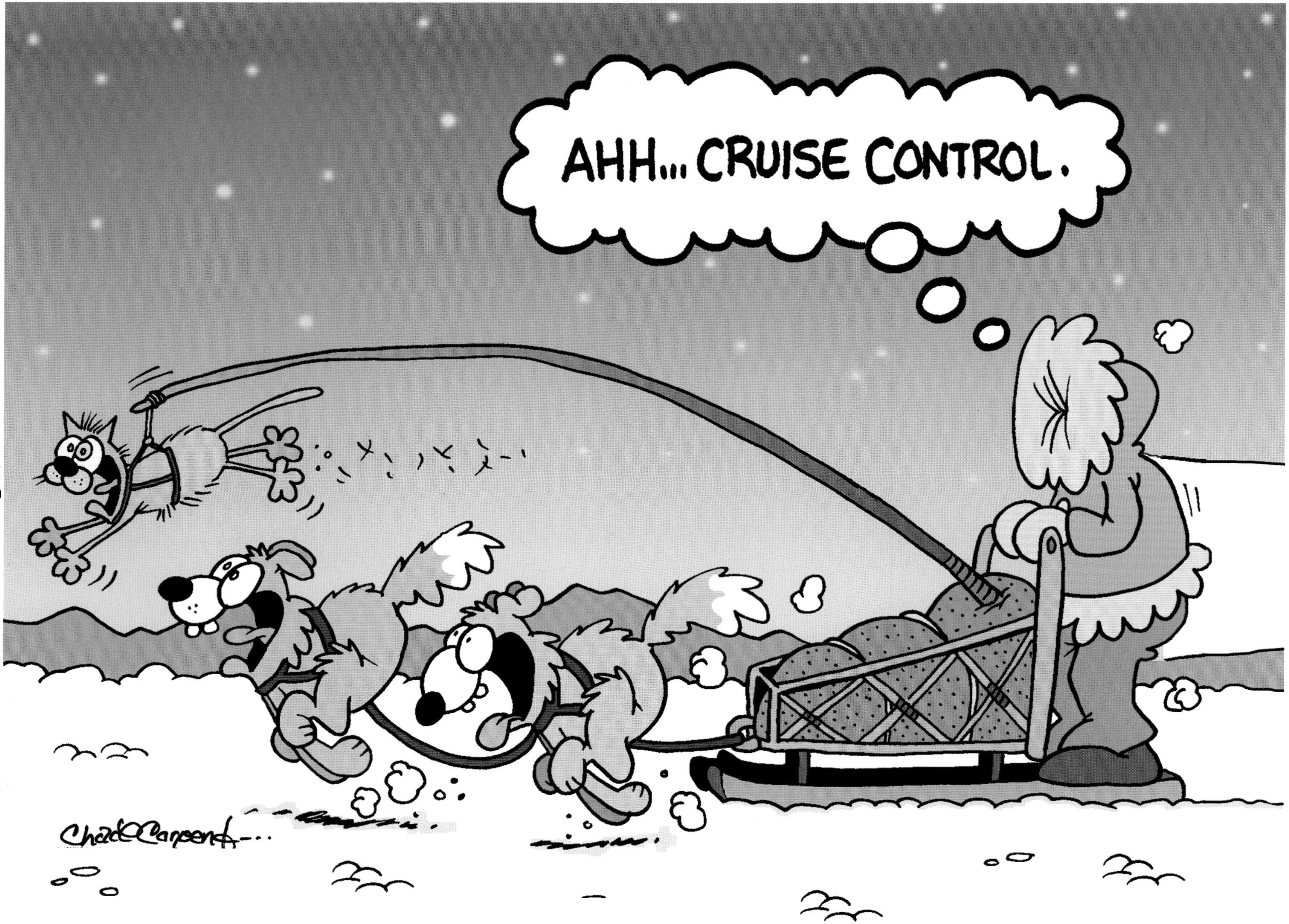
AHH... CRUISE CONTROL.
Chad Carpenter

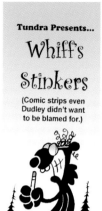

Tundra Presents...

Whiff's Stinkers

(Comic strips even Dudley didn't want to be blamed for.)

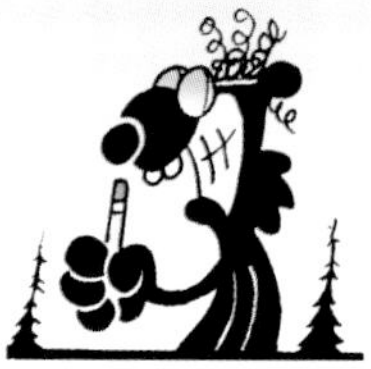

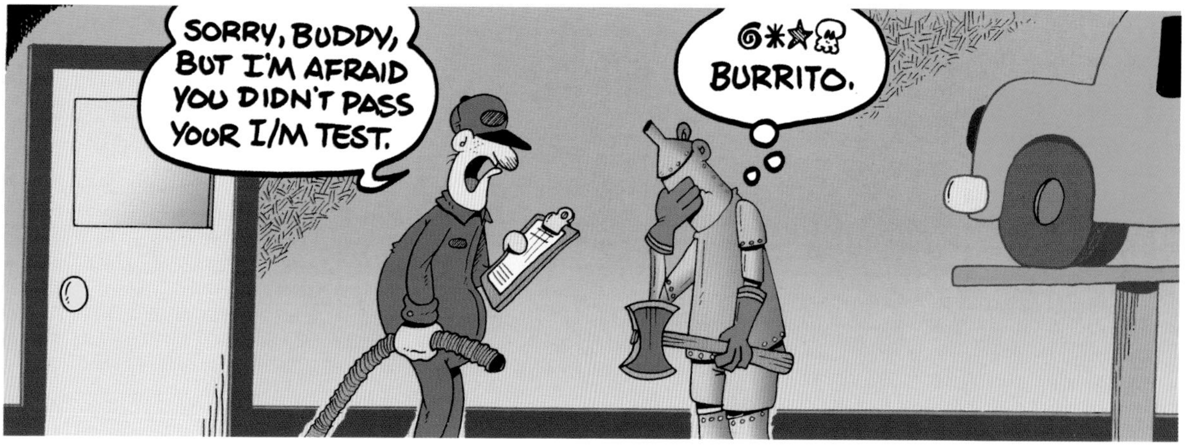
SORRY, BUDDY, BUT I'M AFRAID YOU DIDN'T PASS YOUR I/M TEST.
BURRITO.

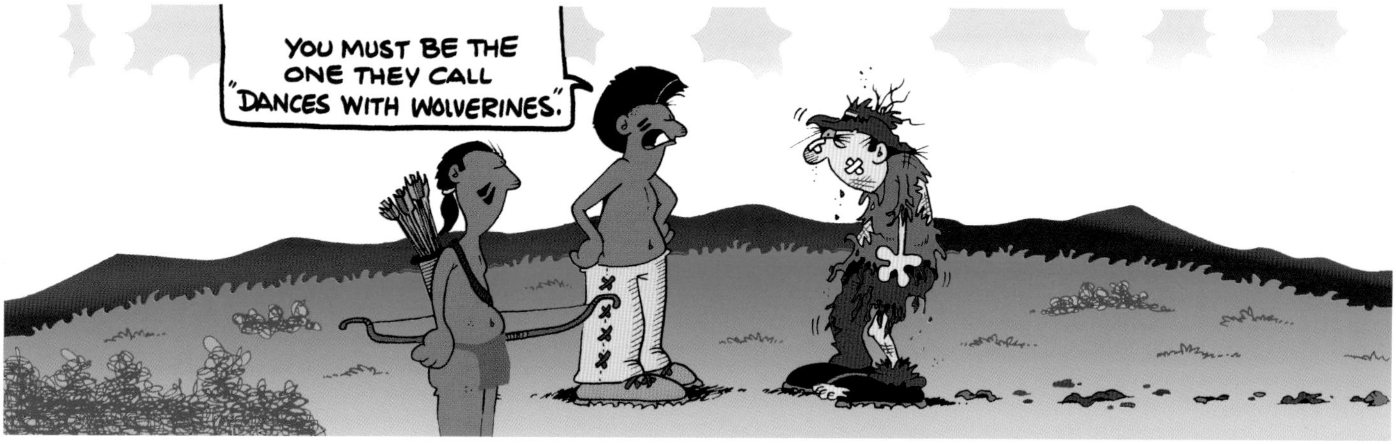
YOU MUST BE THE ONE THEY CALL "DANCES WITH WOLVERINES."

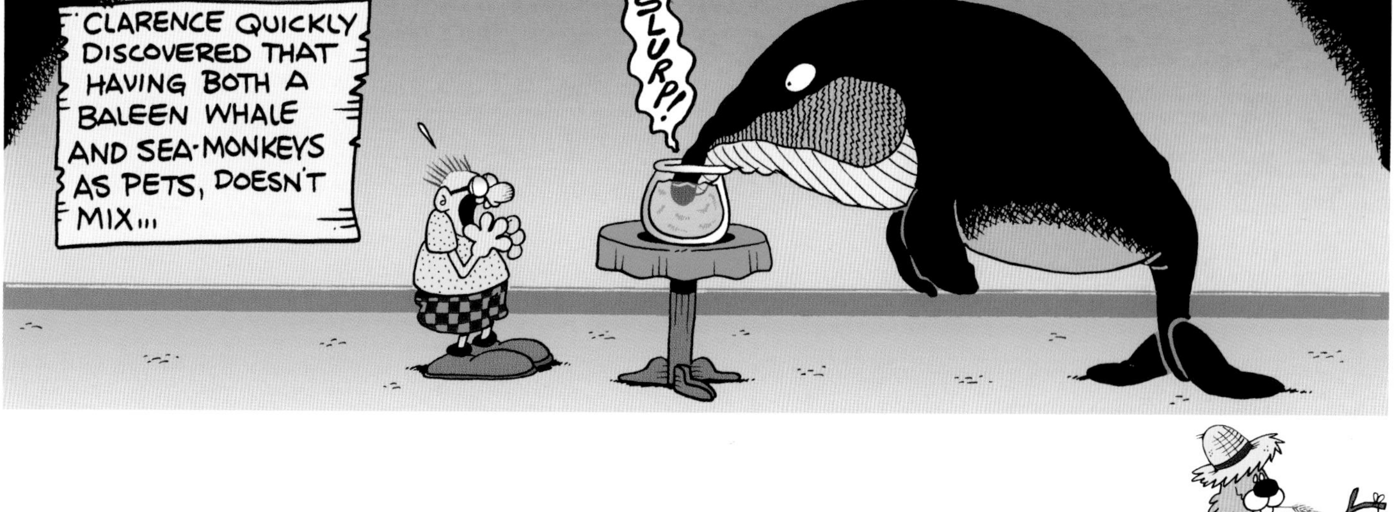
CLARENCE QUICKLY DISCOVERED THAT HAVING BOTH A BALEEN WHALE AND SEA-MONKEYS AS PETS, DOESN'T MIX...
SLURP!

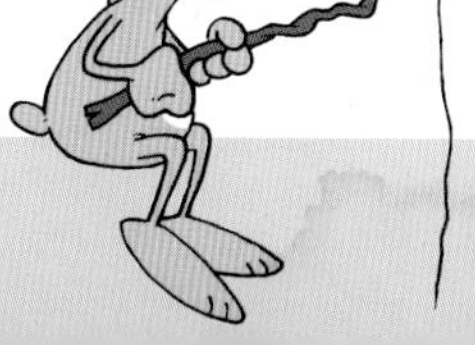

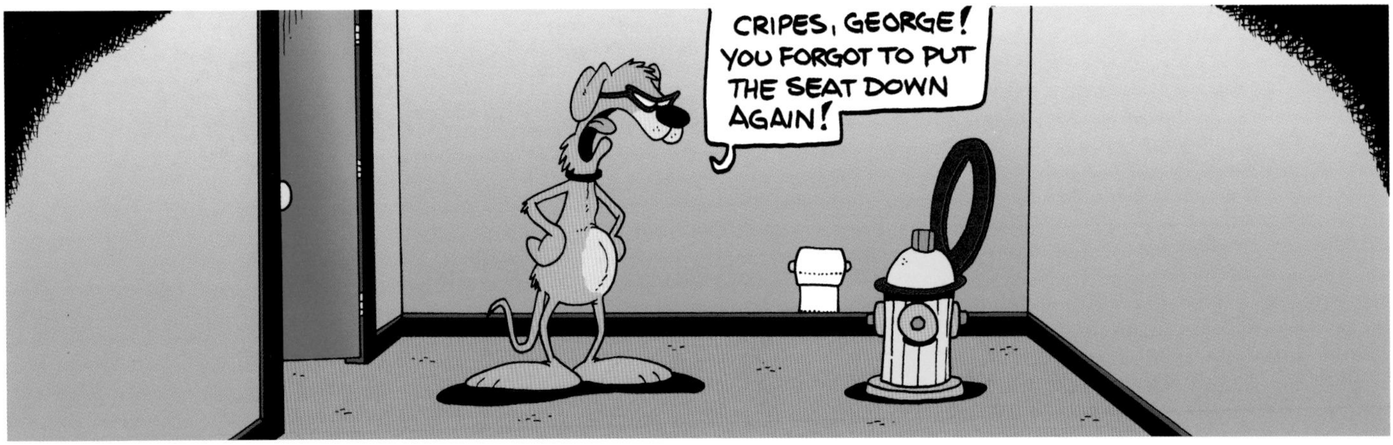
CRIPES, GEORGE! YOU FORGOT TO PUT THE SEAT DOWN AGAIN!

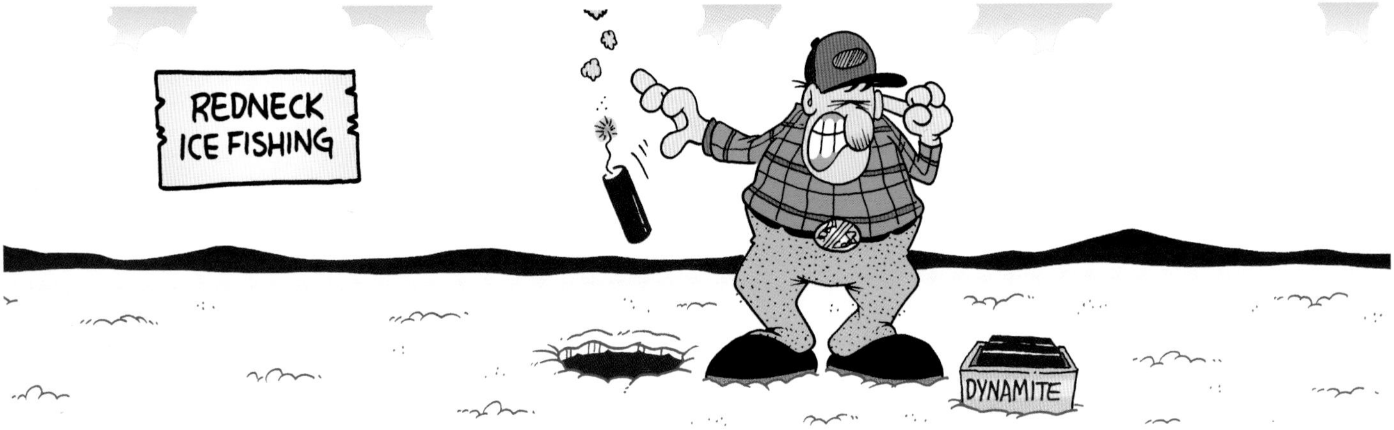
REDNECK ICE FISHING
DYNAMITE

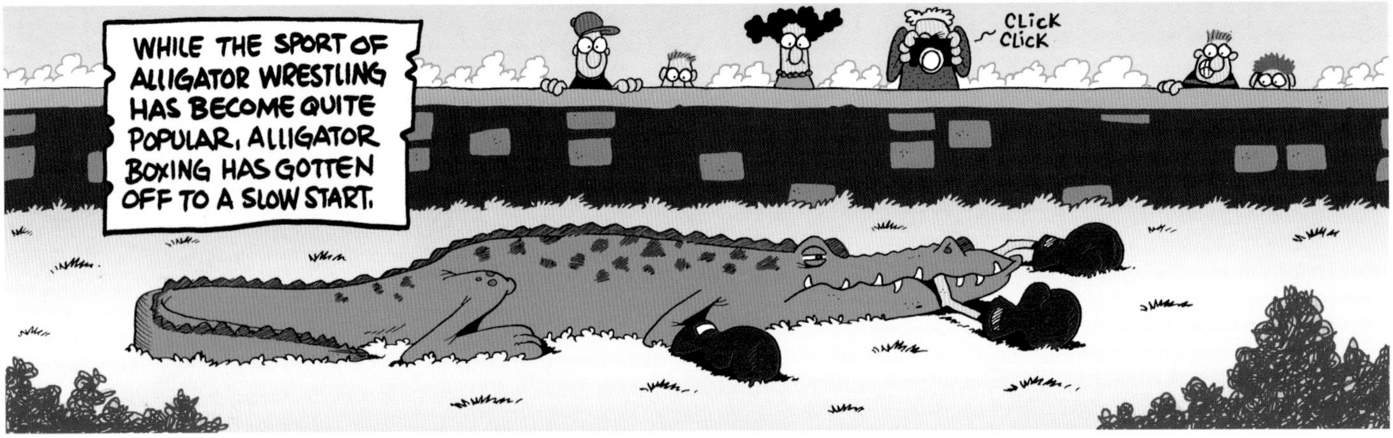
WHILE THE SPORT OF ALLIGATOR WRESTLING HAS BECOME QUITE POPULAR, ALLIGATOR BOXING HAS GOTTEN OFF TO A SLOW START.
CLICK CLICK

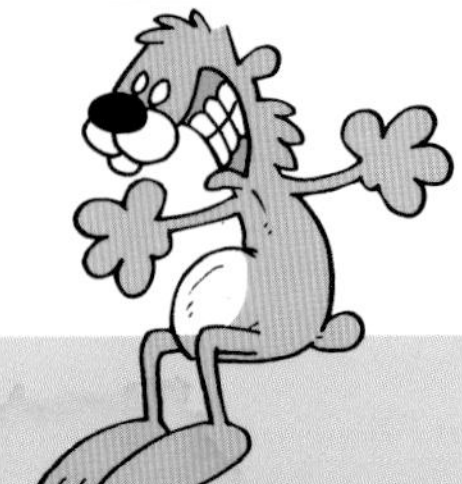

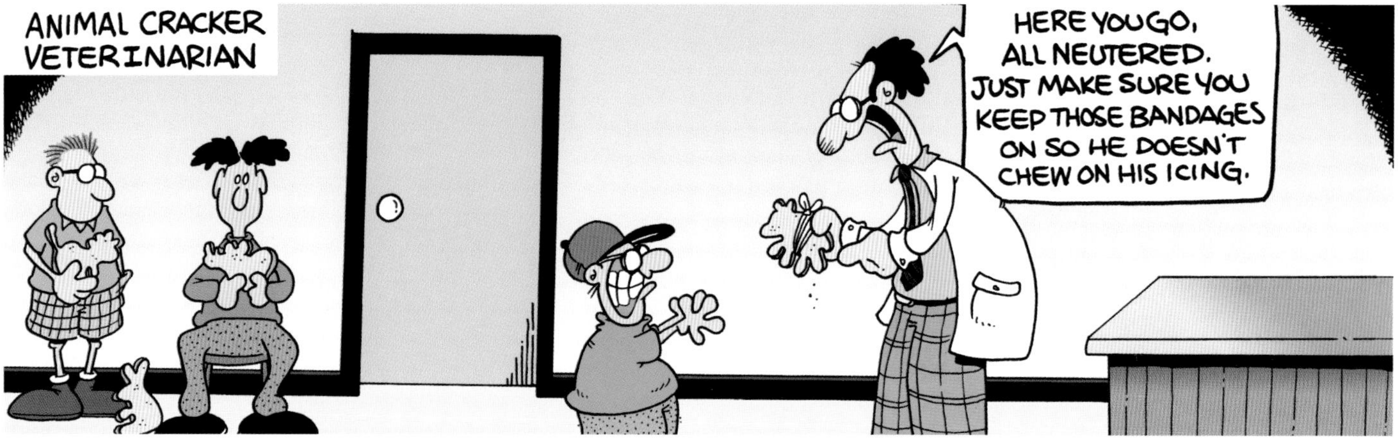
ANIMAL CRACKER VETERINARIAN
HERE YOU GO, ALL NEUTERED. JUST MAKE SURE YOU KEEP THOSE BANDAGES ON SO HE DOESN'T CHEW ON HIS ICING.

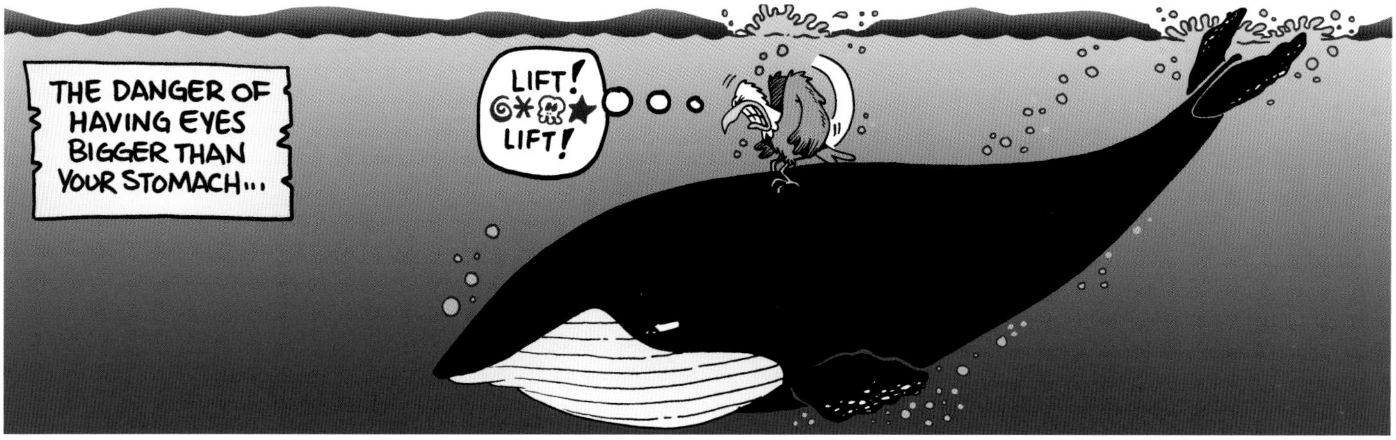
THE DANGER OF HAVING EYES BIGGER THAN YOUR STOMACH...
LIFT! @*#★ LIFT!

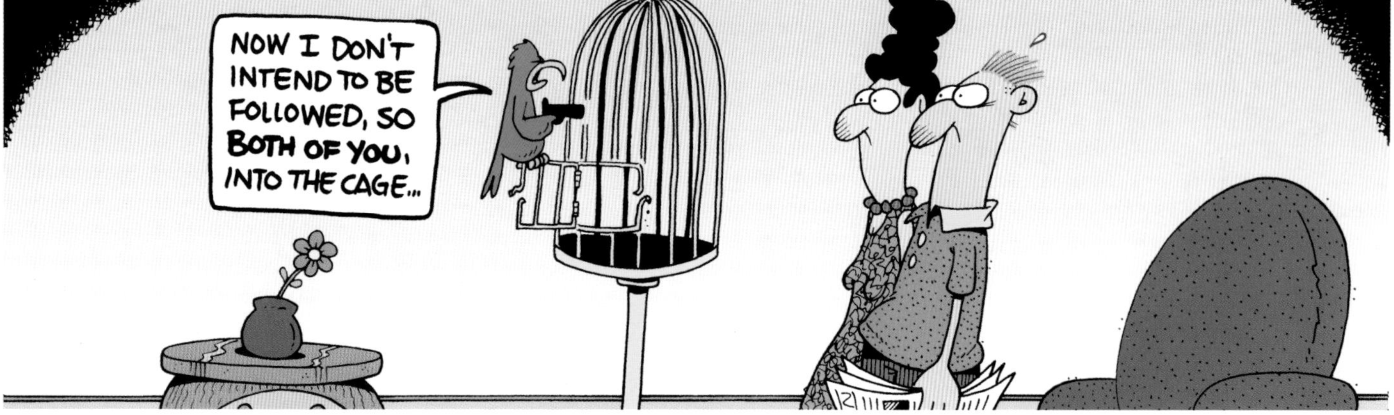
NOW I DON'T INTEND TO BE FOLLOWED, SO BOTH OF YOU, INTO THE CAGE...

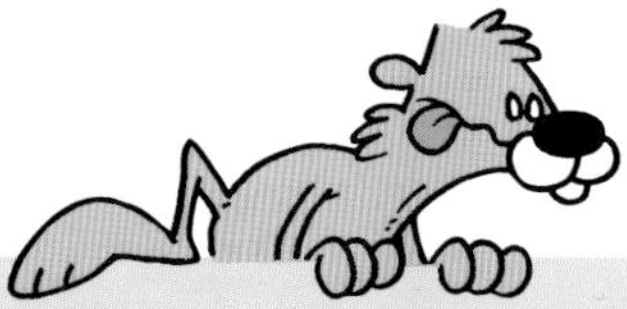

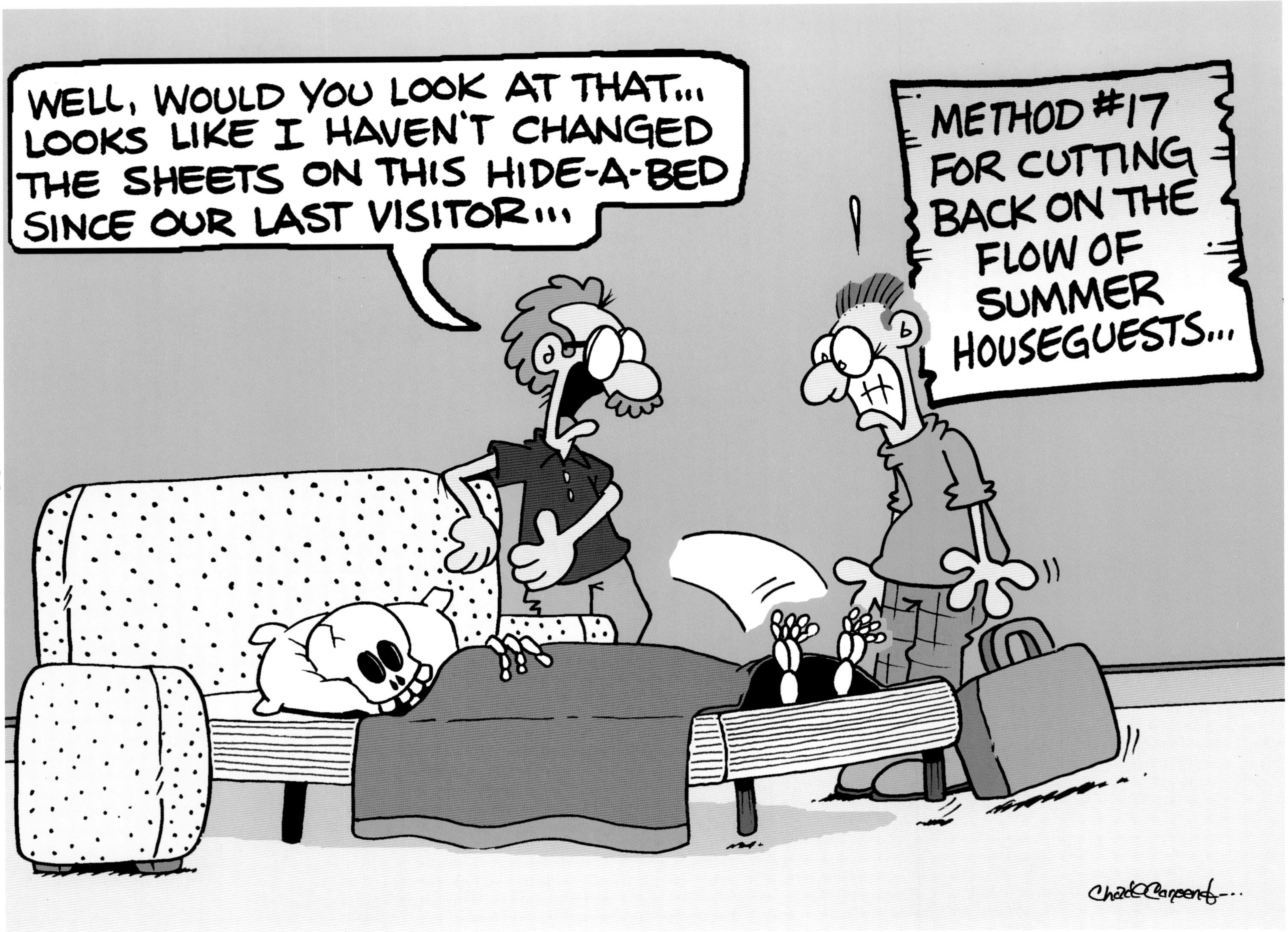
WELL, WOULD YOU LOOK AT THAT... LOOKS LIKE I HAVEN'T CHANGED THE SHEETS ON THIS HIDE-A-BED SINCE OUR LAST VISITOR...
METHOD #17 FOR CUTTING BACK ON THE FLOW OF SUMMER HOUSEGUESTS...

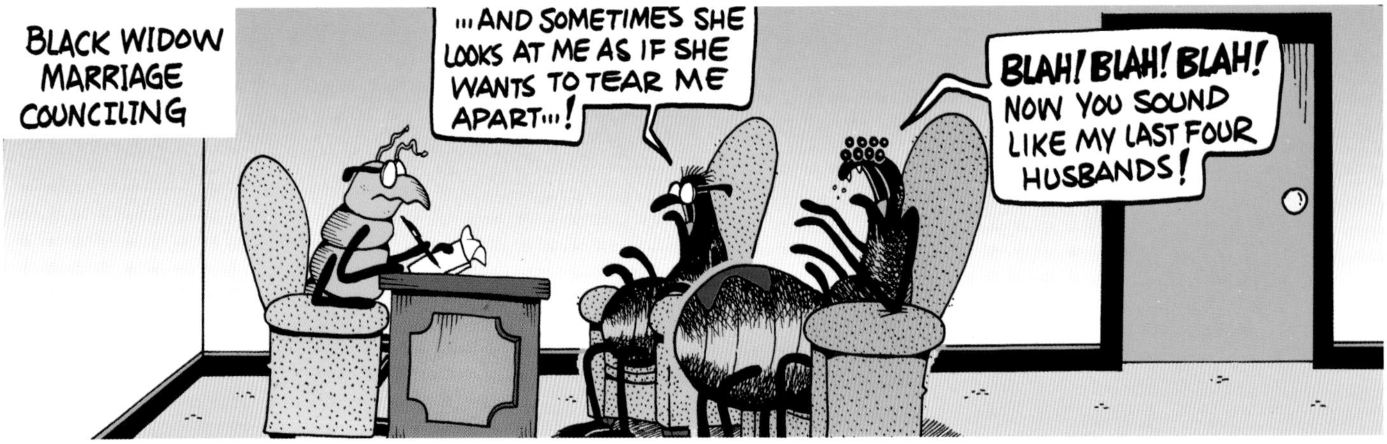
BLACK WIDOW MARRIAGE COUNCILING
...AND SOMETIMES SHE LOOKS AT ME AS IF SHE WANTS TO TEAR ME APART...!
BLAH! BLAH! BLAH! NOW YOU SOUND LIKE MY LAST FOUR HUSBANDS!

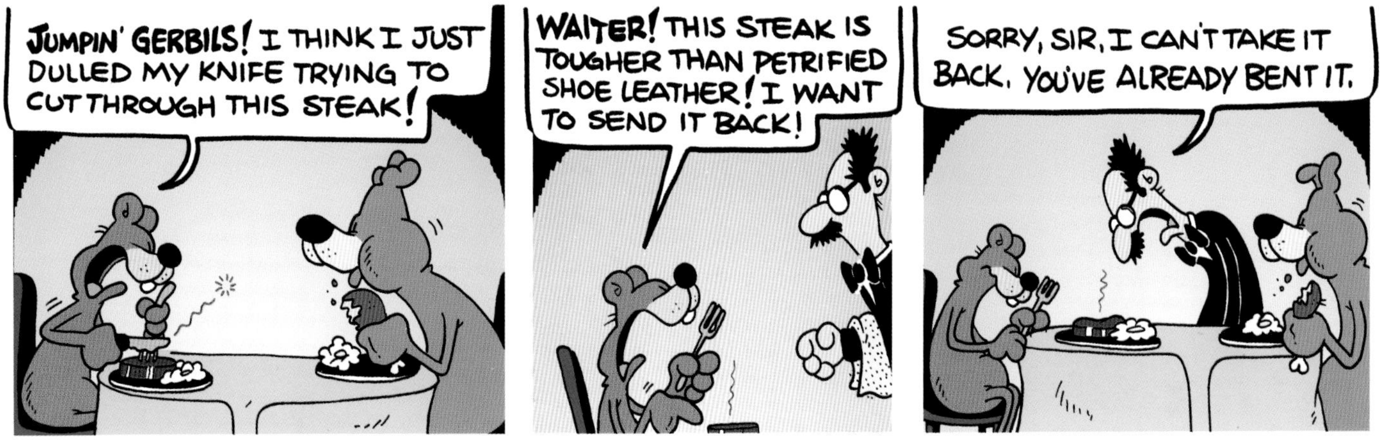
JUMPIN' GERBILS! I THINK I JUST DULLED MY KNIFE TRYING TO CUT THROUGH THIS STEAK!
WAITER! THIS STEAK IS TOUGHER THAN PETRIFIED SHOE LEATHER! I WANT TO SEND IT BACK!
SORRY, SIR, I CAN'T TAKE IT BACK. YOU'VE ALREADY BENT IT.

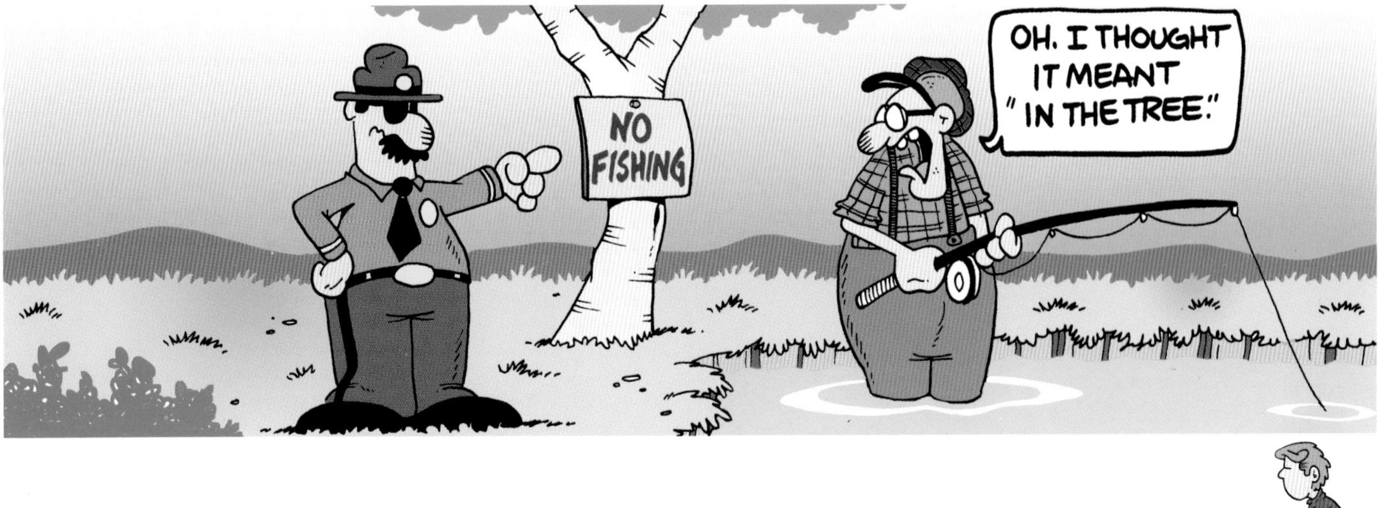
NO FISHING
OH. I THOUGHT IT MEANT "IN THE TREE."

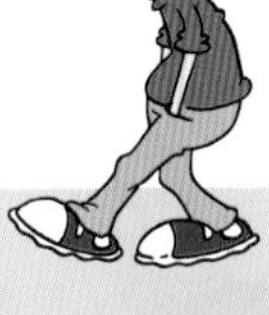

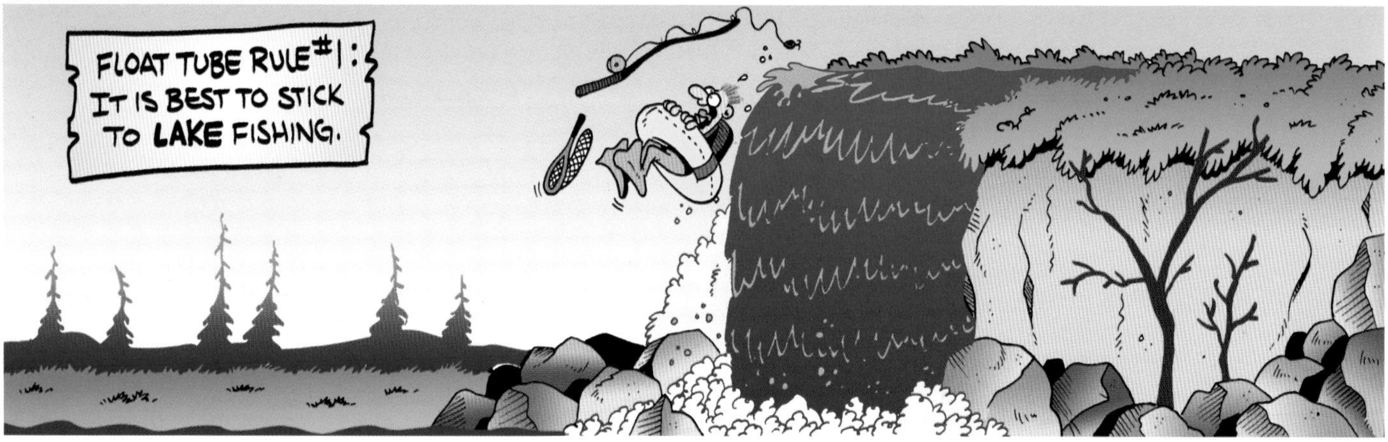
FLOAT TUBE RULE #1: IT IS BEST TO STICK TO LAKE FISHING.

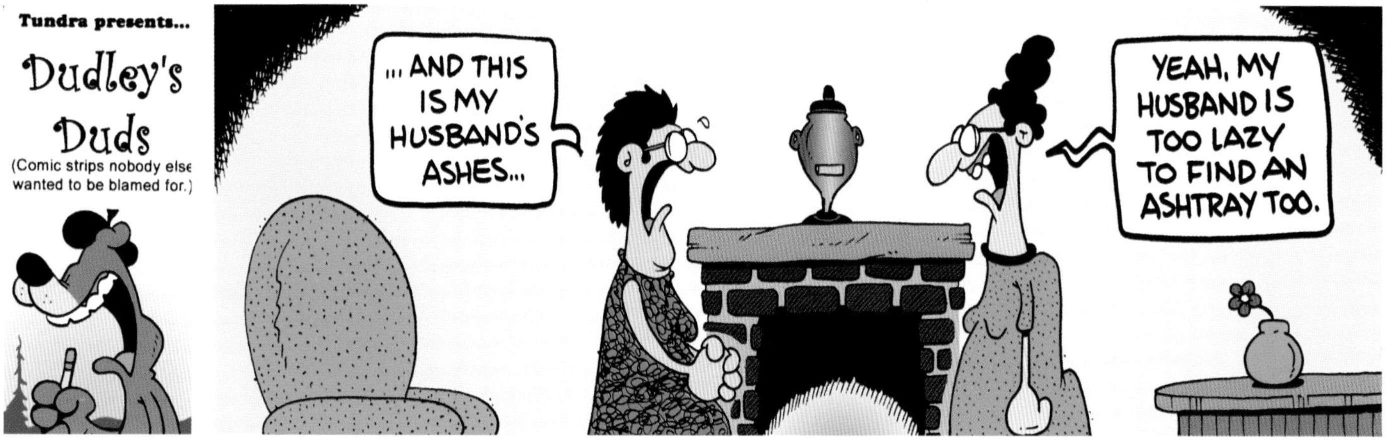
Tundra presents...
Dudley's Duds
(Comic strips nobody else wanted to be blamed for.)
...AND THIS IS MY HUSBAND'S ASHES...
YEAH, MY HUSBAND IS TOO LAZY TO FIND AN ASHTRAY TOO.

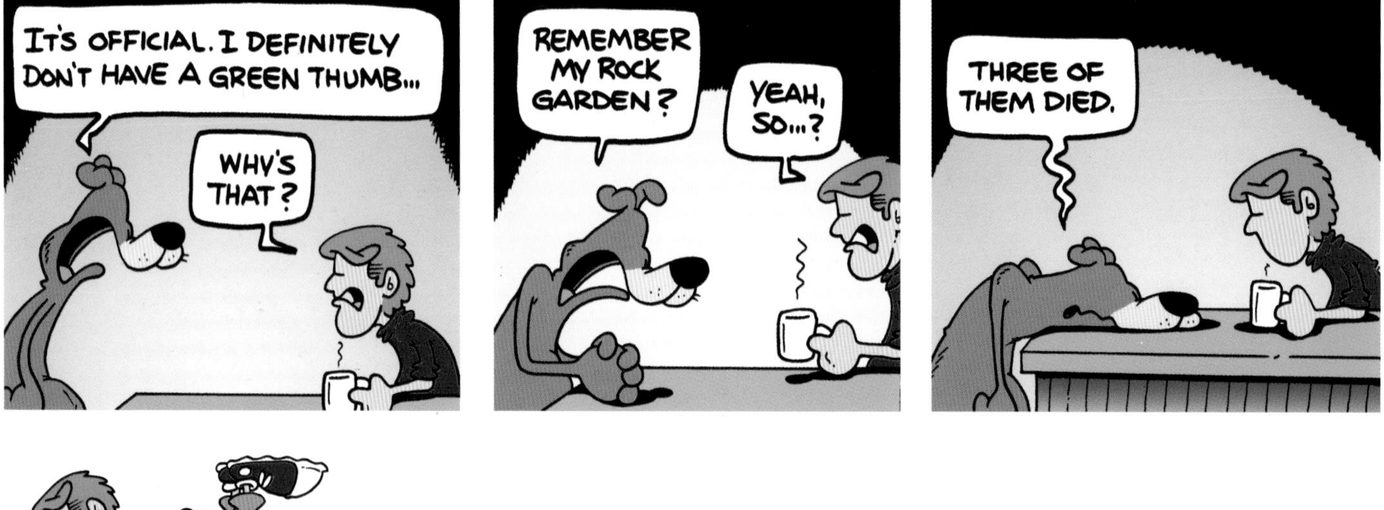
IT'S OFFICIAL. I DEFINITELY DON'T HAVE A GREEN THUMB...
WHY'S THAT?
REMEMBER MY ROCK GARDEN?
YEAH, SO...?
THREE OF THEM DIED.

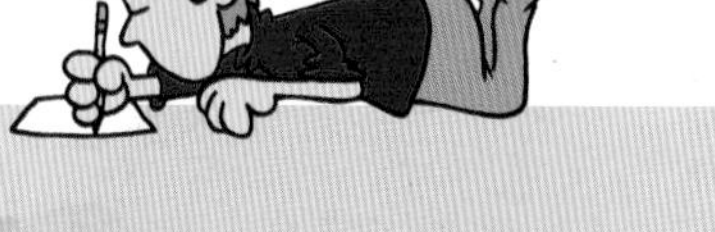

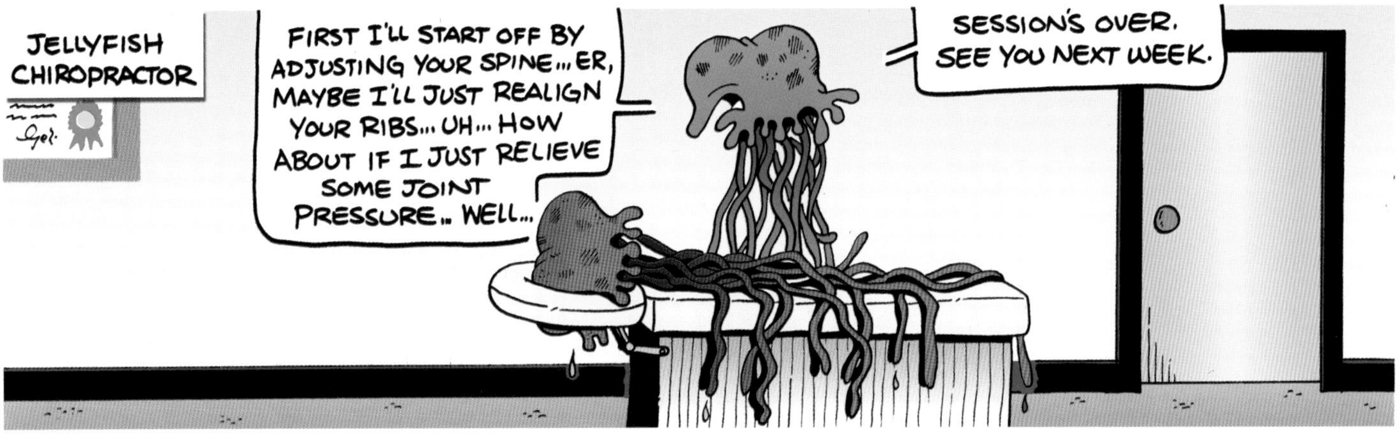

JELLYFISH CHIROPRACTOR
FIRST I'LL START OFF BY ADJUSTING YOUR SPINE... ER, MAYBE I'LL JUST REALIGN YOUR RIBS... UH... HOW ABOUT IF I JUST RELIEVE SOME JOINT PRESSURE.. WELL...
SESSION'S OVER. SEE YOU NEXT WEEK.

This comic strip is based on the idea of

Gerry Hooper
Wasilla, AK

Do you have an idea that would make a great comic strip? Send it to:

www.tundracomics.com

or

TUNDRA IDEAS
PO BOX 770732
Eagle River, AK
99577

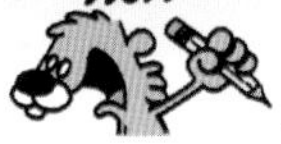

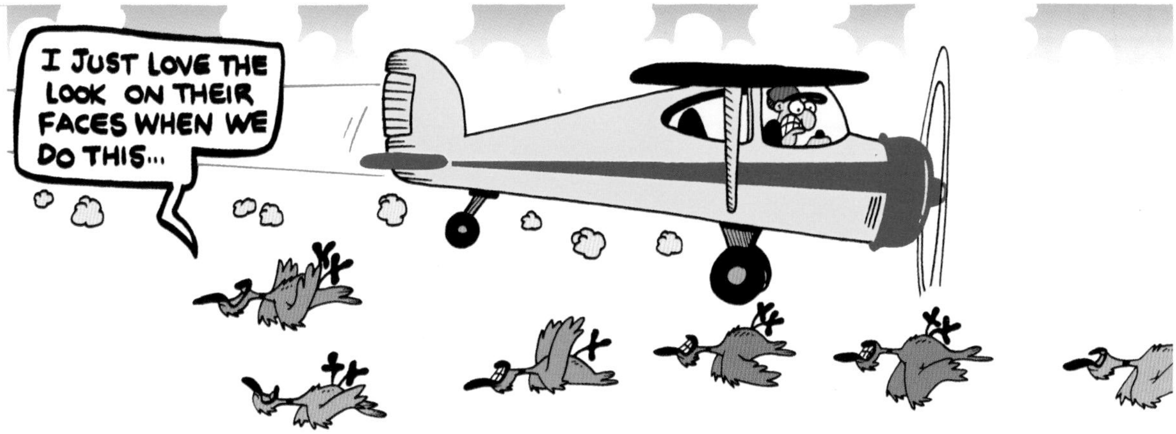

I JUST LOVE THE LOOK ON THEIR FACES WHEN WE DO THIS...

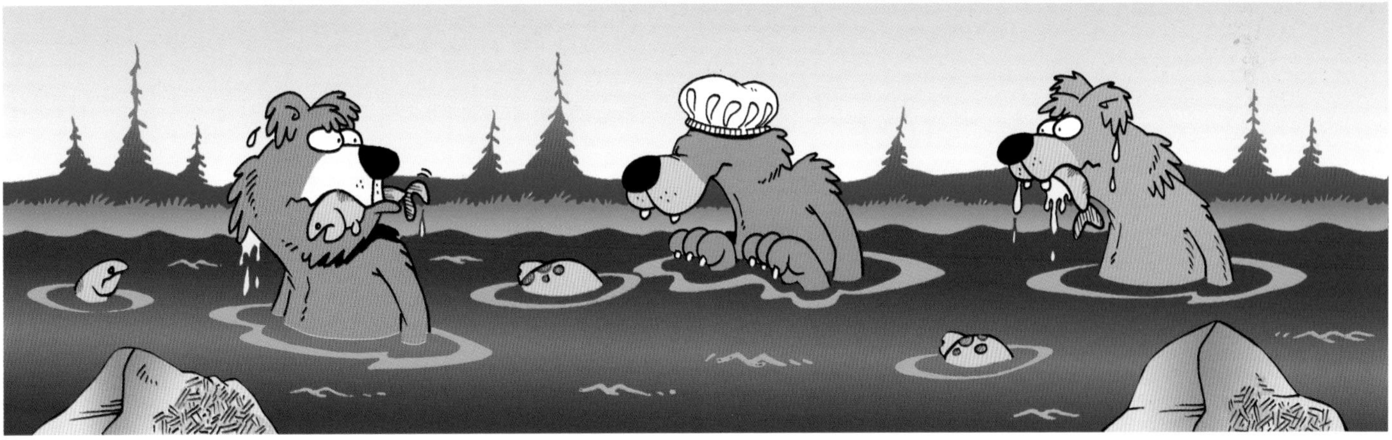

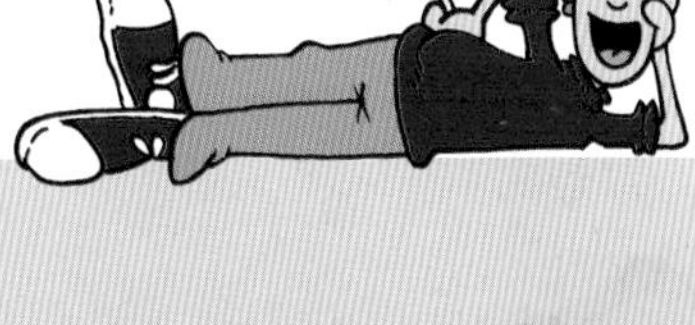

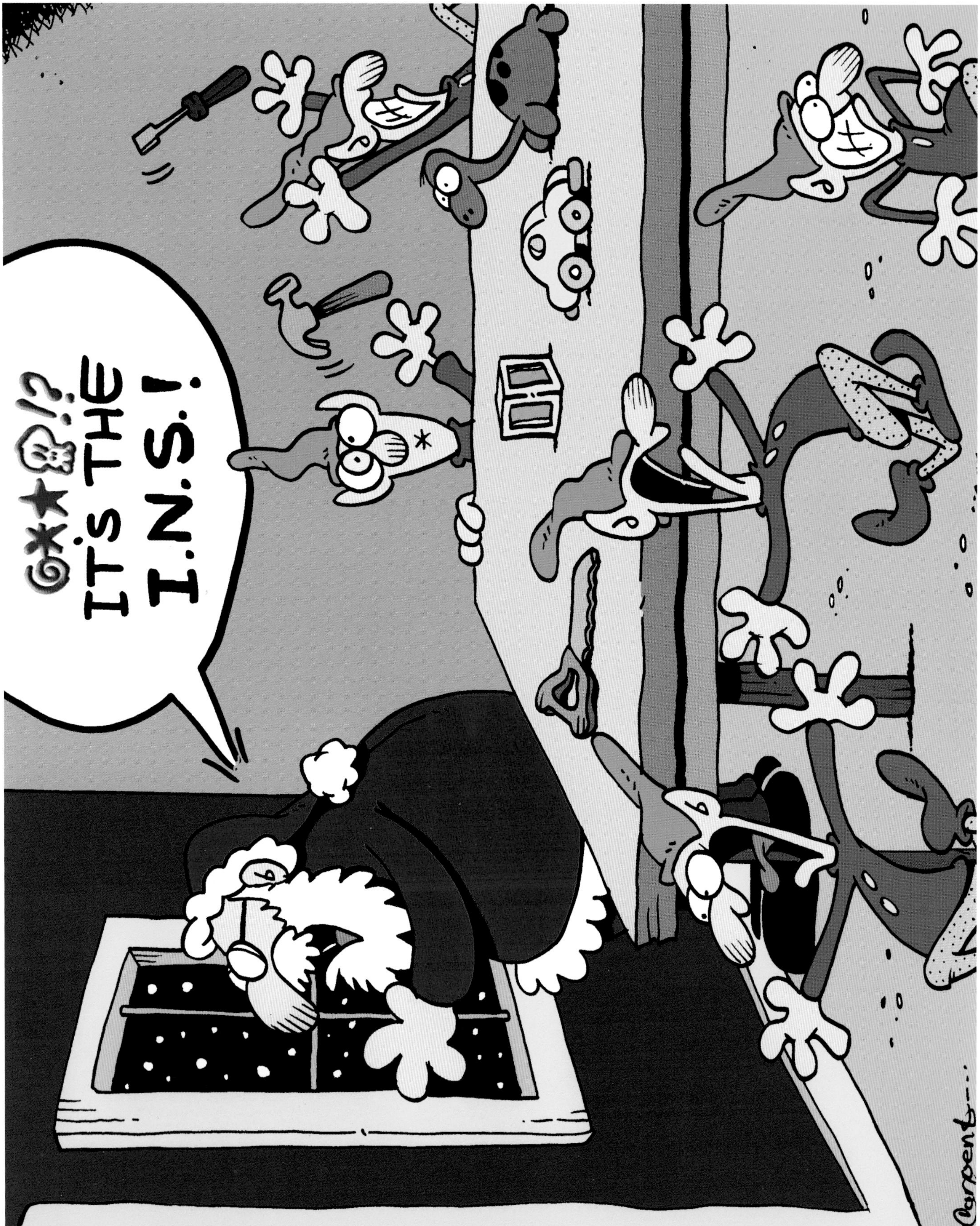
IT'S THE I.N.S.!

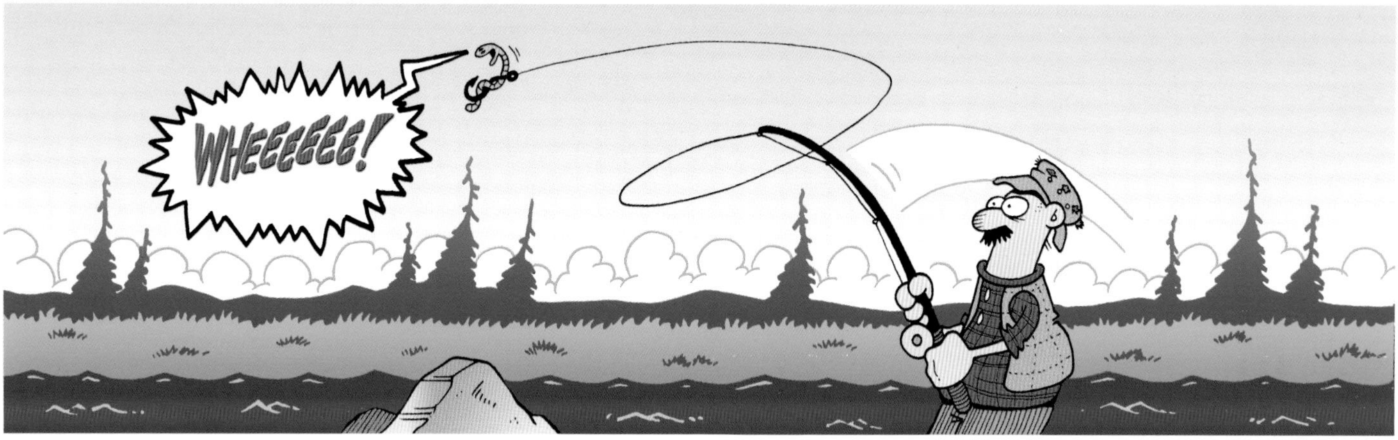
WHEEEEEEE!

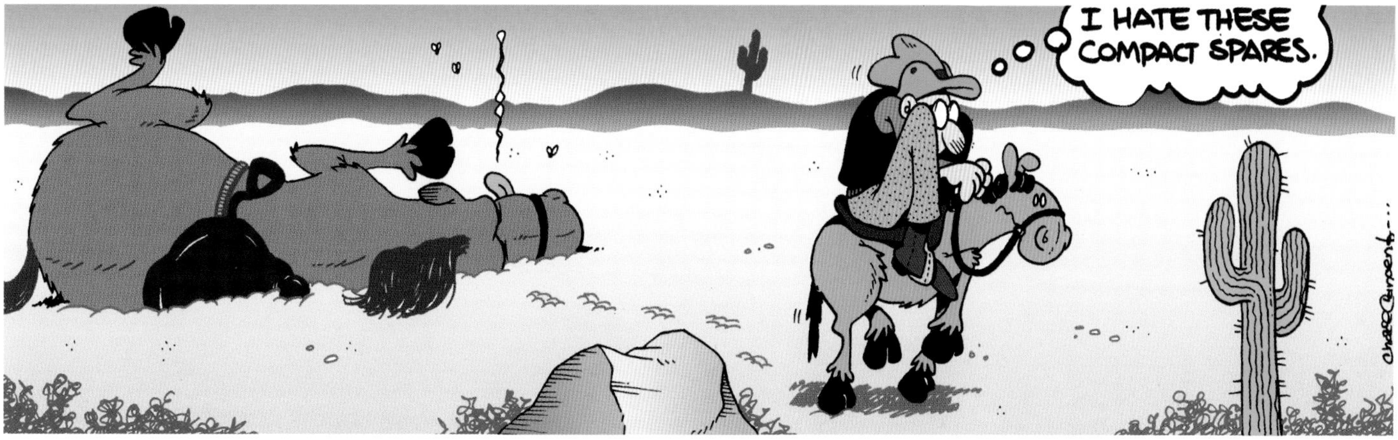
I HATE THESE COMPACT SPARES.

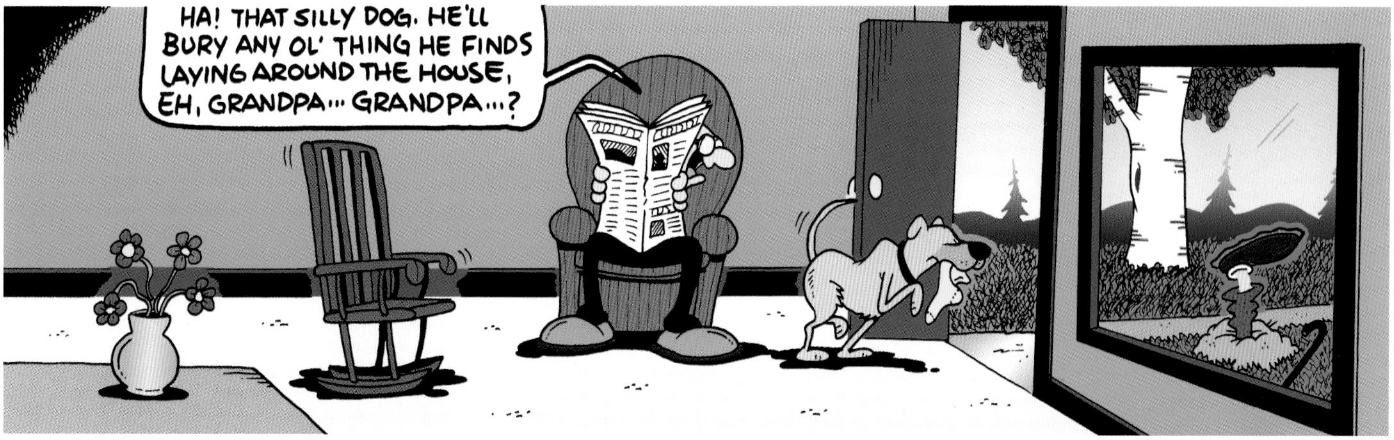
HA! THAT SILLY DOG. HE'LL BURY ANY OL' THING HE FINDS LAYING AROUND THE HOUSE, EH, GRANDPA... GRANDPA...?

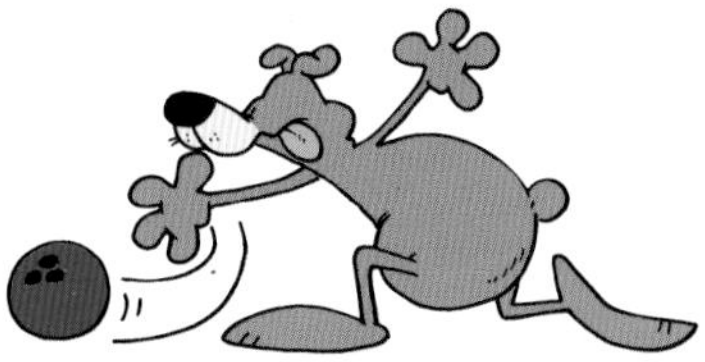

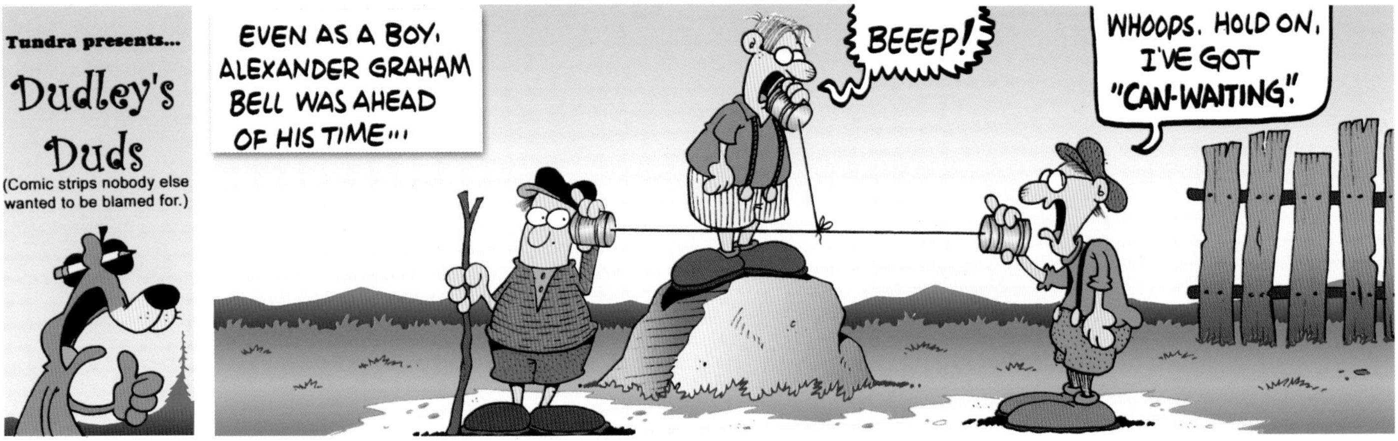
Tundra presents...
Dudley's Duds
(Comic strips nobody else wanted to be blamed for.)
EVEN AS A BOY, ALEXANDER GRAHAM BELL WAS AHEAD OF HIS TIME...
BEEEP!
WHOOPS. HOLD ON, I'VE GOT "CAN-WAITING."

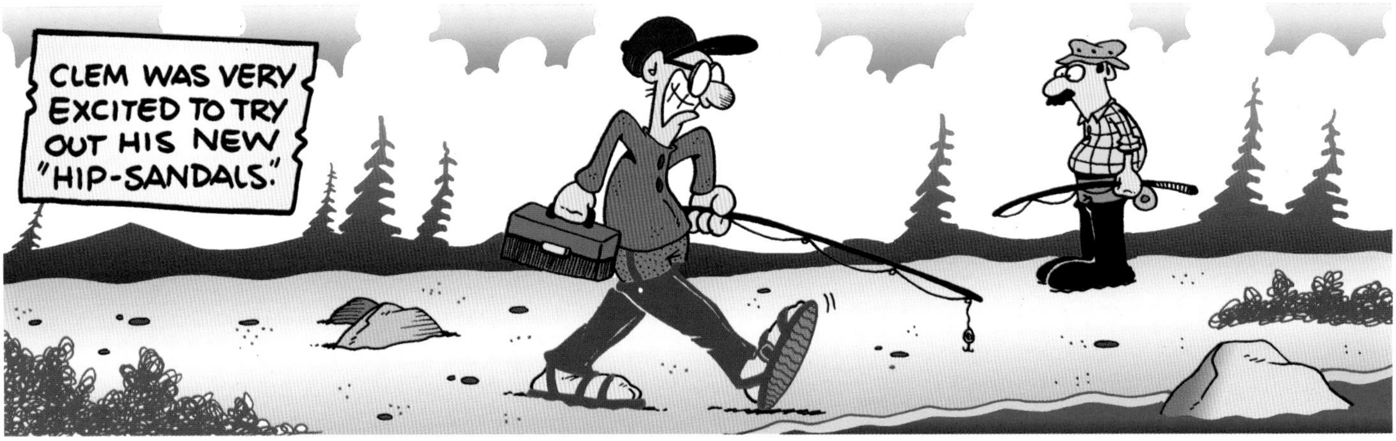
CLEM WAS VERY EXCITED TO TRY OUT HIS NEW "HIP-SANDALS."

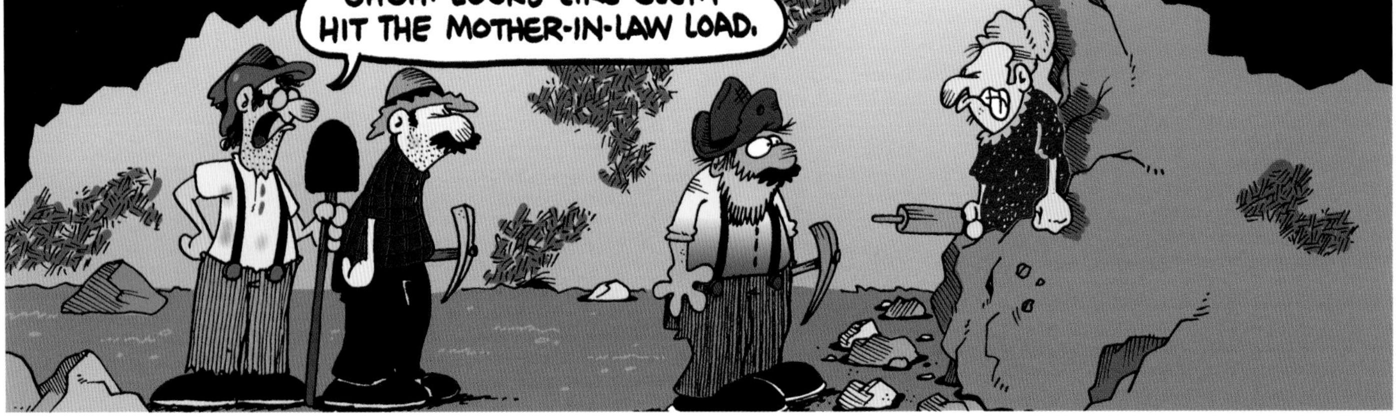
UHOH. LOOKS LIKE CLEM HIT THE MOTHER-IN-LAW LOAD.

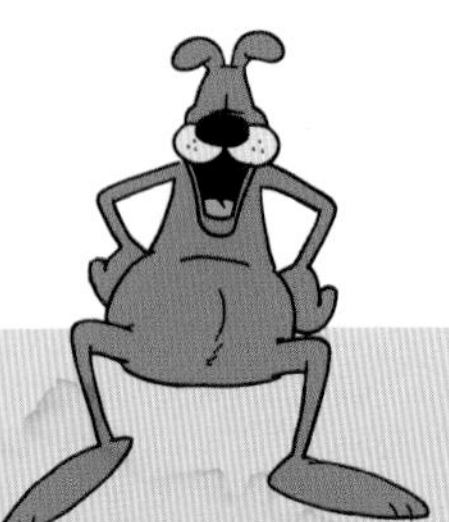

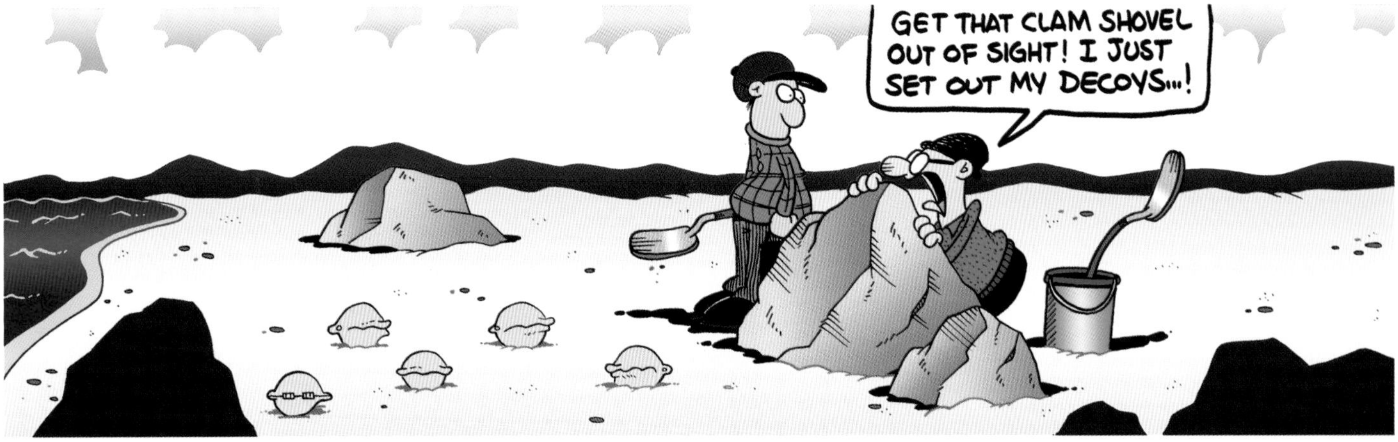
GET THAT CLAM SHOVEL OUT OF SIGHT! I JUST SET OUT MY DECOYS...!

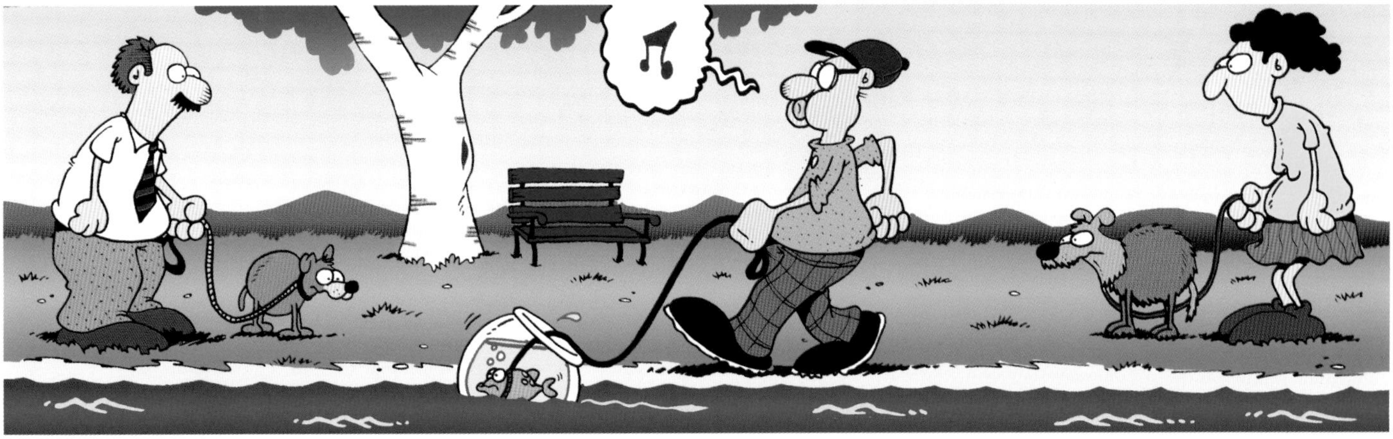

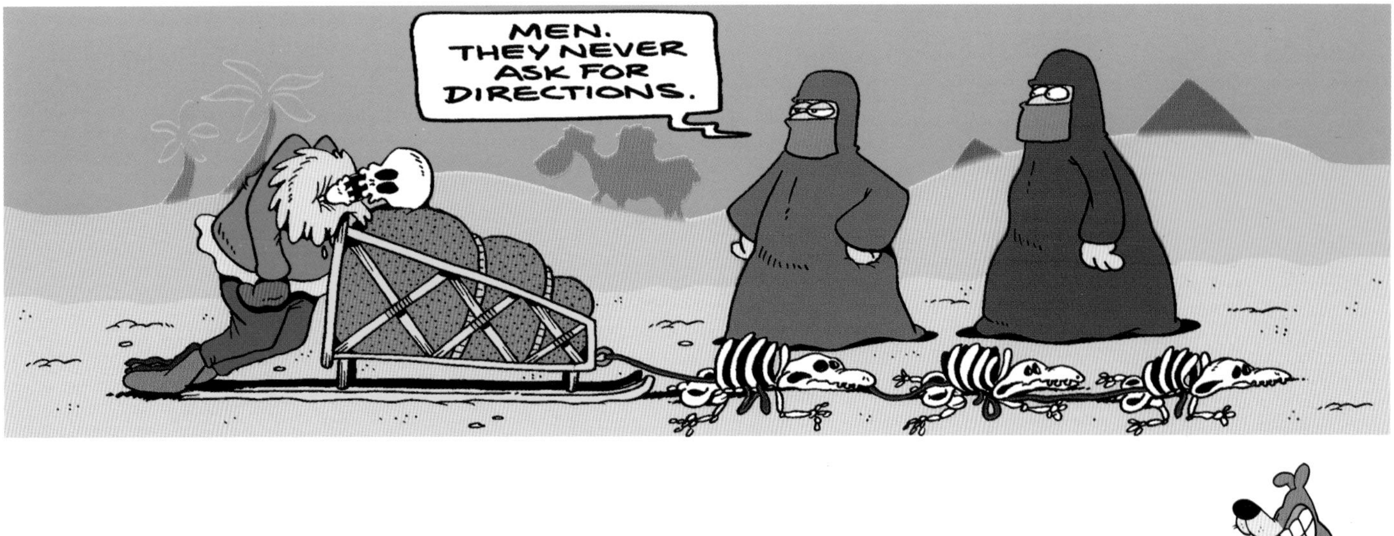
MEN. THEY NEVER ASK FOR DIRECTIONS.

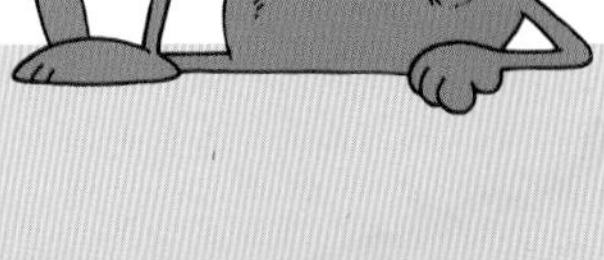

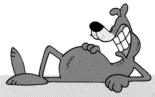

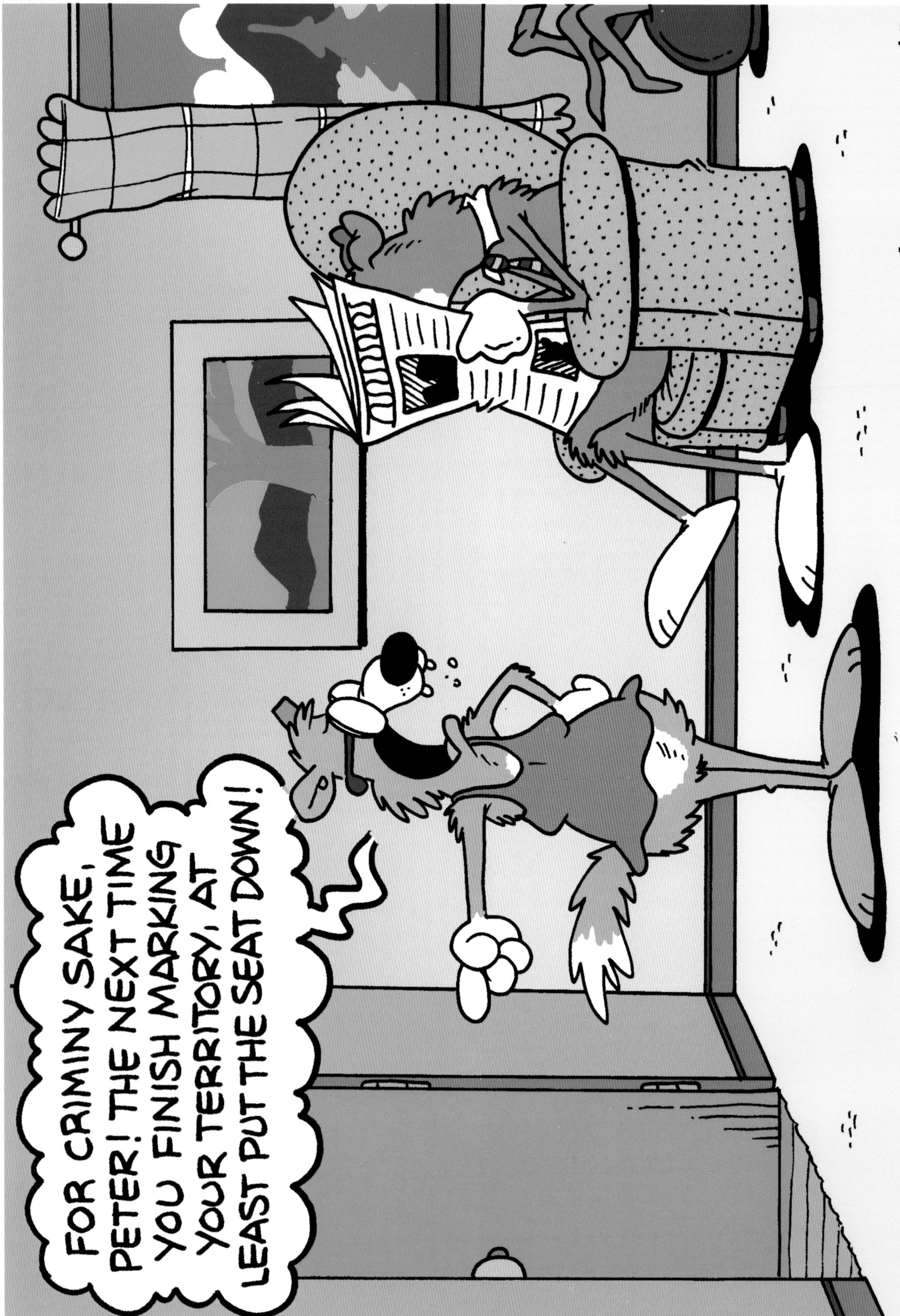
FOR CRIMINY SAKE, PETER! THE NEXT TIME YOU FINISH MARKING YOUR TERRITORY, AT LEAST PUT THE SEAT DOWN!
©TUNDRA 2001

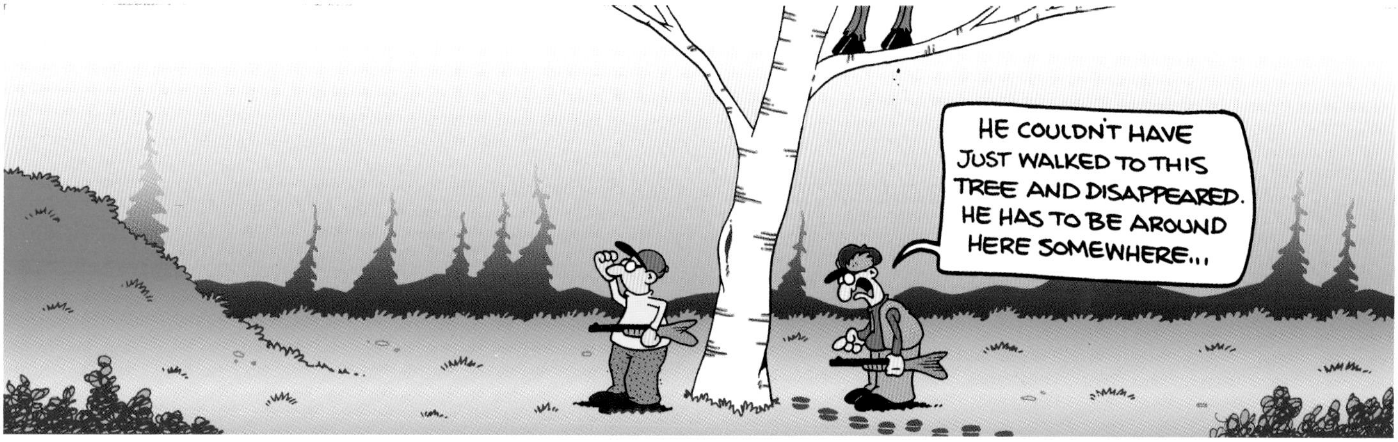
HE COULDN'T HAVE JUST WALKED TO THIS TREE AND DISAPPEARED. HE HAS TO BE AROUND HERE SOMEWHERE...

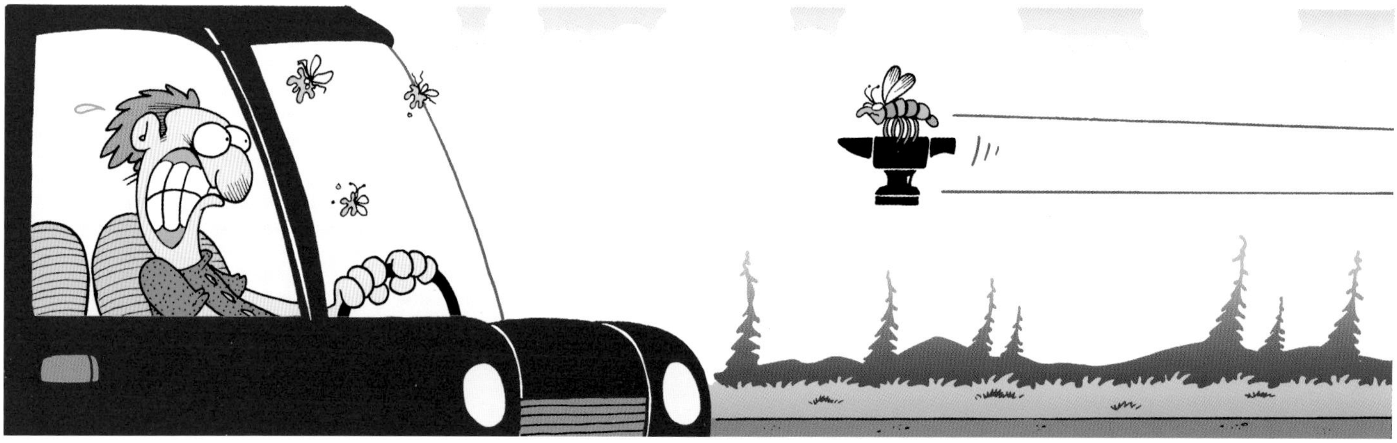

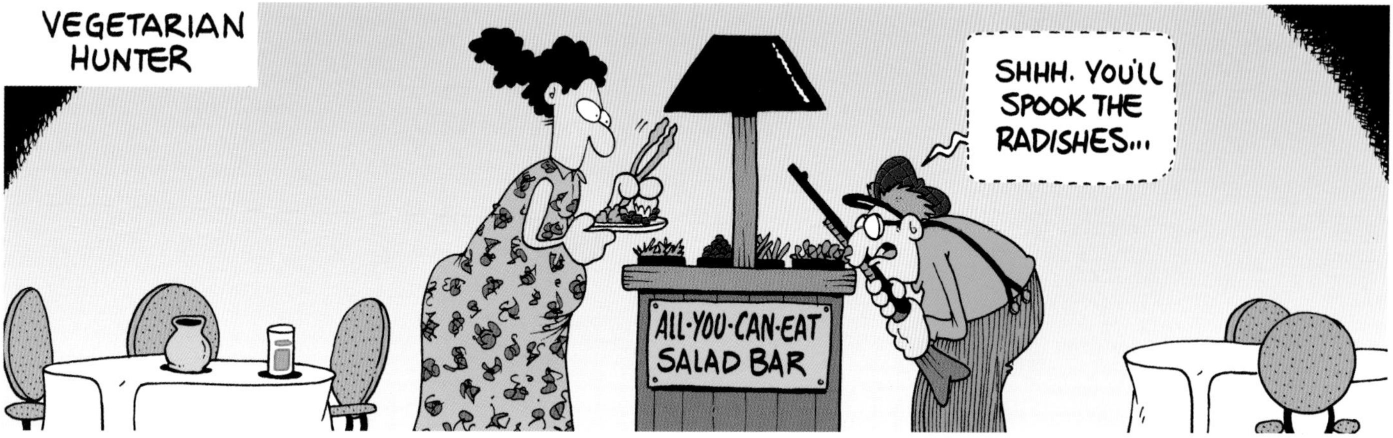
VEGETARIAN HUNTER
SHHH. YOU'LL SPOOK THE RADISHES...
ALL-YOU-CAN-EAT SALAD BAR

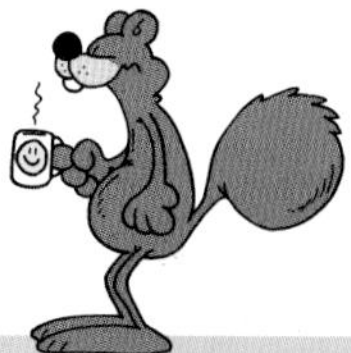

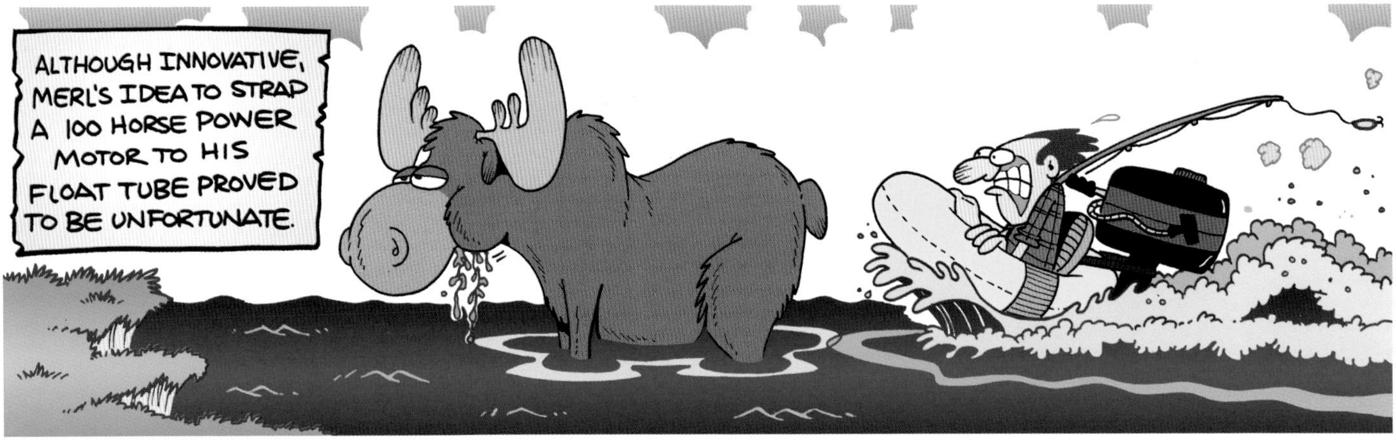
ALTHOUGH INNOVATIVE, MERL'S IDEA TO STRAP A 100 HORSE POWER MOTOR TO HIS FLOAT TUBE PROVED TO BE UNFORTUNATE.

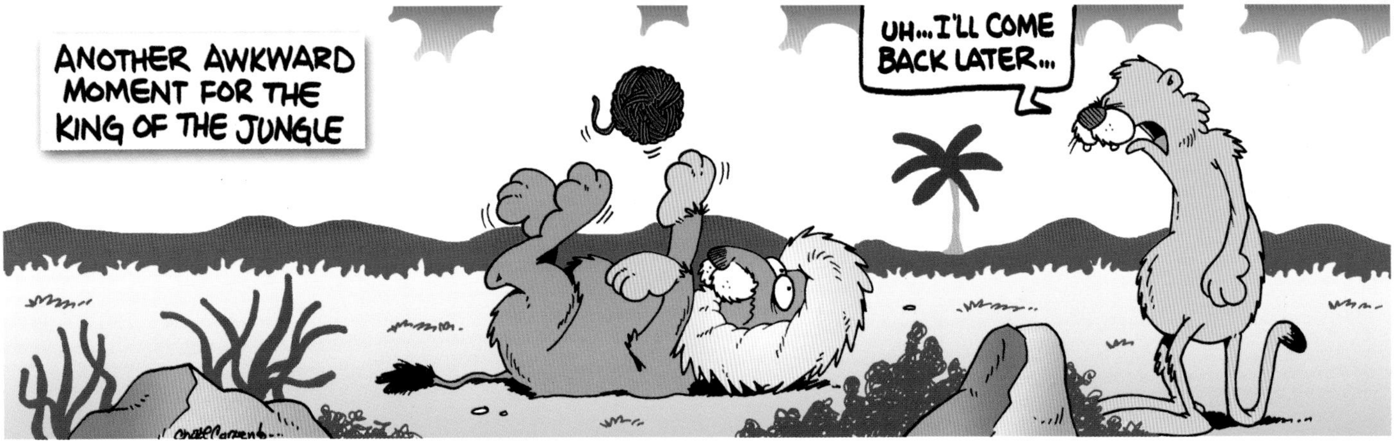
ANOTHER AWKWARD MOMENT FOR THE KING OF THE JUNGLE
UH...I'LL COME BACK LATER...

This comic strip is based on the idea of TONYA DICKERSON Anchorage, AK

Do you have an idea that would make a great comic strip? Send it to:

www.tundracomics.com
or
TUNDRA IDEAS
PO BOX 770732
Eagle River, AK
99577

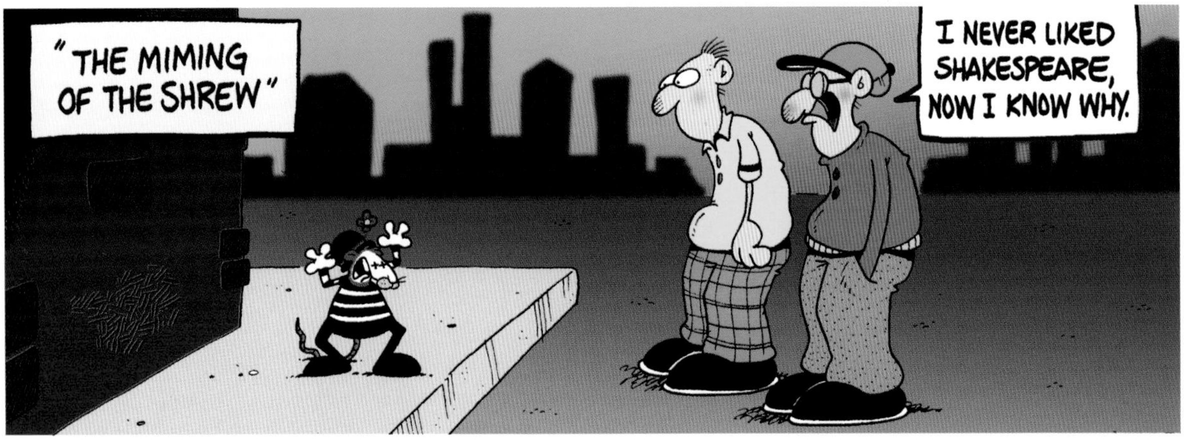
"THE MIMING OF THE SHREW"
I NEVER LIKED SHAKESPEARE, NOW I KNOW WHY.

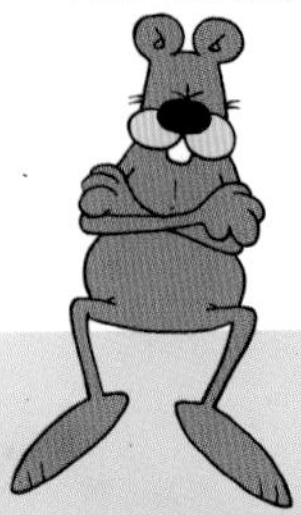

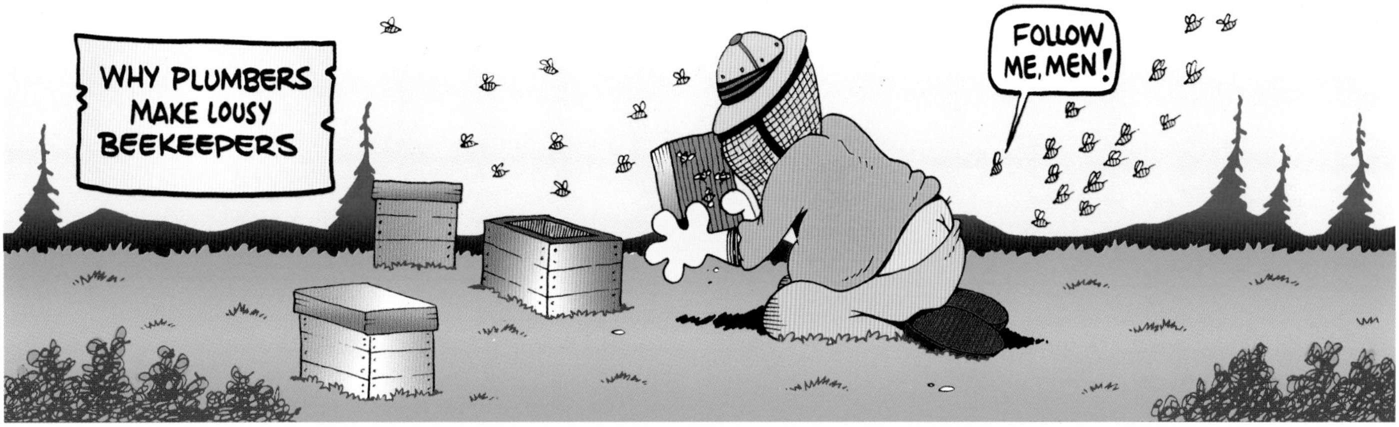
WHY PLUMBERS MAKE LOUSY BEEKEEPERS
FOLLOW ME, MEN!

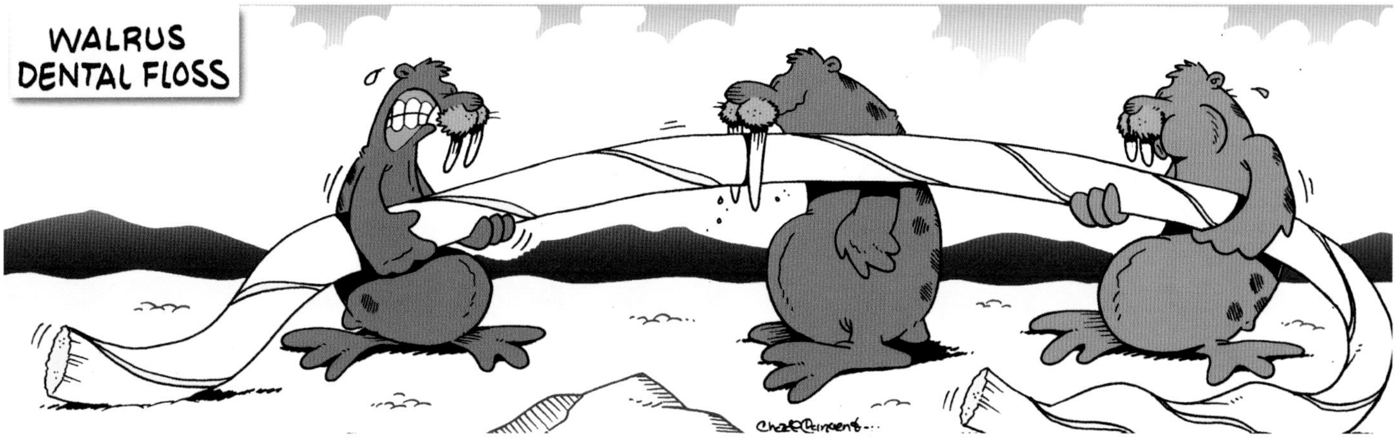
WALRUS DENTAL FLOSS

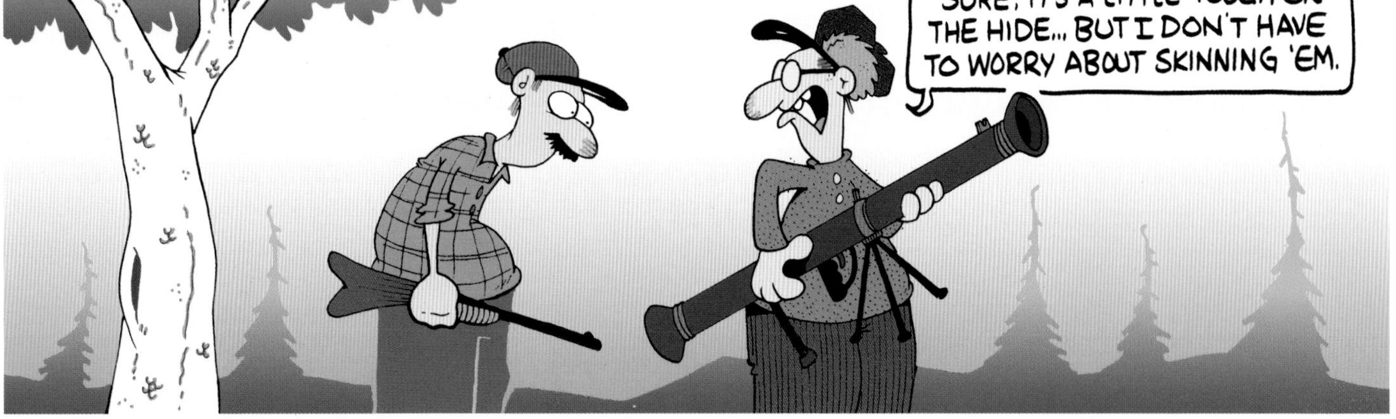
SURE, IT'S A LITTLE TOUGH ON THE HIDE... BUT I DON'T HAVE TO WORRY ABOUT SKINNING 'EM.

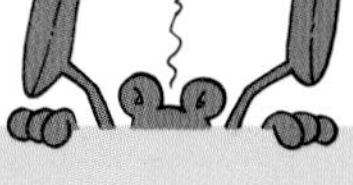

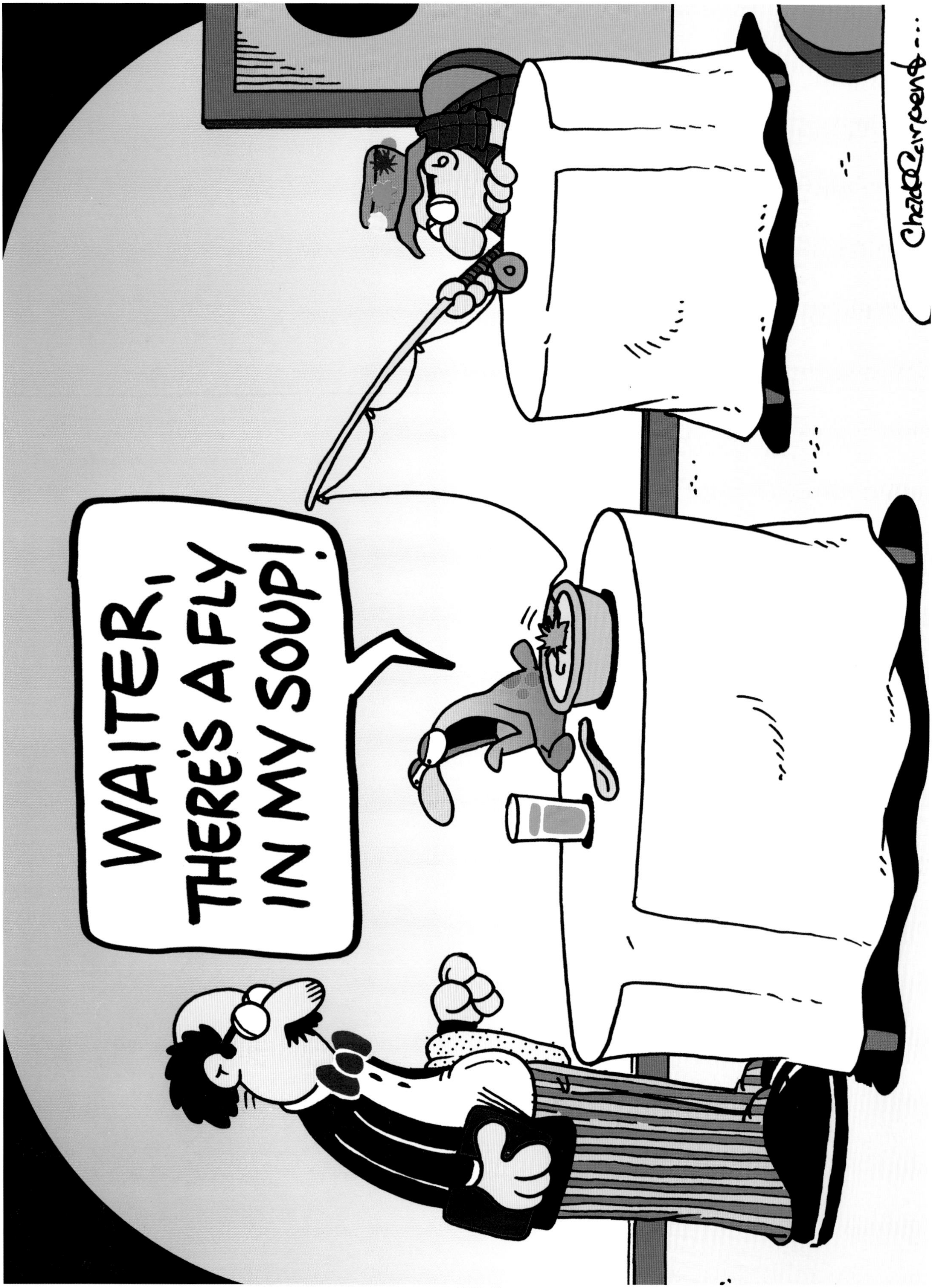
WAITER, THERE'S A FLY IN MY SOUP!
ChadCarpenter...

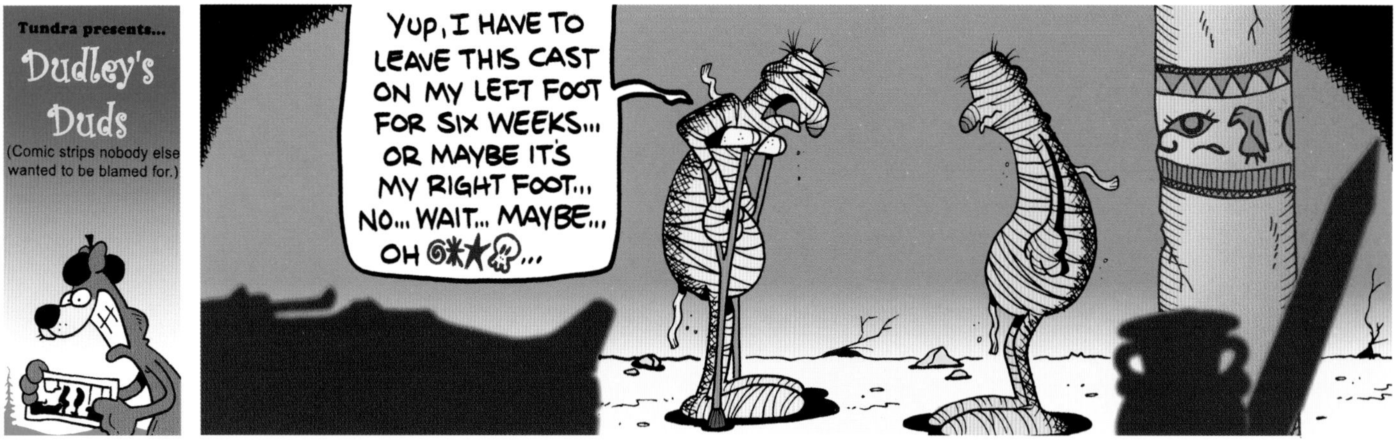
Tundra presents...
Dudley's Duds
(Comic strips nobody else wanted to be blamed for.)
YUP, I HAVE TO LEAVE THIS CAST ON MY LEFT FOOT FOR SIX WEEKS... OR MAYBE IT'S MY RIGHT FOOT... NO... WAIT... MAYBE... OH @*★...

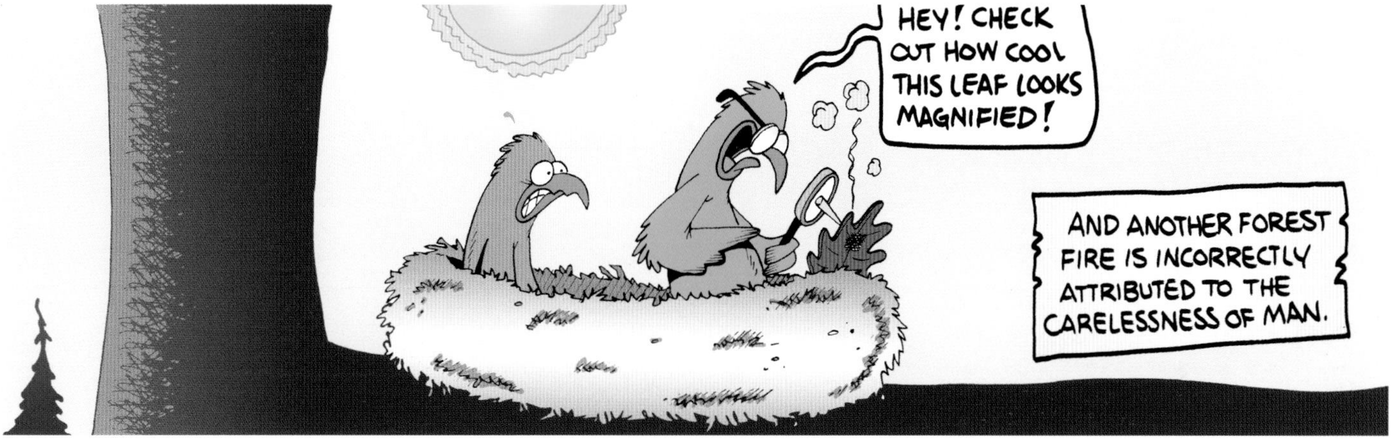
HEY! CHECK OUT HOW COOL THIS LEAF LOOKS MAGNIFIED!
AND ANOTHER FOREST FIRE IS INCORRECTLY ATTRIBUTED TO THE CARELESSNESS OF MAN.

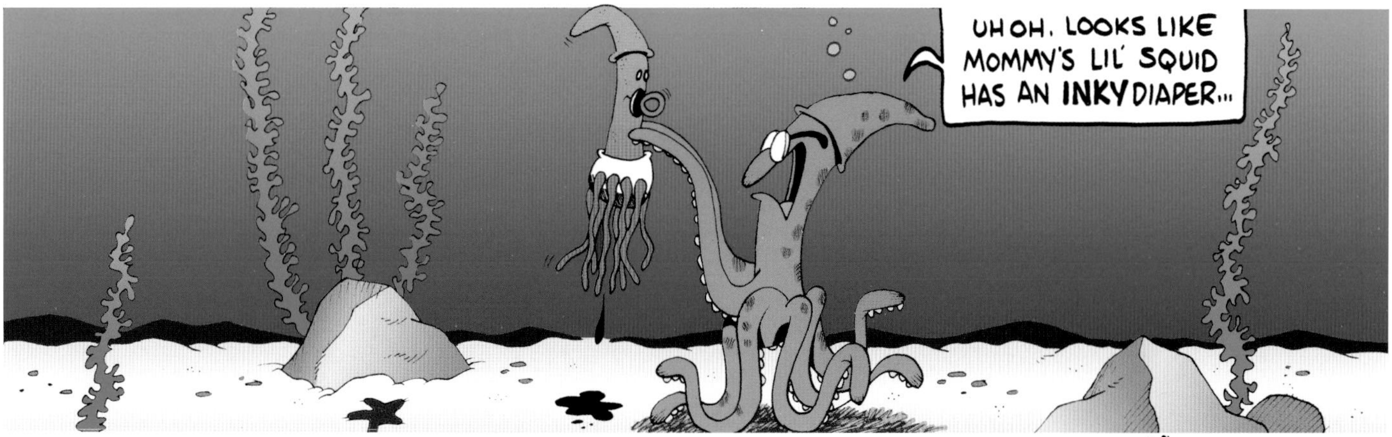
UH OH. LOOKS LIKE MOMMY'S LIL' SQUID HAS AN INKY DIAPER...

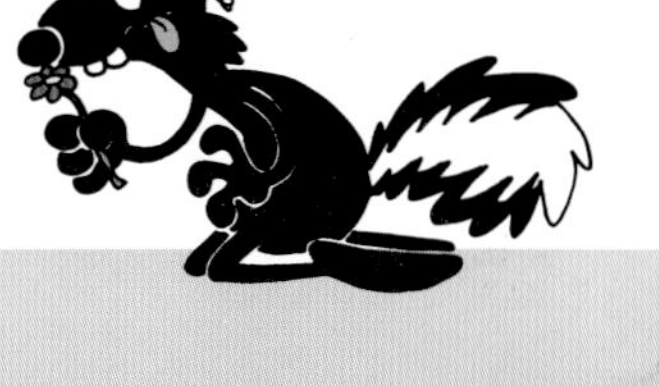

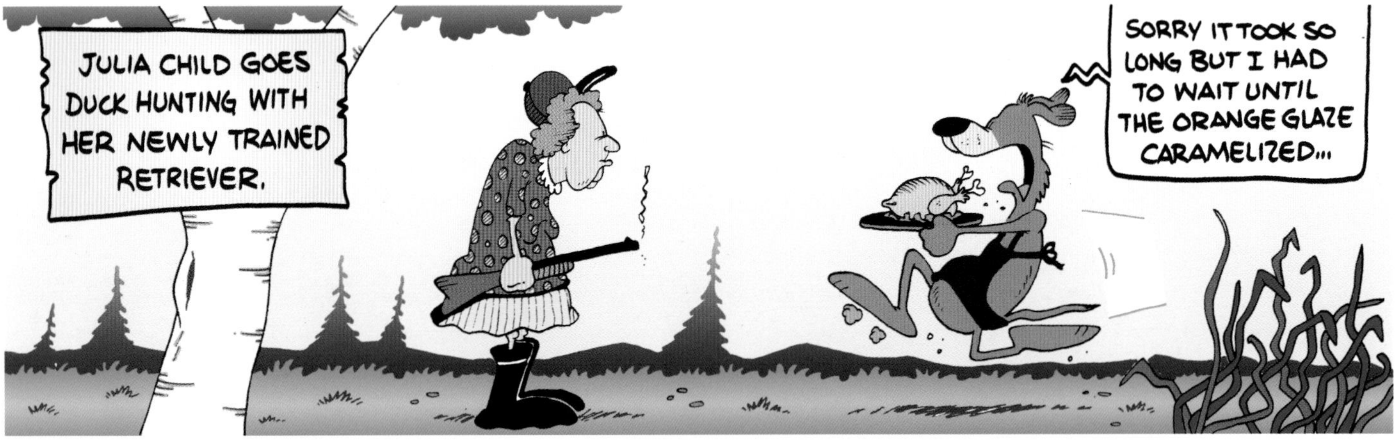
JULIA CHILD GOES DUCK HUNTING WITH HER NEWLY TRAINED RETRIEVER.
SORRY IT TOOK SO LONG BUT I HAD TO WAIT UNTIL THE ORANGE GLAZE CARAMELIZED...

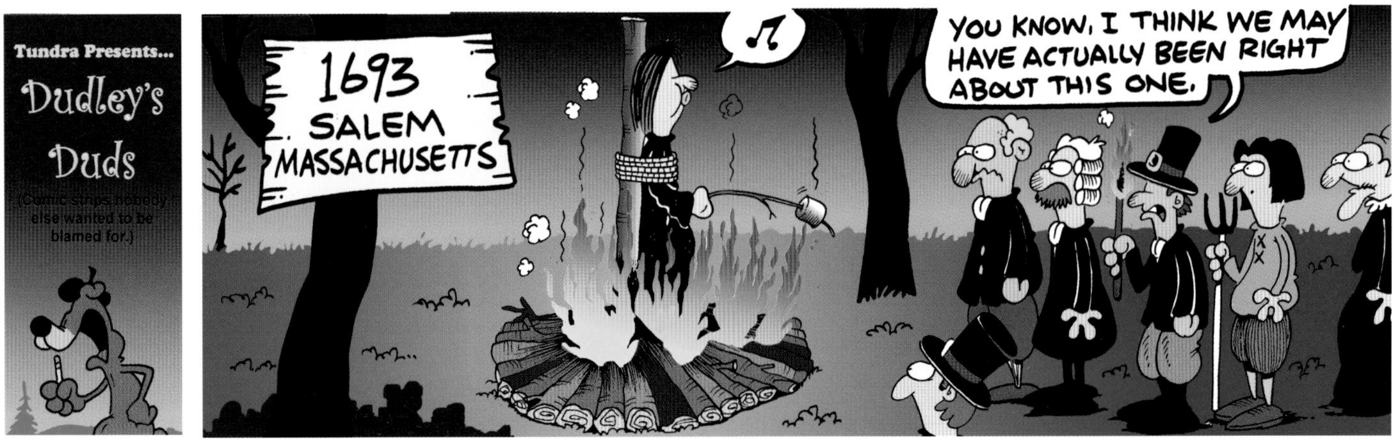
Tundra Presents...
Dudley's Duds
(Comic strips nobody else wanted to be blamed for.)
1693 SALEM MASSACHUSETTS
YOU KNOW, I THINK WE MAY HAVE ACTUALLY BEEN RIGHT ABOUT THIS ONE.

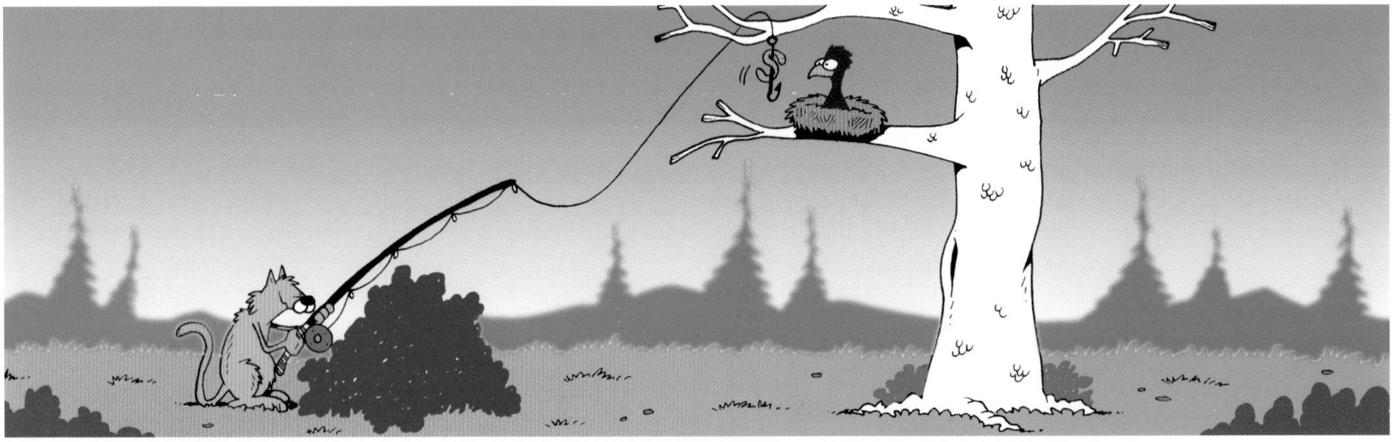

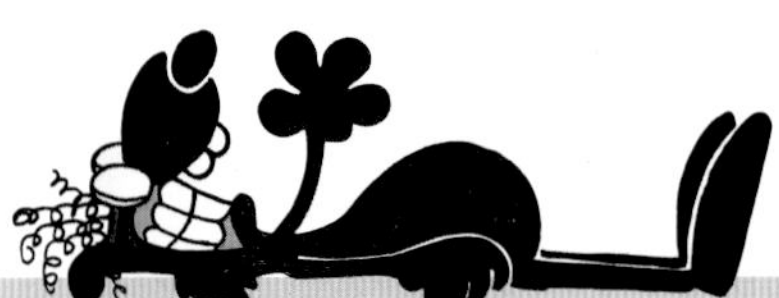

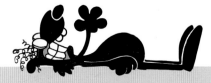

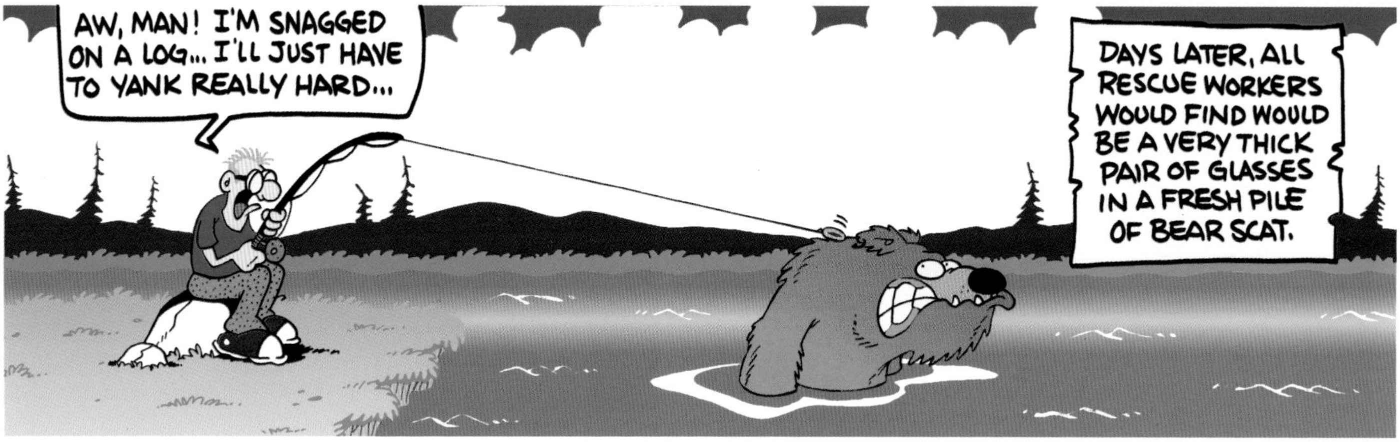
AW, MAN! I'M SNAGGED ON A LOG... I'LL JUST HAVE TO YANK REALLY HARD...
DAYS LATER, ALL RESCUE WORKERS WOULD FIND WOULD BE A VERY THICK PAIR OF GLASSES IN A FRESH PILE OF BEAR SCAT.

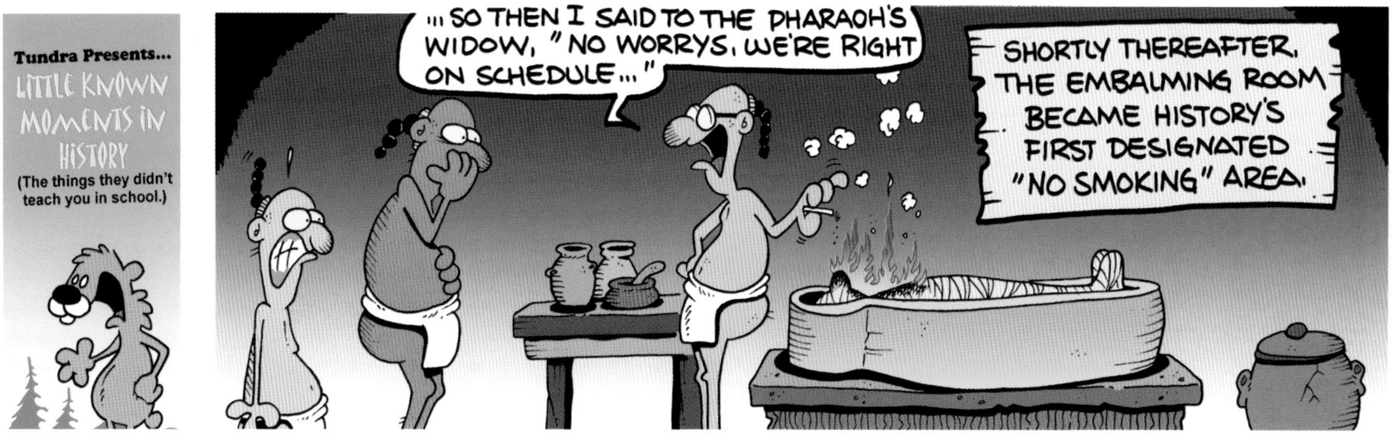
Tundra Presents...
LITTLE KNOWN MOMENTS IN HISTORY
(The things they didn't teach you in school.)
...SO THEN I SAID TO THE PHARAOH'S WIDOW, "NO WORRYS, WE'RE RIGHT ON SCHEDULE..."
SHORTLY THEREAFTER, THE EMBALMING ROOM BECAME HISTORY'S FIRST DESIGNATED "NO SMOKING" AREA.

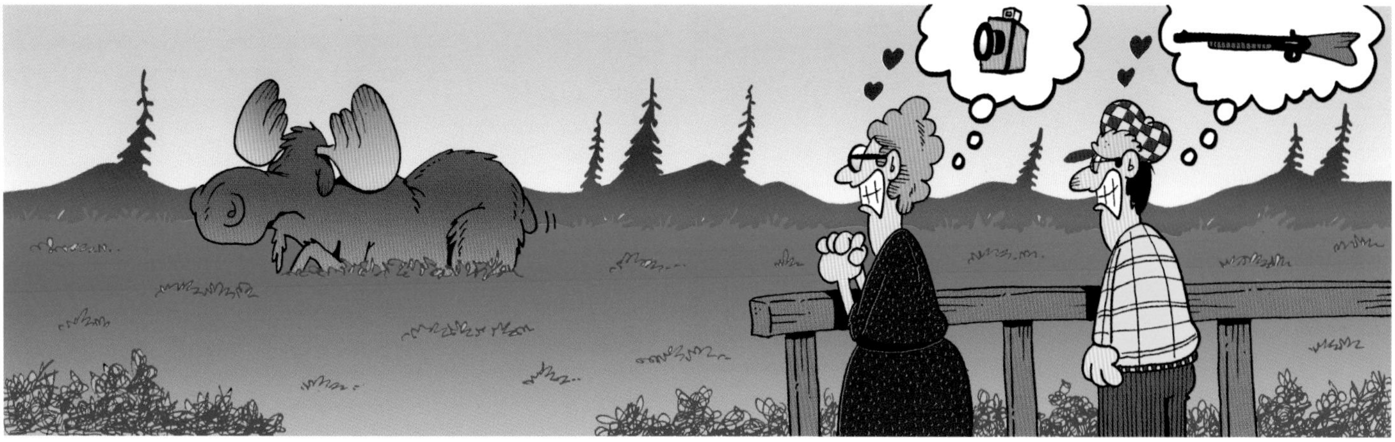

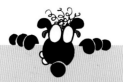

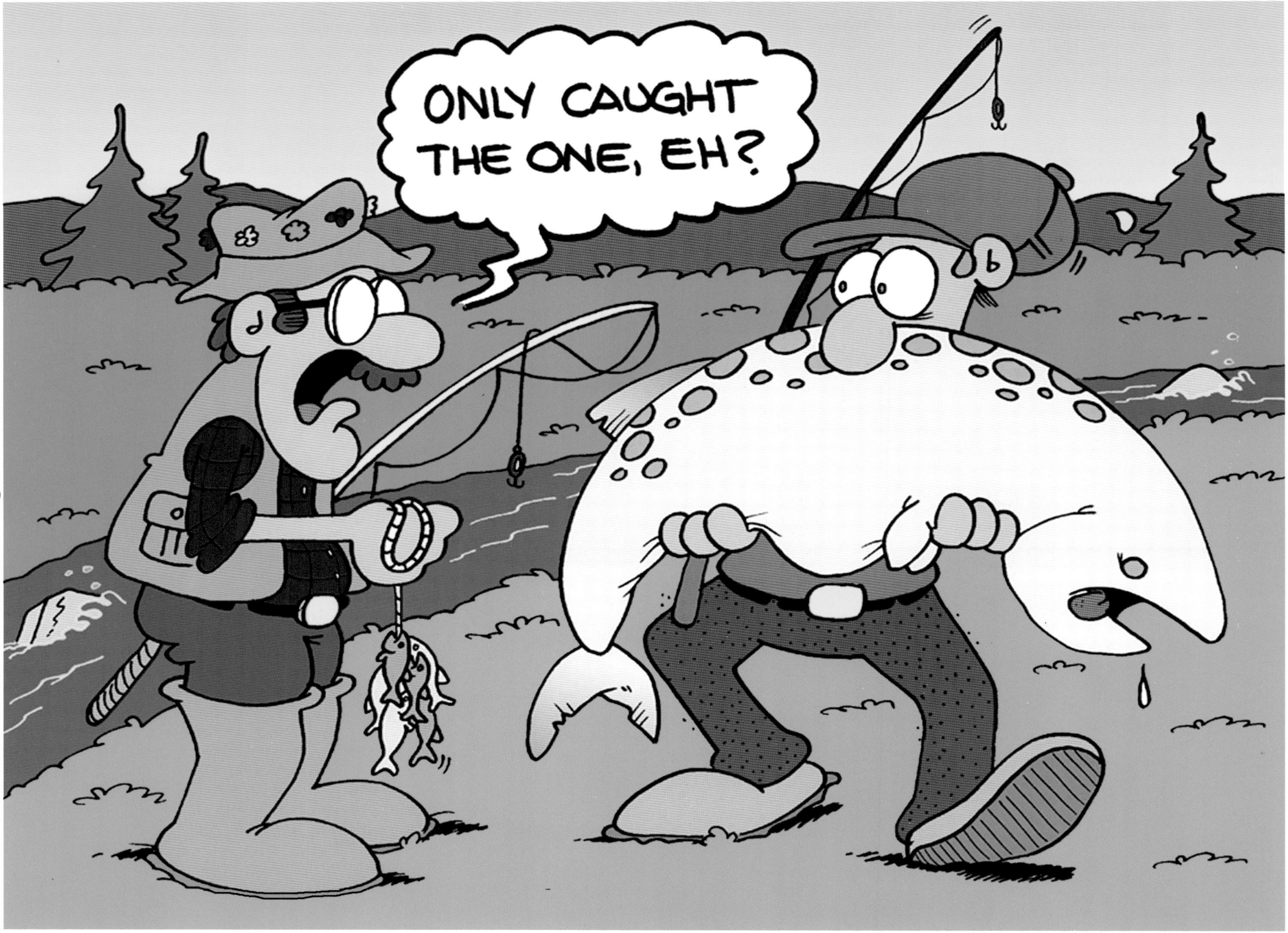
ONLY CAUGHT THE ONE, EH?

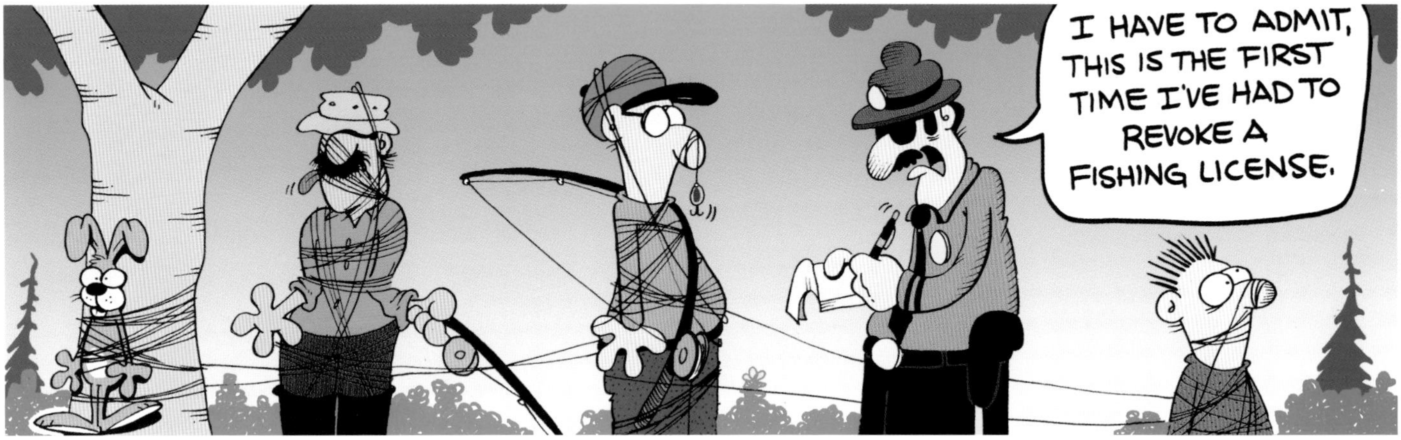
I HAVE TO ADMIT, THIS IS THE FIRST TIME I'VE HAD TO REVOKE A FISHING LICENSE.

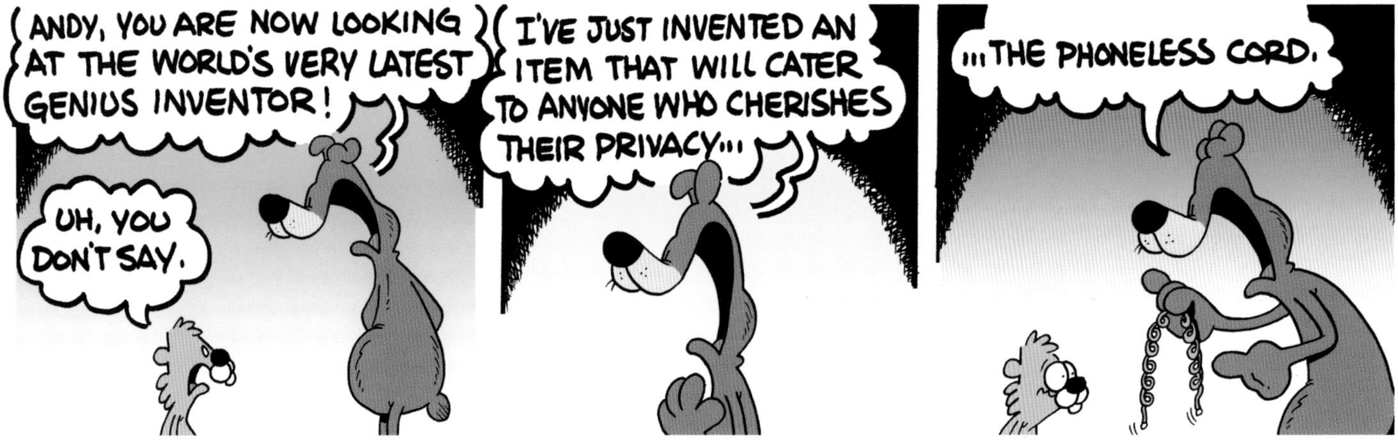
ANDY, YOU ARE NOW LOOKING AT THE WORLD'S VERY LATEST GENIUS INVENTOR!
UH, YOU DON'T SAY.
I'VE JUST INVENTED AN ITEM THAT WILL CATER TO ANYONE WHO CHERISHES THEIR PRIVACY...
...THE PHONELESS CORD.

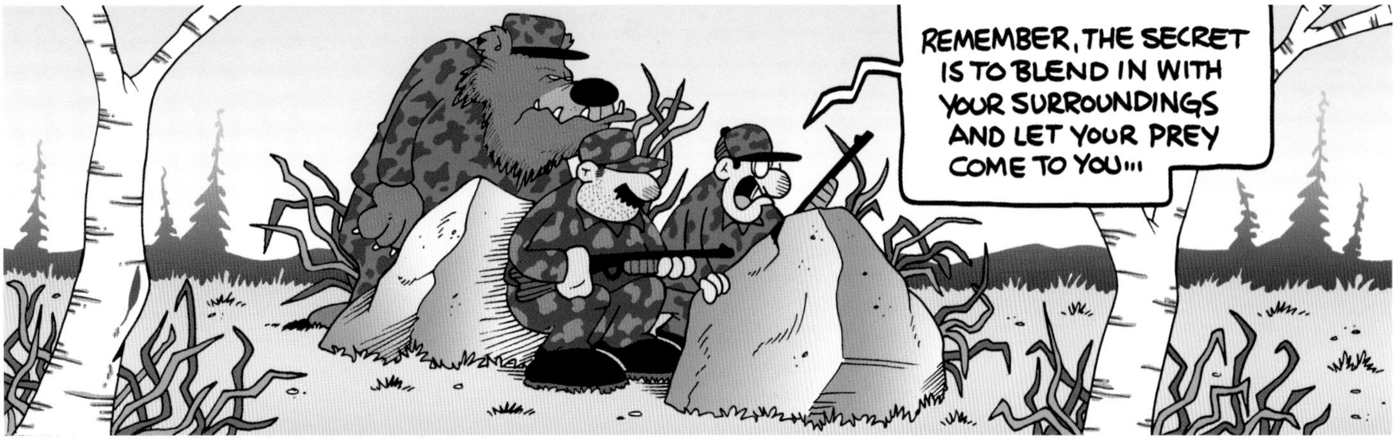
REMEMBER, THE SECRET IS TO BLEND IN WITH YOUR SURROUNDINGS AND LET YOUR PREY COME TO YOU...

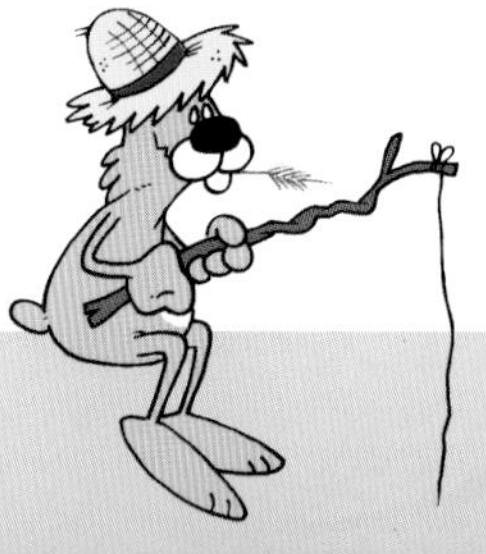

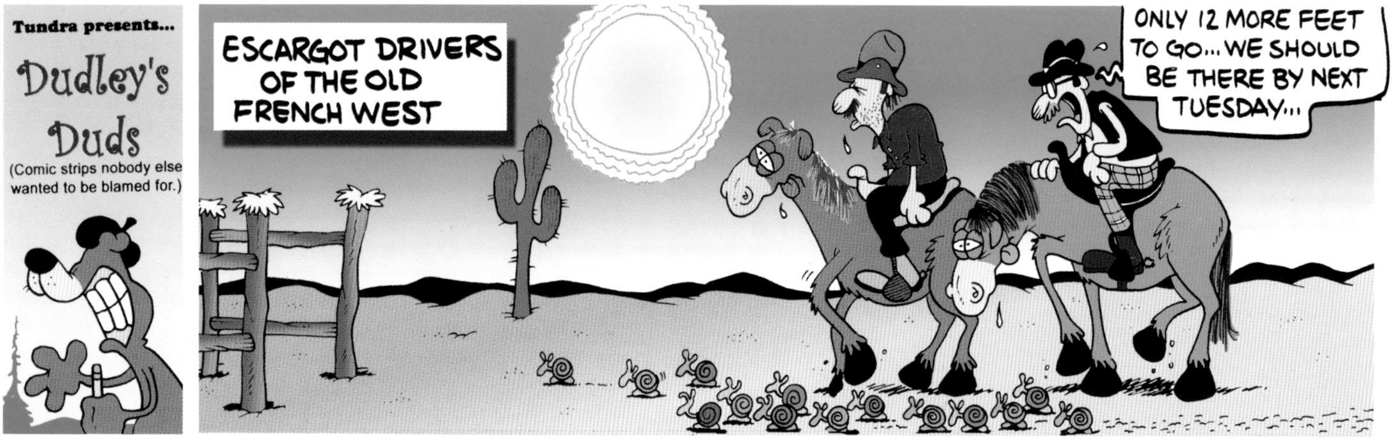
Tundra presents...
Dudley's Duds
(Comic strips nobody else wanted to be blamed for.)
ESCARGOT DRIVERS OF THE OLD FRENCH WEST
ONLY 12 MORE FEET TO GO... WE SHOULD BE THERE BY NEXT TUESDAY...

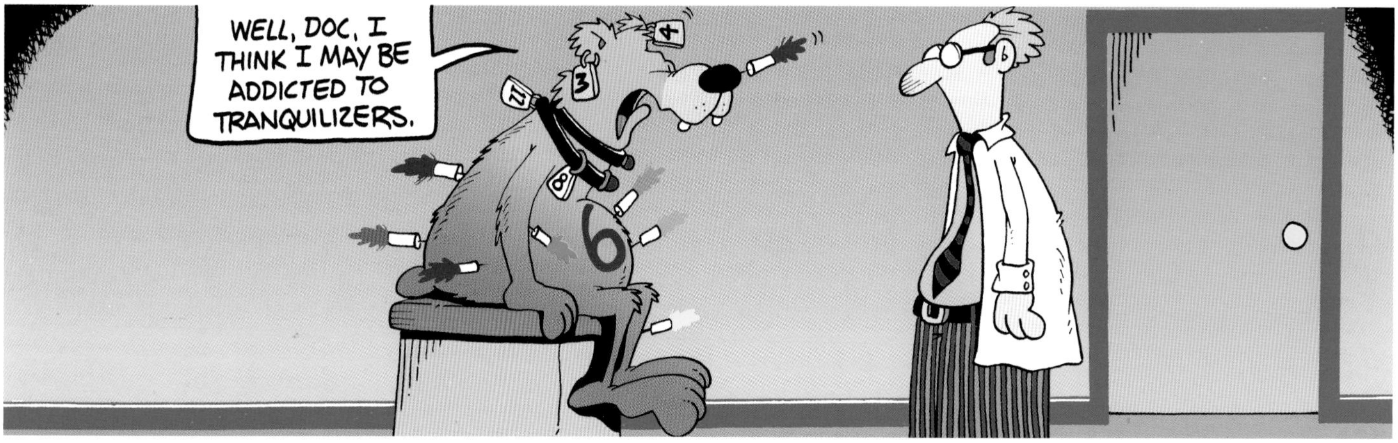
WELL, DOC, I THINK I MAY BE ADDICTED TO TRANQUILIZERS.

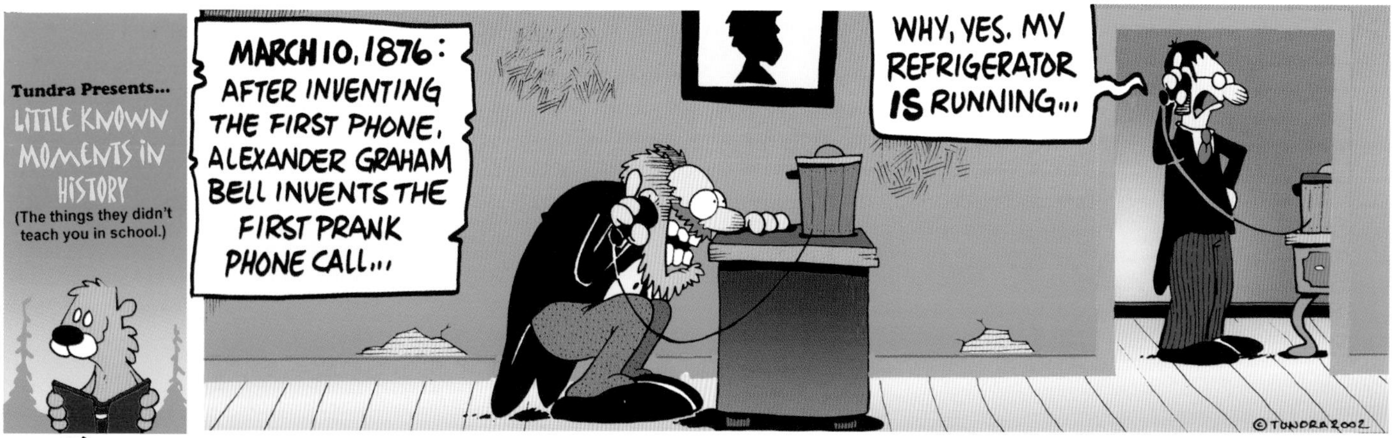
Tundra Presents...
LITTLE KNOWN MOMENTS IN HISTORY
(The things they didn't teach you in school.)
MARCH 10, 1876: AFTER INVENTING THE FIRST PHONE, ALEXANDER GRAHAM BELL INVENTS THE FIRST PRANK PHONE CALL...
WHY, YES. MY REFRIGERATOR IS RUNNING...
© TUNDRA 2002

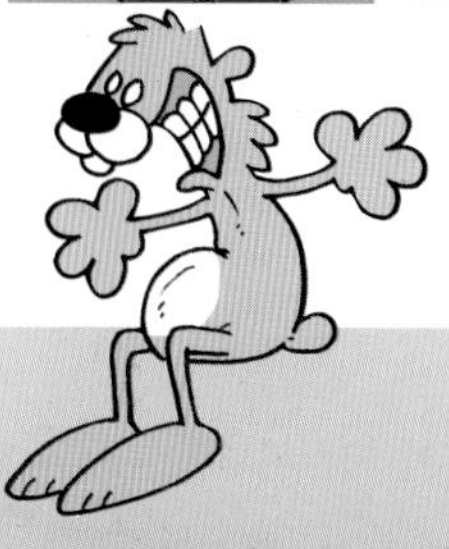

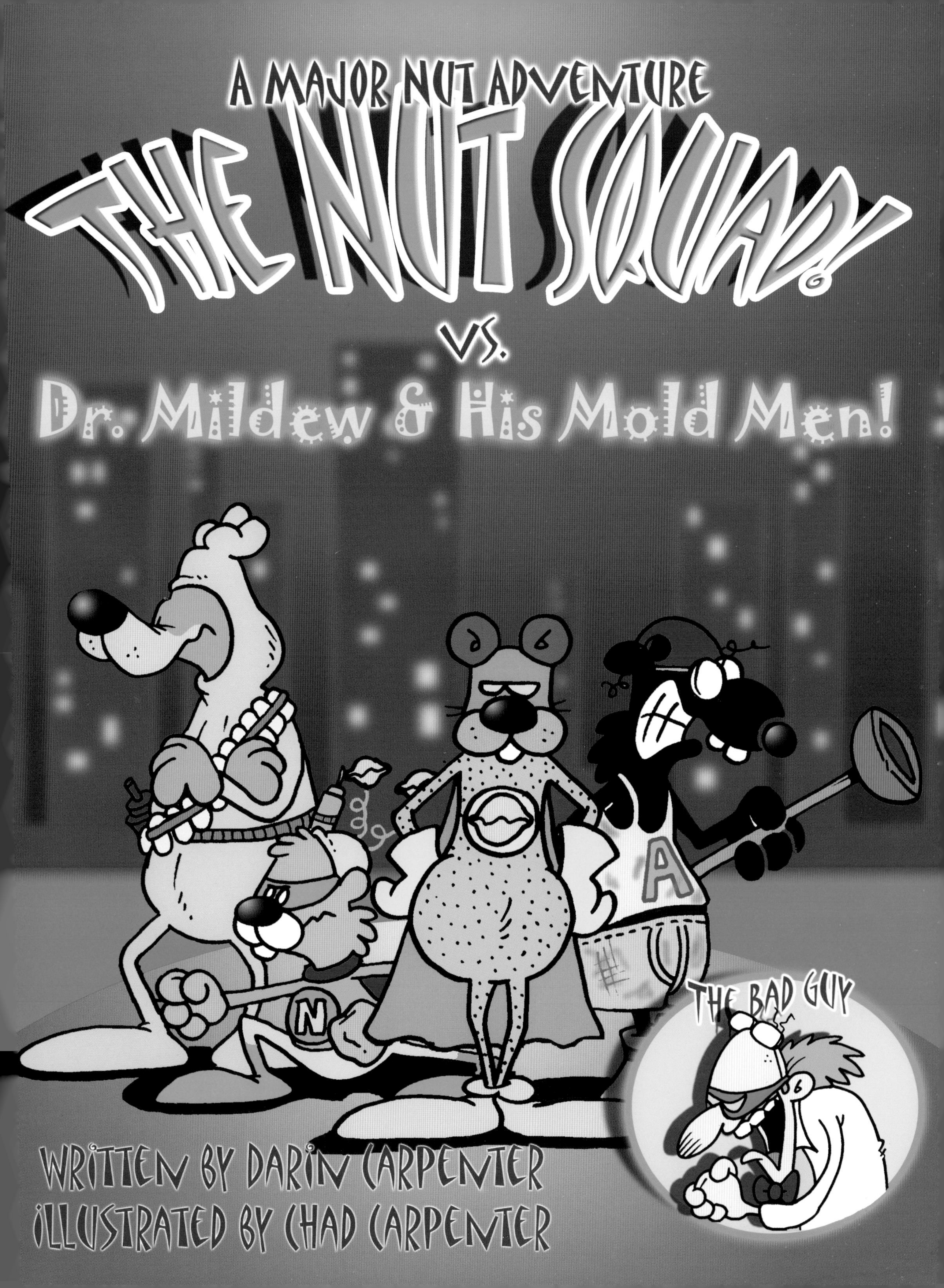
A MAJOR NUT ADVENTURE
THE NUT SQUAD!
VS.
Dr. Mildew & His Mold Men!
THE BAD GUY
WRITTEN BY DARIN CARPENTER
ILLUSTRATED BY CHAD CARPENTER

NEW! From MR. DALE'S NOVELTY EMPORIUM

HOW TO BUILD YOUR OWN REAL X-RAY GLASSES!!!

Are you tired of being ripped off by those "other guy's" phony X-Ray glasses? You send them your money and all you get is cheap plastic frames with cellophane lenses that you couldn't see through a window with? Well never again, because now, thanks to Mr. Dale's Novelty Emporium, you can purchase blue-prints & instructions to build your very own REAL X-Ray glasses!

ACTUAL BLUE-PRINTS

Using nothing more than common household items (and a modest amount of uranium) you'll be able to see through almost any substance known to man!

BRAND "X" X-RAY GLASSES

MR. DALE'S X-RAY GLASSES

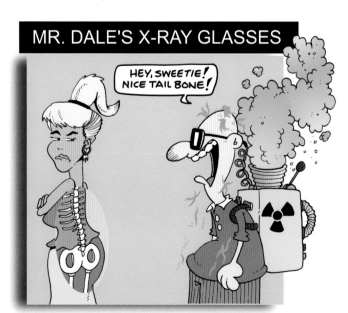

HEY, SWEETIE! NICE TAIL BONE!

AVAILABLE IN FINER BACK ALLEYS EVERYWHERE!

*ALSO RECOMMENDED - MR. DALE'S LEAD BODY SUIT (Sold seperately)

Name: Sherman Squirrel
Hero Name: Major Nut
Profession: Crime Fighter
Height: 3' 5"
Weight: 35 lbs.
Turn-ons: Moonlight walks, cuddling
        by the fireplace, searching
        under couch cushions for
        loose change.

Name: Andy Lemming
Hero Name: Nut Boy
Profession: Sidekick
Height: 1' 6"
Weight: 12 lbs. (Before going through
        the spin-cycle in the
        washer.)
Special Power: Witty retorts

Name: Whiff Skunk
Hero Name: Aromatic Avenger
Profession: Crime Fighter
Height: 3' 6"
Weight: 40 lbs. (Including 12 pounds of stink.)
Super Hero Line: "Pull my finger."
Special Power: "Stench O' Death".
        Able to clear an entire
        elevator before the
        doors even open.

Name: Dudley Bear
Hero Name: Capt'n Gastropod
Profession: Crime Fighter
Height: 6' 4"
Weight: 800 lbs.
Super Hero Line: "You gonna' eat that?"
Special Powers: Ability to gulp down
        entire buffets in single
        swallow.

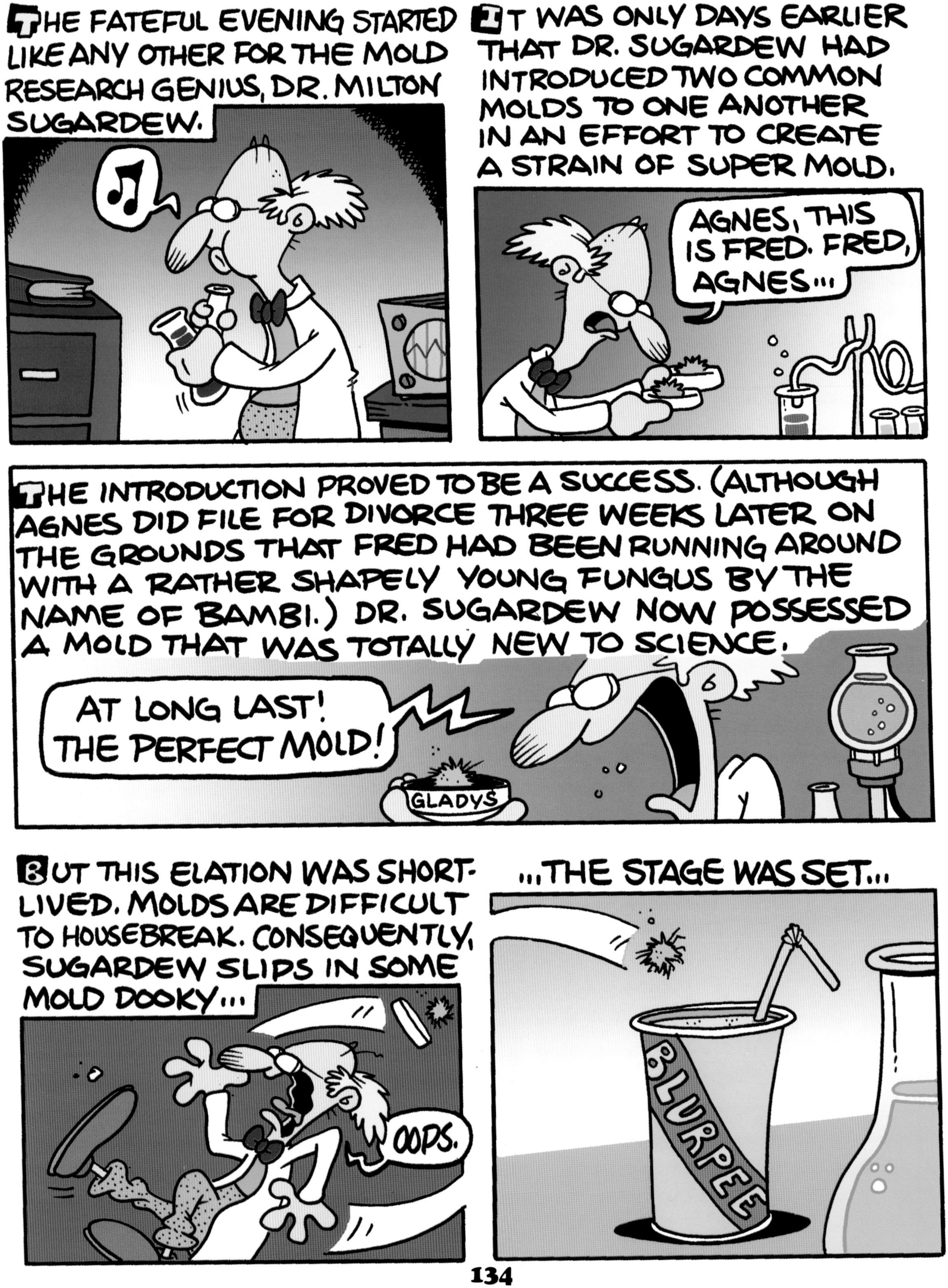
THE FATEFUL EVENING STARTED LIKE ANY OTHER FOR THE MOLD RESEARCH GENIUS, DR. MILTON SUGARDEW.
IT WAS ONLY DAYS EARLIER THAT DR. SUGARDEW HAD INTRODUCED TWO COMMON MOLDS TO ONE ANOTHER IN AN EFFORT TO CREATE A STRAIN OF SUPER MOLD.
AGNES, THIS IS FRED. FRED, AGNES...
THE INTRODUCTION PROVED TO BE A SUCCESS. (ALTHOUGH AGNES DID FILE FOR DIVORCE THREE WEEKS LATER ON THE GROUNDS THAT FRED HAD BEEN RUNNING AROUND WITH A RATHER SHAPELY YOUNG FUNGUS BY THE NAME OF BAMBI.) DR. SUGARDEW NOW POSSESSED A MOLD THAT WAS TOTALLY NEW TO SCIENCE.
AT LONG LAST! THE PERFECT MOLD!
GLADYS
BUT THIS ELATION WAS SHORT-LIVED. MOLDS ARE DIFFICULT TO HOUSEBREAK. CONSEQUENTLY, SUGARDEW SLIPS IN SOME MOLD DOOKY...
OOPS.
...THE STAGE WAS SET...
BLURPEE

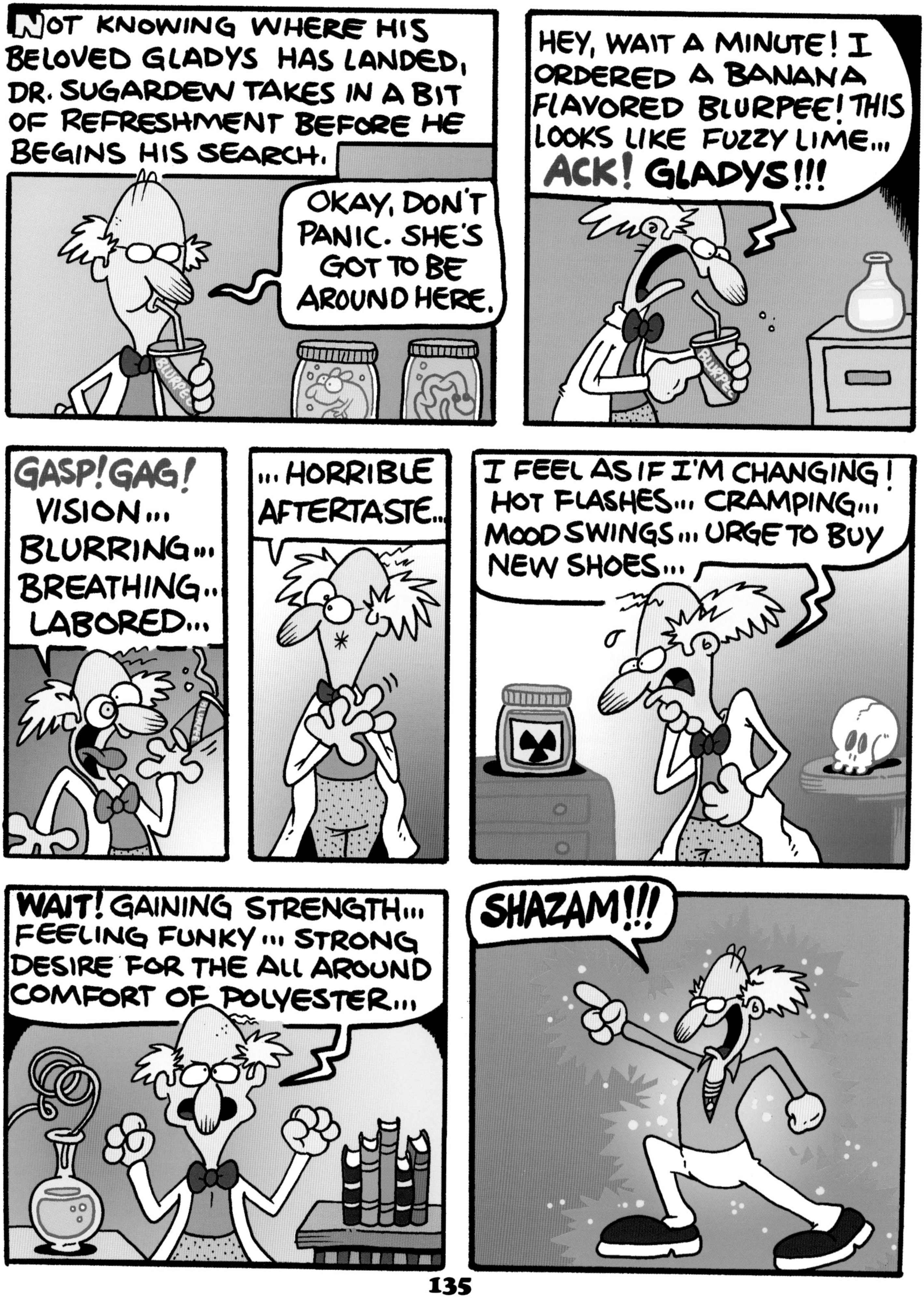
NOT KNOWING WHERE HIS BELOVED GLADYS HAS LANDED, DR. SUGARDEW TAKES IN A BIT OF REFRESHMENT BEFORE HE BEGINS HIS SEARCH.
OKAY, DON'T PANIC. SHE'S GOT TO BE AROUND HERE.
BLURPEE
HEY, WAIT A MINUTE! I ORDERED A BANANA FLAVORED BLURPEE! THIS LOOKS LIKE FUZZY LIME... ACK! GLADYS!!!
BLURPEE
GASP! GAG! VISION... BLURRING... BREATHING... LABORED...
...HORRIBLE AFTERTASTE...
I FEEL AS IF I'M CHANGING! HOT FLASHES... CRAMPING... MOOD SWINGS... URGE TO BUY NEW SHOES...
WAIT! GAINING STRENGTH... FEELING FUNKY... STRONG DESIRE FOR THE ALL AROUND COMFORT OF POLYESTER...
SHAZAM!!!

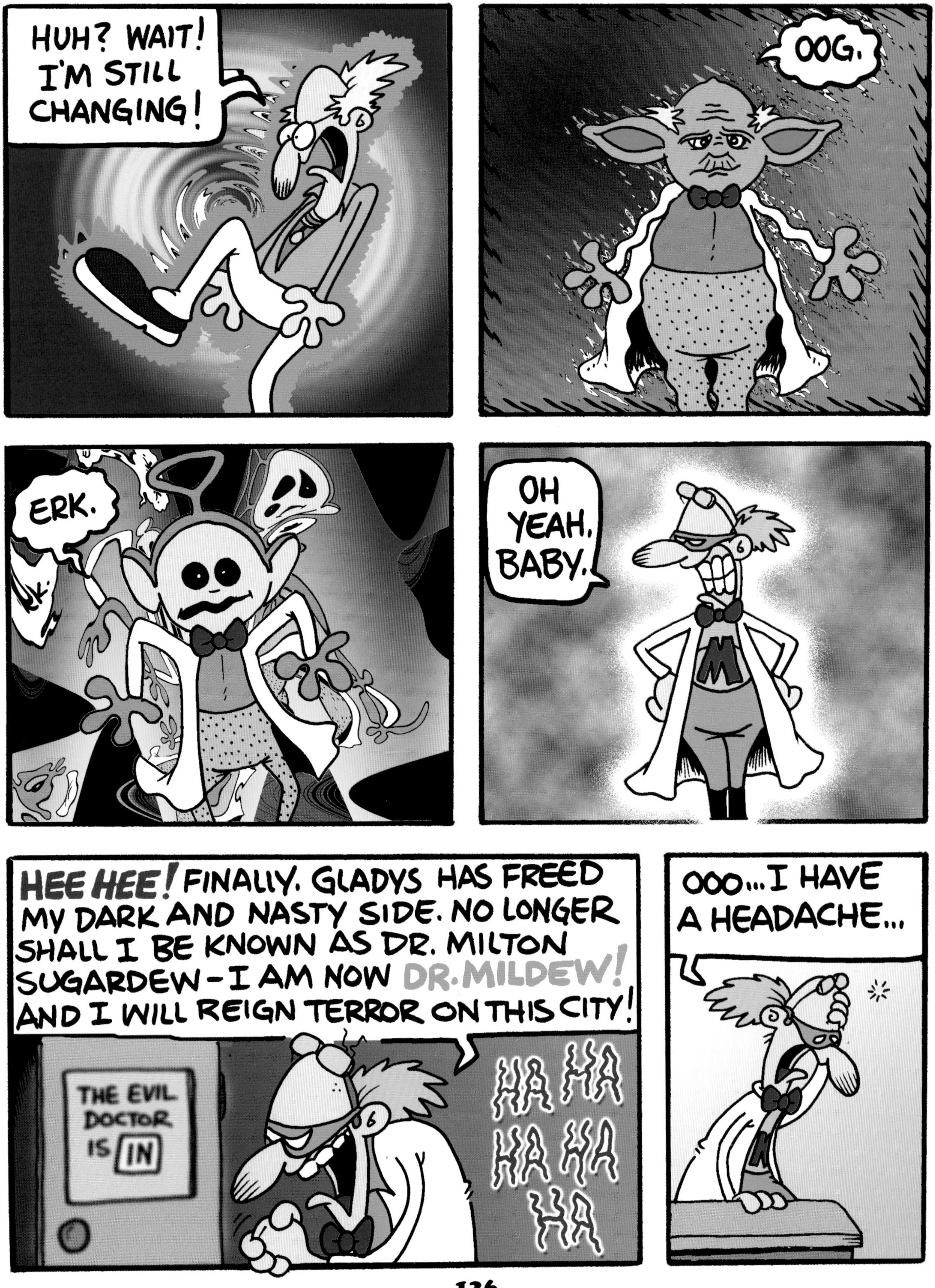
HUH? WAIT! I'M STILL CHANGING!
OOG.
ERK.
ERK.
OH YEAH, BABY.
HEE HEE! FINALLY, GLADYS HAS FREED MY DARK AND NASTY SIDE. NO LONGER SHALL I BE KNOWN AS DR. MILTON SUGARDEW - I AM NOW DR. MILDEW! AND I WILL REIGN TERROR ON THIS CITY!
THE EVIL DOCTOR IS IN
HA HA HA HA HA
OOO... I HAVE A HEADACHE...

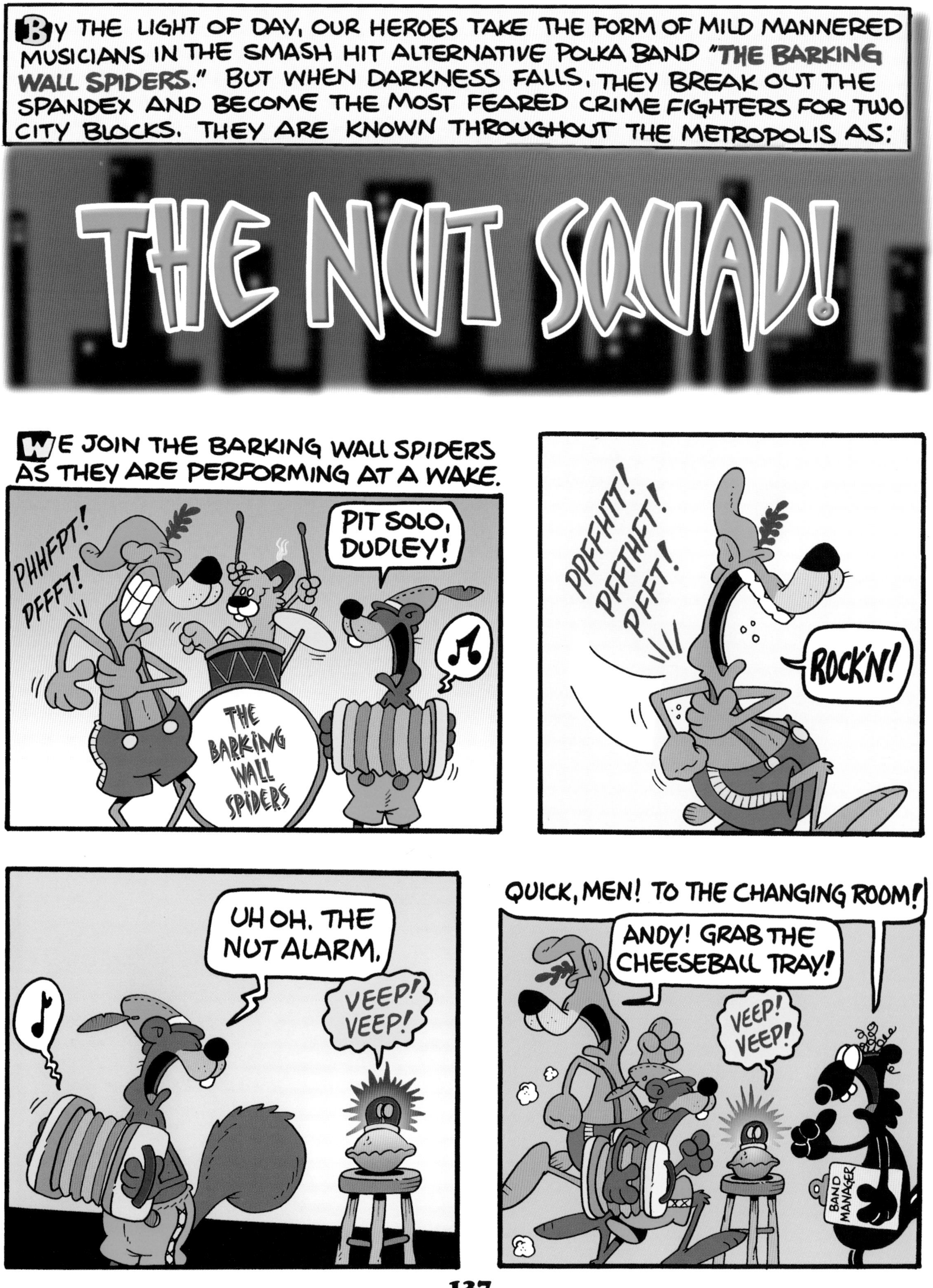
BY THE LIGHT OF DAY, OUR HEROES TAKE THE FORM OF MILD MANNERED MUSICIANS IN THE SMASH HIT ALTERNATIVE POLKA BAND "THE BARKING WALL SPIDERS." BUT WHEN DARKNESS FALLS, THEY BREAK OUT THE SPANDEX AND BECOME THE MOST FEARED CRIME FIGHTERS FOR TWO CITY BLOCKS. THEY ARE KNOWN THROUGHOUT THE METROPOLIS AS:
THE NUT SQUAD!
WE JOIN THE BARKING WALL SPIDERS AS THEY ARE PERFORMING AT A WAKE.
PHHFPT! PFFFT!
PIT SOLO, DUDLEY!
THE BARKING WALL SPIDERS
PPFFHTT! PFFTHFT! PFFT!
ROCK'N!
UH OH. THE NUT ALARM.
VEEP! VEEP!
QUICK, MEN! TO THE CHANGING ROOM!
ANDY! GRAB THE CHEESEBALL TRAY!
VEEP! VEEP!
BAND MANAGER

THE BARKING WALL SPIDERS QUICKLY CHANGE INTO THEIR SUPERHERO OUTFITS:

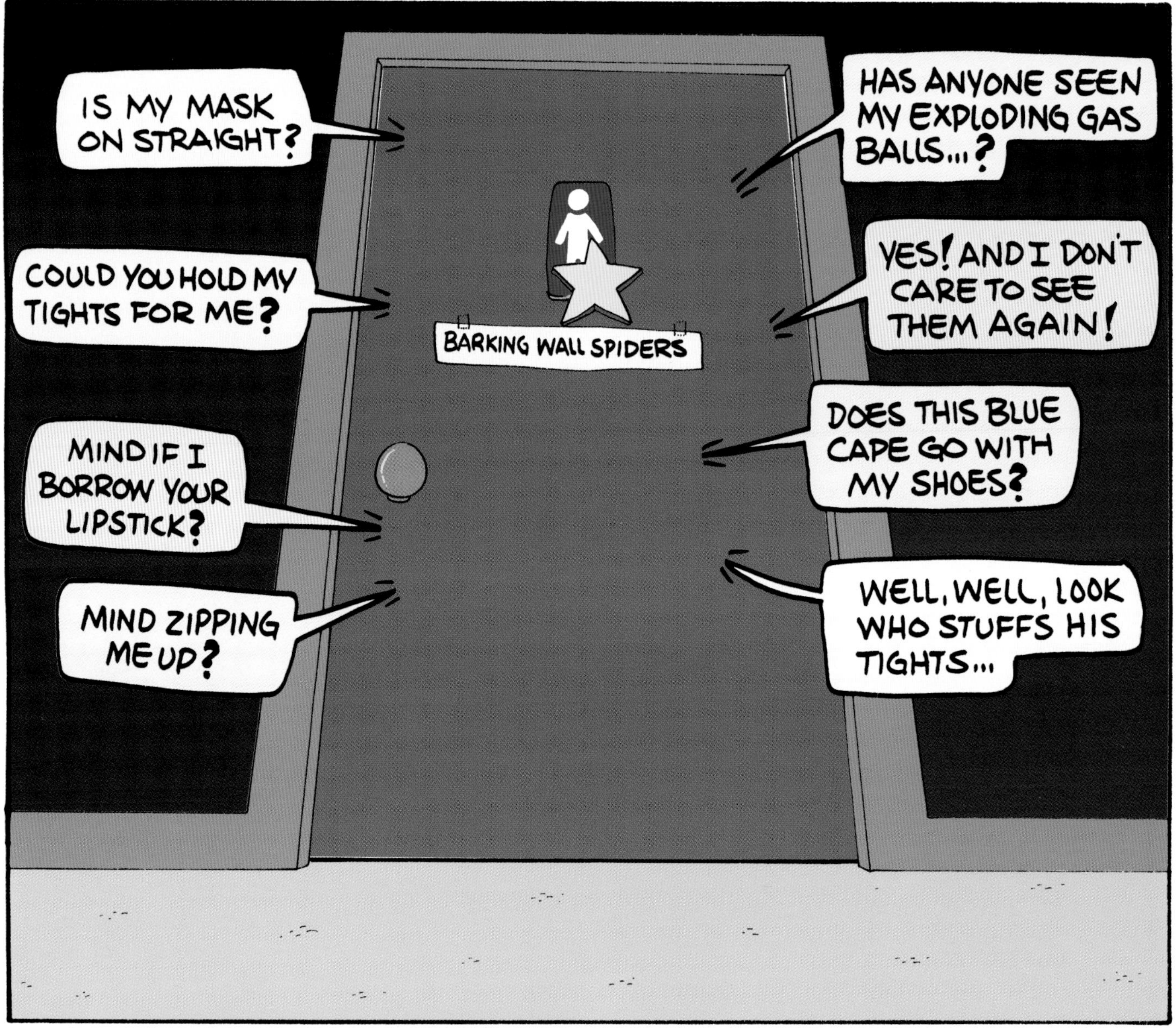
IS MY MASK ON STRAIGHT?
HAS ANYONE SEEN MY EXPLODING GAS BALLS...?
COULD YOU HOLD MY TIGHTS FOR ME?
YES! AND I DON'T CARE TO SEE THEM AGAIN!
BARKING WALL SPIDERS
DOES THIS BLUE CAPE GO WITH MY SHOES?
MIND IF I BORROW YOUR LIPSTICK?
WELL, WELL, LOOK WHO STUFFS HIS TIGHTS...
MIND ZIPPING ME UP?

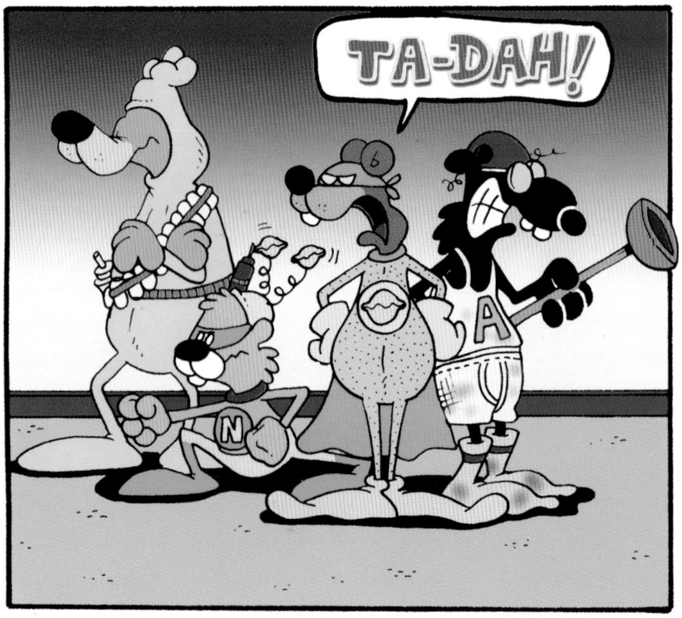
TA-DAH!

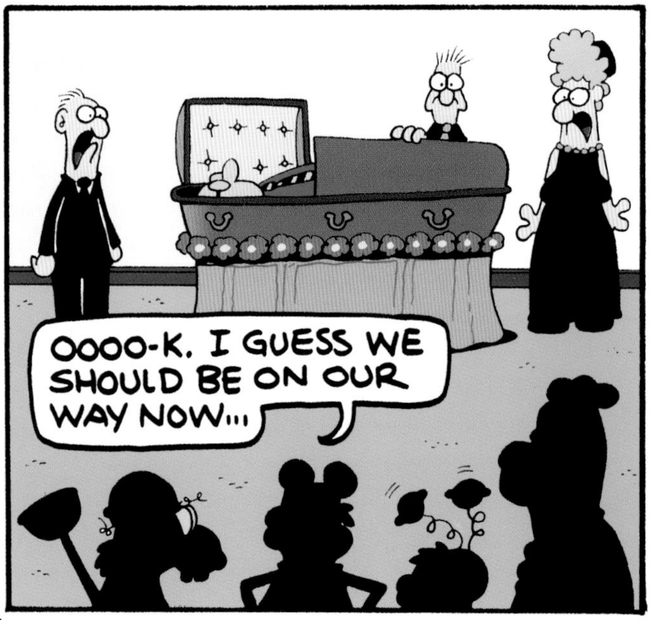
OOOO-K. I GUESS WE SHOULD BE ON OUR WAY NOW...

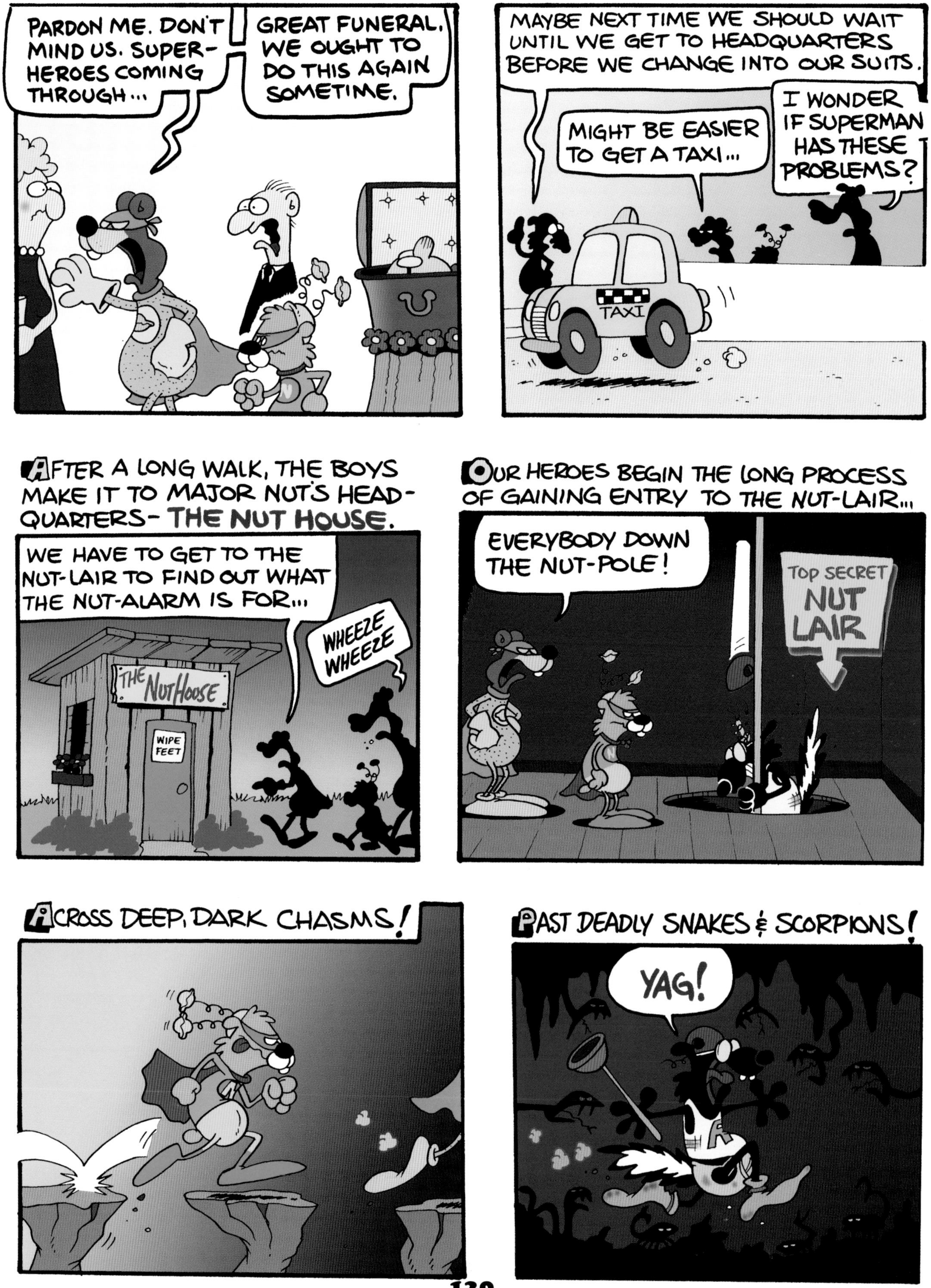
PARDON ME. DON'T MIND US. SUPER-HEROES COMING THROUGH...
GREAT FUNERAL. WE OUGHT TO DO THIS AGAIN SOMETIME.
MAYBE NEXT TIME WE SHOULD WAIT UNTIL WE GET TO HEADQUARTERS BEFORE WE CHANGE INTO OUR SUITS.
MIGHT BE EASIER TO GET A TAXI...
I WONDER IF SUPERMAN HAS THESE PROBLEMS?
TAXI
AFTER A LONG WALK, THE BOYS MAKE IT TO MAJOR NUT'S HEAD-QUARTERS– THE NUT HOUSE.
WE HAVE TO GET TO THE NUT-LAIR TO FIND OUT WHAT THE NUT-ALARM IS FOR...
WHEEZE WHEEZE
THE NUT HOUSE
WIPE FEET
OUR HEROES BEGIN THE LONG PROCESS OF GAINING ENTRY TO THE NUT-LAIR...
EVERYBODY DOWN THE NUT-POLE!
TOP SECRET NUT LAIR
ACROSS DEEP, DARK CHASMS!
PAST DEADLY SNAKES & SCORPIONS!
YAG!

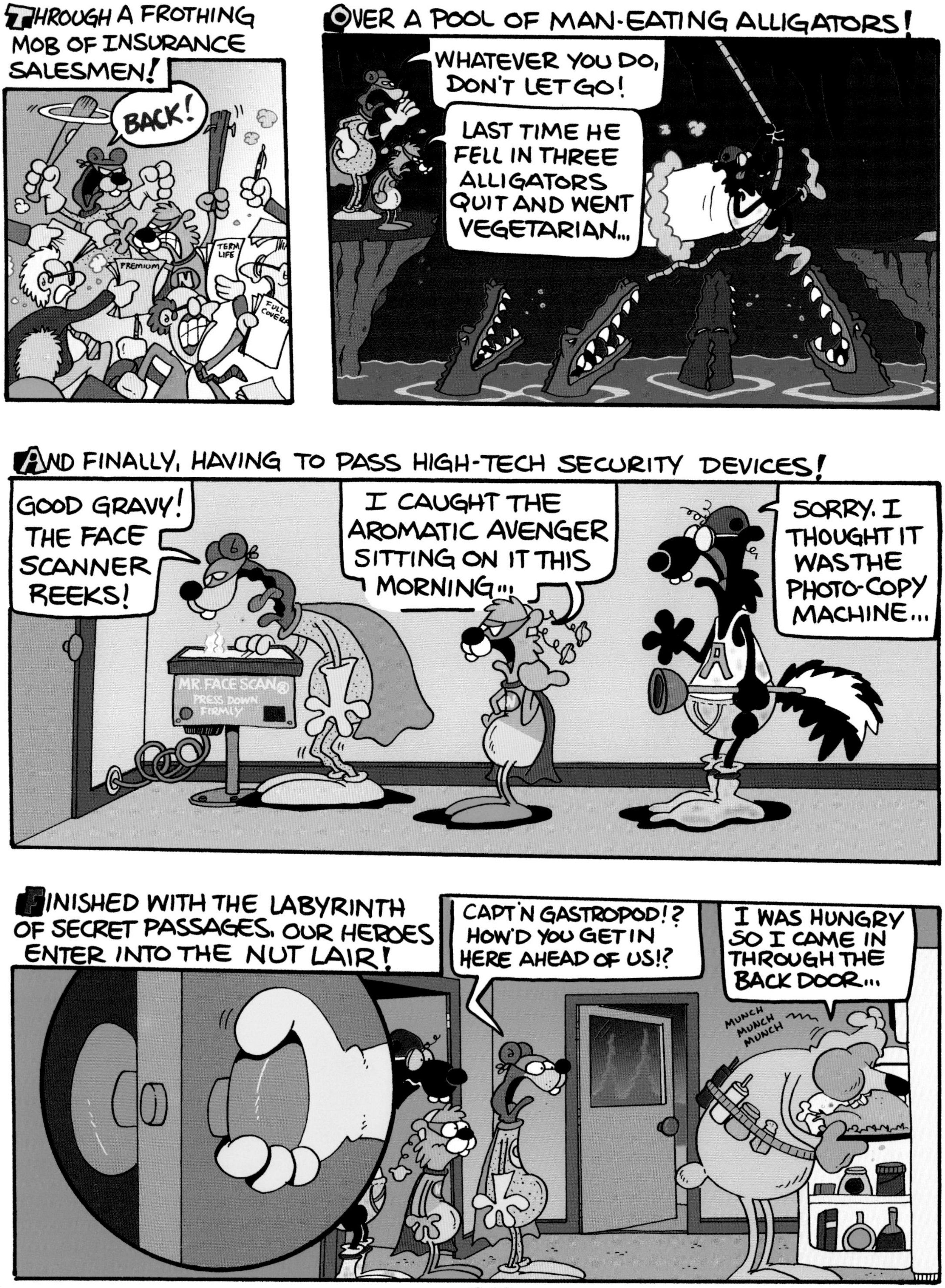
THROUGH A FROTHING MOB OF INSURANCE SALESMEN!
BACK!
PREMIUM
TERM LIFE
OVER A POOL OF MAN-EATING ALLIGATORS!
WHATEVER YOU DO, DON'T LET GO!
LAST TIME HE FELL IN THREE ALLIGATORS QUIT AND WENT VEGETARIAN...
AND FINALLY, HAVING TO PASS HIGH-TECH SECURITY DEVICES!
GOOD GRAVY! THE FACE SCANNER REEKS!
I CAUGHT THE AROMATIC AVENGER SITTING ON IT THIS MORNING...
SORRY. I THOUGHT IT WAS THE PHOTO-COPY MACHINE...
MR. FACE SCAN®
PRESS DOWN FIRMLY
FINISHED WITH THE LABYRINTH OF SECRET PASSAGES, OUR HEROES ENTER INTO THE NUT LAIR!
CAPT'N GASTROPOD!? HOW'D YOU GET IN HERE AHEAD OF US!?
I WAS HUNGRY SO I CAME IN THROUGH THE BACK DOOR...
MUNCH MUNCH MUNCH

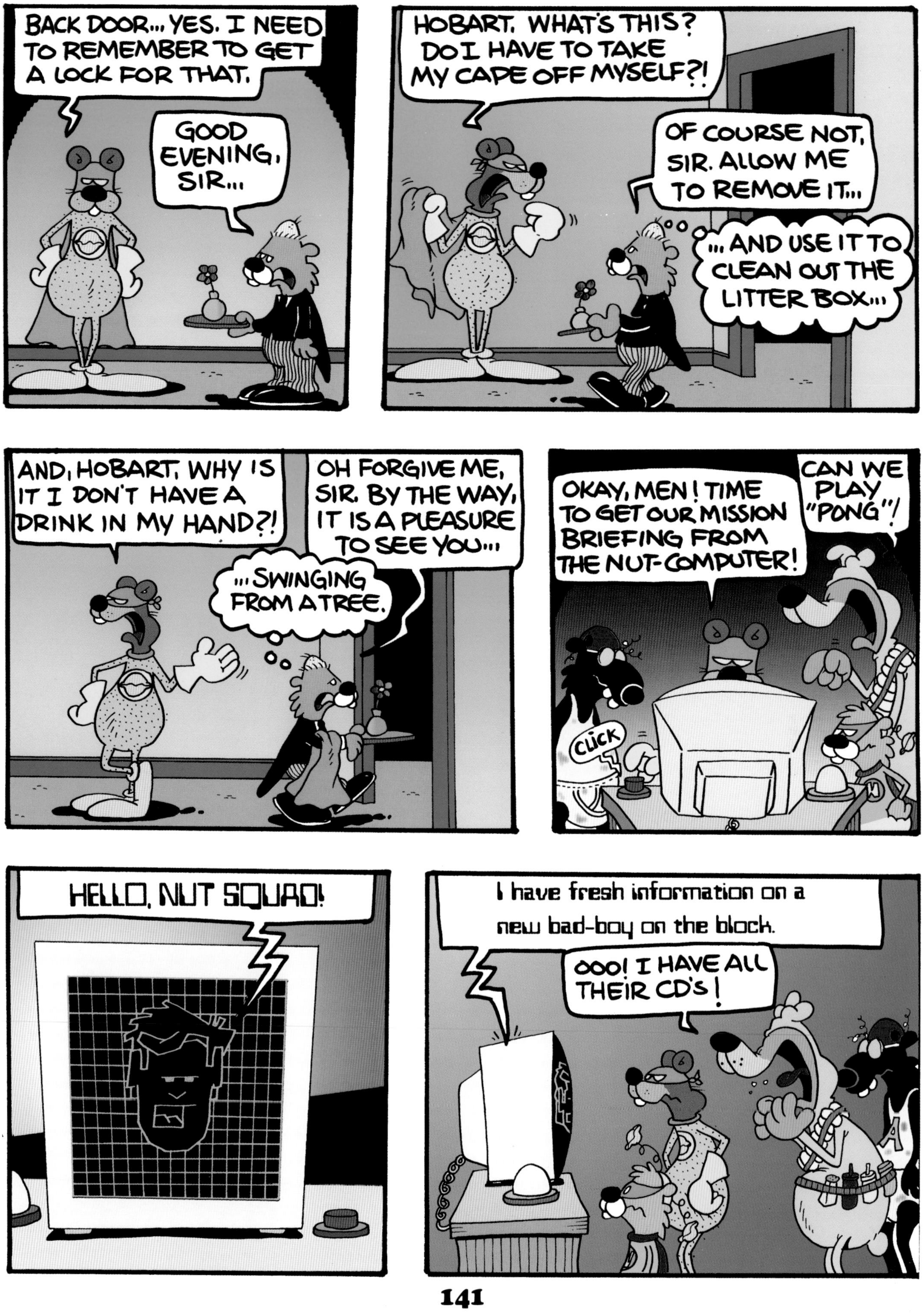
BACK DOOR... YES. I NEED TO REMEMBER TO GET A LOCK FOR THAT.
GOOD EVENING, SIR...
HOBART. WHAT'S THIS? DO I HAVE TO TAKE MY CAPE OFF MYSELF?!
OF COURSE NOT, SIR. ALLOW ME TO REMOVE IT...
...AND USE IT TO CLEAN OUT THE LITTER BOX...
AND, HOBART, WHY IS IT I DON'T HAVE A DRINK IN MY HAND?!
OH FORGIVE ME, SIR. BY THE WAY, IT IS A PLEASURE TO SEE YOU...
...SWINGING FROM A TREE.
OKAY, MEN! TIME TO GET OUR MISSION BRIEFING FROM THE NUT-COMPUTER!
CAN WE PLAY "PONG"!
CLICK
HELLO, NUT SQUAD!
I have fresh information on a new bad-boy on the block.
OOO! I HAVE ALL THEIR CD's!

Mold research genius Dr. Milton Sugardew has created an army of Mold Men and now goes by the name of Dr. Nasty Mildew.

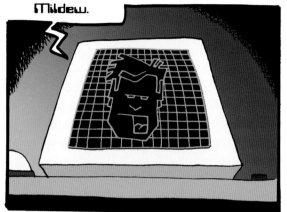

With his evil army he plans to somehow take over the world...

OO-OO! I HAVE A QUESTION...!

JUST WHO IS HE PLANNING TO TAKE THE WORLD FROM?

Why...uhhh... Us, I guess...

WELL I WASN'T AWARE WE OWNED THE WORLD...

...umm... we don't.

THEN HOW CAN WE STOP SOMEONE FROM TAKING SOMETHING WE DON'T EVEN OWN? DO WE HAVE THE RIGHT? THERE'S A REAL PHILOSOPHICAL QUANDRY HERE...!

ME THINKS THE AROMATIC AVENGER HAS BEEN STICKING HIS OWN HEAD UNDER THE COVERS AGAIN...

EXCUSE ME! Can we please continue...!?

OH FINE! NO ONE WANTS TO DISCUSS THE ISSUES!

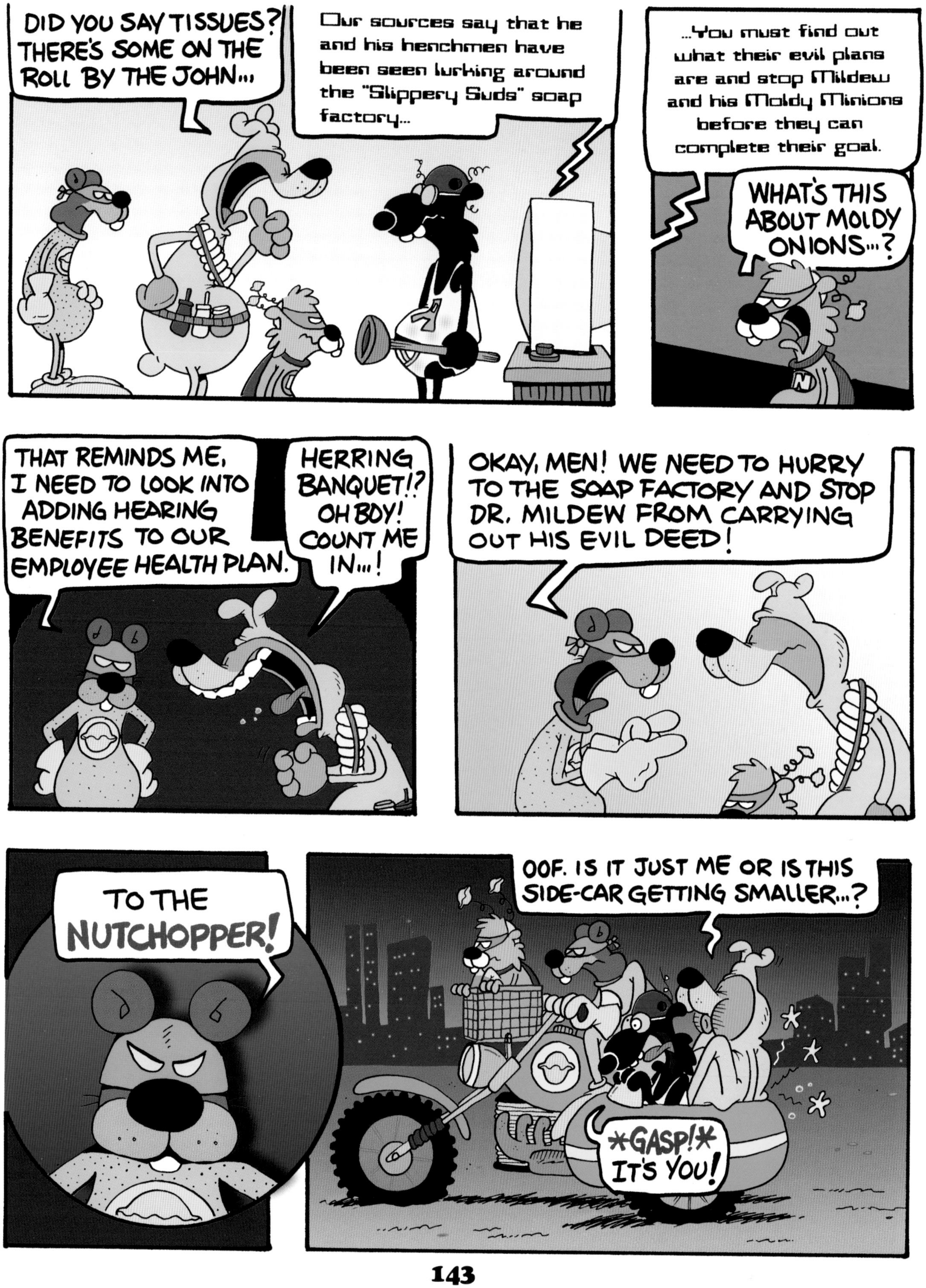
DID YOU SAY TISSUES? THERE'S SOME ON THE ROLL BY THE JOHN...
Our sources say that he and his henchmen have been seen lurking around the "Slippery Suds" soap factory...
...You must find out what their evil plans are and stop Mildew and his Moldy Minions before they can complete their goal.
WHAT'S THIS ABOUT MOLDY ONIONS...?
THAT REMINDS ME, I NEED TO LOOK INTO ADDING HEARING BENEFITS TO OUR EMPLOYEE HEALTH PLAN.
HERRING BANQUET!? OH BOY! COUNT ME IN...!
OKAY, MEN! WE NEED TO HURRY TO THE SOAP FACTORY AND STOP DR. MILDEW FROM CARRYING OUT HIS EVIL DEED!
TO THE NUTCHOPPER!
OOF. IS IT JUST ME OR IS THIS SIDE-CAR GETTING SMALLER...?
GASP! IT'S YOU!

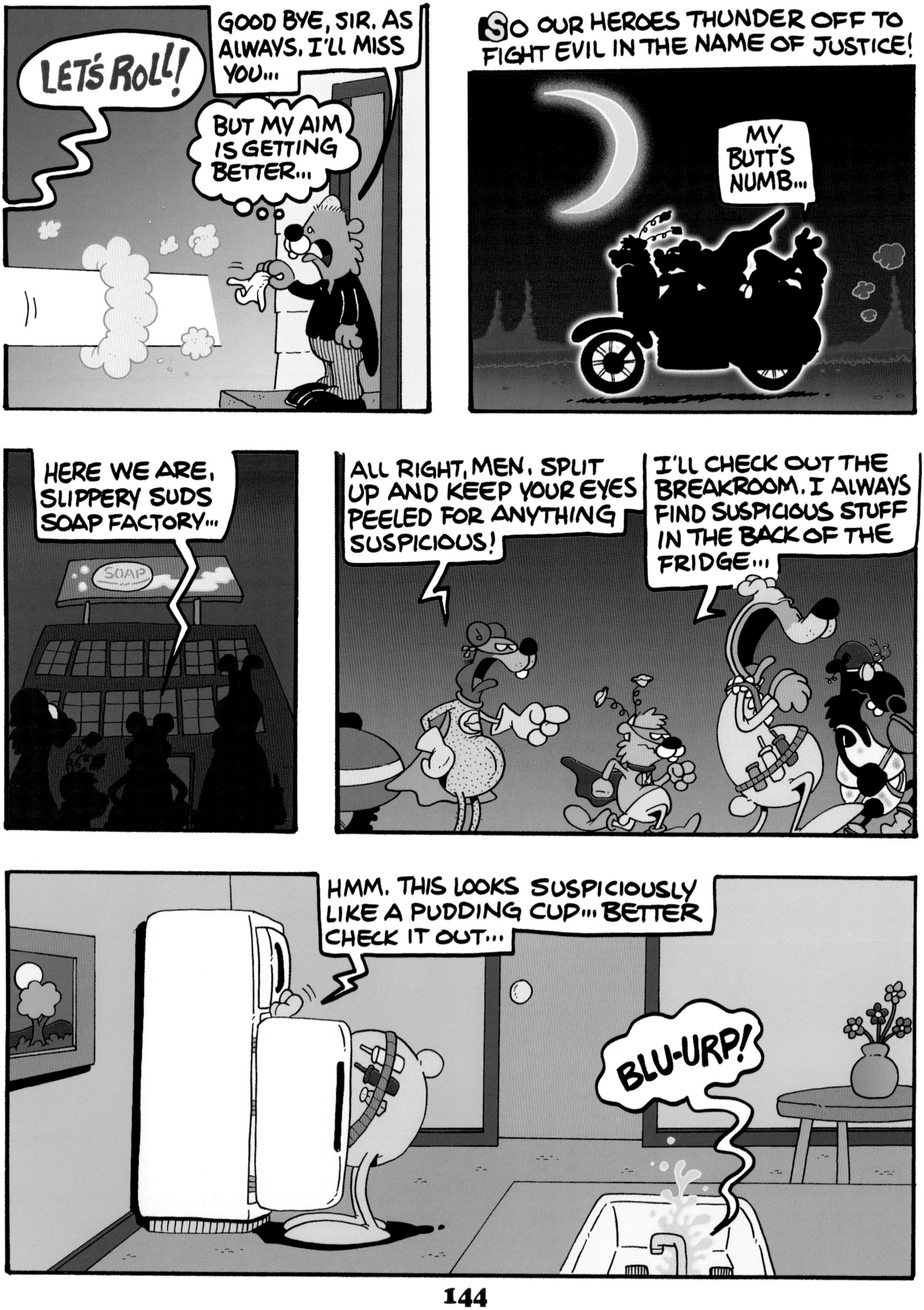
LET'S ROLL!
GOOD BYE, SIR. AS ALWAYS, I'LL MISS YOU...
BUT MY AIM IS GETTING BETTER...
SO OUR HEROES THUNDER OFF TO FIGHT EVIL IN THE NAME OF JUSTICE!
MY BUTT'S NUMB...
HERE WE ARE, SLIPPERY SUDS SOAP FACTORY...
SOAP
ALL RIGHT, MEN. SPLIT UP AND KEEP YOUR EYES PEELED FOR ANYTHING SUSPICIOUS!
I'LL CHECK OUT THE BREAKROOM. I ALWAYS FIND SUSPICIOUS STUFF IN THE BACK OF THE FRIDGE...
HMM. THIS LOOKS SUSPICIOUSLY LIKE A PUDDING CUP... BETTER CHECK IT OUT...
BLU-URP!

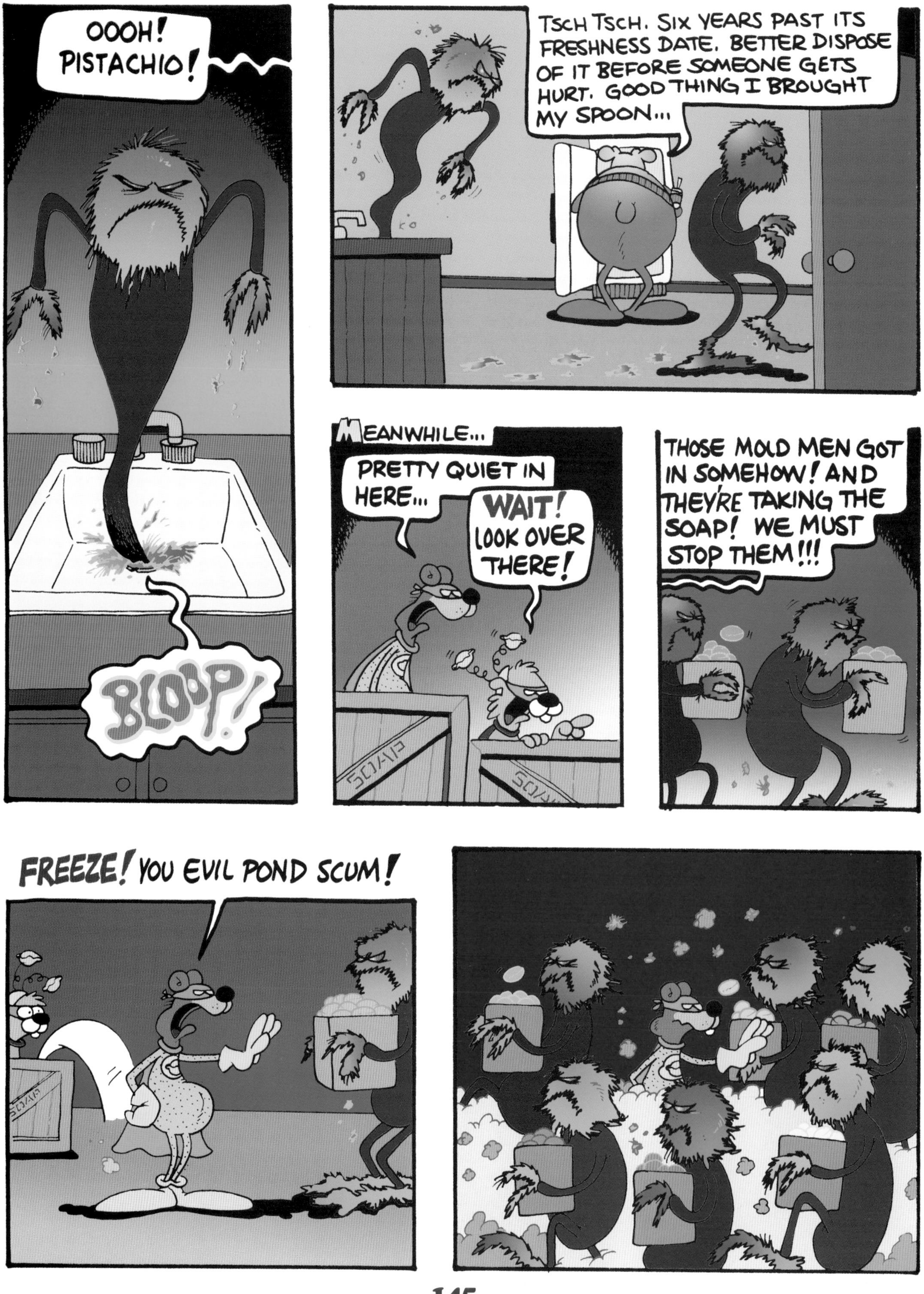
OOOH! PISTACHIO!
BLOOP!
TSCH TSCH. SIX YEARS PAST ITS FRESHNESS DATE. BETTER DISPOSE OF IT BEFORE SOMEONE GETS HURT. GOOD THING I BROUGHT MY SPOON...
MEANWHILE...
PRETTY QUIET IN HERE...
WAIT! LOOK OVER THERE!
SOAP
SOAP
THOSE MOLD MEN GOT IN SOMEHOW! AND THEY'RE TAKING THE SOAP! WE MUST STOP THEM!!!
FREEZE! YOU EVIL POND SCUM!
SOAP

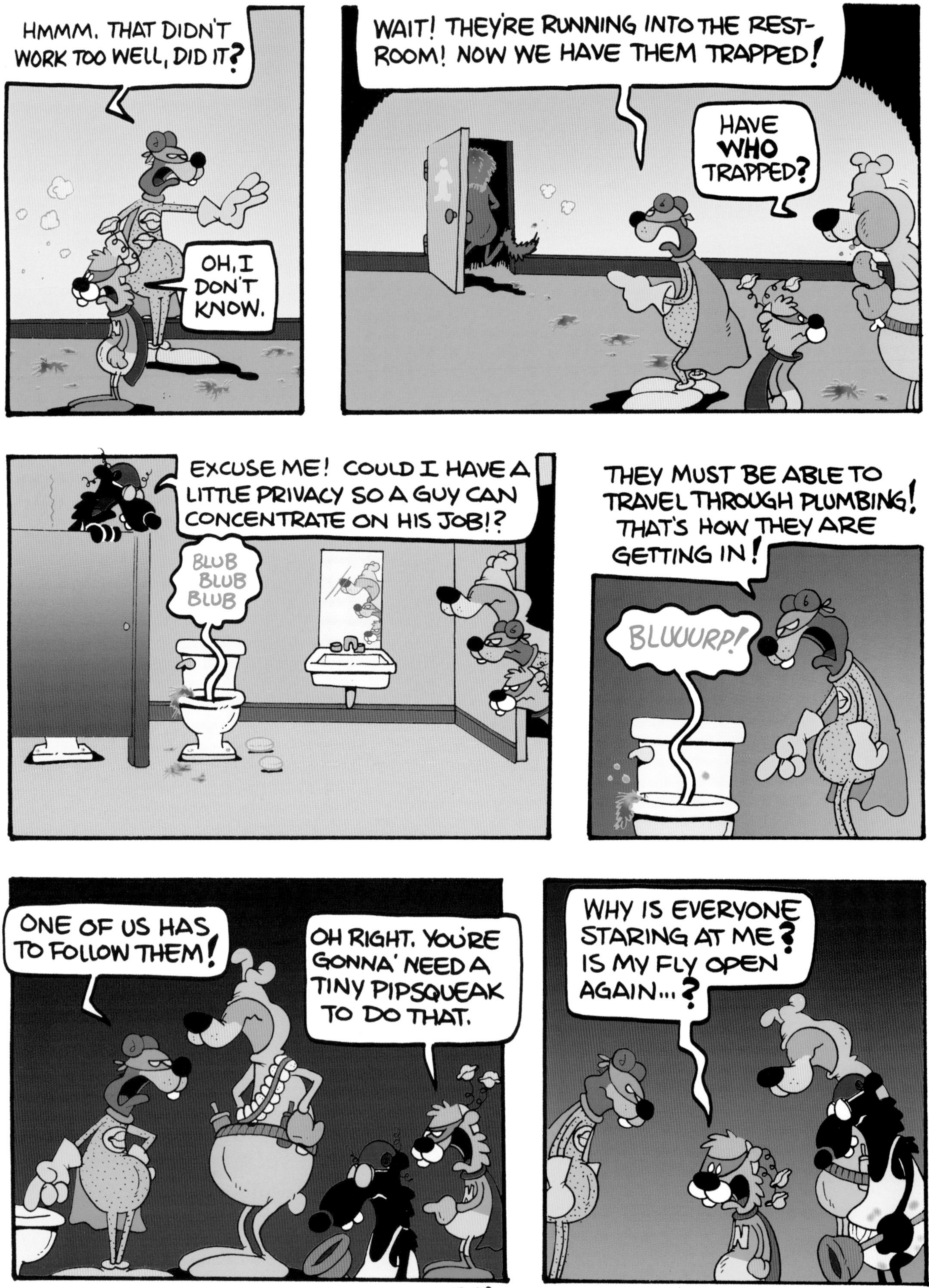
HMMM. THAT DIDN'T WORK TOO WELL, DID IT?
OH, I DON'T KNOW.
WAIT! THEY'RE RUNNING INTO THE REST-ROOM! NOW WE HAVE THEM TRAPPED!
HAVE WHO TRAPPED?
EXCUSE ME! COULD I HAVE A LITTLE PRIVACY SO A GUY CAN CONCENTRATE ON HIS JOB!?
BLUB BLUB BLUB
THEY MUST BE ABLE TO TRAVEL THROUGH PLUMBING! THAT'S HOW THEY ARE GETTING IN!
BLUUURP!
ONE OF US HAS TO FOLLOW THEM!
OH RIGHT. YOU'RE GONNA' NEED A TINY PIPSQUEAK TO DO THAT.
WHY IS EVERYONE STARING AT ME? IS MY FLY OPEN AGAIN...?

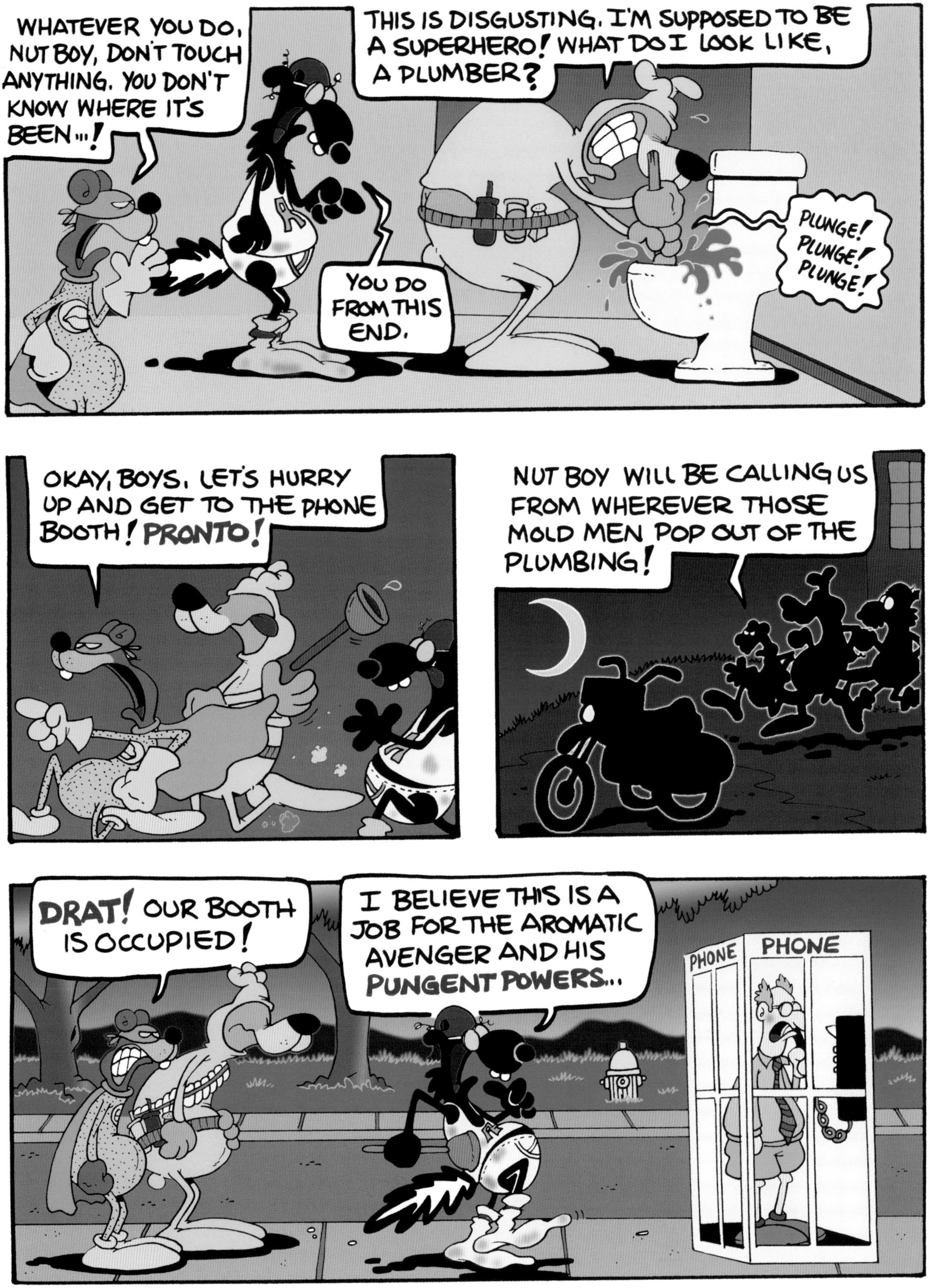
WHATEVER YOU DO, NUT BOY, DON'T TOUCH ANYTHING. YOU DON'T KNOW WHERE IT'S BEEN...!
THIS IS DISGUSTING. I'M SUPPOSED TO BE A SUPERHERO! WHAT DO I LOOK LIKE, A PLUMBER?
YOU DO FROM THIS END.
PLUNGE! PLUNGE! PLUNGE!
OKAY, BOYS. LET'S HURRY UP AND GET TO THE PHONE BOOTH! PRONTO!
NUT BOY WILL BE CALLING US FROM WHEREVER THOSE MOLD MEN POP OUT OF THE PLUMBING!
DRAT! OUR BOOTH IS OCCUPIED!
I BELIEVE THIS IS A JOB FOR THE AROMATIC AVENGER AND HIS PUNGENT POWERS...
PHONE
PHONE

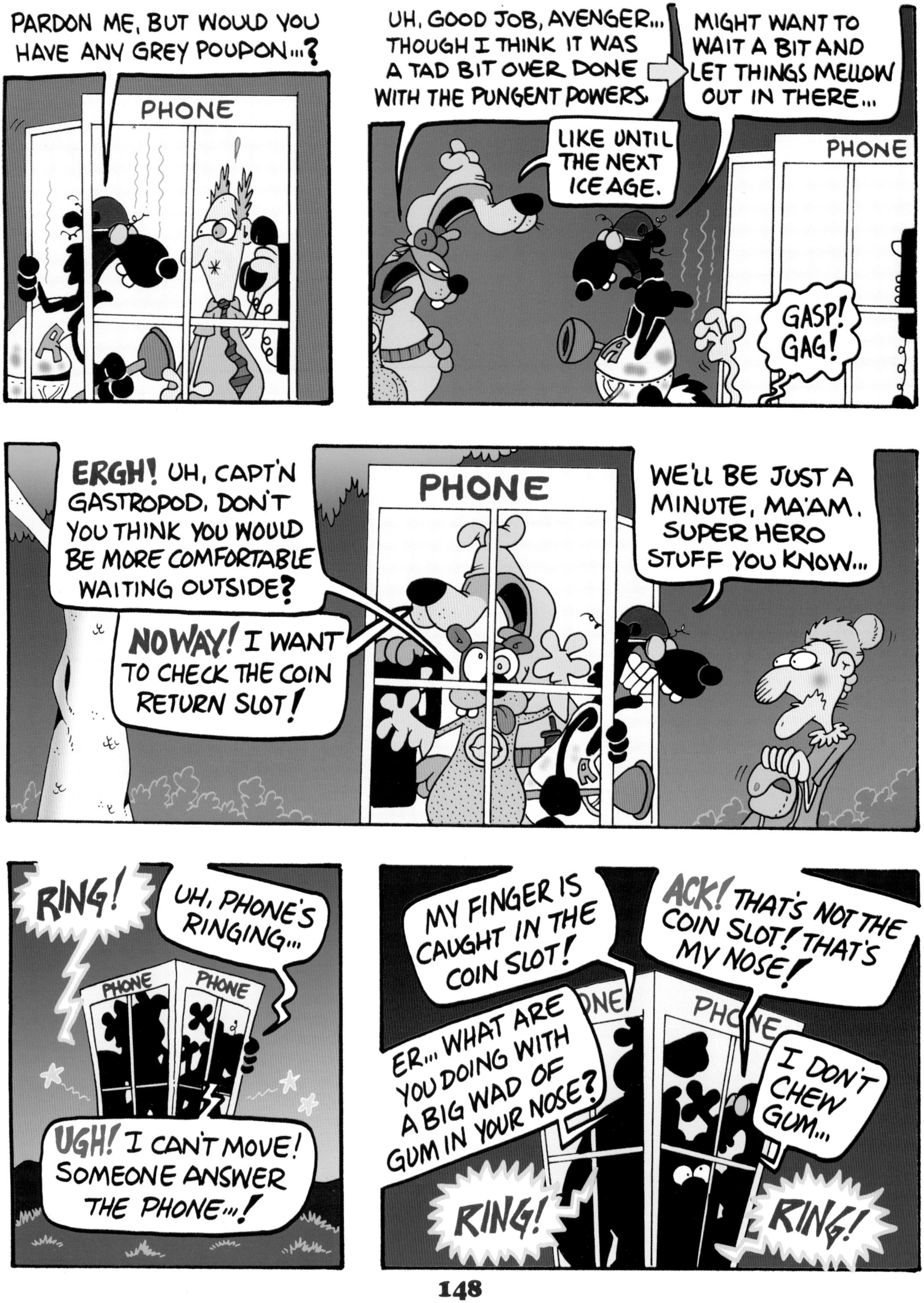
PARDON ME, BUT WOULD YOU HAVE ANY GREY POUPON...?
PHONE
UH, GOOD JOB, AVENGER... THOUGH I THINK IT WAS A TAD BIT OVER DONE WITH THE PUNGENT POWERS.
MIGHT WANT TO WAIT A BIT AND LET THINGS MELLOW OUT IN THERE...
LIKE UNTIL THE NEXT ICE AGE.
PHONE
GASP! GAG!
ERGH! UH, CAPT'N GASTROPOD, DON'T YOU THINK YOU WOULD BE MORE COMFORTABLE WAITING OUTSIDE?
PHONE
WE'LL BE JUST A MINUTE, MA'AM. SUPER HERO STUFF YOU KNOW...
NO WAY! I WANT TO CHECK THE COIN RETURN SLOT!
RING!
UH, PHONE'S RINGING...
PHONE
PHONE
UGH! I CAN'T MOVE! SOMEONE ANSWER THE PHONE...!
MY FINGER IS CAUGHT IN THE COIN SLOT!
ACK! THAT'S NOT THE COIN SLOT! THAT'S MY NOSE!
ER... WHAT ARE YOU DOING WITH A BIG WAD OF GUM IN YOUR NOSE?
I DON'T CHEW GUM...
RING!
RING!

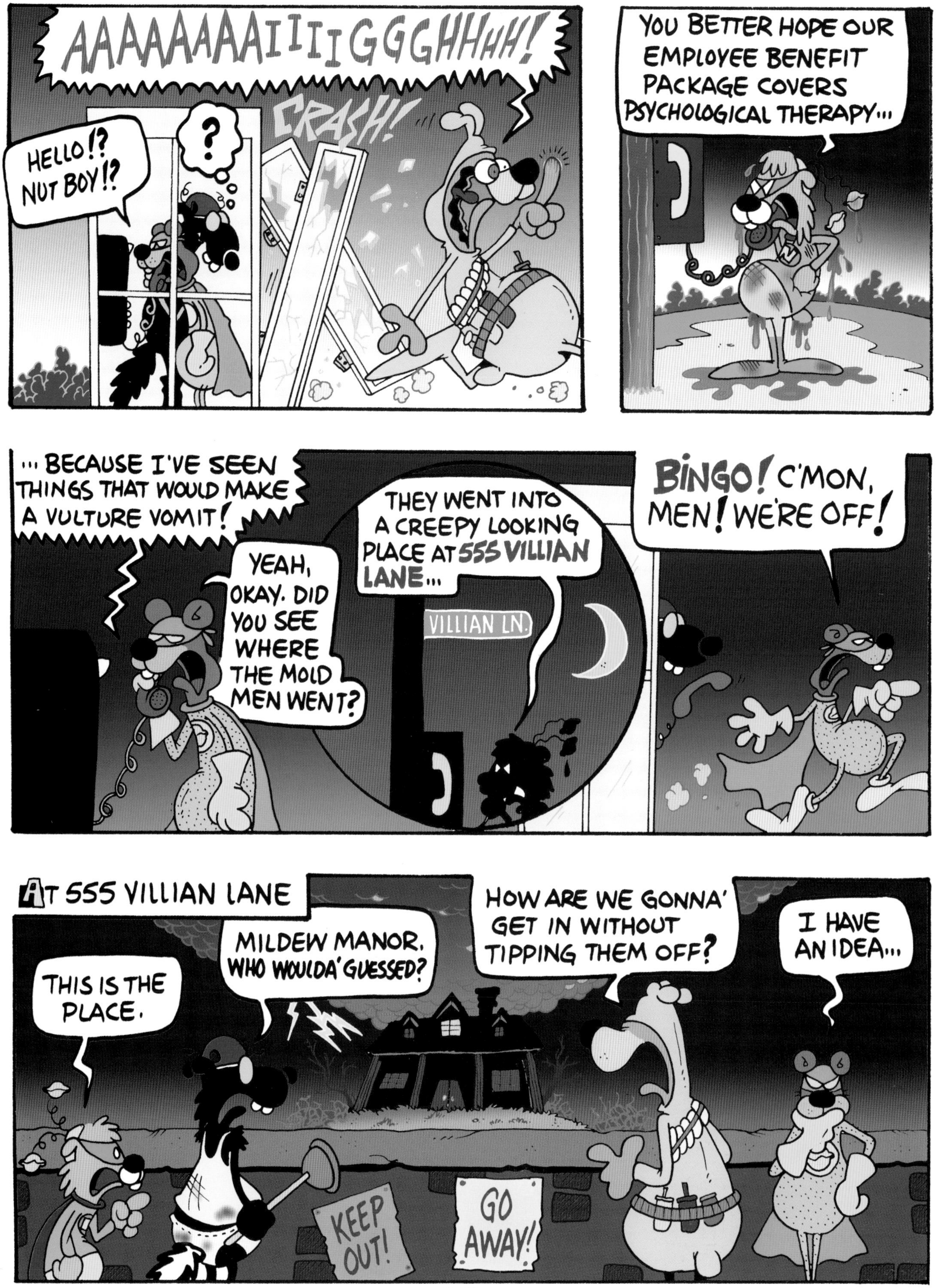
AAAAAAAAIIIIGGGHHHH!
CRASH!
HELLO!? NUT BOY!?
?
YOU BETTER HOPE OUR EMPLOYEE BENEFIT PACKAGE COVERS PSYCHOLOGICAL THERAPY...
... BECAUSE I'VE SEEN THINGS THAT WOULD MAKE A VULTURE VOMIT!
YEAH, OKAY. DID YOU SEE WHERE THE MOLD MEN WENT?
THEY WENT INTO A CREEPY LOOKING PLACE AT 555 VILLIAN LANE...
VILLIAN LN.
BINGO! C'MON, MEN! WE'RE OFF!
AT 555 VILLIAN LANE
THIS IS THE PLACE.
MILDEW MANOR. WHO WOULDA' GUESSED?
HOW ARE WE GONNA' GET IN WITHOUT TIPPING THEM OFF?
I HAVE AN IDEA...
KEEP OUT!
GO AWAY!

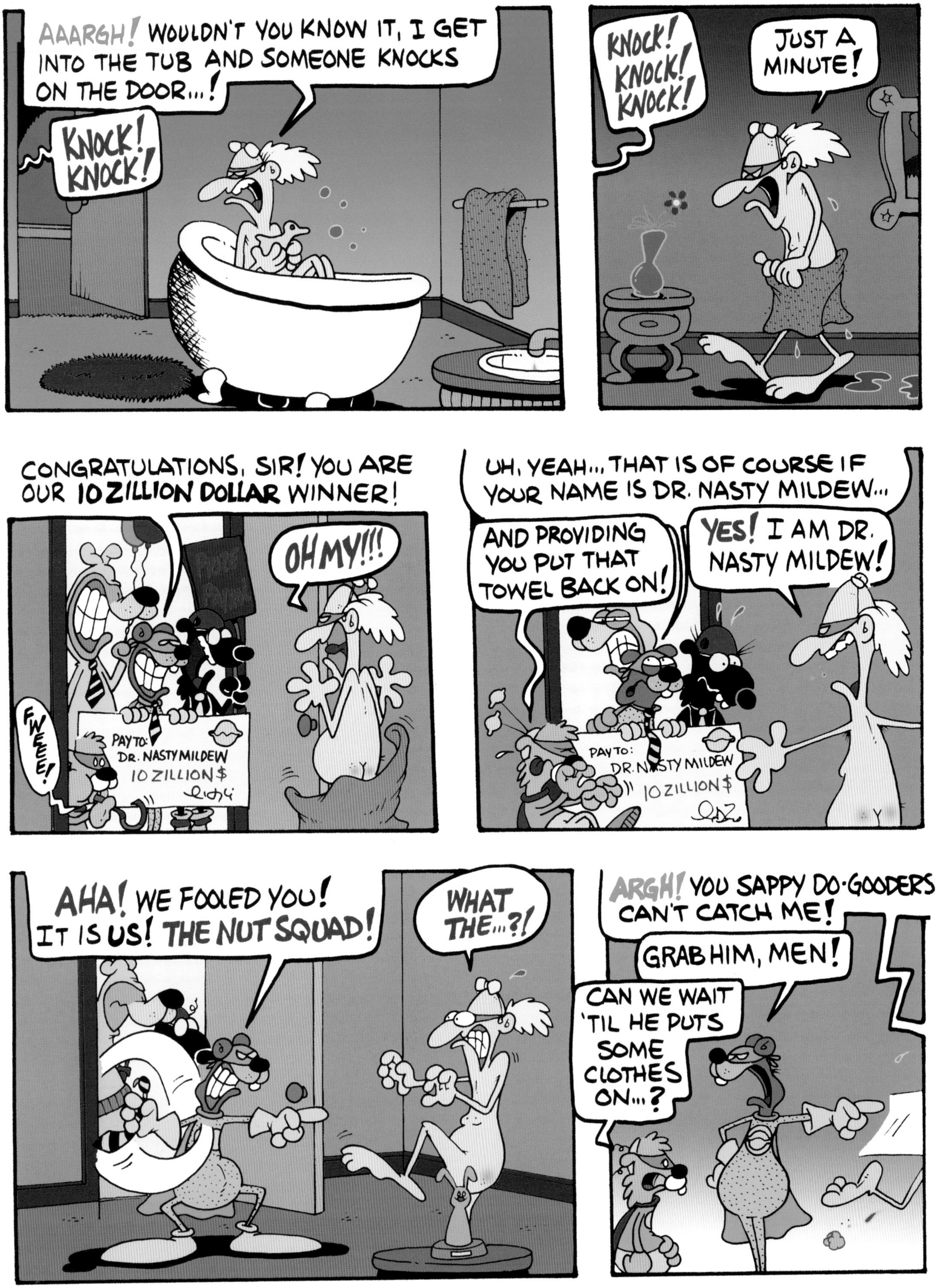
AAARGH! WOULDN'T YOU KNOW IT, I GET INTO THE TUB AND SOMEONE KNOCKS ON THE DOOR...!
KNOCK! KNOCK!
KNOCK! KNOCK! KNOCK!
JUST A MINUTE!
CONGRATULATIONS, SIR! YOU ARE OUR 10 ZILLION DOLLAR WINNER!
OH MY!!!
FWEEE!
PAY TO: DR. NASTY MILDEW 10 ZILLION $
UH, YEAH... THAT IS OF COURSE IF YOUR NAME IS DR. NASTY MILDEW...
AND PROVIDING YOU PUT THAT TOWEL BACK ON!
YES! I AM DR. NASTY MILDEW!
PAY TO: DR. NASTY MILDEW 10 ZILLION $
AHA! WE FOOLED YOU! IT IS US! THE NUT SQUAD!
WHAT THE...?!
ARGH! YOU SAPPY DO-GOODERS CAN'T CATCH ME!
GRAB HIM, MEN!
CAN WE WAIT 'TIL HE PUTS SOME CLOTHES ON...?

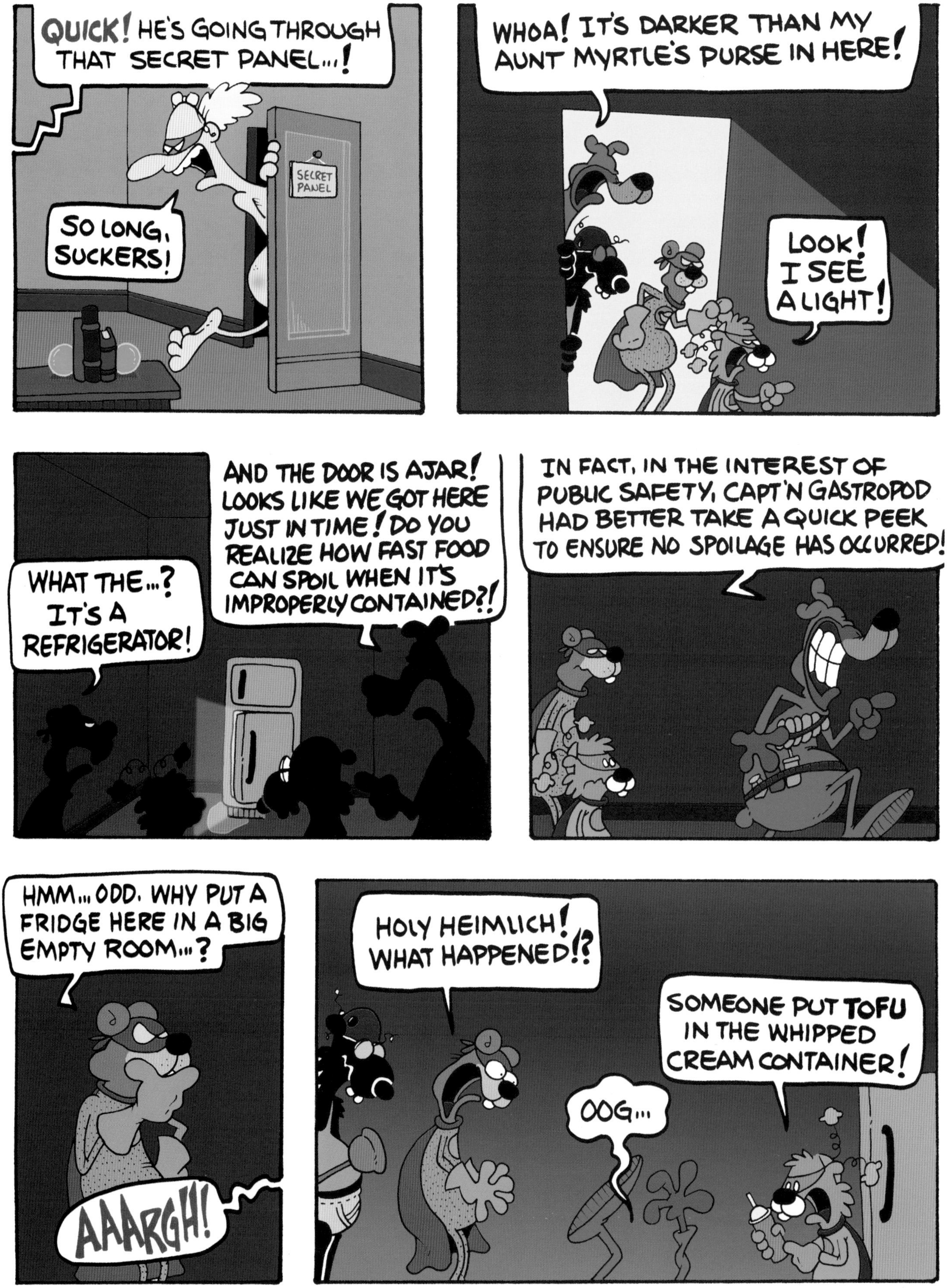
QUICK! HE'S GOING THROUGH THAT SECRET PANEL...!
SECRET PANEL
SO LONG, SUCKERS!
WHOA! IT'S DARKER THAN MY AUNT MYRTLE'S PURSE IN HERE!
LOOK! I SEE A LIGHT!
WHAT THE...? IT'S A REFRIGERATOR!
AND THE DOOR IS AJAR! LOOKS LIKE WE GOT HERE JUST IN TIME! DO YOU REALIZE HOW FAST FOOD CAN SPOIL WHEN IT'S IMPROPERLY CONTAINED?!
IN FACT, IN THE INTEREST OF PUBLIC SAFETY, CAPT'N GASTROPOD HAD BETTER TAKE A QUICK PEEK TO ENSURE NO SPOILAGE HAS OCCURRED!
HMM... ODD. WHY PUT A FRIDGE HERE IN A BIG EMPTY ROOM...?
AAARGH!
HOLY HEIMLICH! WHAT HAPPENED!?
SOMEONE PUT TOFU IN THE WHIPPED CREAM CONTAINER!
OOG...

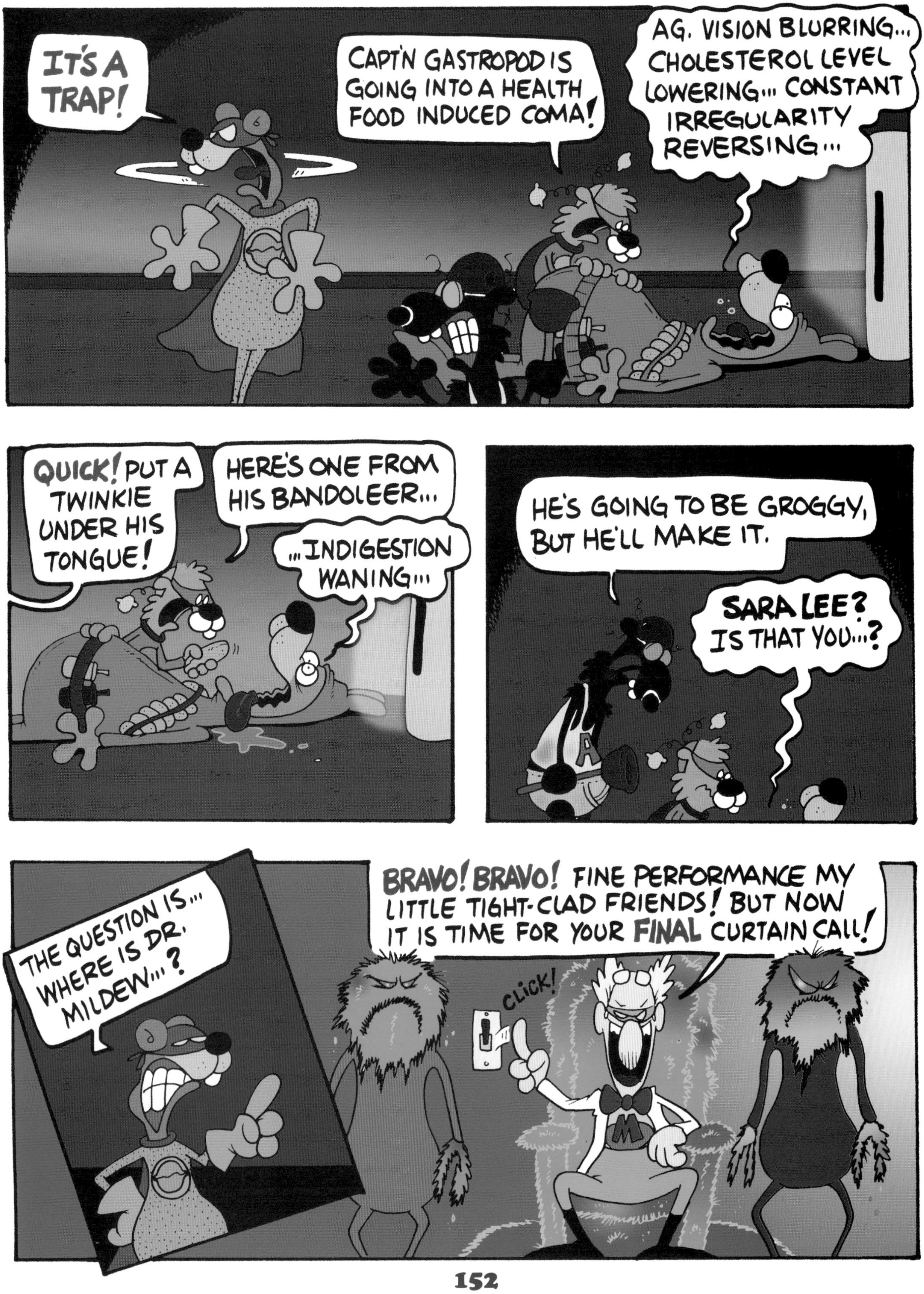
IT'S A TRAP!
CAPT'N GASTROPOD IS GOING INTO A HEALTH FOOD INDUCED COMA!
AG. VISION BLURRING... CHOLESTEROL LEVEL LOWERING... CONSTANT IRREGULARITY REVERSING...
QUICK! PUT A TWINKIE UNDER HIS TONGUE!
HERE'S ONE FROM HIS BANDOLEER...
...INDIGESTION WANING...
HE'S GOING TO BE GROGGY, BUT HE'LL MAKE IT.
SARA LEE? IS THAT YOU...?
THE QUESTION IS... WHERE IS DR. MILDEW...?
BRAVO! BRAVO! FINE PERFORMANCE MY LITTLE TIGHT-CLAD FRIENDS! BUT NOW IT IS TIME FOR YOUR FINAL CURTAIN CALL!
CLICK!

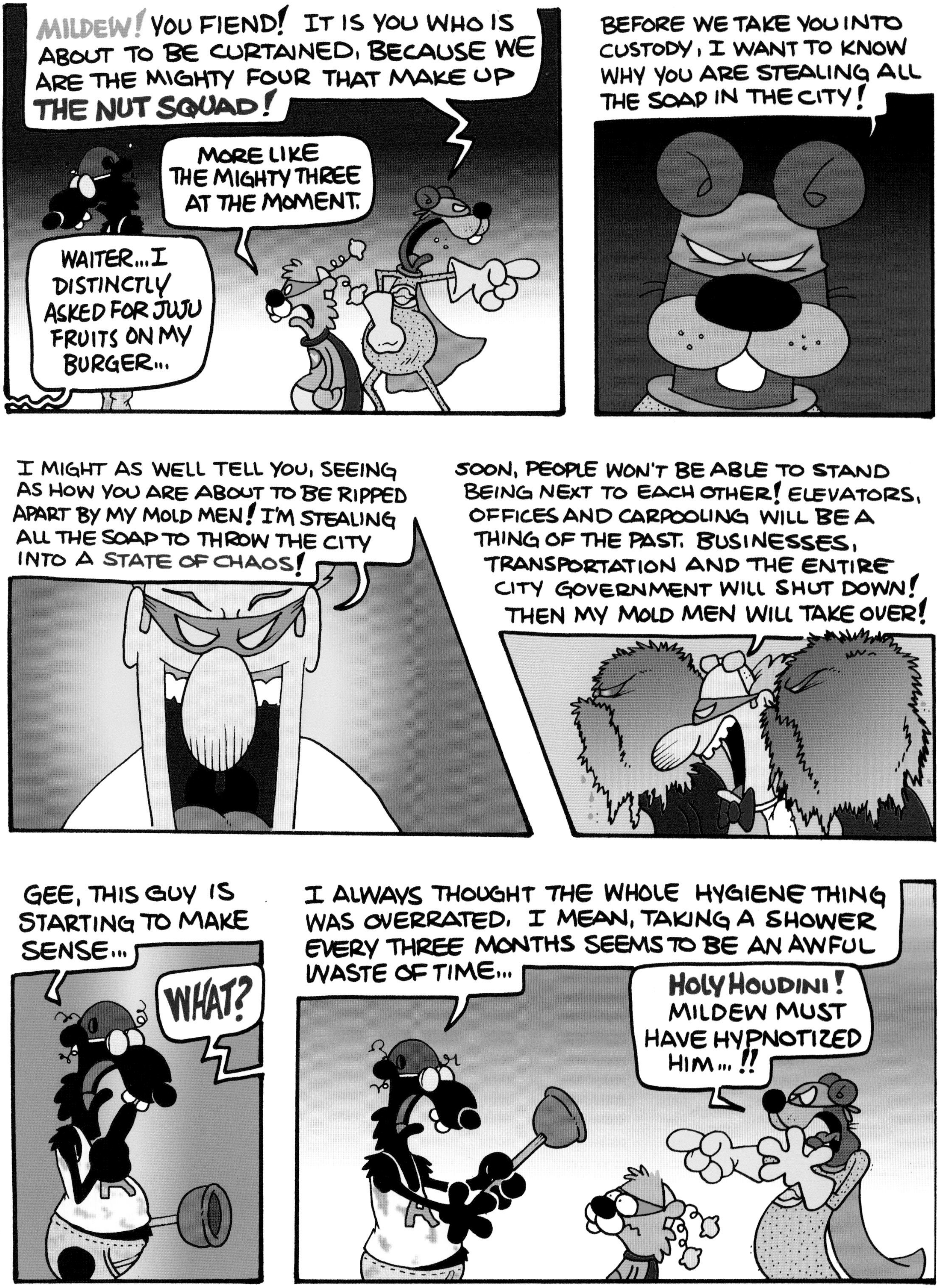
MILDEW! YOU FIEND! IT IS YOU WHO IS ABOUT TO BE CURTAINED, BECAUSE WE ARE THE MIGHTY FOUR THAT MAKE UP THE NUT SQUAD!
MORE LIKE THE MIGHTY THREE AT THE MOMENT.
WAITER...I DISTINCTLY ASKED FOR JUJU FRUITS ON MY BURGER...
BEFORE WE TAKE YOU INTO CUSTODY, I WANT TO KNOW WHY YOU ARE STEALING ALL THE SOAP IN THE CITY!
I MIGHT AS WELL TELL YOU, SEEING AS HOW YOU ARE ABOUT TO BE RIPPED APART BY MY MOLD MEN! I'M STEALING ALL THE SOAP TO THROW THE CITY INTO A STATE OF CHAOS!
SOON, PEOPLE WON'T BE ABLE TO STAND BEING NEXT TO EACH OTHER! ELEVATORS, OFFICES AND CARPOOLING WILL BE A THING OF THE PAST. BUSINESSES, TRANSPORTATION AND THE ENTIRE CITY GOVERNMENT WILL SHUT DOWN! THEN MY MOLD MEN WILL TAKE OVER!
GEE, THIS GUY IS STARTING TO MAKE SENSE...
WHAT?
I ALWAYS THOUGHT THE WHOLE HYGIENE THING WAS OVERRATED. I MEAN, TAKING A SHOWER EVERY THREE MONTHS SEEMS TO BE AN AWFUL WASTE OF TIME...
HOLY HOUDINI! MILDEW MUST HAVE HYPNOTIZED HIM...!!

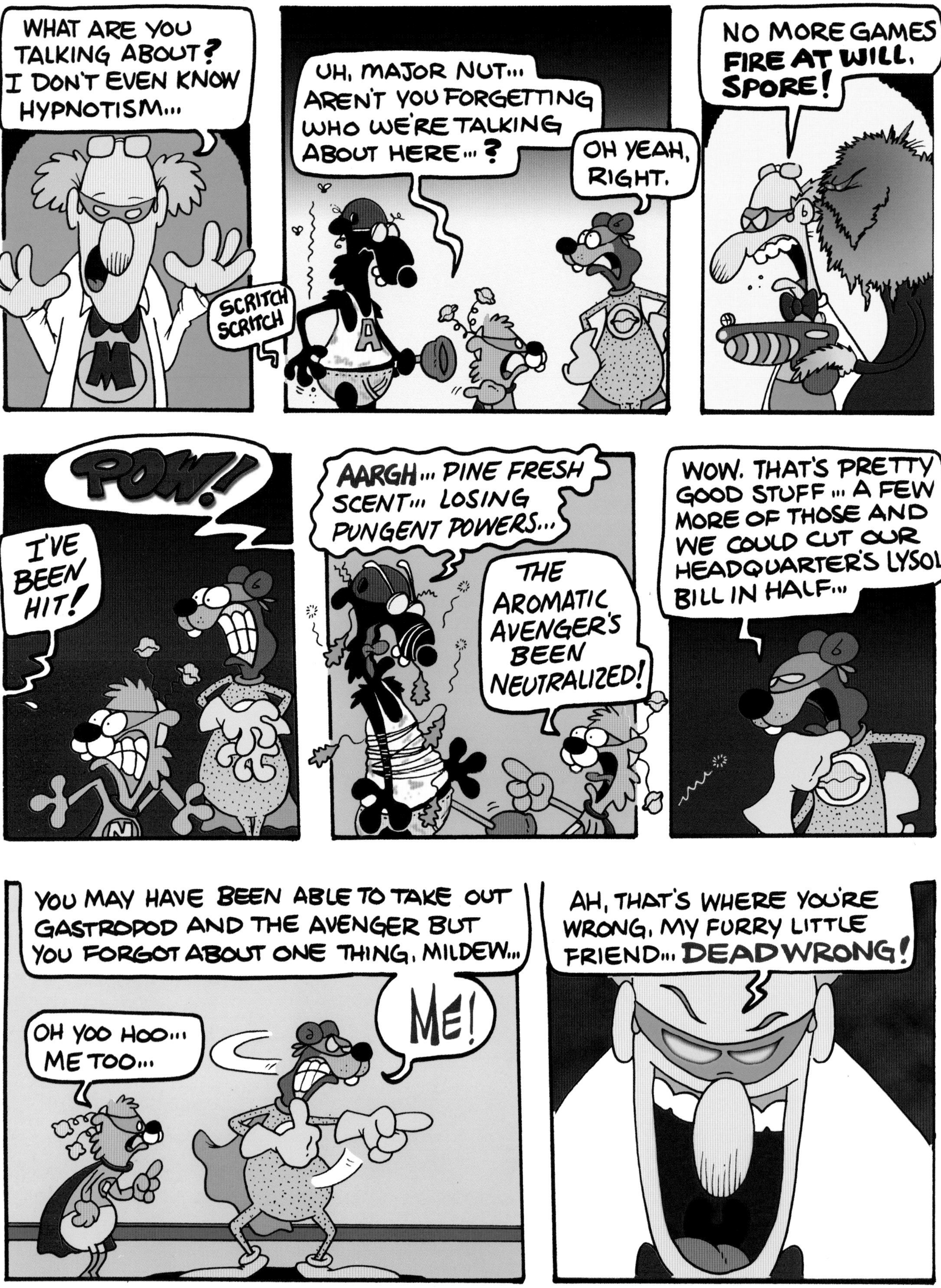

WHAT ARE YOU TALKING ABOUT? I DON'T EVEN KNOW HYPNOTISM...
UH, MAJOR NUT... AREN'T YOU FORGETTING WHO WE'RE TALKING ABOUT HERE...?
SCRITCH SCRITCH
OH YEAH, RIGHT.
NO MORE GAMES FIRE AT WILL, SPORE!
POW!
I'VE BEEN HIT!
AARGH... PINE FRESH SCENT... LOSING PUNGENT POWERS...
THE AROMATIC AVENGER'S BEEN NEUTRALIZED!
WOW. THAT'S PRETTY GOOD STUFF... A FEW MORE OF THOSE AND WE COULD CUT OUR HEADQUARTER'S LYSOL BILL IN HALF...
YOU MAY HAVE BEEN ABLE TO TAKE OUT GASTROPOD AND THE AVENGER BUT YOU FORGOT ABOUT ONE THING, MILDEW...
ME!
OH YOO HOO... ME TOO...
AH, THAT'S WHERE YOU'RE WRONG, MY FURRY LITTLE FRIEND... DEAD WRONG!

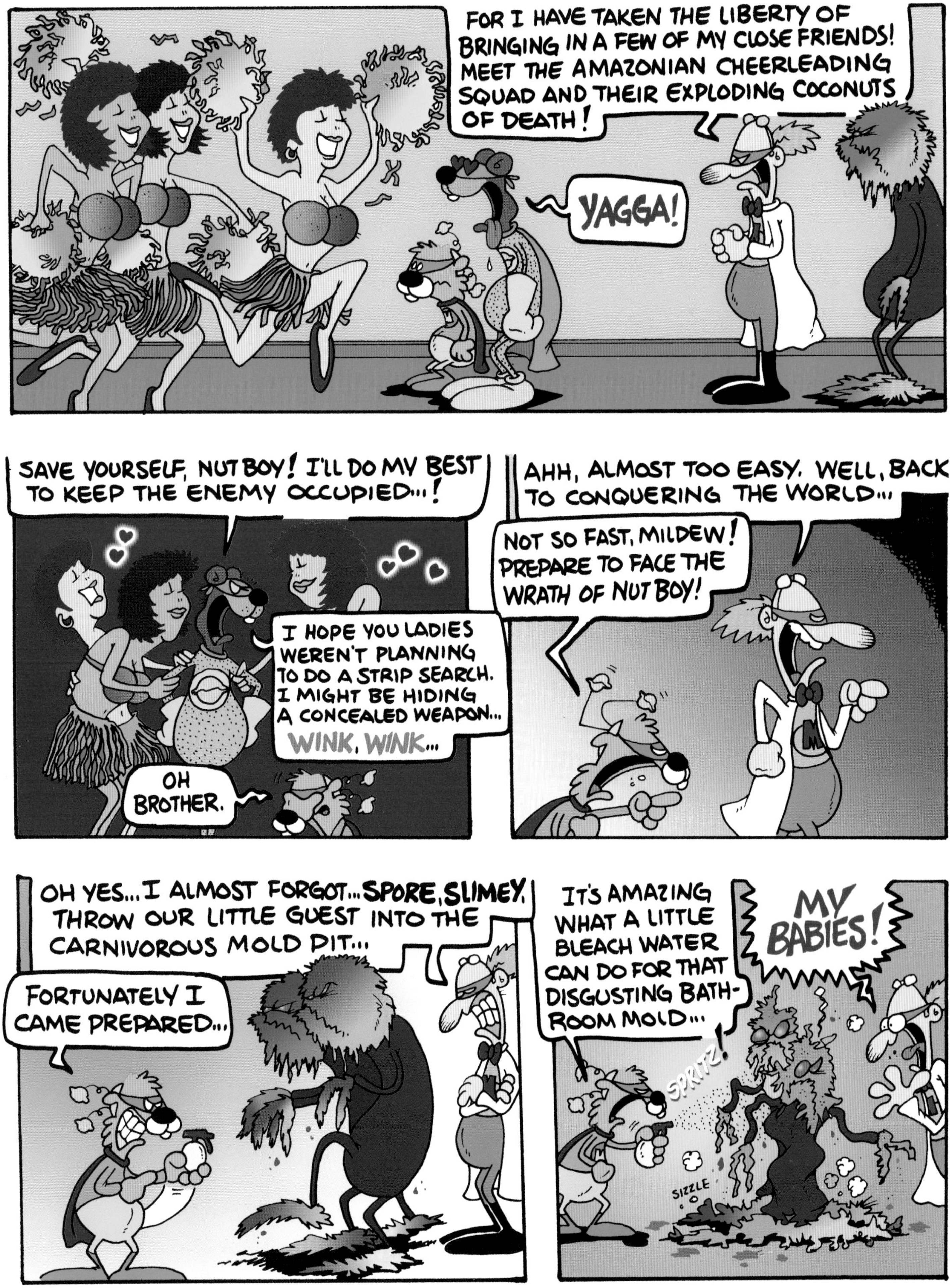
FOR I HAVE TAKEN THE LIBERTY OF BRINGING IN A FEW OF MY CLOSE FRIENDS! MEET THE AMAZONIAN CHEERLEADING SQUAD AND THEIR EXPLODING COCONUTS OF DEATH!
YAGGA!
SAVE YOURSELF, NUT BOY! I'LL DO MY BEST TO KEEP THE ENEMY OCCUPIED...!
I HOPE YOU LADIES WEREN'T PLANNING TO DO A STRIP SEARCH. I MIGHT BE HIDING A CONCEALED WEAPON... WINK, WINK...
OH BROTHER.
AHH, ALMOST TOO EASY. WELL, BACK TO CONQUERING THE WORLD...
NOT SO FAST, MILDEW! PREPARE TO FACE THE WRATH OF NUT BOY!
OH YES... I ALMOST FORGOT... SPORE, SLIMEY, THROW OUR LITTLE GUEST INTO THE CARNIVOROUS MOLD PIT...
FORTUNATELY I CAME PREPARED...
IT'S AMAZING WHAT A LITTLE BLEACH WATER CAN DO FOR THAT DISGUSTING BATH-ROOM MOLD...
MY BABIES!
SPRITZ!
SIZZLE

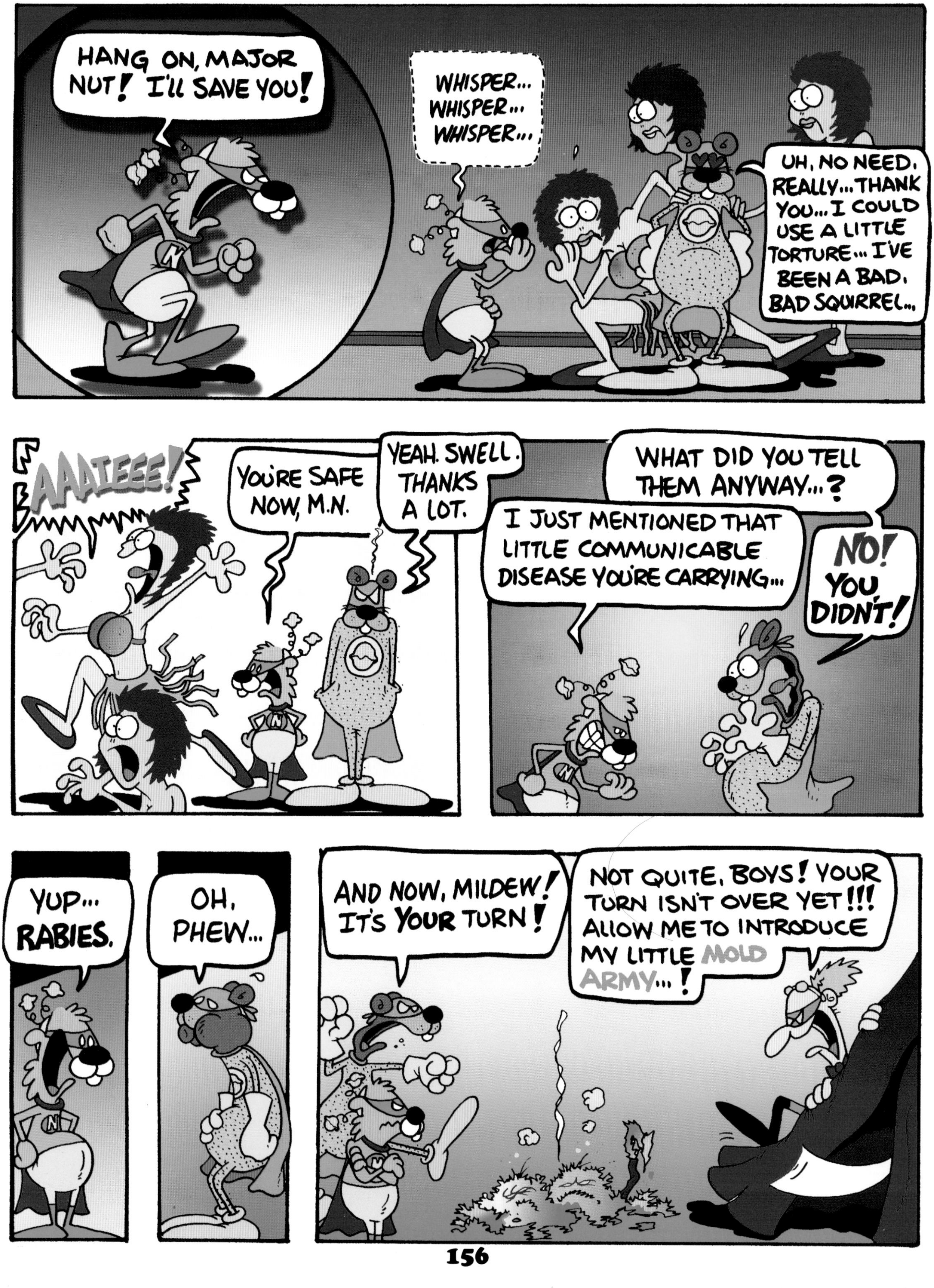
HANG ON, MAJOR NUT! I'LL SAVE YOU!
WHISPER... WHISPER... WHISPER...
UH, NO NEED. REALLY... THANK YOU... I COULD USE A LITTLE TORTURE... I'VE BEEN A BAD, BAD SQUIRREL...
AAAIEEE!
YOU'RE SAFE NOW, M.N.
YEAH. SWELL. THANKS A LOT.
WHAT DID YOU TELL THEM ANYWAY...?
I JUST MENTIONED THAT LITTLE COMMUNICABLE DISEASE YOU'RE CARRYING...
NO! YOU DIDN'T!
YUP... RABIES.
OH, PHEW...
AND NOW, MILDEW! IT'S YOUR TURN!
NOT QUITE, BOYS! YOUR TURN ISN'T OVER YET!!! ALLOW ME TO INTRODUCE MY LITTLE MOLD ARMY...!

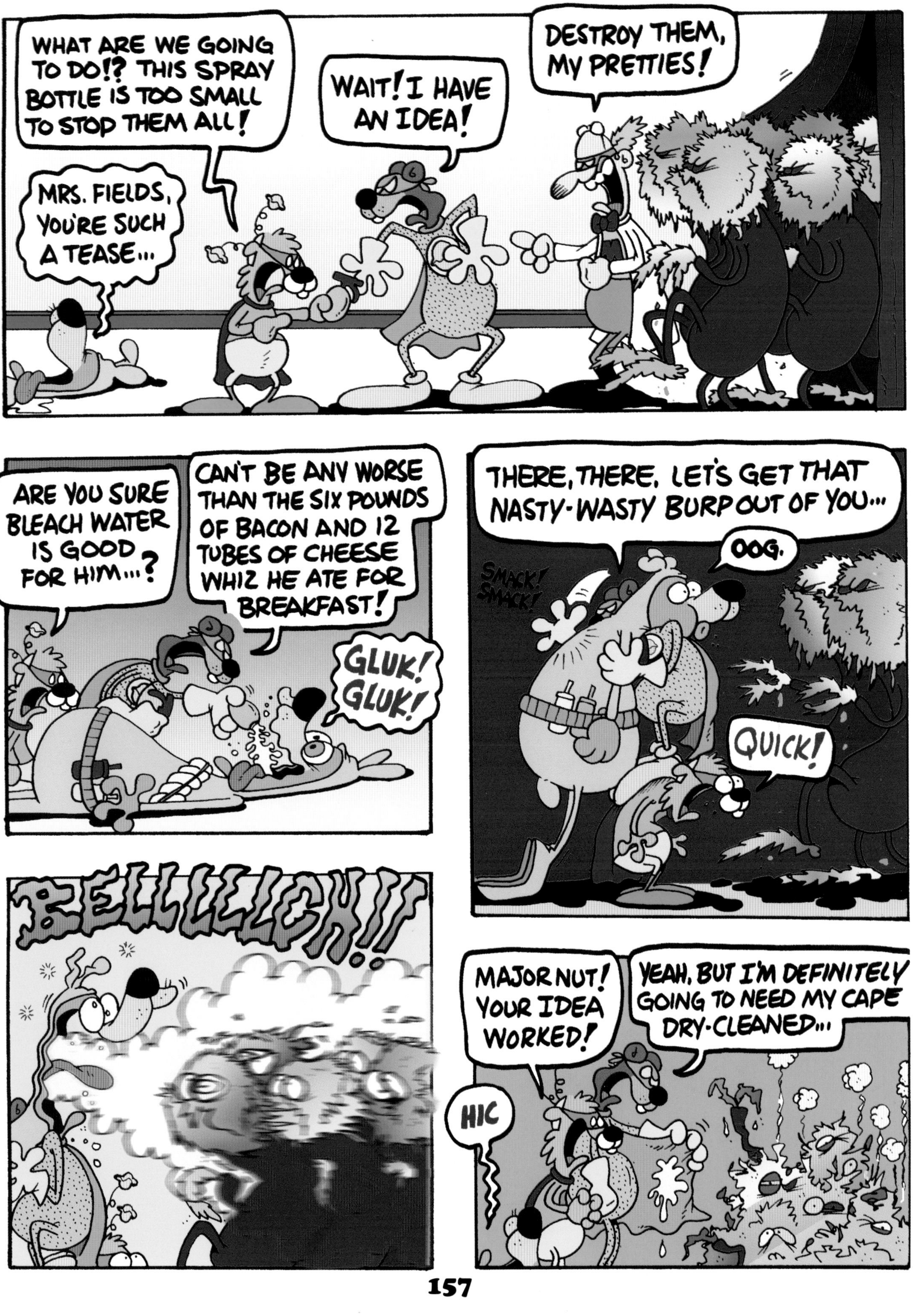
WHAT ARE WE GOING TO DO!? THIS SPRAY BOTTLE IS TOO SMALL TO STOP THEM ALL!
MRS. FIELDS, YOU'RE SUCH A TEASE...
WAIT! I HAVE AN IDEA!
DESTROY THEM, MY PRETTIES!
ARE YOU SURE BLEACH WATER IS GOOD FOR HIM...?
CAN'T BE ANY WORSE THAN THE SIX POUNDS OF BACON AND 12 TUBES OF CHEESE WHIZ HE ATE FOR BREAKFAST!
GLUK! GLUK!
THERE, THERE, LET'S GET THAT NASTY-WASTY BURP OUT OF YOU...
OOG.
SMACK! SMACK!
QUICK!
BELLLLCH!!
MAJOR NUT! YOUR IDEA WORKED!
YEAH, BUT I'M DEFINITELY GOING TO NEED MY CAPE DRY-CLEANED...
HIC

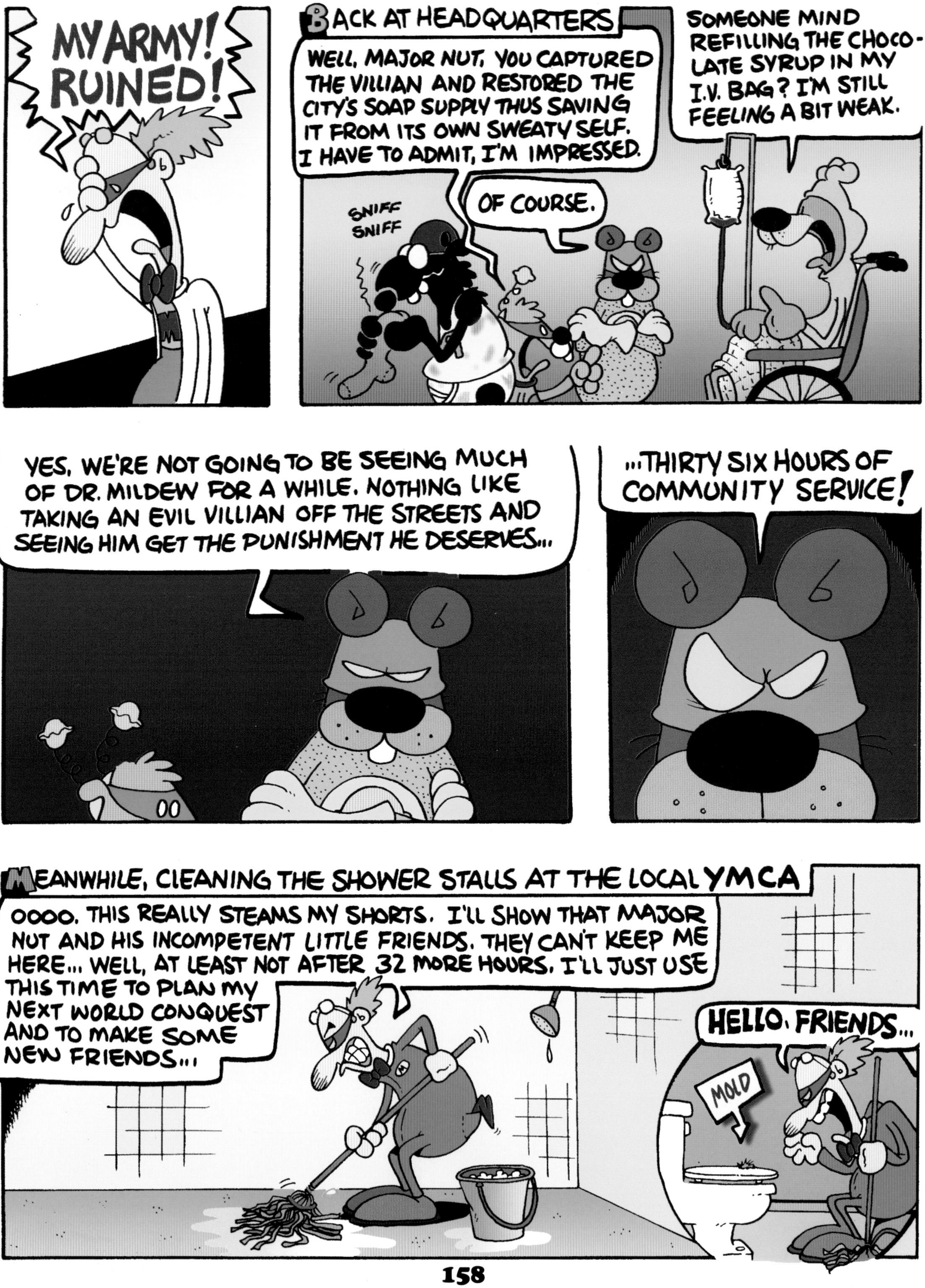
MY ARMY! RUINED!
BACK AT HEADQUARTERS
WELL, MAJOR NUT, YOU CAPTURED THE VILLIAN AND RESTORED THE CITY'S SOAP SUPPLY THUS SAVING IT FROM ITS OWN SWEATY SELF. I HAVE TO ADMIT, I'M IMPRESSED.
SOMEONE MIND REFILLING THE CHOCO-LATE SYRUP IN MY I.V. BAG? I'M STILL FEELING A BIT WEAK.
SNIFF SNIFF
OF COURSE.
YES, WE'RE NOT GOING TO BE SEEING MUCH OF DR. MILDEW FOR A WHILE. NOTHING LIKE TAKING AN EVIL VILLIAN OFF THE STREETS AND SEEING HIM GET THE PUNISHMENT HE DESERVES...
...THIRTY SIX HOURS OF COMMUNITY SERVICE!
MEANWHILE, CLEANING THE SHOWER STALLS AT THE LOCAL YMCA
OOOO, THIS REALLY STEAMS MY SHORTS. I'LL SHOW THAT MAJOR NUT AND HIS INCOMPETENT LITTLE FRIENDS. THEY CAN'T KEEP ME HERE... WELL, AT LEAST NOT AFTER 32 MORE HOURS. I'LL JUST USE THIS TIME TO PLAN MY NEXT WORLD CONQUEST AND TO MAKE SOME NEW FRIENDS...
HELLO, FRIENDS...
MOLD

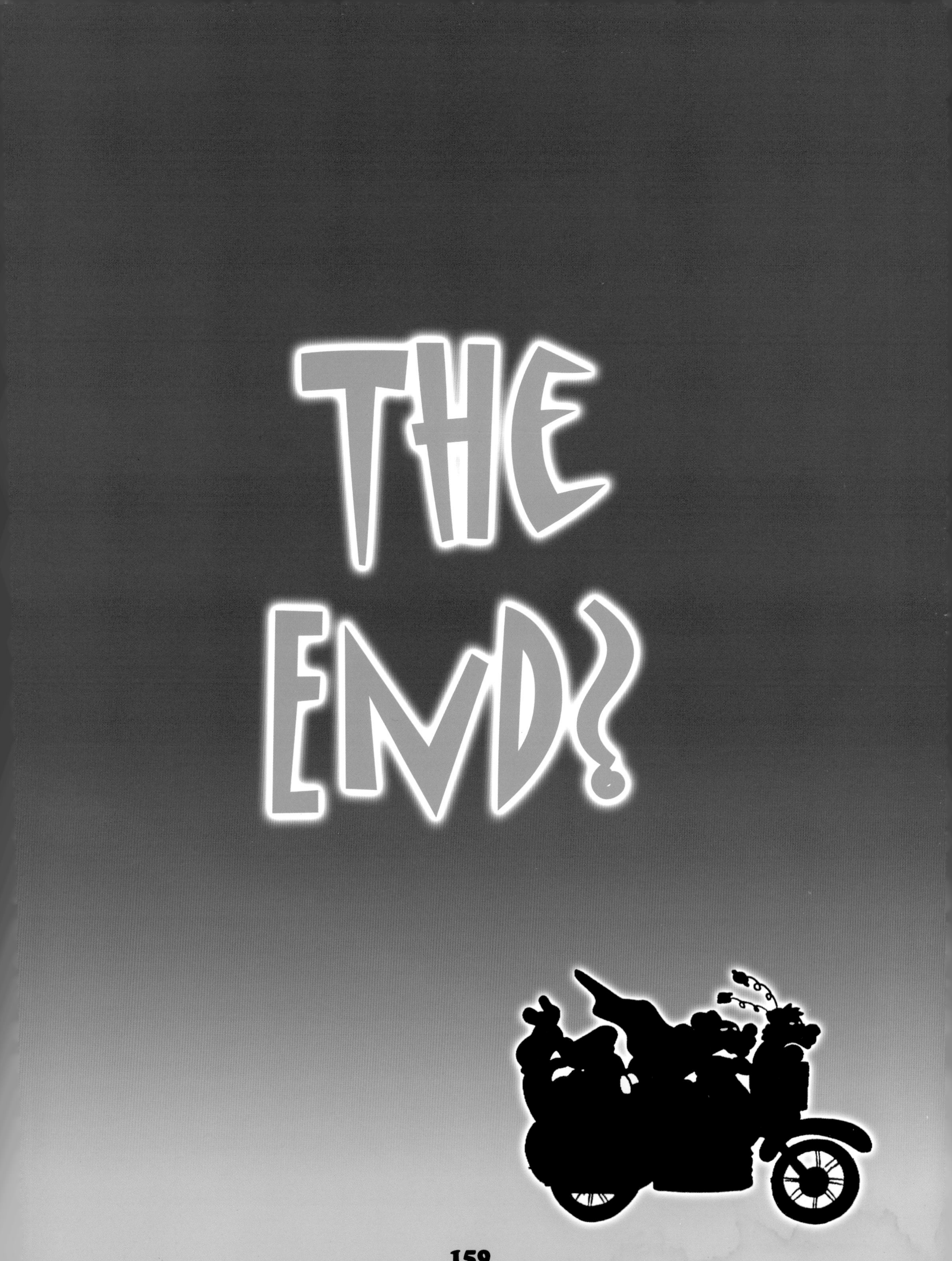
THE END?

ABOUT CHAD & DARIN CARPENTER:

The Amazing Carpdini Brothers began life in a small traveling circus in Eastern Europe. What made The Amazing Carpdini Brothers amazing, had nothing to do with any mystical or acrobatic skills they possessed (for they possessed none) but rather the strange physical attribute of being completely covered in long, luxurious body hair – a hereditary trait they inherited from their mother's side of the family.

They toured hundreds of villages, entertaining masses of people for the first two decades of their lives. Suddenly, disaster struck! It seems they had acquired another hereditary trait, this time from their father's side of the family – premature baldness. No longer were they the Amazing Carpdini Brothers, but simply a couple of bitter, balding guys.

The specter of lost fame haunted them and eventually sent the brothers their own separate ways. Chad, still clinging to the past, went through extensive hair transplant surgeries. Doctors would take hair-plugs from his lower half and plant them on his top half. Then they would take hair-plugs from his top half and plant them on his lower half, only to repeat the cycle (unsuccessfully) dozens of times. Darin, however, fared better. He purchased a used gorilla costume and spent several content years waving at cars during carpet warehouse grand openings.

It was a chance encounter that brought the two brothers back together. While shopping at a carpet store for a suitable body toupee', Chad recognized his brother immediately. It was then they decided to team up once again and step out in front of the masses! Unfortunately, the masses they stepped out in front of was rush-hour traffic.

While recuperating in a local hospital they decided to do comic strip stuff or something.